THE
Musician's Guide
TO
Home Recording

Peter McIan and Larry Wichman

A FIRESIDE BOOK
Published by Simon & Schuster Inc.
New York London Toronto Sydney Tokyo Singapore

LINDEN PRESS/FIRESIDE
Simon & Schuster Building
Rockefeller Center
1230 Avenue of the Americas
New York, New York 10020

Designed by Irving Perkins Associates
Manufactured in the United States of America

10   9   8   7   6   5   4   3
10   9   8   7   6   5   4   3   PBK

Library of Congress Cataloging-in-Publication Data
McIan, Peter.
   The musician's guide to home recording.

   "A Fireside book."
   Includes index.
   1. Magnetic recorders and recording.   2. Sound—
Recording and reproducing.   I. Wichman, Larry.   II. Title.
TK7881.6.M39   1988   621.389′3   88-18369
ISBN 0-671-60189-X PBK
      0-671-65754-2

Grateful acknowledgment is made to Van Nostrand Rheinhold Co.
Inc. for permission to reprint illustrations from *Sound Recording*,
copyright © 1986 by John Eargle.

ACKNOWLEDGMENTS

The authors wish to thank the following people for their contributions and their support:

Leita Purvis, Quita Saxon, Evan Hosie, Joy Harris, Bryan Brown, Allen Peacock, David Oren, Christopher Krause, Erik Scott, Jerry Speiser, Mick Guzauski, and Glen Phoenix.

In addition, we wish to offer a special thanks to our technical adviser, Paul Ray.

Recording-studio photographs by Laura Marenzi.

Some gear on front cover courtesy of TEAC Corporation and Yamaha International.

To my brothers David and Mark

To Leita, Catherine, and Herbert
... for their years of support, caring, confidence, and inspiration.

Stop!!! Read This Page!!! ∿∿∿∿∿∿∿∿∿∿∿∿∿∿∿∿∿∿∿∿∿∿

Before you go any further, we want to let you know about a pair of instructional audio cassettes we've recorded specifically for use with this book. These tapes, which are 45 minutes each, are designed to be a learning tool, and they contain *audio illustrations* of many of the concepts we speak of throughout the text.

Among other things, they include examples of

- the various EQ treatments you can give each instrument and how to adjust that EQ for the special effects you're using
- the effect of using various miking techniques
- techniques that reduce tape noise
- techniques that reduce generation loss during a bounce
- techniques for creating special reverb and echo effects
- techniques for creating a false stereo image
- techniques useful when trying to re-create sounds you've heard on hit records
- techniques for creating a balanced blend of instruments in the final mix

We're making these cassettes available because we realize how hard it is to duplicate a sound or an effect just by reading some instructions in a book. You're much more likely to succeed if you can hear what you're shooting for. After all, you wouldn't expect a visual artist to master his craft without the aid of visual illustrations!

And, no, these tapes are *not* full of songs. We take it one instrument and one concept at a time.

We hope you'll take advantage of this offer. We believe you'll find these cassettes to be an invaluable tool for mastering the art of recording.

To order your set of two instructional audio cassettes, send $17.95 (U.S. dollars) to

Audio Cassettes
P.O. Box 24756
Westwood, CA 90024

- Make check or money order payable to *Musician's Guide to Recording*.
- DO NOT SEND CASH!
- California residents add 6.5% sales tax ($19.12 total).
- Overseas orders add $6.00 for postage (air).
- Be sure to include the tear-out coupon or a note containing your name and address.

If you prefer, you can charge your order to Visa or MasterCard:

Visa _____ MasterCard _____

Account No. _____ Exp. date _____

Signature _____

Please print:

Name _____

Address _____

City _____

State _____ Zip _____

(please allow four to six weeks for delivery)

Contents 〰〰〰〰〰〰〰〰〰〰〰〰〰〰〰〰〰〰〰

Preface ∿∿∿∿∿∿∿∿∿∿∿∿∿∿∿∿∿∿∿

In 1979 I was signed to CBS Records as a solo artist, and as a result of some peculiar circumstances, I was given the opportunity to produce my own album. This was probably due more to good luck than anything else, because my track record as a producer was little more than a drawer full of demos I'd produced over the years.

My album, which was called *Playing Near the Edge,* did moderately well and gave me a Top-Forty single. But more important, it gave me the opportunity to learn professional production on the job.

I quickly discovered that my previous method of inspired improvisation wasn't all that was required. There were new skills to learn, and I found myself using tools I'd never previously been exposed to. And thanks to the project's excellent engineer, Mick Guzauski, who took the time to explain much of what I didn't understand, a whole new world opened up to me: a world where, through the proper use of these tools and techniques, I could more fully realize my musical vision.

During this period, I tried to learn as much as I could about production and engineering. I was fortunate to be surrounded by people who could supply me with answers that suited my level of technical understanding, and thus, when I went to Australia to produce a record for CBS in 1981, I felt ready to take on the engineering duties as well.

Within a week or two of my arrival, I went to see a new band that had been signed to CBS by an A&R director named Peter Karpin. I fell in love with the band's fresh approach, and I was determined to try to find some new production sounds that would complement the band's music. It was through this process of cooperative experimentation that the first Men At Work album, *Business As Usual,* was recorded—an album that netted two number-one singles, a number-one album, and sales of over eight million units.

(Courtesy of Larry Wichman)

The studio we recorded the album in was like most demo studios or advanced home studios found here in the States—meaning that, from a professional standpoint, it had serious limitations. In order to get the most out of what we had available, we had to do a great deal of improvising. So I borrowed some gear from friends in Melbourne, and, applying certain listening techniques I'd learned over the years, I created recording environments in areas that weren't designed as such (we used bathrooms for guitar tracks, a kitchen area for the bass, and so on). And thanks to a lot of careful planning, it all finally came together.

One thing I had missed during my eight months in Australia were the many evenings my friend Larry and I had spent drinking and talking music back in Los Angeles. Being a fellow songwriter, but one only just beginning to take his demo work seriously, Larry would let me ramble on endlessly about the little tricks I'd learned in the studio. In fact, it was during one of these bull sessions that the idea for this book was conceived.

While I was in Australia, Larry had discovered, as I had some years earlier, that there was very little technique oriented information available on recording. All the books he'd read had either been too technical or too general to be of much use. Thus, we thought that a book that taught musicians how to use the available gear, rather than one that explained how the gear worked, would be a great help, since a musician's main interest is in recording *his* music in a way that satisfies *his* musical vision as immediately as possible. Or, to use a metaphor, if a person wants to learn how to drive a car, he doesn't need a book that teaches him how to tear down an engine.

Thus, the purpose of this book is not to supply the technical background for recording (there are already numerous books on that subject), but to provide a hands-on, how-to approach to using technology to create art.

I hope you enjoy using this book as much as we enjoyed writing it.

—Peter McIan

As coauthor of this book, I play a rather unique role. While Peter McIan is a seasoned studio pro, I, like many of you, have never so much as moved a fader in a professional studio. Yet I've been involved with music and recording for more than fifteen years, and I've watched as the quality of home recording gear has evolved to the point where it is now possible to produce demos in your den that sound completely professional.

Yet, unfortunately, the recordist's understanding of how to use this new technology has not kept pace with the technology itself. This is due at least in part to the fact that no one

has bothered to explain how all this gear should be used—at least not in terms I could ever understand. And that's where I come in.

Too often, a book such as this is written over the head of the nonprofessional, so that any useful knowledge it contains is too technical to understand, while all the day-to-day tricks and techniques are ignored altogether. It's almost as if there is a conspiracy among those who know, to keep those who don't know in the dark. Therefore, one of my roles in this project has been to provide a control, so that even when we're explaining techniques a professional songwriter would

(*Courtesy of Leita Purvis*)

be interested in using in his 8-track studio, the concept is clear enough to be understood and applied by someone with less recording experience and less equipment.

I must admit that when we first started out, I was far from convinced that the techniques I'd watched Peter use in professional studios would prove helpful to my recordings. I have the kind of home studio you can put away at night: two small consoles, an old 4-track TEAC 3340, a Yamaha RX11 drum machine, two mikes, and a few signal processing devices. And when I need to do a mixdown, I have to borrow gear from the neighbors. Yet while working on this book, what I discovered was that virtually every operation performed in a pro studio is directly applicable to the home environment—which makes sense when you consider that in essence, high tech has brought scaled-down versions of the professional studio into our basements and living rooms.

It seemed like every time I turned around, I learned something new. And even though I'd always been able to get good reproduction in my recordings, they began to sound even better as I tried out the techniques we were covering in the text. Therefore, to the extent that this book has been written for a person like myself, I find it to be a complete success. Hopefully, it will be just as helpful for you.

Yet if there is one point that needs to be made prior to the text, it is that although this book can provide you with guidelines for improving the scope and quality of your recordings, it cannot, by itself, make your tapes sound better. Only you can do that. And to do so, you need to take the same disciplined approach to recording that you would take when learning to play an instrument.

For example, many of the techniques we outline in the book will need to be practiced over and over. Then, once you've got them down, you'll need to practice them some more. And even though we've done our best to give you quick, easy-to-follow reference material at the end of each chapter, you need to read the preceding text if you want to be able to apply the information in some manner that is totally your own.

It's also very important that you learn to work with the equipment you've got. While my studio can't hold a candle to Peter's, I consider myself lucky to have what I have. I spent many years recording live gigs and song demos with little more than a cheap mike mixer and a 2-track. Yet, working under those limited conditions, I was forced to become more disciplined. Instead of just saying, "Gee, my recordings could be better if I only had this or that piece of gear," I tried to find a way to use what I already had in a more efficient manner. As a result, I learned more about recording than I otherwise would have, and I'm able to get better quality out of my present equipment.

The main thrust of this is that you don't need a zillion tracks and a lot of fancy gear to make a good recording. For example, you can go out and spend a lot of dough on a digital reverb, but if you don't know how to properly apply reverb in the first place, the infusion of "new technology" isn't going to help the sound of your tapes one bit. The same holds true for a song demo: either the song is there, or it's not. If it's there, it can be recorded with a couple of instruments and some reverb, and it will still shine (as evidenced by the Police hit "Every Breath You Take"). If it's not, no amount of studio trickery is going to make it all fall together.

—Larry Wichman

THE
Musician's Guide
TO
Home Recording

Introduction:
Designing a Successful
Demo Tape

Every recording artist I know of began his or her career with a demo tape of one form or another, and because of the rapid growth in consumer electronics, an increasing number of these demos are being done at home. However, before you and the band slap something down on tape and send it off to Capitol Records, you need to understand the various ways demos are used in the industry and the part they play in the artist's career.

WHAT IS A DEMO?

Put simply, the music demo is a sales tool. It's a means of displaying your talents as a performer or as a writer and of showing your *potential* as a recording artist.

Conceptually, a demo is like the scale model an architect builds to convince a client of the quality of the building design. The model has the shape, form, and style of the proposed structure, but it lacks the final details that will be included in the finished product. Thus, all it is meant to convey is the *idea* of the structure, in miniature, and much is left to the imagination.

By the same token, you should never approach a demo as though you were recording a finished album. While the demo needs to contain every important musical element, it is, after all, only a musical model, and you should never think of it as being anything more than a representation of what the music will sound like in its final form.

CREATING AN EFFECTIVE DEMO

The first thing you need to think about when you set out to make a demo is who the audience will be, because that will dictate the style and substance the demo should have.

There are four basic demo types: the demo you submit to club owners in order to get gigs, the demo you send out in order to get a name artist to use one of your songs, the demo you give to an agent or manager in order to get representa-

tion, and the demo you send to record companies in order to get signed to a recording contract.

Each of these demos is directed at a different audience, and that means each requires a different stylistic approach. For instance, the club manager wants to hear what your band sounds like live, while a record company will want to hear a tape that was done in a studio and sounds more like a record. This means that it's very important to design your demo specifically for the audience it's intended for.

"Club Date" Demos

If you're recording a demo that is going to be used to get club dates, your audience will most likely be the club owner, who's interested in the type of music you play and in how well you play it "live." Therefore, you should check out the crowd the club attracts, so that you know what type of music to include on the tape, and you should record the instrumentation with all of the musicians playing at once (although you might want to overdub the vocals). Or, if you have any recordings of previous gigs that are of sufficiently high quality, you might want to edit them down and combine the best material onto one master tape.

"Club" demos should, in some ways, represent your stage act. So, you'll want to include at least ten or twelve tunes that you might do during an evening's performance. However, if you're using tapes made during previous gigs, it's best to edit out any talking that may have taken place between songs. Unless, that is, it shows a particularly strong crowd response to the band, in which case it may be a help rather than a hindrance.

Song Demos

If you're creating a song demo, your primary audience is going to be the artist you're trying to sell the song to, and his or her main concern is going to be the *song,* not the performer or the arrangement. In fact, you want to avoid over-producing a song demo or making it too stylistic, because you want to give the artist an opportunity to imagine what his own arrangement might sound like. This may mean sending off a tape that you feel is instrumentally incomplete, meaning that in your mind's ear you hear a lot of instrumental "finishing touches" that weren't included, but it gives you a better chance of placing the song.

The focus of a song demo should be on the lyrics, the melody, and the feel of the song. It should sound as professional as possible, both in quality of production and in quality of play, and it should include all of the key musical elements that make the song work. Thus, you want to pay careful attention to the vocal and make it a dominant part of the mix, and overall, you want to make sure the production is pleasing to the ear and that it conveys the idea of the song. If you've done that, then you've created a demo that is sufficient for the purpose.

Management Demos

If you're going to be using the demo to look for a management contract, chances are you'll have an opportunity to speak with whomever you're submitting the tape to, and you can find out exactly what they want in advance. However, few managers or agencies will expect the demos to sound as polished as one you might send to a record company, because they assume that you're beginning your career, and that you've reached the stage where you're looking for the sort of expert guidance management can provide.

When you're recording these demos, you should include everything you feel is representative of what you do, whether as a band or as a solo artist, because in order to give you the advice and counsel that will help you develop as an artist, a manager or agent needs to know all of the things that you can do and what musical style you're most comfortable with. This usually means including everything of substance that you've written to date, since you want the demo to have variety, and you want it to convey the totality of your abilities as an artist.

Record Company Demos

Perhaps the most critical demo of all to produce is the one you send to record companies when you're trying to get an album deal. In this case, your audience is the label's A&R director, as he's the one who decides whether or not to sign you. Unfortunately, most people never get the opportunity to sit down and meet these decision-makers until after the decision's been made. But I can give you a few general guidelines from personal experience that can be helpful.

First of all, give the A&R director *three* songs, not ten, to listen to. And make sure that all three clearly convey a similar sense of style. In other words, don't pick three songs that are completely different from each other stylistically, be-

cause to an A&R director, that makes it seem as though you're confused about what your musical identity really is.

Second, the demo you submit needs to sound as much like a finished record as possible, because, quite honestly, if it doesn't sound professional, the music isn't going to be taken seriously.

Third, although you want the demo to convey a strong sense of artistic style, the material needs to sound more commercial than innovative, because you need to convince the A&R director that he can sell records for his company by signing you to their roster. And the truth is that many A&R directors base their decisions upon the type of music the general public is buying at the time, not on what he believes they'll be buying in the future. So, while you don't want to copy someone else's style, or try to forcibly fit your material into a Top-Forty mold, you do want to give the A&R director something that he feels the public will identify with.

And last, you only want to include material that is going to generate interest and excitement. So, if you have a choice between including a song that you think could get a lot of radio play as a single, and a song that you believe to be your most artistic work, give them the single. You'll have plenty of opportunity to express yourself more fully on the album. Remember, the job of the demo is to convince the label to let you do an album, and from their point of view, that will depend upon whether they think your music can generate sales.

As an addendum, it should be mentioned that record labels receive hundreds of demos every week, and it's very rare that an unsolicited tape from an unmanaged band will even reach the A&R director (though members of his staff *do* listen to them). Thus, it's better to seek a management deal first, as demos are taken more seriously when they're brought in by managers or agency reps the label has previously dealt with.

PRODUCTION TIPS

One of the easiest traps to fall into when making a demo—and it's something I'm sure every artist has been guilty of at one time or another—is "production overkill": when the production is so elaborate that the song gets lost. Usually this happens because the artist, who wants his material to sound as exciting as possible, simply tries too hard. So, the thing you need to remember is that a demo is meant to present your artistry, and if "the artist" doesn't shine through, all of the sophisticated electronic tricks in the world aren't going to make it a good sales tool.

This is why, in most aspects of production, I'm a firm believer that "less is more"—in this case meaning that *less* complexity is generally *more* effective. For example, the Men At Work albums I produced included sophisticated production techniques, but they were used only to enhance arrangements carefully worked out to appear simple in approach. And if you listen carefully to albums recorded by groups like The Cars, or Police, you'll see that the records are successful because they feature genuine artists performing genuine music, *not* because the producer used a lot of fancy electronic tricks. The technology is simply a tool.

So, when you approach a demo, you first need to decide how best to present the material. Then you need to determine the least amount you can do in order to achieve the greatest effect. And if you follow that axiom—the least amount necessary for the greatest effect—chances are you'll come up with a winner.

〰〰〰〰〰〰〰〰〰〰〰〰〰〰〰〰〰〰〰

Chapter I

The Art of Listening

The world of audio is a world of sound, and in order to be a good recordist, you need to become a good listener. You need to know what to listen for, and you need to pay attention to what you hear.

Listening comes into play at every step in the recording process. You learn to create an effective recording by listening to records. You analyze the acoustics of the recording environment by listening to the room echoes. You adjust the tonality of the instruments by listening to the effect various EQ levels have on the signal. And so on.

So, don't just skip over this chapter because you figure it's about the "fundamentals of recording." It's not. It's about the fundamentals of *listening*.

THE RECORDIST'S CONCERNS

When Thomas Edison invented the phonograph, he provided musicians with their first means to make audio recordings. Before that, musical performances could only be heard live; but thanks to Edison's invention, music was able to move through time as well as space.

Edison's device gave us the ability to document a musical performance, and in the early days a recording was literally that: an aural documentary of a performance. In fact, up until the mid-fifties, most songs were still being recorded as live studio performances, with the entire band performing the song as they would onstage.

Over the years, however, recording techniques have become much more sophisticated and, as a result, more complex (see "Tape Tip #2," page 29). In modern recording, the instruments are placed on tape at different times, and they're given individual treatment. Yet, each must still be considered as a single component of a much broader picture, and the sound of each must be molded and shaped so that it blends in properly with the whole.

Thus, the recordist must be concerned not only with the sound of the instruments, but also with the acoustical environment in which they're recorded, the electronic effects that are added, the relative levels of the instruments throughout the song, and the internal dynamics (or emotional flow) that they create.

As a consequence, a modern musical recording requires two artistic performances: one by the musicians and one by the recordist. In other words, you're not just recording a performance, you're performing a recording.

THE AESTHETICS OF RECORDING

Throughout the book, we're going to explain the methods used in multitrack recording. Yet these techniques are just tools, and in order to apply them properly, you need to be concerned with the aesthetics of what you're doing, not just with the step-by-step process.

In some ways, producing a multitrack demo can be likened to sculpting a statue from a block of stone; the music represents the raw material and the electronics of your studio represents the chisels and hammers. Thus, just as a sculptor uses his tools to shape and mold his creation, the producer uses his electronic tools to give shape, form, and feeling to the music.

When a sculptor approaches his work, he doesn't just start hacking away at the marble. Before he can begin, he must have a clear picture of the finished statue in his mind. He must be aware of the mood he wishes to create, and he must plan out the proportions and design the anatomical lines of the figures.

The same holds true for a producer. Before he puts anything on tape, he must first determine what he wants the final product to sound like. So, he needs to have a clear picture in his mind as to what kind of mood the music is going to generate and how best to enhance that mood through the various methods at his disposal.

In that conceptual process, he thinks about such things as the musical arrangement and the relative importance of the instruments at given points throughout the song. He also must determine whether he wants the music to sound as though it's being performed in a large hall that's filled with distant echoes, or whether it should be given a more intimate setting. Or whether, in fact, he wants the music to sound natural at all—which is often an issue when heavily synthesized, "electronic" sounds are being used.

These are all concerns the producer must take into account, because his aesthetic goal is to create an environment within the stereo spectrum that enhances the music and reenforces the mood. And he uses the techniques and methods of multitrack production for that purpose. Thus, when you structure a recording, you must keep in mind that your principle purpose for using effects and such is to create a recording that complements the music, not one that rivals it for attention. After all, if the music isn't any good to begin with, fancy production techniques aren't going to help.

LEARNING BY LISTENING

To be a good producer, you must learn to listen. As infants, we learn to use language by listening to, and emulating, the speech patterns of others. And as musicians, much of the flair and technique we develop comes from listening to, and emulating, the work of fellow artists. In many respects, the same holds true for producers. Thus, an excellent way to learn how to structure a mix is to listen to the way others structure theirs.

A record contains a wealth of information for the producer or recordist. A lot of what I've learned over the years has come from listening to records and trying to figure out how the producer created a certain sound or a certain blend of sounds.

Of course, much of that knowledge comes from the experience of having recorded something that sounds similar and by understanding the process. However, you can also learn a great deal by experimenting with the effects and techniques we discuss in later chapters and applying the knowledge you gain as a result.

Critical Listening

Critical listening is not the same as listening for entertainment, and by the time you've finished this book, our hope is that you'll be listening to the sound of a record, as well as to sounds in the world around you, in a totally different way.

Conceptually, critical listening is nothing more than careful, analytical listening, and as such, it has a variety of recording applications. As you'll see throughout this chapter, along with helping you to analyze records and learn from other producers, it plays an important role in determining whether or not a particular acoustical environment is

suitable for recording, and it gives you the ability to evaluate objectively the sound of your own recordings.

The individual who made me rethink my listening habit is an extremely talented recording engineer named Mick Guzauski. He's worked on everything from heavy metal music to Earth, Wind & Fire to Chuck Mangione, and I first m him when he engineered my solo album.

Before working with Mick, I'd listened to records with critical ear and analyzed the production work and the sound that were being created. However, every time I listened something with Mick, he'd point out aspects of the recording that I simply had never heard before. Nor had I ever known to listen for them.

For instance, he pointed out the importance of the reproduction quality in the extreme top and bottom ends of recording. He also made me more aware of things like noise and distortion, and he pointed out the effect that different types of echoes have on the listener.

These were all things that had a subliminal effect upon the way I had perceived the music, and yet, until Mick brought them to my attention, I hadn't consciously considered them as being important to the final product.

Listening to Sound

The first area we're going to apply critical listening to is the physical world itself, which, after all, is the medium in which sound exists.

To begin with, you need to be aware of some of the physical characteristics of sound, as they effect the way sound is heard. For example, if you put on a record and stand directly in front of your speakers, you'll hear the sound one way. However, if you take a few steps backward, you should be able to detect a change in the overall tonality. If the room is small, you'll hear a subtle change. If the room is large, the changes will be more pronounced.

In all likelihood, as you move away from the speakers, you'll start to hear more bottom end. The reason for this is that sound exists as waves. Low-frequency waves, which are at the bass end of the scale, are physically quite long, while high-frequency waves, which are in the treble ranges, are extremely short. Thus, the bass waves take longer to form than the treble waves, and as a consequence they become more pronounced as you move farther from the speakers.

This becomes important while you're recording, because a microphone acts much like a human ear, and the distance between the microphone and the source of the sound will influence the tonality of the track. In fact, in the early days, before the existence of equalizers—which, like tone controls, enable you to boost or reduce specific frequencies—equalization was controlled strictly through mike placement. Thus, the engineers used the physical characteristics of sound (the difference in wavelengths) to control the tone of a recorded instrument.

NOTE—*It is not our intention to go into the physics of sound, as many books have already been written on the subject. However, a more complete explanation of sound waves can be found in chapter 2.*

Listening to the Ambient Environment

Another important aspect of sound waves is that they interact with the physical environment: they reflect off hard surfaces and are absorbed by soft, fibrous materials. Thus, the amount of reflective or absorptive surfaces a room contains will determine its acoustical characteristics. In recording, these acoustical characteristics are referred to as "ambience."

The ambient environment plays an extremely important role in the recording process, as the acoustics of the studio affect the sound of the recorded tracks. So, the more familiar you are with the various ambient environments and the way they can be used, the more control you'll have over the sound of your recordings.

For example, highly reflective environments were used to great effect in creating the huge drum sounds Led Zeppelin became famous for. In at least one case, this was achieved by recording the drums in a castle that had hard stone walls and by allowing the environment to interact with the instrument so that it became a component of the sound.

By the same token, most of the time you will want to keep room reflections from interfering with the sound of the instrument, which is something we discuss in chapter 17, "Studio Acoustics." However, in either case, you need to be concerned with the ambience of the room you record in, and you must learn to distinguish, through listening, between acoustically "live" environments and acoustically "dead" environments.

One excellent way to analyze the acoustics of a room is to use the sound of a hand clap to test the ambient reflections. For instance, if you clap your hands in a very small environment, the reflections will sound very sharp, very bright, and very immediate. However, if you do the same in a larger room, you'll notice that the reflections take longer to develop, and that they sound a bit warmer and have less high end.

To better understand the interaction between room environment and sound, you should pay attention to room ambience as you go through your daily life. For example, if you enter a room that has an unusual characteristic, such as a vaulted ceiling, listen to the way this affects the sound of a person's voice or the sound of his footsteps. If you walk into an unusually large, fully tiled bathroom, compare the way your voice sounds there with the way it sounds in a much smaller bathroom.

The more familiar you become with the sounds of different types of environments, the easier it will be to utilize, or control, the acoustical environment of your studio, and the better you'll understand where amplifiers and instruments should be placed in order to achieve the best effect.

Listening to the Electronic Environment

Another, very important form of ambience is the artificial environment you create by applying reverb and echo to the instruments. Although this is covered at length in chapter 16, "Mixdown Techniques," the basic idea is that if a band is playing live, the ambience of the room they're in will contribute to the sound you hear. And since all the instruments are in the same room, they are all subject to the same ambient conditions. Consequently, the electronic ambience you add to the recording is an integral part of the sound, because it creates the illusion that all of the instruments are being played at the same time in the same room.

This, in turn, is important, because it gives the listener a subliminal point of reference. It gives him a subconscious image of the band, and, because it tends to tie all the elements together, it gives the music a cohesiveness and a sense of reality.

One way to understand this is to listen to a record and to imagine the size of the room in which the song was recorded. Then repeat the same exercise with another record, and another. What you'll find is that your impression of the room size varies according to the amount of echo or reverb that has been applied to the tracks.

LEARNING FROM RECORDS

As I mentioned, analyzing other people's work can be an invaluable tool when you're trying to learn how to create your own recordings.

Listening to the Mix

Before you begin looking at individual components, such as instrumental effects or uses of panning, you should focus on the balance of the recording as a whole. This will help you get used to listening to elements of the mix in the context of how they fit into the broader picture—which is a theme that runs throughout the book.

To gain an overall feel for what a production should sound like, pick out a record you particularly like, and listen first to the general production qualities. Then, listen to the record a second time, and pick out any elements of principle focus. Next, analyze the treatment those elements were given (such as stereo position, effects, volume level, and so on). Finally, listen to the record one last time, and focus on the way those elements interact with the rest of the mix.

You'll notice that the important elements, like the vocals and the drums, are made to stand out above the pack, and that the rhythm tracks, too, are given prominence. This blend of components is extremely important to the success of the recording, as it enables you to manipulate the listener's focus of attention. And in order to create a successful demo, you'll need to devote a lot of care and attention to this blend.

Special Effects

As you listen to your records, you also want to be aware of the special effects that are used. For instance, if a guitar sounds unusual to you, that is to say "processed" in some fashion, try to understand how the effect was created and how it was used.

Hopefully, through the use of this book, you'll be able to understand what that process was and what those sounds were, and you'll be able to generate them for yourself, through experimentation. But the thing to listen for is not so much the sound of the instrument itself, but rather the way the sound helps create the mood that the music is trying to portray.

For instance, in the case of Jimi Hendrix, who was the master of guitar effects, the wa-wa pedal, the phasing, and the feedback from the amplifiers were each as important to the sound of the guitar as the instrument itself. They were also essential in providing the foundation upon which the song was built.

High-End and Low-End Response

Another thing you should listen to is the top end of the recording (the highest sound you can hear on the record). Frequently this highest sound will come from a cymbal, and if that's the case, listen to the way the cymbal decays, or dies out. Try mentally to isolate it from the other instruments, and listen to see if it decays naturally, or if the decay is cut off abruptly. If it ends abruptly, chances are that the high-frequency EQ was not applied properly when it was recorded.

Next, you'll want to check the low-frequency response, which is where you'll find the kick drum and the bass guitar. What you're looking for here is the amount of definition and punch exhibited in the bottom end. In other words, can you hear each note that the bass player is playing, or does the bass sound like a woolly, low rumble? Does the sound of the kick drum hit you in the chest, or is it barely audible?

The low end is extremely important because it establishes a foundation for the other elements. Therefore, it should definitely be audible, and it should definitely be punchy.

When you begin to analyze records sound by sound and instrument by instrument, you get a better understanding of what you need to shoot for in your recordings. It's the way I first gained an understanding of what goes into making a successful recording, and I hope it will be as helpful for you. Of course, much of what I learned, I learned by trial and error. But it was trial and error based on studying the techniques of people whose records I admired.

TAPE TIP #1
A Helpful Hearing Aid

Although it's true that you can gain a great deal of knowledge by listening to finished albums, an excellent way to learn what it is you should be listening *for* is to buy the set of audio cassettes we've recorded specifically for this book (see order form, page 9).

The material included on these tapes covers such subjects as how to apply various types of reverb and echo to a track (and what the effect will be), how to create the proper balance of instruments, how to change the tone of an instrument through the use of EQ, how to generate a false stereo image through the use of effects, and how to re-create sounds you hear on records.

This makes the tapes extremely useful for anyone who's learning what to listen for, because, for example, they let you hear the way an instrument, or vocal, sounds both before and after it's been given an effect. So, instead of analyzing one component of a finished mix, you're able to hear each of the stages it goes through in order to reach that point.

We wouldn't offer these cassettes if we didn't feel they were useful at every stage of production. However, because we've isolated so many different sounds, the tapes are particularly valuable at this stage of the learning process.

TAPE TIP #2
The Process of Multitrack Recording

In the *very* early days of rock 'n' roll, a band would come into the studio, set up, and record each song in one take. And all the reverb and echo effects were added right then and there.

However, thanks to the capabilities of multitrack tape machines, contemporary studio recordings are made in a totally different fashion. Instruments are recorded either separately or in bunches, and there may be as many as 48 overdub tracks laid down before it's over. Plus, instead of adding effects to the instruments as they are being recorded, most effects are now added to tracks *after* they've been laid down, either during a bounce or during the final mix, which produces the finished, master copy of your work.

Those of you who have only had live, onstage experience may find this manner of recording to be somewhat foreign, since live music dictates the immediate use of effects on an instrument. However, by laying down "dry" tracks and adding effects at the end, you have more control over the use of the effect and over the way each instrument fits into the final blend of elements.

For example, if you add echo to a guitar track as it's being recorded, you need to guess at the amount of echo that's added. If you guess wrong, you may later find that you've given the guitar too much echo, and as a result it has sunken into the background. However, if you add the effect during the mix, at which point you're blending all of the instruments together at once, you'll be able to vary the amount of echo and establish the exact depth you want the guitar to have.

There is, in fact, a standard set of procedures for multitrack recording that we suggest you follow. However, they are fairly general in nature, and, as you'll see throughout the book, there are times when you'll need to make adjustments. Basically, however, multitrack recording is accomplished as follows:

1. *The instruments are recorded.*
   At this time, EQ is applied, and the tracks are recorded "raw" (without effects).
2. *Additional tracks are laid down.*
   At this point, overdubs and insertions are performed.
3. *Effects are added to the instruments.*
   This is done either during a bounce or during mixdown (see step 4).
4. *The instruments are re-EQed and blended together during the final mix—which is recorded onto a 2-track.*
   This step generates a master copy of your song.

TAPE TIP #3
What Is Stereo?

By recording in stereo, you open up a three-dimensional world of possibilities for your music. Because of the properties of stereo reproduction, you're able to give the same "illusionary" perspective to your music that an artist is capable of creating on a canvas. You have a linear stereo field extending between the left and right speakers, and, because of the effect of reverb and echo, you can create foreground and background placement (or depth).

Conceptually, then, the stereo spectrum is a three-dimensional space emanating from two sources: the speakers. So, even though the sound itself is being reproduced in two dimensions (the plane of the speakers), it gives the illusion of existing in three dimensions.

A stereophonic recording is created by capturing the sound with two microphones that are placed some distance apart. The idea here is that even though both mikes are recording the same source, they are picking up different aspects of the sound because they're in different locations. Thus, they function just like a pair of human ears.

This means that you can't create a stereo recording with just one microphone (a stereo mike is, in fact, two microphones in one). So, for example, if you were to take the signal from one microphone and record it on two tracks, even if you panned one track hard left and the other hard right during playback, you'd end up with a monaural recording, because both tracks would contain exactly the same signal. (For details on the principles of panning, see chapter 16.)

Instead, if you want to record and playback in stereo, you must use two microphones and record the signal from each onto a separate track. Then one track must be played back through the left speakers and the other through the right speakers, so that you have full, stereophonic separation.

This last bit is important, because if you were to pan the two signals to the same stereo location, thus eliminating the separation that allows you to hear the differences between the two signals, you would again end up with a monaural recording.

It's critical that you understand the principles of stereophonic reproduction, because, as you'll see later, effective use of the stereo spectrum is essential if you want to create a successful recording.

TAPE TIP #4
Frequency Ranges of Musical Instruments and the Human Voice

Equalization is the process of controlling the level of specific frequencies within the response range of an instrument. It is used to enhance particular aspects of the instrument's sound, such as, in the case of a guitar, the sound of the pick hitting the strings.

Figure 1a represents the response range for most musical instruments and for the human voice, so if you need to determine the upper and lower reaches of an instrument's frequency response, all you need to do is refer to this chart (although we do offer specific EQ suggestions in each of the instrumental chapters).

In this chart, the solid black areas represent the body of the instrument's tonal response, while the grayish areas represent the instrument's upper harmonics.

Figure 1a

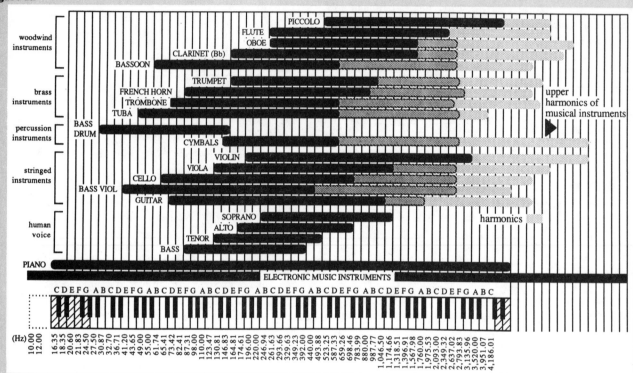

(Courtesy of TEAC Corporation of America)

hapter **2** 〰〰〰〰〰〰〰〰〰〰〰〰〰〰〰〰〰〰〰〰

Microphones

Microphones are, quite literally, your electronic ears. They convert sound waves into signal, which can then be fed to an amplifier, in much the same way the human ear converts sound into a signal that is fed to the brain.

While it may sound silly to equate microphones with ears, the sooner you begin to think of a microphone as being *one* of your ears, the more sensitive you'll become to its appications and abuses. For example, you'd never want to place a mike an inch away from a fully cranked-up Marshall guitar amp, just as you'd never want to put your ear that close to one. The sonic bombardment would have the same distorting effect on a mike that it would have on your ear, although the *mike* wouldn't suffer any permanent damage.

HOW THEY DO WHAT THEY DO WHEN THEY DO IT

To use microphones properly, you need to have at least a general understanding of how they operate. However, this does not mean that you have to know everything about the technology involved. Therefore, we've chosen to take a more general approach to microphone operation, and even though the following material is accurate, you may want to look to technically oriented texts for more details.

A microphone is a *transducer,* meaning that it converts the acoustic energy represented by sound waves into an electronic signal current. It does so in a fashion that is quite similar to the technique nature worked out some time ago for us: microphones all have some type of thin, flexible "eardrum," or diaphragm device, that responds to the changes in air pressure we *hear* as sound waves. As a series of waves impacts with this surface, the material vibrates back and forth in response to the rising and falling pressure, and the rate at which it vibrates dictates the frequency level of the signal.

As we'll see in the next section, each different type of microphone has a different way of converting this movement

into electrical energy. However, these are not critical concepts to understand, because the quality of signal reproduction in a microphone depends more heavily upon the efficiency of this diaphragm response.

To some extent, this response is affected by the material the diaphragm is made of. A lighter, thinner material, such as the metal ribbon in a ribbon microphone, will produce better high-end response than you'd get from the heavier diaphragm found in most other dynamic mikes.

Yet the efficiency of the response is also dependent upon proper mike techniques. For example, when you distort a mike by bombarding it with sound, you literally destroy the ability of the diaphragm to respond. What you're doing is subjecting it to so much pressure that the diaphragm expands to its limit (much like a blown-up balloon) and is no longer flexible enough to vibrate. By the same token, if the source is too quiet, too little pressure will reach the diaphragm, and you won't receive a complete signal (only the highs and lows will be represented).

One thing about transduction that does affect the quality of the signal is the noise that is created when the diaphragm vibrations are changed into electronic signal. As you'll see in the next chapter, this is the noise that, like a birthmark, stays with the signal until it is changed back into an acoustic form. And it is this hisslike noise that you begin to hear as the signal-to-noise ratio drops.

This becomes important when you look at the quality of a microphone, because if it exhibits a poor signal-to-noise response, it will create more noise during the birth of the signal, and it will be just that much more difficult to retain a strong signal-to-noise ratio throughout the rest of the recording process.

MICROPHONE TYPES

Microphones are categorized according to both the directional response patterns they exhibit and the method they use to change the vibrations of the diaphragm into electronic signal. In the latter case, which we'll discuss in this section, microphones fall into one of two fundamental classifications: dynamic and condenser.

Dynamic Microphones

Dynamic microphones are the most common type of home studio mike, and they operate on relatively simple electromagnetic principles. The diaphragm on a dynamic mike, which is like those we've been describing (made of flexible material that vibrates in and out), is connected to a movable "voice" coil (Figure 2a). As the diaphragm vibrates, the coil moves, which alters the magnetic flux and causes current to flow.

This process requires a minimum of electronic circuitry and therefore results in a durable microphone that requires little more than commonsense handling and care. Most bands use dynamic mikes for concert sound reinforcement, and since they are capable of exhibiting excellent response, they are perfect for professional as well as home use.

A more unusual type of dynamic mike is the "ribbon microphone," so named because, though operating on "dynamic" principles, it uses a thin metallic ribbon in place of the diaphragm and voice coil. This type of mike is usually very large, and as they were the state-of-the-art mike in the fifties, you often see them in old TV game show reruns.

Although there are a few models of ribbon mikes being manufactured for home use, these microphones are seldom found outside of the studio. They are particularly useful when you wish to capture the warm tones of a bass or low horns. However, while most other dynamic microphones are excellent for recording very loud sources, ribbon mikes are extremely sensitive to sudden gusts of wind and high acoustic pressure and will not perform well under such circumstances.

Condenser Microphones

Condenser (or capacitor) microphones are the mikes that most commonly used in the studio or under controlled conditions. They're also very expensive. In this case, a crothin diaphragm is stretched parallel to, but not touching a thin perforated plate (Figure 2b), and current is through both elements. By adding current, each element begins to act as the opposite pole of a capacitor, so that the diaphragm vibrates, it causes the output current to fluctuate.

As you can see in Figure 2c, which gives you a good look at the innards of a condenser mike, there is a lot of inter

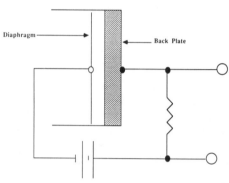

Figure 2b: Condenser microphone elements. On a condenser microphone, fluctuations in the diaphragm create slight changes capacitance, which generates the signal that eventually is sent tape. (*Illustration from* Sound Recording *by John Eargle*)

Figure 2c: The guts of a Neumann U-89 condenser mike. (*Courtesy of Gotham Audio Corporation*)

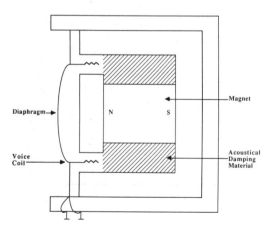

Figure 2a: A dynamic microphone's diaphragm and voice coil. (*Illustration from* Sound Recording *by John Eargle*)

cuitry involved. This is at least partially due to the necessity of maintaining a flow of current in the elements and cause they generate a low impedance output of between 0 ohms and 200 ohms.

There is one type of condenser mike that is, in fact, frequently found in home studios. It's called an "electret condenser," and it costs little more than a good home dynamic ike. Unlike the studio condensers, these mikes produce a 00-ohm signal that can be sent directly into a tape recorder r into the high-impedance inputs of a console, and they are owered by a very small, low-voltage battery. Yet they have xcellent frequency response, due to the low mass of the iaphragm, and they are quite durable.

ZM

A PZM, or "pressure zone microphone," is the newest type f microphone to hit the market (Figure 2d). It works off of a relatively technical principle involving acoustic pressure buildup on a surface as a sound wave strikes it and bounces off and is technically a condenser. However, the bottom line is that it produces a very clear, clean signal.

PZMs are not general-use microphones, but they can serve a number of functions. They can be used to pick up room acoustics, and by taping them to a resonating wall or a sounding board, they are capable of producing quite a bit of bass. In this regard, PZMs work very well as piano mikes, and when using them as such, you should tape them to the shell, or lid, of the instrument.

MICROPHONE RESPONSE PATTERNS

As we mentioned, microphones are also classified according to their directional response patterns, which reflect their ability to pick up sound from anywhere in a 360-degree radius. These classifications, which are represented by the illustrations in Figure 2e, include "omnidirectional" and "unidirectional."

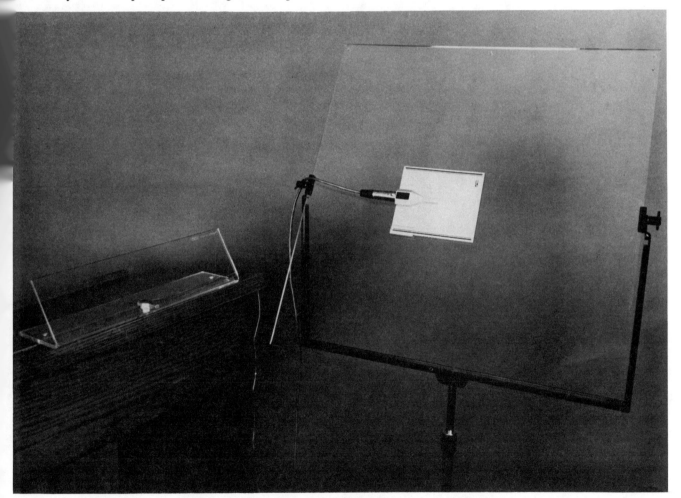

Figure 2d: Although a "pressure zone microphone" (PZM) can be attached directly to the sound board when recording piano, for other instruments it is generally mounted on a wall or on a reflective surface of its own. The larger the surface, the greater the bass response—up to a point. (*Courtesy of Crown International, Inc.*)

Figure 2e

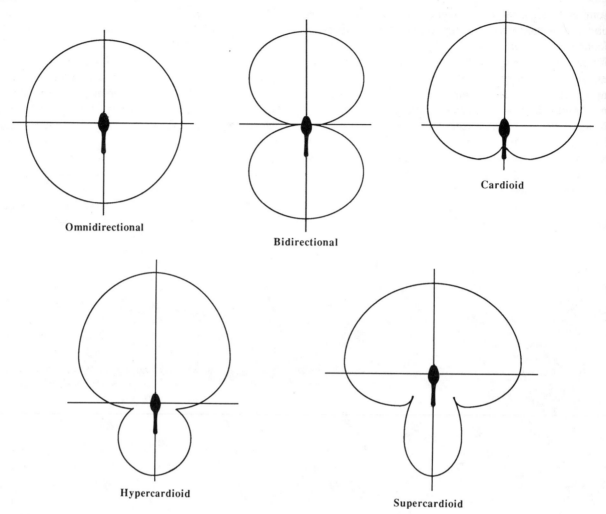

Omnidirectional

Bidirectional

Cardioid

Hypercardioid

Supercardioid

1. Polar response patterns of omnidirectional and unidirectional microphones. (*Courtesy of Audio Technica U.S., Inc.*)

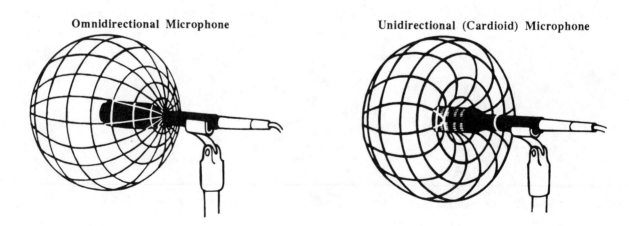

Omnidirectional Microphone

Unidirectional (Cardioid) Microphone

2. Three-dimensional polar response patterns. (*Courtesy of Audio Technica U.S., Inc.*)

Omnidirectional

An omnidirectional response pattern is one that attempts to exhibit an equal response to sound, no matter what direction it's coming from. This means that an omnidirectional microphone is able to pick up sounds coming from the front, sides, and rear and give them equal treatment—although there is a certain amount of high-end loss in any sound that comes from behind.

Because these mikes cover such a wide field, they are rarely used to isolate an instrument. However, they are excellent mikes to use when you want to capture ambience, and they are very useful during backing-vocal overdubs when you have more singers than you have mikes.

Bidirectional

A bidirectional microphone exhibits a response pattern that resembles the figure "8," meaning that it will pick up sound from both the front and rear equally well, while rejecting any sound that strikes it from the side. Thus, bidirectional (or "figure-8") mikes are used primarily either to generate stereo mike fields or to capture room ambience when recording backing vocals or amplified guitars. Outside the studio, they are often used to record classical music in a live environment.

Directional

A directional response pattern is one that exhibits a concentration of response in the direction the mike is aimed. In most cases, this means that the mike will reject any sound coming from the side or from the rear. Therefore, to pick up the complete signal, a directional microphone needs to be pointed at, or just to the side of, the source.

As you'll see throughout the remainder of this section, there are many different directional patterns in use. And although most less expensive mikes will exhibit just one or another of these patterns, many condenser mikes offer variable settings that allow you to choose from between two and four different patterns.

Cardioid (Unidirectional)

A cardioid (or unidirectional) microphone exhibits a heart-shaped response pattern that vaguely resembles an inflated balloon you're poking with your finger. As the shape of this pattern indicates, a cardioid mike will give you full response when pointed at, or slightly to the side of, the source, while rejecting any sound coming from the sides or from the rear.

This pattern of response makes cardioid mikes excellent multipurpose studio mikes, since they can be used as close mikes to isolate an instrument while retaining a wide-enough field of response to serve as a distant mike with which to pick up the ambience of the room.

Hypercardioid

A hypercardioid pattern is shaped somewhat like a mushroom, but with a tighter frontal field of response than the normal cardioid. This means that a microphone exhibiting a hypercardioid response will pick up any source it is pointed toward, plus it will pick up many sounds coming directly from the rear. Under studio conditions, when only one instrument is being recorded, this mike is thus able to focus its attention on the source but at the same time pick up room ambience in the form of reflections off the walls and ceiling.

Supercardioid

This is another variation on the cardioid theme, and like the hypercardioid pattern, it responds to sounds behind it. However, the supercardioid has a narrower rear field of response, so the only ambience it will pick up will be from sound that is being reflected off the opposite wall.

Yet the frontal field on a supercardioid extends a full 180-degrees, which can make it very useful for recording horn sections and multivoice backing vocals.

TAPE TIP #5
Polar Response Patterns

Microphones exhibit different patterns of response at different frequencies. When a mike is tested, these patterns are determined and placed together on a round chart to form what is called a "polar response pattern."

These patterns can tell you a great deal about how your microphone performs. For example, if you look at the polar pattern of a typical cardioid mike (Figure 2f), you see that the pattern of rejection is most pronounced for signals of 8K and above, meaning that it just won't pick up the high-frequency portion of any signal that is not directly in front of it (on axis). At 1K, the classic cardioid pattern can be found. Yet at lower frequencies, this pattern begins to break down, and by the time you reach 100 Hz, the response almost resembles that of an omnidirectional mike.

Unfortunately, there are a lot of things these patterns don't tell you, such as the overall quality of the mike. Plus, these microphones are tested under ideal conditions, just as when they rate cars for fuel efficiency, so you can't always accurately judge how the mike will perform in your studio.

Figure 2f: Polar pattern of cardioid mike. (*Courtesy of Audio Technica U.S., Inc.*)

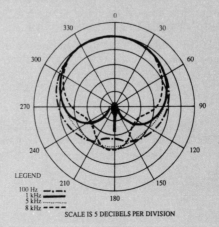

LEGEND
100 Hz
1 kHz
5 kHz
8 kHz

SCALE IS 5 DECIBELS PER DIVISION

IMPEDANCE

Another way to categorize microphones is according to the level of their output impedance. For example, condenser mikes are considered to be low-impedance because they exhibit an output impedance level of between 50 ohms and 200 ohms, depending upon the mike. In fact, any mike with an impedance level under 1,000 ohms, which includes most "home" mikes, is considered to be low impedance.

Yet the real importance of output impedance is that it affects how the mike needs to be treated as it is brought into the console, because *if the output impedance of the mike is greatly different from the input impedance of the desk,* the signal quality will suffer. For example, you would not want to plug a microphone that has an output impedance of 200 ohms into a high-impedance, line-level input on the console, because the signal would be too weak to properly record. Instead, you'd want to plug the mike into a low-impedance "Mic" input (which uses an XLR connector), where it would receive a boost up to line level.

Condenser mikes are the only microphones that *must* be brought in on a low-impedance input. On the other hand, dynamic mikes usually operate at between 500 ohms and 600 ohms, so they can be plugged into any console mike input or directly into any tape recorder, and they'll sound just fine. *However, 600 ohms is still low impedance, and you'll find that you'll improve the signal quality of almost any dynamic mike if you bring it in on a low-impedance mic input* (although the degree of improvement will depend upon the mike, so experiment and see what works best).

A console's low-impedance mike inputs utilize an XLR format, and in order to use them, you'll need a mike cable that has an XLR plug (see Figure 2h, page 39). So if your cable is equipped with a standard, ¼-inch phone plug, you have one of two options: buy a mike cable that is equipped with an XLR plug or buy an input transformer/adapter.

Your first choice should be to buy an XLR-equipped cable and plug it directly into the low-impedance mike input on the console. However, if for some reason you can't outfit your mike with an XLR cable, you can try using a high-to-low-impedance input transformer. These devices function as adapters, as they have a standard, ¼-inch, female phone plug at one end, and at the other end a male XLR connector that can be plugged into the low-impedance mike input on the console. Yet because they also act as transformers, the signal will not be as strong or as clean as what you'd get using the XLR mike cable and going directly into the low-impedance input.

PHANTOM POWER

Phantom power is a specially designed console circuit that is used in conjunction with low-impedance condenser mikes. In order for a condenser to function properly, it must receive a constant supply of power. Normally, this power is supp[lied] either by a portable battery pack or by a stationary po[wer] supply unit. However, if you have a console that is equip[ped] with a phantom power circuit, this circuit will effectiv[ely] take care of the microphone's power needs, and no outs[ide] power source will be required.

Phantom power is fully compatible with dynamic mic[ro]phones, and it will not harm them when engaged. Howev[er,] not all condenser mikes will operate at the 48-volt level t[hat] phantom power supplies, so you should check your owne[r's] manual before proceeding. If it is compatible, all you ha[ve] to do is switch on the phantom power and plug the mi[ke] directly into the low-impedance input of the console.

MICROPHONE SENSITIVITY

The "sensitivity" of a microphone is directly related to t[he] level of output it sends to the console. For example, a high[ly] sensitive mike is one that generates a strong signal, eve[n] when it's being applied to a very soft sound, while a lo[w-] sensitivity mike has very little output at those low volumes[.]

This particular response characteristic will determine ho[w] well a microphone performs in a given situation, because t[he] output level of a mike will vary according to the volum[e] level of the source. If a mike is highly sensitive and pro[-] duces a strong signal at low volumes, it will generate a[n] extremely powerful signal if it is used to mike somethin[g] like a stack of Marshalls or a snare drum. This, then, woul[d] not be an ideal situation, since you'd have to strongly pa[d] the signal upon input into the console, and even if you coul[d] avoid distortion in the console, the mike itself would likel[y] go into distortion.

Therefore, when recording extremely loud sounds, it'[s] much better to use a mike that has a lower level of output[,] given that it has the same level of quality. It will send a les[s] powerful signal to the console and reduce the amount o[f] padding needed. Plus, such mikes go into distortion less eas[-] ily because their diaphragms are less sensitive.

When recording quiet passages, you want to stick with a more sensitive mike because it would send a stronger signal to the console. This will allow you to keep the level on the console down, and you'll avoid adding any console noise to the recording.

Typically, nonribbon, dynamic mikes are the least sensitive, and condenser mikes are the most sensitive.

MIKE TECHNIQUES

Specific mike techniques are outlined in each of the instrumental recording chapters. However, the examples we provide are to be used as guidelines with which to experiment and build upon, because the methods you use will depend upon the particulars of your situation.

Before you can begin to experiment, it's important that you know what tools you have available. So it would be a

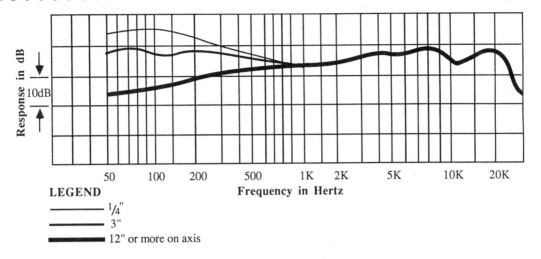

Figure 2g: Proximity effect is shown in this unidirectional microphone response graph. When the source is one-quarter inch away from the mike, the bass response is much higher than when the source is three inches from the microphone. Thus, if the source is too close to the mike, the signal loses definition and becomes overloaded with bass. (*Courtesy of Audio Technica U.S., Inc.*)

good idea for you to test your microphones for response and sensitivity, and try them out under various recording conditions. It would also be a good idea to try pairing different mikes together and listening to the results.

If you've kept any of the literature that came with the mikes, check out the polar response patterns, and try recording from different angles and from different distances to see how that alters the response. And if one of your mikes sounds like a real dud, double-check the wiring, and make sure you're running it at the proper impedance level.

And remember that the better you know your mikes, the easier it is to improvise when you run into a snag.

PROXIMITY EFFECT

One term you will encounter throughout our discussions on mike technique is "proximity effect." This is the increase in bass response that occurs the closer the mike is to the source (Figure 2g).

To understand this phenomenon, all you have to do is stand in front of a mike and monitor the difference between the way your voice sounds when you're twelve inches away from the mike, and the way it sounds when you're an inch away. If you have a thin, weak voice, you'll sound like a baritone when you're right on top of the mike. But if your voice is normally strong and clear, it will begin to get muddy when you move close in, and the bass will be too strong relative to the rest of the signal.

The proximity effect can be extremely detrimental to your recordings, particularly if you have limited EQ capabilities. With proximity effect, you'll find a continual buildup of signal around the 200 Hz range, and this will destroy much of the clarity of the recording. One way to get rid of this 200 Hz "hump" is to reduce the EQ at 200 Hz, and yet, as you'll

see in our instrument chapters, there are many other EQ levels you'll want to be treating. So if you can keep proximity effect out of your recordings, you won't have to concern yourself with this 200 Hz dip.

One area in which proximity effect truly takes its toll is during vocal performances. Most singers who have only worked in a live situation are going to want to be eating the mike as they sing, since that is what is required of them onstage. Yet, as you'll see in our chapter on vocals, that is not what's best in the studio, where vocal performances need to be recorded at least eight inches away from the mike.

PHASE CANCELATION

Phase cancelation is the resulting alteration in normal frequency response that occurs when a mike is either out of phase with its acoustic surroundings or with a second, closely positioned mike.

Single-Mike Cancelation

When a mike is placed in highly reverberant surroundings, after it responds to the direct sound, it is subjected to reflections that arrive an instant or so later. If these secondary waves are strong enough, and their delay times are just right, the low-frequency sound waves will cancel each other out, and as a result the recording will lose much of its bass response.

The worst offender for the creation of such bounce waves is a highly reflective floor. Therefore, if you find that you have to keep boosting the low-end EQ on a signal, but you're getting very little added response, you'll either have to alter the mike position or cover the floor with an acoustically absorptive material like carpeting.

Multiple-Mike Cancelation

Phase cancelation can also occur when you are using two mikes to record an instrument. In this case, while you may not hear any difference in tone when the microphones are listened to individually or in stereo, when they are panned together to form a monaural image, you will notice an immediate drop off in bass response, or a "tubular" sound.

This can be due to one of two factors: either one of the mikes is wired out of phase, or the mikes are improperly positioned relative to the acoustic source.

It's not unusual to run across a mike that's wired out of phase, so the first thing you'll want to do is replace both sets of cables. Then, if you still have a problem, try flipping the reverse-phase switch on your mixer (if it has one), or just try using a different mike. Yet although this may get rid of the problem for the moment, it would be a good idea to have the out-of-phase mike repaired.

It's more common that two mikes will be *acoustically* out of phase, which means that because of their relative distance from the source, the sound waves are causing the diaphragms of both mikes to vibrate sympathetically. To rectify this situation, you need to monitor the signals and slightly alter the position of the mikes until the cancelation problem disappears.

Again, you may not hear the cancelation if the two signals are allowed to remain stereophonic. However, if they are to be combined at some point to form a monaural track, you have to make sure that the mikes are in phase before they are recorded. The phase problem won't go away just because the signals are recorded on separate tracks, and even if they remain stereo, you may find that when listening to the final mix, the phase problem will arise if the speakers are too close together. Therefore, it is always a good idea to listen to a monaural mix of the mikes after you've positioned them, and to take care of any problems at that point.

NOTE—*For the specific mike techniques used on individual instruments, see chapters 9–15.*

TAPE TIP #6
Plugs, Wires, and Soldering Tips

Most musicians are familiar with the plugs and cables they use with their instrument. However, it's equally important that you familiarize yourself with the connectors that are used in the studio—particularly if you intend to make or repair any of those cables yourself.

If you enjoy soldering, and you have the temperament for it, you can save a lot of money patching up cords that you would normally throw away. However, the work requires patience as well as an understanding of the hardware.

Plugs

Plugs come in all shapes and sizes, but the three most common to pro and semipro gear are phone plugs, RCA plugs, and XLR connectors. Each type of plug has a variety of applications, but in general, RCAs are used to run line-level signals to and from tape recorders, small mixers, and hi-fi gear; phone plugs (these are the plugs used for guitar cables) are used to run everything from low-impedance to high-impedance signals; and XLRs are used to run balanced, low-impedance signals such as those associated with a direct box or with microphones (Figure 2h).

Wires

When putting your own cables together, you should always use shielded wire (although speaker wire can be unshielded). Shielded cable has a braided, wire jacket that surrounds and grounds the cable, thus "shielding" it from radio interference and eliminating buzzes and hums.

As a ground, the shield needs to be treated as an individual wire and soldered to the ground terminal of the plug. This means that the cable needs one less wire than there are terminals on the plug. So, mono phone plugs and RCA plugs, which have *two* terminal contacts (ground and "+"), require shielded, *single-strand* cable, while stereo phone plugs and XLR plugs, which have *three* terminal contacts (ground, "+," and "−"), require shielded, *two-strand* cable.

Soldering Tips

It's impossible to cover every aspect of soldering in the limited space available. However, if you already have some understanding of the techniques, the following tips should help make the work a lot easier.

1. Whenever you're attaching a plug to a cable, the *first* thing you want to do is slip the plug's protective shell (or housing) onto the cable. This is an easy thing to forget, in which case you'll have to redo all the work.
2. It's most important to have a good, temperature-controlled soldering iron (such as the Weller Solder Station) and a supply of fresh tips. Cheap irons, like worn tips, can behave erratically, and if the iron is too cold or too hot, you can end up with a bad solder joint or a damaged plug.
3. Two useful accessories to have are a pair of variable-gauge wire strippers and a vise or a clamp, which can be used to secure the plug while you solder. They will help make your work neater and more precise.
4. Always use rosin core solder. Acid core solder will eat through the wires.
5. Always heat the solder joint with the iron before applying any solder. But be careful not to overheat the plug.

continued . . .

Figure 2h: Plug types normally found in the studio.

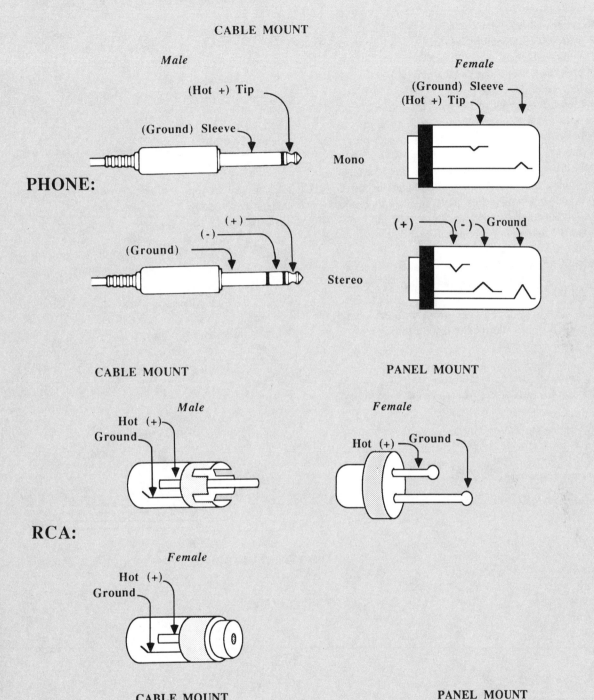

CABLE MOUNT

Male

(Hot +) Tip

(Ground) Sleeve

Mono

Female

(Ground) Sleeve
(Hot +) Tip

PHONE:

(+)
(-)
(Ground)

Stereo

(+)   (-)   Ground

CABLE MOUNT   PANEL MOUNT

Male   *Female*

Hot (+)   Hot (+)   Ground
Ground

RCA:

Female

Hot (+)
Ground

CABLE MOUNT   PANEL MOUNT

Female   *Male*   Pin 1   *Female*   *Male*
                        Pin 2
                        Pin 3

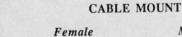 **XLR:**

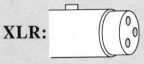 PIN #1 is usually ground. PIN #2 is usually (-) but sometimes (+).
PIN #3 is usually hot (+) but may be (-).

continued . . .

6. Never use Scotch tape or masking tape to insulate the wiring. Instead, cover any exposed wires or connections with "heat-shrinkable" tape (or heat-shrinkable Teflon tubing), as it will provide a tighter, more secure layer of insulation than electrical tape. To use it, just wrap the exposed area, then heat it with a heat-shrink gun, which operates like a hair dryer but is much hotter.

7. Always keep a moist sponge or rag nearby so that you can regularly clean the tip. Often, it will pick up old solder (particularly if you're rewiring a used plug), which will not melt as cleanly as fresh solder.

8. Never pile layers of solder onto a connection, because the larger the solder joint is, the more chance it has of coming in contact with other parts of the plug and shorting out. Besides, if the solder joint has been properly preheated, and the iron is hot, it'll take very little solder to secure the connection.

9. Never begin soldering until you've stripped all the wires in the cable and made sure that each reaches its respective terminal. In other words, *first* prepare the cable, *then* begin soldering. And as you finish with each connection, wrap it in heat-shrinkable tape or tubing.

Phone Plug Terminals

10. The nice thing about phone plugs is that each of the terminals has a small hole in it. So, if the wire is thin enough, you can pass it through the hole and wrap it back around on itself to form a closed loop (Figure 2i). Then, by applying solder both to the area of the hole and to the length of wrapped wire that closed off the loop, you have a connection that is quite strong.

11. On the other hand, if the wire is too large for the hole, the other alternative you have is to simply lay the wire on top of the connector and solder it firmly into place. Then, make certain to wrap it in heat-shrinkable tape, as this will strengthen the joint.

XLR Connectors

12. XLR plugs are pin connectors, which means that all three wires need to be the same length. Therefore, the easiest thing to do is create a third wire out of the shield. So, after you've unwrapped the shield, twist it gently so that it will hold its shape. Then, cover it either with heat-shrinkable tape or Teflon tubing to insure that it will remain insulated (Figure 2j). It's also a good idea to wrap the area where the wires emerge from the cable, to insure that no shield wire is left exposed.

13. When soldering XLR plugs, leave about 1/16-inch of stripped wire above the connector. This will make for a clean, easy solder joint when inserted into the pin (Figure 2k).

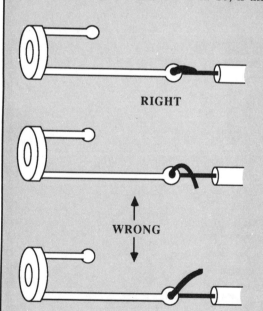

Figure 2i: Closed-loop soldering technique used on ¼-inch phone plugs.

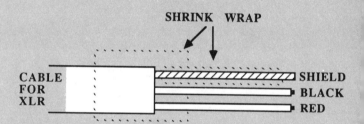

Figure 2j: Preparing the cable when soldering an XLR plug.

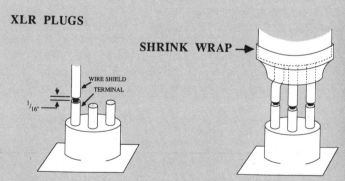

Figure 2k: Soldering the XLR plug.

3

Multitrack Tape Recorders

The tape recorder is undoubtedly the most important component in the audio chain. After all, without it there would be no such thing as a recording, and in a very real sense, *its* limitations are *your* limitations.

By the same token, the more you understand about how tape recorders actually work, the easier it is to make them work *for* you. And the more familiar you are with their capabilities, the less you need to worry about their limitations.

OWNER'S MANUALS

The best way to learn about your machine is to read the owner's manual, which is something too few people do. It contains all the specific details of operating and servicing the unit, as well as a list of precautionary measures. And, as you

go through the next few chapters, you may need to refer back to it to see how, or if, your unit performs the various functions that are discussed.

FORMATS AND TRACK CAPACITIES

Multitrack tape recorders are available in two basic formats: reel-to-reel and cassette. The reel-to-reel *(open reel)* format, which has existed in its present form since the 1940s, utilizes a double-reel configuration in which the tape passes from a supply reel, across the tape heads, to a take-up reel (Figure 3a). The cassette format, which has only been in existence since the late 1960s, utilizes the same tape path but packages the tape in a cartridge.

The open-reel format offers a rich variety of multitrack

Figure 3a: Tape path on an open-reel tape machine.

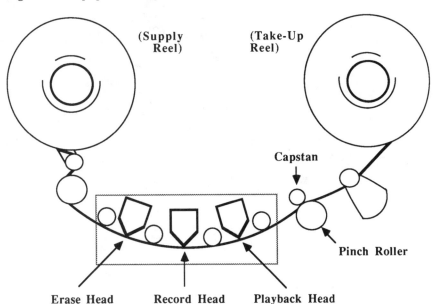

(Supply Reel) (Take-Up Reel)

Capstan

Pinch Roller

Erase Head   Record Head   Playback Head

TAPE TIP #7
Tracks vs. Channels

Two of the most confusing terms for the recording novice are "tracks" and "channels." These words are often used in ways that make them appear to be interchangeable, while in fact they have two distinct meanings.

"Track" refers to a location on the tape. More precisely, a *track* is a strip, running the length of the tape, which is assigned to one of the record head/playback head pairs. If you have eight of these pairs, you have eight tracks, each running side by side along the tape. So, to "record a track" is to print a signal onto one of these strips.

A "channel" is the electronic circuitry through which a signal flows. In the case of a tape recorder, it's the circuitry that sends the signal to, and through, the tape heads as you're recording a track and later *channels* the playback signal to an output. This circuitry can also be that within a mixing console or a playback amplifier.

Once you understand these concepts, you can see why they might *appear* to be interchangeable. For example, a 4-track recorder can quite properly be called a 4-channel recorder, but only because in order to record four tracks, the tape deck needs to have four channels.

But if you still need some easy way to tell the two apart, just remember that you don't make channels, you *make tracks*. . . .

---

equipment. There are 2-track, 4-track, and 8-track machines available in a ¼-inch tape format; 8-track and 16-track machines in both ½-inch and 1-inch tape formats; and studio-quality 24-track, 32-track, and even 40-track machines, which use a 2-inch tape format.

Unfortunately, the cassette format does not yet offer quite as large a selection. For the most part, these decks are only available in 2-track and 4-track formats, which use standard, ⅛-inch (0.15-inch) tape. In 1984 Akai introduced a cassette deck that uses ½-inch tape and provides 12-track capabilities, but with the exception of the new 2-track digital decks, which have limited applications (see "Digital Tape Decks," page 277), this deck has been the only unit to break the standard cassette mold.

TAPE HEADS

Tape recorders may come in all sizes and shapes, but matter what kind you own, be it open reel or cassette, track or 24-track, the principles of analog recording are same.

Figure 3b shows a typical tape head configuration. As tape passes over these heads, it is either erased, record onto, or played back. Each head governs one of these three functions and is, in fact, a "stack" of smaller heads which are each assigned to a separate track. This allows each head in the head stack to function independently of the others, so for instance, you can record on one track while simultaneously listening to another.

Figure 3b: Tape path across tape heads. (*Courtesy of TEAC Corporation of America*)

Erase Head

The erase head is the first head to come in contact with the tape. The function of this head is to erase any existing signal from the track (or tracks) of tape you are recording onto. This head is only "active" when the machine is in the record mode.

Record Head

The record head is the head stack that actually places, or transfers, the signal onto the tape. It does so by electromagnetic induction, which creates kind of a "picture" of the sound at the molecular level.

Playback Head

The playback head reads the pattern that has been imprinted on the tape by the record head and sends the resulting signal through the tape recorder's output circuitry. Normally, this head is only used during playback, as the record and Sel-Sync functions are monitored off the recorder head.

HOW SIGNAL IS PLACED ON TAPE

In order to use a tape recorder properly, you really do need to understand the process by which signal is recorded. So, to make the concepts easier to grasp, we'll be drawing analogies between the way photographs are printed on paper and the way sound is printed on tape. These analogies are not meant to be full technical explanations, but rather they are meant to provide a way for you to visualize the concepts.

Recording tape is called "magnetic tape" because it is coated with a thin film of fine metallic-oxide particles. During record, these particles become energized by the flow of electricity running through the record heads, and they form patterns along the lines of the magnetic field. The shape and density of these patterns dictate the texture, volume, and clarity of the recorded signal.

In order to help these magnetic particles overcome inertia, a machine-generated, high-frequency signal current (known as bias) is also sent to the tape during record. As you'll see in chapter 4, this increases the high-frequency response of the recording. However, it also produces tape noise, because the particle pattern it creates reproduces as hiss.

The quality of the signal you send to the tape heads will greatly determine the amount of bias noise the recording contains. This is because it is the function of bias to make sure that every particle on the surface of the tape receives a charge, and any particles left uncharged by signal will be charged by bias. *Therefore, anything that is not signal will be noise!*

The effect of sending a weak signal to the tape heads is illustrated by comparing the lightly printed photograph in Figure 3c, with its properly printed counterpart in Figure 3d. If you think of the white areas in the two frames as representing tape hiss, and the inked dot patterns that create the photographs as representing signal, you can see how the

Figure 3c: This photo is a representation of a poorly recorded signal. In this case, all the white areas represent tape hiss. (*Courtesy of Laura Marenzi*)

Figure 3d: This photo is a representation of a properly recorded signal. It has a minimum of tape hiss, as it is a much more complete signal. (*Courtesy of Laura Marenzi*)

Figure 3e: This photo is a representation of tape saturation, in which, because of excessive volume, the recorded signal is distorted and all definition is lost. (*Courtesy of Laura Marenzi*)

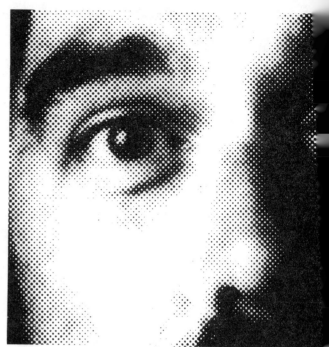

Figure 3f: This photo is a representation of the loss of definition due to slow tape speeds. With fewer magnetic particles available during the signal pulse, the "picture" of the recorded signal is less complete. (*Courtesy of Laura Marenzi*)

amount of signal can affect the amount of bias noise on the tape: when you reproduce a more complete signal, you generate less noise.

You can "reduce" bias noise by increasing the volume of the signal. This increases the number of organized particles in the pattern and reduces the number of uncharged particles. However, if you boost the volume too much, you create distortion.

In this sense, increasing the volume is like adding more ink to the dot pattern of the photograph. When you add more ink to Figure 3c, you allow the softer tones to appear, which gives the photograph better definition, as in Figure 3d. However, as you add more and more ink, the lighter tones get darker and darker, until they're as black as the rest of the dots in the pattern. As a result you get a picture that looks like Figure 3e: totally black.

This is much the same way that too much volume can destroy the "shape" of the signal—the highs and lows within the sound. You see, there are a finite number of particles on any given length of tape, and when *all* of the particles have become equally energized, you reach the point of "tape saturation." This is a form of signal distortion where all of the frequencies respond at the same level, and as a consequence the signal loses all definition and sounds flat.

Though a form of distortion, as you'll see in later chapters, tape saturation can be used as an effect. However, should the signal get any louder, the particles become *ultracharged,* and the molecular patterns break down. And since these patterns no longer have any shape to them, they just produce "noise," in the form of crackly, high-end distortion.

Another relationship that exists within these patterns is also important: the more particles you have available to be charged, the better the fidelity of the sound. This is why the speed at which you record is so important. With the tape moving at a faster rate, more particles pass over the head during the duration of the signal pulse. And that means more particles are available to the softer tones that otherwise wouldn't find room on the tape. As a result, there is more high end on the recording, cleaner bass response, and slightly less hiss, all of which means better overall definition.

In Figure 3f, you see that when, for example, you use half the normal number of dots to reproduce a photograph, the photo loses definition. In terms of recording, you'd get similar results at half speed: only the loudest parts of the signal would make it to tape, and they'd provide very little shading or detail.

Putting all these elements together, then, this basically means that to get the best reproduction quality from your machine, you should record at a fast speed, use quality tape, and send a signal to the heads that is loud but doesn't distort.

TRANSPORT SYSTEMS

The tape transport system is the part of your tape recorder that controls the flow of tape across the heads. You'll find examples of the two basic types of transport—open loop and closed loop—in Figures 3a and 3g (see pp. 41 and 45 respectively).

In principle, each of these transport systems operates in the same way: the tape winds through a path of "pinch rollers," "capstans," and "tape guides," which is designed to maintain a consistent tape speed across the heads. Without this, you would encounter wow and flutter, which occurs when the tape speed begins to wobble. And since these systems also serve to prevent your tape from snapping or stretching during start-up, they're a part of your deck you can't do without.

Open Loop

This is the most widely used reel-to-reel transport system. As the tape leaves the supply reel (Figure 3a), a wheel-hub brake system, which keeps the reel from spinning wildly out of control with the first forward tug, is engaged. If this brake system is faulty, and it applies too great or too small a pressure on the supply reel hub, your tape could snap or simply pour out onto the floor when you put the machine in a motion mode.

This brake system also insures that there will be constant tension on the tape as it travels across the heads. However, it can't do the job alone. A pair of spring-loaded guidance arms, placed at either end of the transport assembly, assist in this function by taking up any slack that might result from the initial "tug" on the tape. They also serve to restrict any lateral movement of the tape so that it maintains a consistent path across the heads.

After passing around the first guidance arm, the tape winds past a stationary "idler" post that sets the tape up for its pass across the tape heads. The three heads are positioned in a semicircular configuration to insure that the tape will in fact come in contact with each, while avoiding any sharp angles that might cause the tape itself to stretch.

Positioned in between the heads are a set of small, movable posts, called "lifters," which extend out during the fast-forward/rewind mode and lift the tape away from the heads. This saves a lot of wear and tear on the head stacks.

After passing across the heads, the tape passes through a pinch-roller/capstan assembly, which is the main stabilizing force in the transport system. The capstan is an extension of the motor drive shaft and turns at a constant speed. During record/playback, the pinch roller squeezes the tape against the capstan, and this forward pull, combined with the reverse torque from the wheel-hub brake system, insures a smooth, even tape flow.

When you take your tape machine in for its annual servicing, the technician will probably replace the pinch roller, whether you've been having trouble with it or not. That's because it's such an important part of the system and quite inexpensive. If the pinch roller is worn, or if it's excessively greasy or dirty, it won't apply an even amount of pressure on the capstan. As a result, the tape may have a tendency to slip off the capstan and either fold in half or crease along the edge.

After exiting the capstan assembly, the tape winds around the second guidance arm (which usually controls an automatic shut-off switch), after which it makes its way to the take-up reel. Like the supply reel, the take-up reel is driven by a separate motor and has its own brake system. When in a forward mode, the take-up reel motor engages and the supply wheel brakes. During rewind, it is just the opposite.

Closed Loop

The closed-loop transport system (Figure 3g) functions a bit differently from its open-loop counterpart. Instead of using a single pinch roller, the closed-loop design utilizes a dual-capstan assembly that effectively isolates the tape loop ("closes" it off) from the inconsistent tugs of the supply and take-up reels.

SUPPLY REEL AND TAKE-UP REEL ALIGNMENT

There is nothing more irritating than hearing tape rub against a moving take-up reel. Often, this is just the result of using plastic reels, which, unlike metal reels, tend to warp with age. Or it may be that the reel is loose, and you need to tighten the locking hub that holds it in place. However, the problem may also be due to an improper alignment of the wheel hubs.

Figure 3g: A closed-loop transport system. (*Illustration from Sound Recording by John Eargle*)

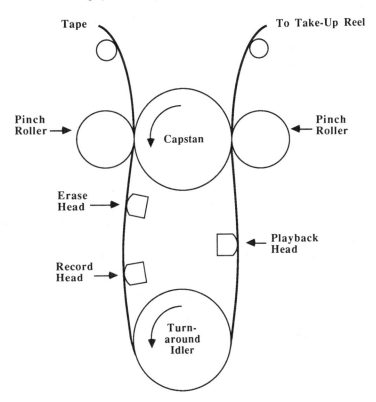

The wheel hubs, upon which the supply and take-up reels ride, are adjustable. So if your tape isn't sitting in the center of the reel, and is rubbing the sides, the hub can be moved in or out accordingly. Unfortunately, in order to make these adjustments, you have to get to the part of the hub that is *inside* the deck. And since it's not advisable to dig around in the guts of your equipment, most manufacturers provide thin rubber pads that can be placed behind a reel should the hub be sitting in too close against the machine.

Another sign that your reels are off line is the appearance of a crease or bevel along one edge of the tape, which occurs when the tape rubs up against one of the inside walls of the control arm groove. And if one of the hubs is *really* out of whack, you may suddenly hear a grinding sound coming from the hub axle assembly. When this happens, you should take your machine in for repairs—although, if you're handy, the repairman can probably show you how to do the repairs at home should it happen again.

MAGNETIC TAPE

Magnetic tape comes in many widths, thicknesses, and qualities, and knowing which tape to use in any given situation is important. Your choice will depend primarily upon the demands of your equipment and the recording quality you are trying to achieve.

Tape Width and Head Size

The width of the tape you use is governed by your deck's tape format. For instance, standard cassette decks use ⅛-inch (0.15 inch) tape. On the other hand, open-reel decks might use anything from ¼-inch to 2-inch tape, depending upon their track capacity and upon whether or not they have been designed for professional use. For instance, a professional 16-track is designed for 2-inch tape, while some of the new, home-studio 16-tracks are available in 1-inch or ½-inch formats.

The reason studio decks use such wide tape is that there is a limit to how small you can make a record head and still have it produce a high-quality signal. That's because smaller heads can't charge as many particles as larger heads, so they provide less signal definition. Therefore, if a manufacturer wants to fit more tracks on a machine without hurting the recording quality, his only alternative is to increase the size of the head stack and use wider tape.

To some extent, tape speed can compensate for head size, as faster speeds present the head with more particles per second. This technique is used by multitrack cassette deck manufacturers, for whom the issue is critical because of the even smaller cassette tape widths. That's why it is important to use high-quality tape in these machines and to run them at high speed (3¾ ips).

The two head stack diagrams in Figure 3h illustrate the dimensions of the heads and the head gaps on standard ¼-

Figure 3h

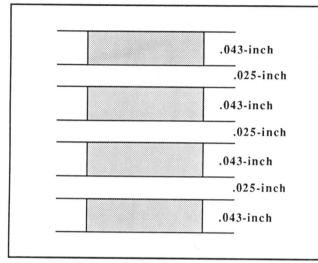

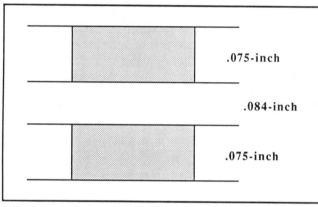

1. The dimensions of a standard, 4-track head stack. (*Illustration from* Sound Recording *by John Eargle*)

2. The dimensions of a standard, 2-track head stack. The larger heads and gap widths produce recordings that are superior to those produced by the 4-track, which is why 2-tracks make excellent mixdown decks. (*Illustration from* Sound Recording *by John Eargle*)

inch 2-track and ¼-inch 4-track machines. The first thing you'll notice about the head stack is that it looks, in fact, like a stack of heads—which it is. In order to insure the integrity of each head, and to reduce crosstalk (which is when the signal from one track leaks onto another), strips of nonconductive metal are sandwiched between the heads. The space this creates between the heads is the "head gap."

As you can see, the distances we're dealing with are extremely small: the standard gap on a professional 2-track playback head is twenty-five *thousandths* (.025) of an inch! Yet more important is the size of the head itself, because the larger the head, the more particles it can charge, which translates into better frequency responses. So, when you compare the size of the head on a standard ¼-inch 4-track (.043 inch) with its counterpart on a standard ¼-inch 2-track (.075 inch), it's easy to see why 2-tracks make excellent mixdown machines: the tape heads are half again as large!

Tape Thickness

Although your tape recorder is formatted to accept only one tape width, it will readily accept tapes of different thicknesses. At least it's supposed to. Unfortunately, if you have a "touchy" machine, thin tapes may have a tendency to snap or get mangled. Therefore you should monitor your deck's response to various tape thicknesses and steer clear of any that cause problems.

Tapes are manufactured in a variety of standard lengths and widths. So when you shop for open-reel tape, be sure to check the labels. The standard lengths for 7-inch reels are 900, 1,200, 1,800, 2,400, and 3,600 feet, and the respective thicknesses of the tape are 2.0 millimeters, 1.5 millimeters, 1.0 millimeter, 0.75 millimeter, and 0.5 millimeter.

The two problems you're most likely to run into when you use the ultrathin tape are "print-through" and creasing. Print-through occurs when you've encoded the tape with a signal that is so strong, some of its magnetic pattern is transferred to the next layer of tape on the reel. To some extent this occurs on all tape, but thinner tapes provide much less of a barrier between layers, so print-through is more likely to occur.

Creasing occurs when you use tape that is too thin for your pressure roller to handle. As a result, the tape either folds in half or develops a bevel along one of the edges, which destroys the response on one of the outer tracks.

The most devastating form of creasing occurs when an open-reel deck chews the tape up while coming out of fast forward or rewind. In this case, the thin tape isn't able to handle the stress of abrupt deceleration and either slips off the stack of tape already on the reel or snaps.

The bottom line is, if you want to avoid difficulties, especially if your deck isn't "fresh off the assembly line," stick to using tape with the thickness of 1.0 millimeter or better (in cassettes, never use a tape that runs longer than 90 minutes). You may not be able to fit as much music on the reel, but at least it won't end up in the garbage.

Tape Quality

Basically, there are three levels of tape quality: high bias, metal bias, and normal bias. High-bias tapes use superior-grade coatings of chromium dioxide (CrO_2) or ferric oxide (FeO), and, like metal-bias tapes, in order to use them you need to set the bias controls on your machine to the appropriate setting. If your machine cannot accommodate metal-bias or high-bias tapes, you shouldn't use them, because the recordings you'll generate will sound as if you covered the microphone with a sock.

However, if your tape machine does have variable-bias controls, you can produce some very interesting effects. For instance, you can record on high-bias chromium tape and play back at a normal-bias level. Although this makes the

---

TAPE TIP #8
Tape Storage: Heads Out or Tails Out?

"Heads out?" "Tails out?" No, it's not a coin toss. In fact, these are two alternatives for tape storage.

At home, you probably put a tape on the machine, play it, rewind it, and put it away. This is known as storing your tape "heads out," meaning that the beginning (or *head*) of the tape is on the outer layer of the reel. So, if you want to hear the first song on the tape, all you need to do is thread the machine and put it in play. However, in professional studios, tapes are stored "tails out," so that the *tail* end of the tape is on the outer layer, and in order to get to the beginning of a song, the tape needs to be rewound.

This practice dates back to when tapes were stored like stacks of pancakes rather than on individual flanges, and it was necessary to store them in a tight, evenly wound condition so that the edges of the tape were better protected. Unfortunately, rewind produces a very loose, uneven wind and can cause the tape to stretch, so it has become customary to either spool the tape or play it back from start to finish before taking it off the machine.

Today, if you want to know whether a particular reel has been stored heads out or tails out, all you need to do is check the color of the adhesive tape that was used to secure the loose end of leader tape to the reel. If it's red, the tape is heads out; blue, and it's tails out.

---

recording a bit noisy, it gives more apparent top end, which you may find pleasing.

There is not a great deal of difference between the chromium and ferric tapes, but as high-bias tapes, they'll give you better high-frequency response than you would get from normal-bias tape. Metal-bias tape, on the other hand, is widely regarded as being superior to both—although it's only available in a cassette format.

"Old" Tape

Don't use old tape! At least not to record on. If you ever had a magnet as a kid, you know that over time magnets lose strength. Well, the same sort of thing happens to magnetic tape: over time, it loses its ability to respond to the heads.

Recording tape also has a tendency to dry out after a few years, and *very* old tape can get so brittle that you can scrape pieces of the coating off with your fingernails. Of course, the tape may take ten or twenty years to reach that point, but if you're trying to get the best recording quality possible, you just don't want to mess around with anything but a fresh tape.

By "fresh" I don't necessarily mean "virgin"—at least not as far as recording tape is concerned. Magnetic tape does not lose its effectiveness just because it's been recorded on. When tracks are cut in recording studios, they are often repeated time and time again on the same piece of tape, and there is no loss of quality because there is no significant loss in the ability of the charged particles to re-form into a different pattern.

Tape Storage

Magnetic tape is quite sensitive, so if you want to keep your existing tracks from getting screwed up, you need to keep your tapes away from any strong magnetic fields.

For instance, if you have a bulk eraser or a head demagnetizer, you never want to bring a tape *anywhere* near them while they're operating. Neither do you want to bring a tape in contact with, or store it close to, a magnet. And if you think about it, there are plenty of magnets around a studio, the most powerful of which are on your speakers. So you never want to store tapes on a speaker cabinet or transport them in a guitar amp.

MULTIPLE TAPE SPEEDS

As we mentioned, the speed at which you record has a telling effect on the audio quality of your recordings. Most professional machines operate at 30 ips (inches per second), but the three speeds most generally available on semipro, open-reel gear are 15 ips, 7½ ips, and 3¾ ips. Some older machines even have speeds as low as 1⅞, ips, but by today's standards speeds of less than 7½ ips are virtually unusable for high-quality recording. So, if you can, always record at 15 ips. And since you use up a lot of tape in a hurry at high speeds, you'll want to use 10-inch reels if your deck can accommodate them.

You'll find that some cassette decks also offer multiple-speed settings: either 1⅞ ips or 3¾ ips. Again, you will want to run the tape at the higher speed, as you will get better fidelity.

Most new multitrack cassette and open-reel decks offer both multiple-tape speed and variable-tape speed, the latter of which allows you to increase or decrease the speed up to 15 percent. This "pitch control" feature can be extremely useful in situations where you've done most of your recording, and suddenly you find that either the song is in the wrong key for the singer or you need to add an instrument like a piano, which, for whatever reason, is not in tune with the other tracks. By using the pitch control, you can effectively alter the pitch of the recording to suit the new track.

However, you do need to be careful with pitch controls, because they are indeed *variable*. And if you record one of your first tracks at anything but the normal speed, you may find it impossible to duplicate the pitch throughout the rest of the recording.

4 〰〰〰〰〰〰〰〰〰〰〰〰〰〰〰〰〰〰〰〰〰〰〰〰〰

Reducing Signal Noise

In order to produce a clear, clean recording, whether at home or in a professional studio, you need to understand what signal noise is and how it can be reduced.

Although in this chapter we've attempted to be as accurate as possible in our technical explanation of this relationship, it should be noted that certain technical information has been simplified in order to make the material easier to understand and apply. So if you want to study the subject in depth, we suggest you look at one of the technical books listed in appendix A.

SIGNAL-TO-NOISE RATIO

The signal-to-noise ratio is not just a meaningless piece of numerical data used to fill up space on spec sheets. To your ears, it's the volume of the music in relation to the volume of hiss, or noise, in the recording. And just as the signal-to-noise ratio is often used to gauge the quality of a piece of gear, the signal-to-noise ratio of your recordings can affect the listener's evaluation of your material.

There is no way to eliminate signal noise in analog recording—there are only ways to reduce it. Therefore, as you'll see in this chapter, the key to signal management is knowing how to process and record a signal while generating the least amount of noise.

BIAS NOISE

The first type of noise you need to concern yourself with is the tape noise generated by bias, which is sent to the tape heads as you record.

As we discussed in chapter 3, bias is a high-frequency signal current used to excite the magnetic particles on the surface of the tape throughout the duration of the recording. These particles require a great deal of energy in order to overcome inertia in the initial stages of magnetization, and bias provides that initial surge. In fact, without some sort of

pregenerated energy floor (such as bias) to use as a jumping-off point, many frequencies—particularly those in the high ranges—would never make it to tape.

Yet bias is a trade-off, because although it allows your machine to add more high-end definition to the recording, it also adds noise, in the form of tape hiss. You can hear what this hiss sounds like by turning the record levels down on your tape deck and recording over a few feet of virgin tape. Upon playback, you'll notice that the portion of tape you recorded over has a certain amount of background hiss, while the rest of the reel is completely silent. That hiss is bias noise.

BIAS NOISE REDUCTION

You're always going to have some level of bias noise on a recording, but you should never be hearing excessive amounts of the stuff. If you are, the problem is either in your gear or in your technique.

Bias Adjustment

When you're having trouble with bias noise, the first place to look is in the bias control circuitry. If the internal bias controls are set improperly, the quality of your recordings will suffer dramatically. If the bias is set too high, the bias will be *over*compensating, and as a result your recordings will sound too bright and noisy. If the bias is set too low, it will not be compensating enough; the high frequencies, which most need that magnetic "push," will drop from the tape, and your tracks will sound dull and muddy.

You can get a good idea of what overbiased and underbiased recordings sound like by purposely misrecording a tape. For example, if your deck has "Normal Bias" and "High Bias" settings, in order to hear what an overbiased signal sounds like, set the controls to "Normal Bias" during record and playback and record a portion of one of your

49

favorite records on high-bias tape. With these settings, the recording will sound thin and unstable compared with the way it would sound using high-bias settings. To produce an underbiased signal, set the deck on "High Bias" and use a normal-bias tape for your recording. The signal will sound duller than if you'd recorded it using "Normal Bias" settings.

If the internal bias controls are malfunctioning, they probably just need to be reset. So if your deck was designed to let you realign the settings yourself, simply play the manufacturer's "alignment tape," and follow the instructions in the owner's manual. If not, you can take the unit into the shop and have the controls adjusted for a minimal charge. This should, in fact, be part of the normal servicing your unit receives during its annual check-up.

Of course, the problem may be due to something as simple as using the wrong external bias settings (such as recording high-bias tape with the bias switch set to normal) or using the wrong kind of tape for your machine. This is easy to check, since most owner's manuals will list the specific tapes the unit has been calibrated to use. Still, if your tapes sound bad, the best thing to do is have *everything* checked by a qualified technician.

High-Bias Tape

One way to solve the problem of excessive hiss is to use high-bias tape. This tape is designed for higher levels of bias than normal-bias tape, and as a result it gives your tracks better high-end definition. (High-frequency signals require a stronger magnetic "push" onto tape, so the greater the amount of bias, the better the high-frequency reproduction.)

This limits the amount of hiss you hear because it adds more signal (and therefore less noise) to the tape. Plus, since there is more high-frequency information present in the recording, you'll need to apply less high-frequency EQ—which otherwise would make the hiss more audible.

Tape Speed

Running your tapes at higher speeds is another way of limiting bias noise. As we've explained, the speed at which you record has a telling effect on the fidelity of the recording, and for this very reason it also affects the amount of bias noise you hear.

Faster tape speeds create a much fuller "picture" of the signal, and since creating a more complete picture literally means adding *more signal* to the tape, there will be *less noise* on the track.

Recording Levels

Likewise, if you send a weak signal to tape, you'll hear more bias noise. Thus, when you record, you want to send enough level to tape so that the VU meters are registering a little into the red—although you never want the transient peaks (for example, the loud smack of the kick drum) to push the needle off the scale. And if your unit has "peak indicator" lights, which respond much more quickly than the meters, use these to set your levels. In this case, the lights should be flashing occasionally, because if they remain brightly lit for long, it means the signal is too hot and will distort.

HEAD ALIGNMENT AND HEAD WEAR

Noisy recordings are often caused by malfunctioning head stacks. In order for the tape recorder to perform the record and playback functions properly, each of the three heads must be perfectly aligned with the others and must be at a ninety-degree angle to the tape. This means that each head in each head stack must be touching the tape at exactly the same lateral spot on the tape, and that the length of each

---

TAPE TIP #9
Oh, Mr. Repairman . . .

The Maytag repairman may have it easy, but it seems that recording gear breaks down with disgusting regularity at my house. Luckily, I have a good repairman.

Some of the things you should look for in a repair shop are friendly service, relatively quick turnaround time, reasonable prices, and, of course, *quality* workmanship. For instance, if, after the shop has your gear, you can't get a straight answer about what's wrong with it, how long it will take to fix, and how much it will cost, don't go back. And be wary of shops that promise to have your gear back to you within twenty-four hours. You might think it'll save you downtime (time during which your equipment is not working), but if you have to take the gear back a second time, you're not saving a thing.

If you do need to have a repair redone, you shouldn't have to pay for it. After all, you will have already paid through the nose: a technician's *time* will cost you about thirty dollars an hour, and there is usually a minimum fee for diagnosing the glitch, whether you have it repaired or not (though this is not included in the final bill if it *is* repaired). And, of course, there are always parts to be paid for.

You definitely should have your deck serviced at least once a year, depending upon how often you use it. A good shop will give your machine a complete check-up and cleaning inside and out, and they'll probably ask for a sample of the tape you use so they can adjust the bias to suit your needs. The work they do should also include cleaning, demagnetizing and aligning the heads, adjusting all levels, lubricating the motor assemblies, cleaning the switches, testing the unit for proper frequency response, and possibly replacing the pinch rollers. Your cost: about $90–$100. Your saving: a lot of aspirin!

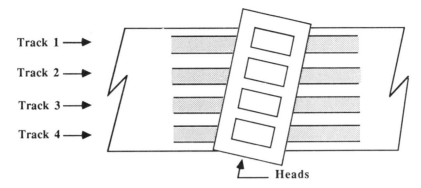

Track 1 →
Track 2 →
Track 3 →
Track 4 →

Heads

Figure 4a: When the azimuth of the tape heads is out of alignment, the full length of the head is no longer parallel to the flow of tape. As a consequence, there will be a loss of high-frequency response.

head must be positioned parallel to the movement of the tape.

If this is not the case, the heads are said to be "out of alignment." As a result, your recordings could suffer either a loss of high-frequency response or excessive crosstalk, which is when the signal from one track bleeds onto the next.

One of the most common forms of misalignment is an improperly set azimuth (Figure 4a). Azimuth is the angular relationship between the tape head and the tape's movement. The ideal azimuth would be when the tape head sits at a ninety-degree angle to the tape flow, so that the length of the individual heads in the head stack run parallel to the tape. However, if the azimuth is off even a bit, the heads won't be able to make proper contact with the tape, and your recordings will sound muddy.

Other misalignment problems can cause the signal to get noisy, so if you're having difficulties generating clear, clean tracks, you should have your heads checked out by a competent technician. Your repair shop can realign the heads for a small fee and run a check on the machine to see if you may also be having problems with excess bias.

Another factor that will determine the reproduction quality of your tape recorder is the amount of wear on the tape

TAPE TIP #10
Keep a Clean Machine!

Cleanliness is the first step toward a clean recording. And that means keeping your tape machine clean inside and out.

If you don't keep your tape heads clean and free of the residue magnetic tape tends to leave behind, they will have almost no high-frequency response, and you'll get flat, muddy tracks. If you let the interior of your machine get dirty, you'll have problems with the solenoid switches that you push to set the machine in motion, and that can result in a runaway tape deck, or worse yet, one that won't start or record when you want it to.

Keeping the inside of the deck clean is a simple matter: keep it covered when you're not using it. This is particularly important if you live in a dusty area or if you're a heavy smoker and your room/studio is poorly ventilated.

If you can't buy a cover for your machine, craft one from the heavy plastic sheets people use for storm windows (available at most hardware stores). Or better yet, the next time you take your machine in for repairs—like having your solenoid switches cleaned—ask if they have any plastic bags around. Many repair shops automatically provide these for the protection of your gear during the ride home.

Keeping the heads clean is also easy: just use some tape-head cleaner. Ampex makes a good product, as does TEAC and Nortronics. Many brands come with their own applicators, the best being those with foam-padded tips. Cotton swabs (Q-tips) can be used as a last resort, but you must be careful, because the fibers can get stuck between the heads.

This cleaner can also be applied to capstans, but you should never apply it to the pinch rollers, because it contains alcohol, which has a tendency to harden the rubber over time. So buy some rubber-cleaning fluid instead, and make sure it doesn't smell like alcohol.

Another excellent product to use on your heads is "stainless polish" (made by TEAC, for one). This does an excellent job of reducing head wear to the point where, if you use it each time you clean your heads, it can reportedly double the life expectancy of the head!

How often you clean your heads depends on how often you use your equipment, as well as how old your tapes are. Old tape can coat your heads with residue after only a few passes, and some new tape is not much better. So you should clean your heads before every session, or at least before each set of takes that you deem important. After all, a good cleaning doesn't in any way harm the heads, and it would be a shame to lose a good take to dirt.

heads themselves. The life expectancy of a tape head is relatively short. On average, after about 600 to 800 hours of operation, they begin to wear out. This is due to the constant flow of tape across the surface of the head, which has an eroding effect much like a river carving out a canyon—though the result is not nearly so dramatic.

In most cases you'll be able to hear the effects of head wear long before you'll see any evidence of it. When the record or playback heads start to go, your recordings will begin to lose their sparkle, and excessive amounts of tape hiss will start creeping in. These heads will need to be replaced immediately, and although the cost is relatively high (¼-inch 4-track heads, installed, cost about $125 apiece), if you want quality, it's got to be done.

When the erase head begins to wear, you'll lose the ability to wipe a track clean. Luckily, however, erase heads can often be polished by a technician and used for an additional 100 hours or so. Otherwise, it will cost about $150 to have a new one installed.

The hours of operation, by the way, are not computed in terms of the amount of time the tape deck is turned on, but on the amount of time the machine spends in the record/playback modes. When the tape is not moving, for instance, it's not causing any wear on the heads, and during fast forward or rewind, the machine moves the tape away from the heads.

SIGNAL NOISE

Unlike bias noise, which is added as you record, signal noise is contained within the electronic signal itself, prior to its being placed on tape.

There will always be a certain amount of noise in a given signal, because when a sound wave is transferred from an acoustic state to an electronic state (via, for instance, a microphone), the energy it takes to "create" the electronic pulse leaves a static imprint on the signal—sort of like a birthmark (Figure 4b).

This imprint, which is the "noise" you would hear if you monitored the signal direct from the mike, will always be there in exactly the same amount—from the moment of transition *into* the electronic environment, until the moment the sound waves are re-created by a speaker. However, what will vary is the amount of "clear signal" that exists in relation to the amount of noise it took to create it (such as the "signal-to-noise ratio" of the pulse). And when this ratio is altered, it changes the amount of noise you hear coming from the signal.

The important thing to remember here is that what changes is the amount of noise you *hear,* not the amount of noise that *exists* within the pulse. Figure 4c, for instance, shows what happens to a signal when it loses strength and the signal-to-noise ratio is lowered. In its initial state, the pulse exhibits a nominal ratio of signal to noise. By Stage B, however, the pulse has suffered a loss of clear signal, and the signal-to-noise ratio has deteriorated. If at this point you record the signal as is, which means that the ratio of signal to noise becomes fixed on tape, and you boost the level of the *total* signal back up to where it was (Stage C), you'll hear more noise. But as you can see, you haven't *added* any noise to the pulse, you've just lost some of the clear signal.

The fact is, every time a signal passes through an electronic "control" circuit, such as a volume fader or a tone regulator (EQ), it loses strength. And that worsens the signal-to-noise ratio, which is why your equipment can *appear* to be adding noise to the signal.

If the process of signal loss within the circuits were to continue unaltered, the situation would eventually become critical, because the amount of pure signal could theoretically become so low that noise would be about all you'd hear. For that reason, when electronic circuits are designed, small, clean amplifiers are placed at various points along the signal path. So every two or three strength reductions are followed by a boost, which brings the clear signal back up to level.

The difference between the boost these amps give (Stage D), and the boost that resulted in the noisier Stage C signal, is that here we're not amplifying a tape-recorded "picture" of the pulse, which has a *fixed* signal-to-noise ratio. Instead, we're applying a boost to the pulse itself, which adds strength to the *signal* and not the noise, because, as we already discussed, the noise portion of the pulse never changes.

SIGNAL NOISE REDUCTION

This whole concept is very important to the overall quality of noise reduction achieved during recording, because to eliminate noise, you want to do exactly what those circuit amps do: enhance the signal-to-noise ratio of the pulse *be-*

Figure 4b: A diagrammatic representation of an electronic signal.

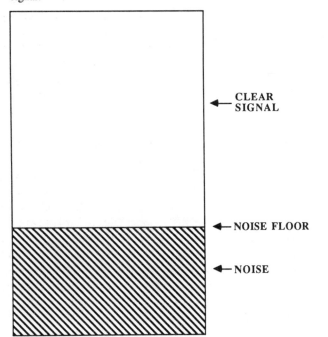

← CLEAR SIGNAL

← NOISE FLOOR

← NOISE

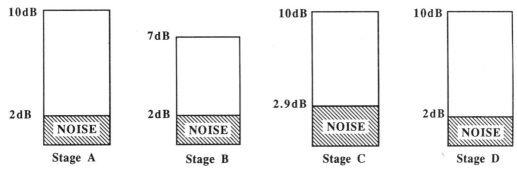

Figure 4c: When a clear, strong signal (STAGE A) suffers a loss of strength (STAGE B) by passing through an electronic circuit, its signal-to-noise ratio deteriorates. If the signal is then recorded and boosted back up to its prior volume level (STAGE C), the "noise" portion of the signal rises as well. However, if the signal is boosted *before* it is recorded (STAGE D), the boost would only affect the "clear signal," and the level of noise would not increase.

fore it reaches the tape heads. This means paying close attention to the treatment the signal receives from the time it's generated until the time it's recorded, making sure that *each successive link in the chain receives the strongest and cleanest signal possible*.

Mike Choice

The first link in the chain is the microphone, where the signal is "created." The more careful you are here the better, because after all, the best way to reduce noise is not to create it in the first place. In this respect, your choice of a suitable microphone and an appropriate miking technique is crucial.

A really cheap mike, for instance, will have poor frequency response, *and* it will create excessive noise. Even an expensive mike can cause trouble if it's brought in at the wrong impedance level, as it will require additional amplification. Or, if it's the wrong mike for the instrument, the signal may need additional tonal (EQ) enchancement, which can cause an increase in the noise level during later stages of the recording.

Mike placement is also important. If the mike sits too far from the source, it will produce a weak signal pulse that has very little clear signal relative to noise. Thus, it will carry excessive amounts of hiss directly to tape unless the high frequencies (and thus a good deal of tone) are completely removed.

TAPE TIP #11
Mixer/Recorder Calibration

When you're using a mixing console in conjunction with your tape recorder, you'll get cleaner recordings if you calibrate the input levels of the tape deck with the output from the console. This will give you the optimum signal-to-noise ratio for recording, and it will take much of the guesswork out of setting levels.

The first thing you need to do is find a continuous, non-undulating 1K signal that you can put through the mixer. If you have an automatic tuner with a "tone" production mode, or a synthesizer, either will do, because the tone produced by the C that is two octaves above middle C (C-1046) approximates 1K (see Figure 1a, page 30) and can be sent through the console. Your console may, in fact, come with its own 1K "oscillator" signal. Or you may want to buy an oscillator at your local music or electronics store.

The idea is to run this 1K signal into a mixer channel and center the pan control so that it will register on both left and right VU meters. Then, set your mixer's master output to the nominal level, marked "0," and raise the fader on the channel module so that it, too, is set at the "0" mark. (On powered PA consoles, these "0" marks are usually placed at the very top of the scale, while on recording consoles, the top of

the scale is usually marked as +10, and to set it at "0" you must pull back a bit on the fader.)

The "0" settings represent the manufacturer's nominal output levels, so at this point the VU meters should themselves be registering at their nominal "0" mark (which is at the very edge of the red). If this isn't the case, adjust the console input gain (or trim) by raising or lowering it until the needles are properly positioned. If you're not applying any gain reduction, and the meters still don't read "0," turn up the output level of the 1K signal until they do.

By setting the output level to "0," you are sending the best-possible signal to the tape deck. Therefore, what you want to do is use this to set the record levels of your tape machine, so that when it is receiving the optimum signal, it is recording at the optimum level and thus generating a minimum amount of noise.

This is done by sending the 1K signal from the console to the tape deck and setting the record levels so that the VU meters on the deck also register "0." As long as you mark these input settings, you should never have to recalibrate your equipment, unless one of the two pieces is sent out for repair. And you should never have to touch your tape recorder input levels again, either. If you want to make an instrument louder or softer, do so on the mixer's individual channel controls.

Sit down right now and try this simple little process. You'll find that it'll make recording a lot easier.

Equalization

While the principle function of EQ is to shape the total characteristics of the signal, it *can* play a role in noise reduction. EQ allows you to control the level of specific sections of the audio spectrum, so if you locate the set of frequencies in which the hiss is occurring, which is generally between 16K and 20K, you can simply eliminate them from the signal.

The problem is that noise is not the only thing being generated in those frequencies. All of the sibilants that give you the ambience of the room and its natural reverb are there, as is the "air" that seems to surround a vocal. So if you just cut out a block of these frequencies, your recording will lose a great deal of texture.

Still, if you have EQ, and you have a noisy signal, you may as well do something about it. The first thing you can do is experiment with the EQ in the highest range you have available, remembering that the lower the frequency, the more it will affect the body of the signal.

Begin by turning the EQ volume down (with graphic EQ, push the fader to the bottom), and gradually raise the level, listening carefully as you go, until you hear a balance of noise and signal that you're comfortable with. Of course, if you're EQing a bass drum or a bass guitar, you won't hear any signal in the 16K range, so you can generally eliminate the upper registers (and the hiss) altogether.

Parametric EQs allow you to limit the bandwidth to a very narrow range, which means that you can zero in on a specific frequency, remove it, and still leave that section of the spectrum relatively unscathed. This makes the parametric EQ a much more desirable tool for noise reduction. But you still have to be careful.

Tone Controls

Very simply, tone controls do the same job as the controls governing EQ, but they do it much less efficiently.

Your tone controls allow you to affect a wide range of frequencies at one time, and this can help reduce noise in the same way EQ does. However, tone controls affect a greater part of your total signal, and cutting down on the high end by turning down the treble may eliminate more of the signal than you'd like. Therefore, be careful if you're trying to use this control to reduce noise.

DOLBY/DBX NOISE REDUCTION

Although all noise reduction systems basically work the same, this is definitely one case where understanding exactly how something works is not essential to knowing how to use it properly.

So, to keep it simple but correct, we'll just say that noise reduction systems take a signal prior to recording and compress it. When this compressed signal is played back through the playback heads, it picks up a certain amount of noise—which is the case whether noise reduction is being used or not. However, during playback, the noise reduction system expands the signal, and the signal-to-noise ratio expands right along with it. This means that more clear signal is available, and the level of noise that would have been added to the output signal is effectively reduced (Figure 4d).

One important thing to remember about all this is that if you use noise reduction when you record the signal, you must also use it during playback, or the signal will be noisier than when you began. Therefore, whenever you send someone, like a record company exec, a tape copy of your material, make sure you *do not* apply noise reduction to *the copy*. You never know if the person at the other end is going to have the same capability, and you don't want to risk destroying the effectiveness of the production.

By the same token, Dolby and DBX systems can be very sensitive, and if the compression-expansion actions are not matched perfectly, you won't even get a good sound from *your* machine. So you should have these systems checked if your tapes begin to sound too dull or too bright.

NOISE FROM OUTBOARD EFFECTS

In discussing the signal noise generated by outboard effects, we are jumping ahead a little. Yet some of the noise in your recordings may come from either the misuse of effects or from the use of cheap effects gear. And since special effects are such an important part of the recording process, they deserve special consideration.

Most such signal noise is the result of using effects gear that was designed for stage use rather than studio use (such as guitar pedal effects). Here, the problem is one of noisy, inefficient circuitry.

As you'll see in upcoming chapters, there are a variety of ways to limit the amount of noise an outboard effect generates. This includes the use of direct box transformers (which allow you to use the more efficient console circuits to boost the signal), as well as the use of your console's effect send/return circuitry (which is designed to "limit" such noise).

However, in all cases, the basic concept remains the same. That is, you always want to send the strongest, nondistorting signal to the effect and then balance the level of the return signal against the level of noise being generated. So if the device is generating a fairly clean signal, you should return a strong signal to the console. But if you're getting a lot of noise from the effect, reduce the output level of the device and let your console boost the level of the return signal.

In addition, when you're using an effects pedal (or, for that matter, any other non-studio-quality gear), *never* use an AC adapter to power the equipment. These adapters are much noisier than batteries, and they'll make the job of reducing signal noise almost impossible. And if you *are* using batteries, be sure to listen for distortion in the effect, as this is a sign that the batteries are running out of juice.

Figure 4d

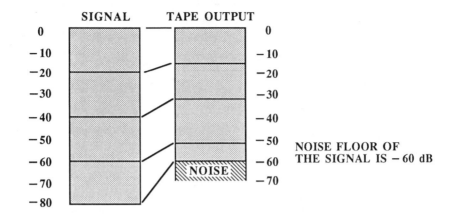

1. The noise level of a signal recorded without noise reduction circuitry using a tape recorder that has a -60 dB dynamic range. (*Illustration from* Sound Recording *by John Eargle*)

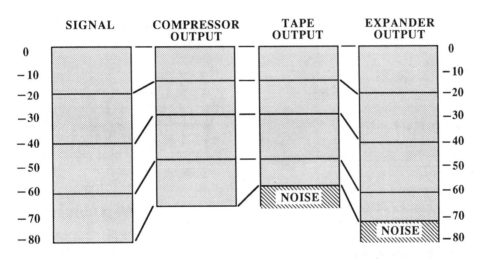

2. How a typical noise reduction system affects the signal. By using the compression/expansion technique, the noise reduction circuitry has effectively lowered the noise floor to -70 dB and thus increased the dynamic range of the signal from 60 dB to 70 dB. (*Illustration from* Sound Recording *by John Eargle*)

ROOM NOISE AND BAD WIRING

The most easily remedied recording noises are generated by poor equipment and bad playing habits. For instance, a noisy amp or a badly shielded guitar or mike cable will create hiss and pop and should be replaced. It's also important that the musicians *not* fiddle with strings or tap drum rims or do anything else that's going to be picked up and put on tape. These noises can be as detrimental to the recording as any others.

Another important source of noise to keep in mind is the room environment—especially if you're recording at home. To insure that you're not picking up things like the refrigerator or the air conditioner, or even crickets out in the yard, be sure to double-check your mike positions and test the room sounds by monitoring the mike feeds with the volume cranked up.

TAPE TIP #12
Demagnetizing the Heads

Over the course of hundreds of hours of use, your tape heads are going to become slightly magnetized. In extreme cases, this results in the loss of high-frequency response and/or an increase in tape noise.

If you have your machine serviced regularly and ask the technician to *de*magnetize, or "degauss," the heads (which they normally do anyway), this will never cause you to suffer any loss in recording quality. If, however, you make a habit of operating a bulk eraser near your gear, or waving a horseshoe magnet in front of your heads, you'll want to buy yourself a "head demagnetizer" at your earliest convenience.

These gizmos come in different forms, but most look pretty much like a bulky ice pick and cost less than $15. Read the instructions before you use it, and make sure that you *never* place the metal tip in direct contact with the running surface of the heads. This could create a scratch on the surface and damage the heads severely. Instead, cover the tip with a scrap of cloth before bringing it anywhere near your machine.

And *never* degauss the heads while the tape deck is turned on, or you will severely damage the machine.

SIGNAL NOISE CHECKLIST

You will always have a certain amount of noise in your recordings, but if you're careful, you should be able to keep it to a level where it does not interfere with the material. If you're having trouble with tape noise, chances are that you've either got a problem with your equipment or a problem with your technique. The following checklist includes the most common sources of, and reasons for, excessive track noise and is designed to provide you with a guide to clean recording.

Ambient Noise

1. After setting up your mike, boost the level of the input and monitor the "room." Make sure you aren't picking up the sound of an appliance, like air-conditioning, and if you are recording in the same room as the tape deck, make sure you aren't hearing any noise from the machine when it's in motion.
2. During vocals, make sure the singer doesn't hold the mike, as this will create unwanted noise.
3. After recording a track, monitor the playback for any squeaks or clicks from room furniture the musicians might be using during the performance (such as piano benches or stools).
4. Also monitor the track for any noise that may have been created by musicians fiddling with strings or tapping their feet or whatever.

Reducing Bias Noise

1. Calibrate the input levels of the tape recorder with the output levels of the console.
2. Clean the record and playback heads with head cleaning fluid.

3. Align the internal bias controls on your tape deck using the manufacturer's test tape. If you cannot perform this operation at home, take your machine to a repair shop and have them align the machine according to the type of high-bias tape you use in your recordings.
4. Regularly have the tape heads realigned and checked for wear.
5. If possible, use high-bias tape for your recordings, and make sure that the bias switch on your machine is set in the high-bias position ("CrO_2" or "FeO") during both record and playback.
6. If you are not using high-bias tape, make sure that the bias switch is set to "Normal" during both record and playback.
7. If your tape machine has multiple operating speeds (such as 15 ips, 7½ ips, and so on), record your material at the fastest speed offered.
8. Do not send a weak signal to the tape heads. If the VU meters are not registering at their nominal level ("0"), boost the level of the signal until the needles are peaking just inside the red.
9. If this boost in itself creates noise, check to see that you are using the proper mike for the particular situation, and that it is being brought into the console on the low-impedance mike input (generally this requires that you use the console's XLR input jacks). Also, try moving the mike closer to the source so that you can lower the amount of boost supplied by the tape deck or console.
10. If your tape machine offers noise control circuitry, use it if you like the way it makes your material sound. However, if you use it during record, make sure you also use it on the playback.
11. Refer to the troubleshooting guide at the end of chapter 5 for any noise problems having to do with consoles or outboard gear.

5

Recording Consoles

As you'll see throughout the book, it's our policy to stay away from the *technical* side of recording and to concentrate on *techniques*. Thus, the following chapter is meant to serve as a quick, easy guide to operating a console, and it does not provide a lot of "textbook" explanations of why they do what they do. You'll find, however, that it does include both a troubleshooting guide and a set of easy-to-read operational diagrams that are designed to be used as a reference while you're recording. Any technical explanations that have been included are geared toward these real-world applications.

THE CONSOLE IN RECORDING

Next to the tape recorder, the recording console is the most important piece of recording gear in your arsenal. (Note that recording consoles can also be called "desks," "mixers," "mixing consoles," and "mixing boards." These terms are interchangeable, and they are used as such throughout the book.) It is an extremely versatile home studio tool, and it performs a multitude of functions that have become essential to the process of making a quality, contemporary recording.

For example, when you record a signal, you EQ it in the console before sending it to tape. When you add a new track to a recording, you use the console to monitor the existing tracks. When you bounce, or combine, tracks, you run them through the console in order to balance the levels. And during mixdown, you use the console to add effects to the signals, to re-EQ them, and to balance their relative volume levels.

Yet the mixing console is not a difficult piece of equipment to use once you understand the basic principles of its operation. In very simple terms, the console gives you control over the quality and the movement of signals to and from tape, and it enables you to monitor your work.

At the most basic level, a console functions on the same principle as a mike mixer—which is the simplest form of mixing "console." With a mike mixer, you can bring two or more mike lines into the unit on individual channels, blend them together at different volumes, and send them out a single line. Sophisticated recording consoles do the same thing, though they provide for an even greater variety of signal sources (including line level) and for a greater variety of output options. And no matter how complex the operation appears to be, it's really just that simple.

CONSOLE AS PREAMP

The main difference between mike mixers and mixing consoles is that consoles function as preamps, while mike mixers have no internal amplifiers of their own. In chapter 4 we talked about preamplification as being a means of enhancing the signal-to-noise ratio of a recording, and consoles are designed around these principles. In fact, there are preamps at each stage of the console's circuitry (EQ, trim, and so on), so that any energy that is drained from the signal gets replaced immediately.

By functioning in this manner, the console helps reduce noise at every stage of recording, including the processes of adding effects and bouncing tracks.

CONSOLE AS MIXER

A console's primary function is to serve as a mixer. The fact is, although you can split one signal with a Y-cord and send it into two different inputs, you can't use a Y-cord to send two different signals into one input. By doing so, you over-tax the circuits and create "an impedance load." However, mixers are designed to prevent such occurrences and thus allow you to mix many signals together in as many different ways as you like—and for that reason alone they're invaluable.

CHANNEL MODULES

A multichannel console can look rather awesome to someone who doesn't know how to use it. But you shouldn't let all the dials and lights on the control panel intimidate you. After all, you only have to know how to use one channel on a 32-channel studio console in order to operate the other thirty-one.

The console is a collection of channels and circuits that are grouped together according to their function (Figure 5a). For instance, there are "input channels," which are used to bring the signal into the console and to add EQ; there are "buss channels," which are used to send the signal out of the console; and there are auxiliary circuits, such as the "cue send" and "effect send/return," which are used to split the signal so that it can be monitored or sent to outboard effects such as reverb.

Each of the input channels and buss channels has its own "channel module," which is basically the collection of circuits and panel controls that comprise, or are associated with, the individual channel. And each module is an identical, self-contained unit, which you see as a vertical strip of controls on the panel.

INPUT CHANNELS

In a sense, the input channel serves as an electronic platform or home base for the signal, so that once you get it into the console, you can establish it, EQ it, and send it along on the path you've designed. Basically, then, this channel provides a jumping-off point for the signal, and it gives you the initial control over its movements to tape, to effects, and to monitors.

Figure 5b is a detailed representation of the controls on an average input module. These modules can be broken down into five individual sections ("input," "EQ," "auxiliary," "buss assigns," and "status"), each of which controls a different function of the channel.

Channel Input Section

This section of the module, which controls the process of bringing the signal into the console, is used to establish the optimum level of signal to noise at input. On some consoles, these circuits enable you to reduce the strength of the input signal so that you can bring the strongest-possible signal into the unit, yet keep it from distorting. On other consoles, this section also offers control over circuits that can process signals of extremely low impedance, which eliminates any loss in quality from impedance mismatches.

Your console will probably have an input configuration consisting of one, or all, of the following three controls: a "mic/line" impedance switch, a "pad" switch, or a "trim" ("pad attenuation") knob.

MIC/LINE. The tape/line impedance switch, which can

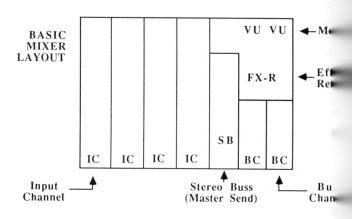

Figure 5a: Modular layout of a typical 4 × 2 × 2 console (*four input channels, two buss channels, and two effect sends*).

Figure 5b: A typical input channel module.

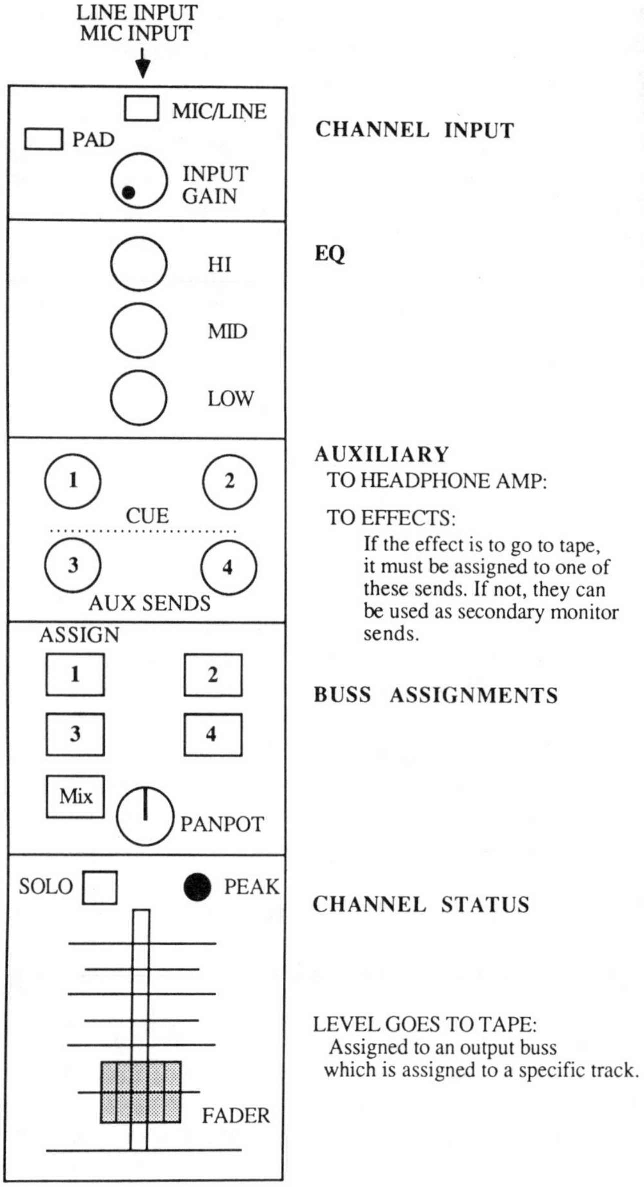

lso be called a "mic-pre" or an "LI" (line input), tells the console to treat the source as either a high-impedance or a low-impedance signal (see glossary). It is important to have his switch set for the appropriate level, because if, for instance, a low-impedance source is sent in at high impedance, the console won't give it the initial boost required to bring it up to the impedance level of the channel circuits, and it will be too weak to record.

It should also be noted that some manufacturers apply the "mic/line" label to their *pad* switches (see below), so, before assuming that it has any bearing on impedance, check your owner's manual.

PAD. A "pad" is little more than a muting circuit that lowers the level of the input signal a set amount. In essence, it is a safeguard device that protects against the distortion that might be caused by a sudden surge in signal strength, and when you turn it on, it sounds as if you've thrown a blanket over the signal. This level reduction can be as great as 50 dB or as little as 10 dB, although some consoles offer three-stage switches that give you the option of reducing the gain 20 dB, 35 dB, or 50 dB.

TRIM (Attenuation Pad). This is also a "volume" control, but unlike the pad switch, an attenuation pad offers *variable* gain reduction. This gives you more precise control over the amount of reduction you apply, and as a result you should get better overall signal quality. Usually an attenuation pad will allow you to reduce the input gain by any amount between 1 dB and 50 dB. However, the less gain you reduce the better, because with a stronger signal you'll hear less noise. So the idea is to use only as much gain reduction as is necessary to keep the signal from distorting, and the way you do this is to reduce gain until the channel's peak indicator light is only dimly flashing on and off.

Equalizer Section

The controls within this section of the module enable you to regulate the level of specific frequencies within the signal. Thus, they provide you with your first real opportunity to alter the texture and character of the sound.

In general, you will find one of four different types of EQ on your console: R/C, click stop, sweepable, or parametric. Each provides a different level of control over the frequency makeup of the signal (Figure 5c).

R/C (resistance/capacitance) EQ is provided by treble and bass tone controls. However, although it is used on everything from home stereos to PA mixing consoles, it is of limited value in the home studio, because it only enables you to boost or cut a fixed band of frequencies.

Click-stop (and graphic) EQ also uses a fixed-bandwidth format. However, in this case, the center position of the band can be moved to fixed positions *(click stops)* along the frequency spectrum, so that you can alter the *range* of frequencies being EQed. Graphic EQ is simply a different way of doing the same thing, so it, too, falls into this category.

Figure 5c: How each EQ format functions.

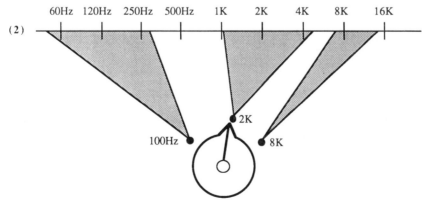

1. R/C EQ: Boost or cut applied to a fixed position, using a fixed bandwidth.

2. Click-Stop EQ: Boost or cut applied using a fixed bandwidth.

Figure 5c (cont.)

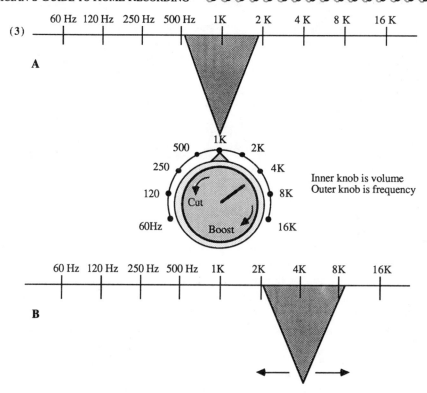

3. Sweepable-Band EQ: Boost or cut applied using a fixed bandwidth (A), but band moves up and down the spectrum (B) and can stop at any point along the scale.

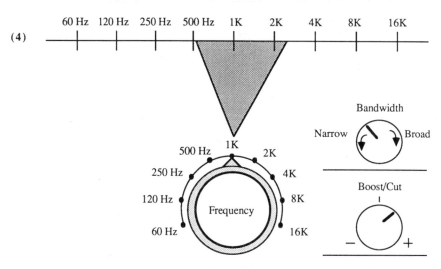

4. Parametric EQ: Boost or cut applied using a variable bandwidth, plus offers sweepable-band control.

Sweepable-band EQ also has a fixed bandwidth, but unlike click-stop EQ, the variable positions are not fixed. Thus you are able to manually *sweep* the band from one end of the spectrum to the other and stop at any frequency you wish.

Parametric EQ is the most sophisticated of the lot. Not only is it sweepable, but it also has a flexible Q—meaning that the bandwidth (or range of affected frequencies) can be broadened or narrowed as much as you like. Thus you can control precisely where you want the EQ treatment placed, how wide a range of frequencies you want it to affect, and how strong the boost or reduction will be in that range.

NOTE—*For more information on EQ formats, see Tape Tip #17, pages 104–106.*

uxiliary Section

his section of the module is used to send the signal to utboard effect units and headphone amplifiers.

CUE/EFFECT SENDS. These controls, which on your onsole might instead be called "monitor" sends or "aux" ends, regulate the amount of signal sent to the cue and ffect busses on the rear panel. From there the signal can be ed into the desired piece of outboard gear and, if used to dd effects, returned either through a second input channel r an effect return buss.

Each of the sends is a separate, monophonic circuit, so it s possible to route the signal to as many locations as there re sends. However, if you have four sends, two are normally used for effects and two are used as cue sends for the eadphone mix. If you have two sends, one can be used as a nonaural cue send and the other for an effect, or they can be used together as a pair of cue sends or as a pair of effect ends.

Buss-Assign Section

This section of the channel module is used to route the signal to one or more of the console's buss channels. The buss channel then controls the process of sending this signal, along with any others sent through the same buss, to tape, thereby allowing you to balance and send a number of sources to the same track.

The number of buss assignment switches on your console is determined by the number of buss channels it has. Each of these assigns represents a single monophonic output, but they can be paired together in order to provide a stereo feed: 1 and 3 being assigned a left channel, 2 and 4 a right channel.

PANPOT. When engaged in stereo mixing operations, this control is used to route the channel's monaural signal to any point left or right of stereo center. However, it only affects a signal if the channel has been assigned either to the stereo buss or to a pair of busses that are being used as a stereo send.

MIX. This control assigns the channel to the stereo buss, which is used as both a monitor source and, during mixdown, as a stereo send.

Channel Status Section

This section of the module contains a variety of basic channel control circuits.

SOLO. The solo switch enables you to isolate and monitor the channel without altering any other settings on the console. However, although the other channels will disap-

pear from the monitor mix, this control does not affect the mix that is being sent to tape.

PEAK LIGHT. This red light is an indicator lamp that safeguards against signal distortion in the channel. It lights up just *below* the point at which distortion would occur, so it's okay if, on occasion, it dimly flashes on and off. Should it be producing a bright flash or a steady glow, you'll want to lower the input gain of the signal. However, excessive boosts in EQ can also produce peaks, so be sure to check your EQ levels before cutting the gain.

CHANNEL FADER. The channel fader controls the volume of the signal that is sent to the buss channels.

Direct-Outs

Many consoles provide direct-out sends for each input channel, and these can be used in conjunction with, or instead of, buss channels. You'll need to consult your owner's manual to determine how the direct-outs on your console function, but normally the signal level is controlled by the channel fader. Also check to see if the channel's EQ affects the signal. If it doesn't, don't use it.

BUSS CHANNEL MODULES

A "buss" is a means of transporting the signal out of the console (if it helps, you can almost think of it as being a "bus"). Therefore, the primary function of any buss channel is to provide output control over the signal.

The buss channels on your mixer may not resemble the buss channel in Figure 5d. They may only be represented by a pair of control panel faders marked "Sub-Main" or "Buss Out." This is because on some semipro gear, all this channel really does is govern the level of the signal that is being sent to tape, and all that requires is a fader control. However, on more sophisticated consoles, the buss channels can also be used to return signals from the tape recorder, which is when the input controls and aux sends come into play.

Output Section

This section of the module controls the level of signal leaving the console.

CHANNEL FADER. Since you can assign more than one signal to a given buss channel, this control provides a master output level to tape, while the faders on the input channels are used to generate the specific mix of signals being recorded.

SOLO. This switch allows you to isolate and monitor the buss and operates just like an input channel solo switch.

TAPE INPUT

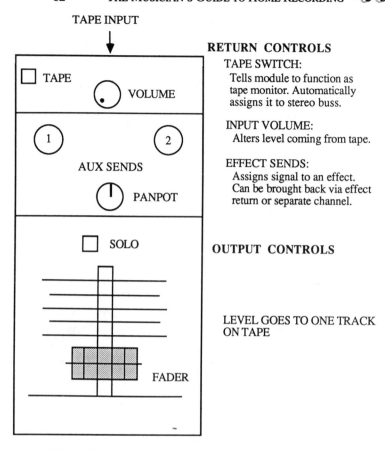

Figure 5d: A typical buss channel module.

RETURN CONTROLS

TAPE SWITCH:
Tells module to function as
tape monitor. Automatically
assigns it to stereo buss.

INPUT VOLUME:
Alters level coming from tape.

EFFECT SENDS:
Assigns signal to an effect.
Can be brought back via effect
return or separate channel.

OUTPUT CONTROLS

LEVEL GOES TO ONE TRACK
ON TAPE

Return Section

This section of the module controls the process of returning a signal from tape for the purpose of monitoring. Often it is used for overdubs, but it should never be used for mixdowns, as it does not provide EQ control.

Since a buss channel cannot simultaneously be used to monitor both the output and the return from tape, when this section of the module is disengaged, you'll hear what is being sent to tape. When it *is* engaged, you'll hear what is returning from tape.

TAPE SWITCH. When this switch is engaged, the buss channel functions in the input mode. It is at this point, and this point *only,* that the other controls in this section of the module come into play.

VOLUME. The volume pot is used to vary the input level of the signal. And, since any signal returned to a buss channel is sent to the stereo buss, it also controls the relative level of the signal in the monitor mix.

EFFECT SENDS. Like their input channel counterparts, these sends enable you either to add an effect to the signal or to route it to the headphone (cue) mix. Each send provides independent level control over the signal.

PANPOT. This pot gives you pan control over where stereophonically, the input signal will appear in the stereo buss monitor mix.

STEREO BUSS

Though not a channel module per se, the stereo buss is the console's master send circuit. Its purpose is to provide stereo monitor send (separate from the individual busses) and it automatically receives any signal that is returned to a buss channel. It is also capable of receiving signals directly from an input channel, and if any effect is brought back into the console on an effect return circuit, it, too, shows up on the stereo buss.

As you'll see in "Console Operational Diagrams," page 66, this buss circuit, which may have a single, stereo plug or a pair of L-channel/R-channel plugs, can be used to supply signal for everything from studio monitors to the 2-track mastering deck you use during mixdowns.

SIGNAL PATHS

The operational diagrams provide detailed examples of how you can route a signal through the console channels in order to accomplish a specific goal. For instance, we'll show you how to place an effect on a signal you're sending to tape, how to give the headphone mix an effect that *isn't* being sent to tape, how to monitor existing tracks during an overdub, and so on. However, even though the section is designed so that it can be used by persons with little hands-on experience, it is important that you understand the basic concepts that apply to signal paths within the mixer.

This is particularly important for those of you who are using mixers that have limited buss capabilities, or have only four input channels, because you may not always be able to use the signal path we recommend. However, if you understand the basic options your particular system offers, it is often possible to find ways to work around your console's limitations.

A "Normal" Signal Path

Mixing consoles offer so many recording options that the hands-on operation of a console can appear to be much more complex than it really is. In reality, each option is just a variation or a reapplication of the "normal" path the signal takes when it's being sent through the mixer. So once you understand the normal signal path, you're much less likely to be confused by the options.

A "normal" signal path is the path a signal takes as long as you don't interfere with it. For instance, *normally* the

BUSS OUT ———————————————————————————— TAPE IN

(normaled)

BUSS OUT ————————— in │ **EFFECT** │ out ————————— TAPE IN

[breaking the normal]

Figure 5e:　The buss output from the console is normaled to the tape input (top). But when an effect is inserted in the line (bottom), the normal signal path is altered. This is called "breaking the normal."

utput of the console would be sent to an input on the tape ecorder. This would be the *normal* signal path, and you would say that the console was "normaled" to the tape deck. However, if you decided to plug the console into an echo evice, and send the output from *that* unit into the tape deck (Figure 5e), you would be "breaking the normal," as the signal would no longer be following its normal path.

Normaled Console Paths

Essentially, the console performs two basic functions: (1) it rocesses and sends the signal to tape; and (2) it provides a return for the recorded signal so that it can be monitored. Since each of these is a separate function of the console, we an break the normal signal path down into two component arts and look at each individually, which in turn makes the entire process more easily understood.

Figure 5f illustrates the normal path of a signal that is being sent to tape and returned to the console. During the first half of the operation, the signal is brought in through input Channel 1, where it is processed. The signal is then assigned to Buss 1, which is used to send it to tape. When

the signal is returned to the console, it is brought in through a line input on Buss 2, and the channel is switched to a "tape monitor" mode.

The monitor sources available along this signal path are displayed in Figure 5g. In the return portion of the process, the stereo buss is used as a source for the studio monitor mix, because buss channel returns are normaled (automatically routed) to the stereo buss. In turn, the cue sends provide a separate mix for the musician's headphones. This gives both the musician and the engineer the ability to monitor separate mixes.

Our "Normaled" Paths

Most consoles are designed to use signal paths that are normaled in the above manner. However, there are alternative applications of these normaled paths that will enable you to get a lot more out of your unit.

We will be giving you detailed diagrams of these alternatives in the following section. However, to understand how these alternatives are derived, it helps to see how they relate to the normaled paths we've been discussing.

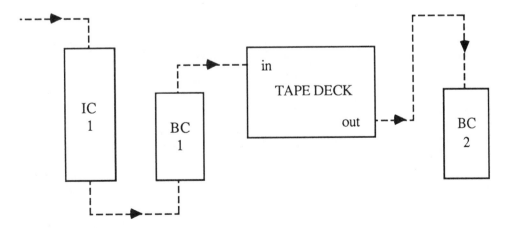

Figure 5f:　When routed along its *normal* path, the signal enters the console on an input channel and is sent to tape via a buss channel. The recorded signal is then returned through a separate buss channel's line-in circuitry.

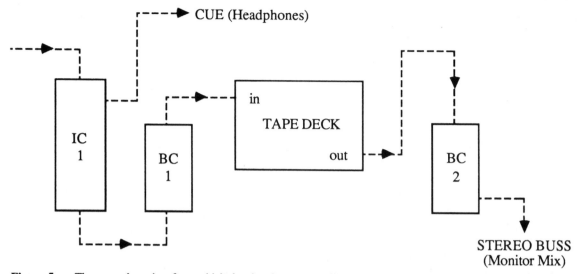

Figure 5g: These are the points from which the signals are normally monitored. The cue mix, having been assigned by the input channel's cue sends, is pulled from rear-panel jacks and sent to a headphone amp, while the stereo buss feeds the monitor amp, which is used to drive control room speakers.

Figure 5h illustrates the basic output/return signal path we will be using in our routing diagrams. This is the "ideal" path through which the signal could be normaled, as it offers you the greatest amount of control over both the record and monitor processes.

In our system, the signal is sent to tape in exactly the same manner as before. However, instead of bringing the signal back on a buss channel, we return it on an available input channel, which provides greater control over the signal and over the headphone and monitor mixes.

Procedurally, all we're doing in Figure 5h is assigning Input Channel 1 to Buss 1 in order to send the signal to tape. Then we're using Input Channel 2 as a return from tape, and we're assigning it to the stereo buss.

Figure 5i is a representation of how this would translate into the functional use of a console under ideal circum-

stances—meaning that the unit had at least one input cha[n]nel available for each possible return. In this configuratio[n] anything sent out of the tape deck is routed in a norm[al] fashion (such as buss channels to tape deck, effect sends [to] effect packages, and so on). However, *all returns*, wheth[er] from the tape deck or from an outboard effect, *are broug[ht] in on their own individual input channels*.

Under less-than-ideal circumstances, when the number [of] input channels available is limited, the console can still [be] used in this manner. However, to do so you'll only be ab[le] to record one or two instruments at a time, and you'll prob[a]bly have to repatch for each situation. Then again, you ma[y] find that in some situations you just can't route everythi[ng] this way. And when that happens, you'll need to refer bac[k] to those original normaled paths and just use the console [as] it was intended to be used.

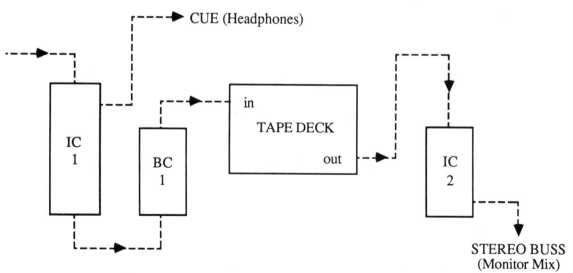

Figure 5h: Our "normaled" signal path is designed to use input channels, rather than buss channels, for all returns. This provides more control over the incoming signal, as you are able to apply EQ as well as input gain reduction.

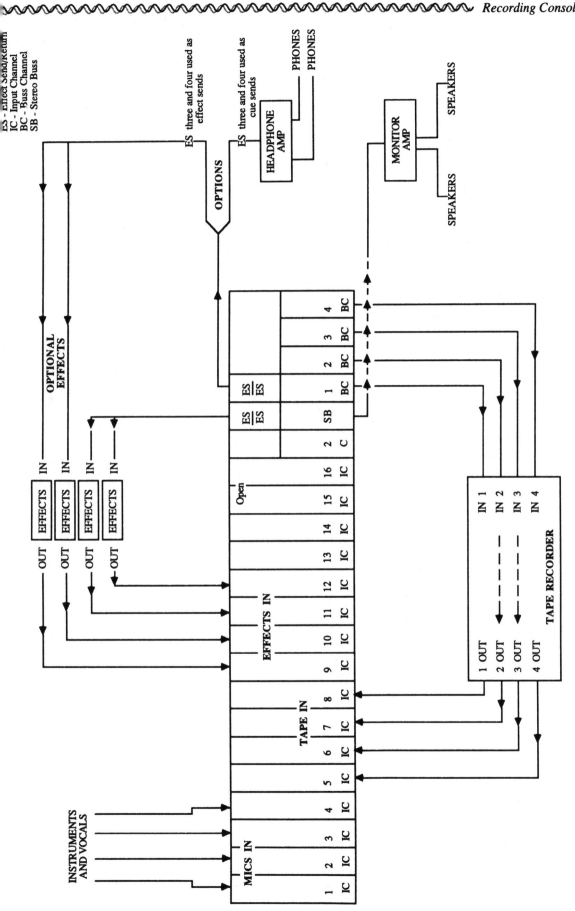

Figure 5i: This is an example of how a 16-channel, 4-buss console would be set up using input channels as returns. In this configuration, Input Channels 1–4 are assigned to Busses 1–4, and the signal from Tracks 1–4 are returned to Input Channels 5–8. Either two or four different effects can be added and returned to Input Channels 9–12. The monitor mix is pulled from the Stereo Buss.

CONSOLE OPERATIONAL DIAGRAMS: FIFTEEN PRACTICAL APPLICATIONS

The following diagrams are designed to provide a quick-reference guide to operating your console in "real world" situations. If you are unsure about how to apply them to your particular unit, you may find it helpful to read "Signal Paths," the preceding section of this chapter.

HOW TO USE THIS GUIDE

On each of the following fifteen pages you will find a diagram that illustrates a particular recording procedure. Each is accompanied by a list of the applications it's best suited for and by an explanation of the advantages and disadvantages of its use. At the bottom of each page, you'll find a step-by-step "walk-through" of the operation.

Channel capacities and auxiliary capabilities differ from console to console, so we've included certain programs that are particularly well suited for less versatile desks ("limited capacity consoles"). However, this does not mean that owners of small home consoles can't also apply some of the other recording procedures to their work.

In most cases, the procedure you'll be able to use will depend upon the number of input channels you have available and not upon whether your modules match the ones in our diagrams. And just as small consoles can sometimes handle the more complex programs, owners of large desks may occasionally have use for one of the "limited" programs.

Therefore, it is best to look upon this collection as a set of basic formulas that you can refer to as you record. And if one of the formulas is unworkable in a given situation, just look to one of the alternatives.

1. Using a Mike Mixer to Premix Mikes

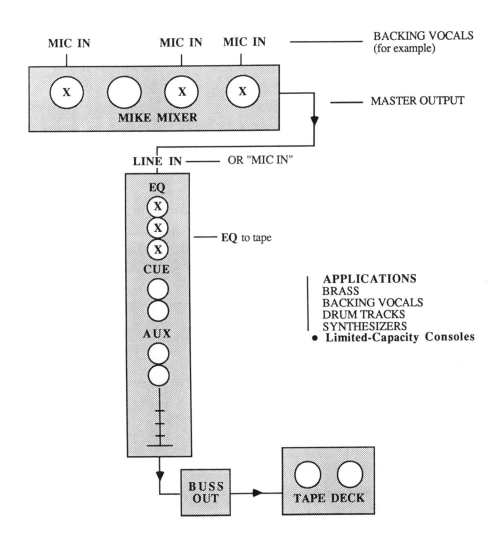

APPLICATIONS
BRASS
BACKING VOCALS
DRUM TRACKS
SYNTHESIZERS
• **Limited-Capacity Consoles**

Advantages: By premixing the mikes, you save console channels—which can be very useful when you are recording a live band, and there are more mikes than you have channels.

• Plus, this allows you to balance the levels of the microphone mix before it reaches the console.

Disadvantages: The impedance load to input can cause distortion, and a pad might be necessary.

• Also, if you want to apply effects to one of the vocals after the mike mixer stage, the effect will be applied to all vocals equally.

Procedure:

1. Plug mike into mike mixer.

2. Patch mixer's master output to a console input channel and treat it as you would a single mike input. (Patch it into a low-impedance Mic In if the mixer is running a low-impedance out.)

3. Assign channel to the desired buss.

4. Monitor the channel and balance the mikes.

#2. How to Monitor the Signal Through an Input Channel

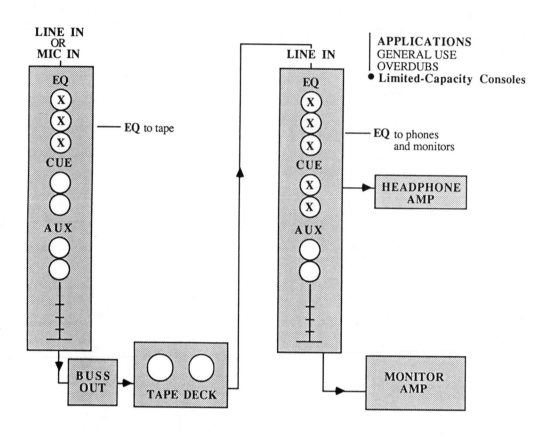

LINE IN
OR
MIC IN

EQ
X
X
X

—— EQ to tape

CUE

AUX

BUSS
OUT

TAPE DECK

LINE IN

APPLICATIONS
GENERAL USE
OVERDUBS
• Limited-Capacity Consoles

EQ
X
X
X

—— EQ to phones
and monitors

CUE
X
X

AUX

HEADPHONE
AMP

MONITOR
AMP

Advantages: This allows you to EQ the recorded signal and the monitored signal separately. So, as you listen, you can experiment with the EQ on the monitors without altering the signal going to tape.

• This also allows you to EQ the musician's headphone mix, which gives the player a better feel for the music. This can be particularly helpful when the musician happens to want to hear the track EQed in a way that makes it totally unsuitable for recording.

Procedure:

1. Bring mike or line into a console channel and assign it to a buss (bring mike into low-impedance input, line into high-impedance input).

2. Patch the output of the buss to the desired input channel of the tape deck.

3. Patch output of the tape deck to the Line In of the return module.

4. Patch the cue output to the input of the headphone amp.

5. Patch the console's stereo buss to the monitor amp.

6. Set EQ and levels on the input module.

7. Set EQ and levels on the return module after bringing up level on the tape deck.

3. How to Monitor an Effect on Monitors Without Sending It to Tape or to Headphones

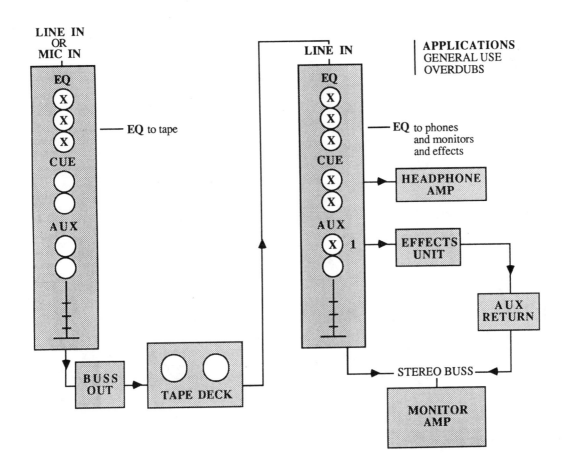

Advantages: This allows you to monitor the effect in conjunction with the original signal (both are sent to the stereo buss), so that you can hear an approximation of the way it will sound in the final mix.

- It also allows you to experiment with effects in the monitors that might otherwise distract the musician if they were added to his headphone mix.

Disadvantages: Because the effect is being brought in on the aux return, you will not be able to EQ the effect separately.

Procedure:
1. Bring mike or line into a console channel (bring mike into low-impedance input, line into high-impedance input).

2. Assign the channel to the desired buss.

3. Patch buss output to tape input.

4. Patch tape output to Line In on the return module.

5. Patch Aux Send 1 to input of the desired effect.

6. Patch output of the effect to console's aux return.

7. Patch cue to headphone amp and stereo buss to monitor amp.

8. Bring up levels.

#4. How to Monitor an Effect on Monitors and Headphones Without Sending the Effect to Tape

APPLICATIONS
GENERAL USE
OVERDUBS

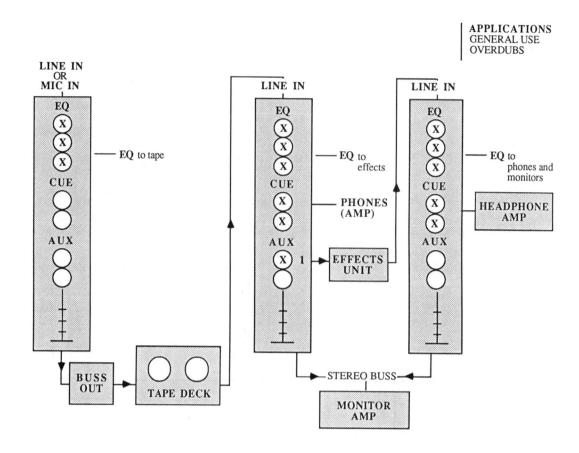

Note: 1. When using a console that operates at +4 dB, you may wish to send the effect output through a direct box before bringing it into the return module. This will reduce the amount of noise generated by the effect unit.

2. The cue mix is generated by blending the preeffect and posteffect signals, as indicated.

Advantages: This gives you all of the capabilities listed in Diagram #3, plus it allows you to add an effect to the musician's headphone mix, which is essential if you're not adding it to the recorded signal until mixdown.

• This also gives you the capability of EQing the effect separately.

Procedure:

1. Bring mike or line into a console channel (bring mike into low-impedance input, line into high-impedance input).

2. Assign the channel to the desired buss.

3. Patch buss output to tape input.

4. Patch tape output to Line In on the return module.

5. Patch Aux Send 1 to input of the desired effect unit.

6. Patch output of the effect unit to Line In on a secon return module. (If sending the effect through a dire box first, send the low-impedance output of the D [direct box] to the low-impedance Mic In of the secon return module.)

7. Patch cue to headphone amp and stereo buss to moni tor amp.

8. Bring up levels and EQ signals.

5. How to Monitor an Effect on Monitors and Headphones Without Sending the Effect to Tape

Limited-Capacity Consoles

APPLICATIONS
GENERAL USE
OVERDUBS

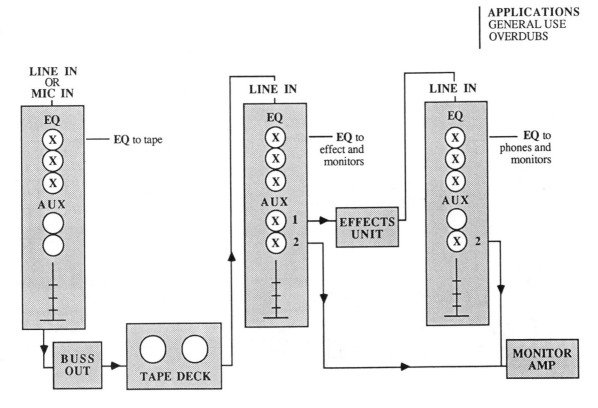

Note: When using a console that operates at +4 dB, you may wish to send the effect output through a direct box before bringing it into the return module. This will reduce the amount of noise generated by the effect unit.

Advantages: This allows you to monitor the effect in conjunction with the original signal so that you can hear an approximation of the way it will sound in the final mix.
- It also allows you to EQ the effect separately.

Disadvantages: Because the headphones are being fed by the same signal source as the monitors (Aux Send 2), the musician's headphone mix will have to be the same as the mix you're using for the monitors.

Procedure:
1. Bring mike or line into a console channel (bring mike into low-impedance input, line into high-impedance input).

2. Assign the channel to the desired buss.

3. Patch buss output to tape input.

4. Patch tape output to Line In on the return module.

5. Patch Aux Send 1 to input of the desired effect unit.

6. Patch output of the effect unit to Line In on a second return module. (If sending the effect through a direct box first, send the low-impedance output of the DI [direct box] to the low-impedance Mic In of the second return module.)

7. Patch Aux Send 2 to monitor amp and headphone amp.

8. Bring up levels and EQ signals.

#6. How to Monitor an Effect on Monitors and Headphones Without Sending the Effect to Tape

Limited-Capacity Consoles

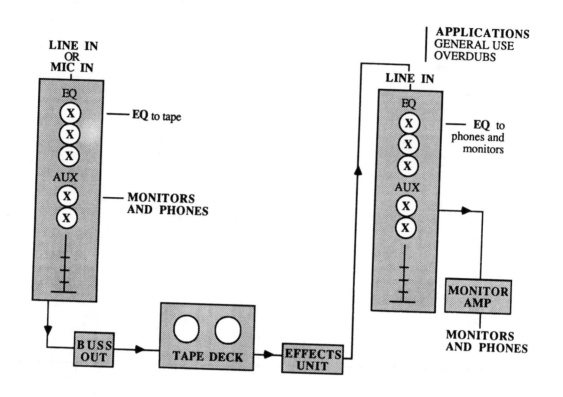

Advantages: When doing overdubs, this allows the musician to hear both the original signal and the effect through his own separate headphone mix.

- Also, this gives you the ability to EQ the effect before it is monitored.
- Plus, you need only use two input channels, and if you only have one pair of aux sends, this allows you to use them both for the phones.

Disadvantages: Doing this, you must rely more heavily on the effect unit's controls, and that makes it more difficult to control the quality of the signal and the amount of effect you hear.

Procedure:

1. Bring mike or line into a console channel (bring mike into low-impedance input, line into high-impedance input).

2. Assign the input channel to a buss.

3. Patch buss output to tape input.

4. Plug tape output to effects unit input.

5. Plug effects unit output to Line In on the return module.

6. Assign and send cues.

7. Establish signal level to tape.

8. Set effects unit levels and return levels.

7. How to Send an Effect (Echo, Phaser, etc.) to Tape

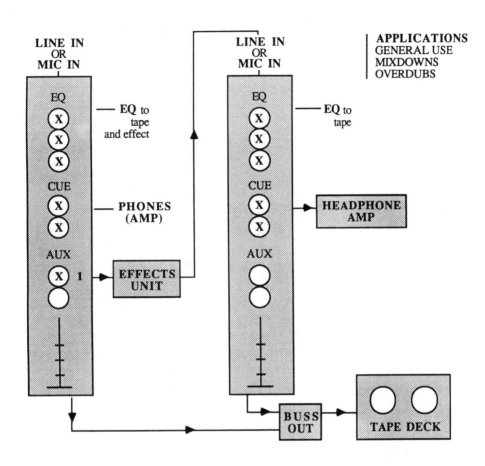

Note: 1. When using a console that operates at +4 dB, you may wish to send the effect output through a direct box before bringing it into the return module. This will reduce the amount of noise generated by the effect unit.

2. The cue mix is generated by blending the preeffect and posteffect signals, as indicated.

Advantages: By returning the effect on an input channel, you are able to add the effect to the musician's headphone mix.

- This also allows you to EQ the effect signal separately, which is very helpful during mixdown.
- Plus, you have better control over the amount of effect placed on the track because through this process you blend the original signal with the effect before it is sent to tape.

Procedure:

1. Bring mike or line into a console channel (bring mike into low-impedance input, line into high-impedance input).

2. Patch Aux Send 1 to the input of the desired effect.

3. Patch the output of the effect into the Line In of the return module. (Or, if you are using a direct box, patch the effect into the high-impedance input of the direct box, and patch the low-impedance output of the direct box into the low-impedance Mic In of the return module.)

4. Assign both channels to the desired buss and balance the two channel levels.

#8. How to Add an Effect to an Effect (Placing Reverb, or Delay, on an Echo)

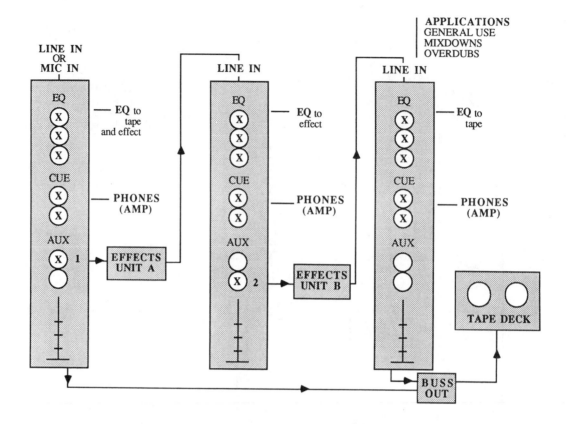

Note: 1. Though not shown, it is advantageous to send effect signals through direct boxes before returning them to a +4 dB console.

2. The cue mix is generated by blending the preeffect and posteffect signals, as indicated (see "Advantages").

Advantages: This procedure allows you to perform certain complex mixdown operations, such as placing reverb on an echo. (See chapter 16, "Mixdown Techniques.")

- It also allows you the flexibility of blending the cue sends from any or all of the three channels, which makes for a better headphone mix.
- Although pictured as a recording process, this can also be used to monitor signals from tape during overdubs.

Disadvantages: It means using two additional input modules.

- It also means using both aux sends, which can be a problem if you only have two—especially if one of them is normally used for a monaural headphone mix.

Procedure:
1. Bring mike or line into an input channel and assign it to a buss (bring mike into low-impedance input, line into high-impedance input).

2. Patch Aux Send 1 to the input of Effects Unit A.

3. Patch Effects Unit A output to the return module input. (If sending Effect A or B through a direct box before bringing it into the respective return module, bring the signal in through a low-impedance Mic In on the channel.)

4. Patch Aux Send 2 to the input of Effects Unit B.

5. Patch Effects Unit B output to a second return module.

6. Assign this return module to the same buss as the input channel.

7. Bring up level on the input module and EQ the signal.

8. Bring up level on the Aux Send 1 pot and solo the first return module so that you can set level and EQ of the first effect.

9. Mute the first return channel by pulling back on the fader level and turn up the Aux Send 2 pot after placing it in a prefader mode (if it only operates postfader, you will have to leave the fader up in order to send level to Effects Unit 2).

10. Bring up level on the second return module and solo it in order to set EQ.

11. Balance the mix to achieve the desired blend of instruments.

#9. How to Record a Direct and Amplified (or Affected) Signal from the Same Instrument

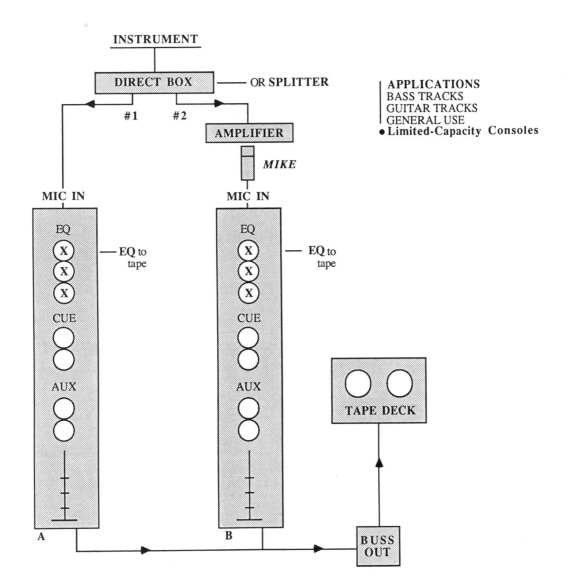

APPLICATIONS
BASS TRACKS
GUITAR TRACKS
GENERAL USE
• Limited-Capacity Consoles

Note: This same configuration can be used to send two direct signals into the console when one of those signals is to receive an effect. To do so, an outboard effect unit would take the place of the amplifier in this diagram, and the signal would need to be sent through a second direct box, where it would be transformed to low impedance, before entering Channel B.

Advantages: This method gives you greater control over the blend of the original and the effect signals.
- This is particularly useful for bass tracks, when both signals are being sent direct into the console.
- Also, this gives you the ability to compress each signal individually or to compress them both as a group.

Procedure:
1. Plug the instrument into the direct box/splitter ("DI").
2. Plug low-impedance DI output (#1) into the low-impedance, Mic In of console Channel A, and plug the high-impedance DI output (#2) into an amplifier.
3. Mike the amplifier, and bring the signal into the low-impedance Mic In of console Channel B.
4. Assign Channels A and B to the same buss.
5. Blend signal as desired.

#10. How to Send an Effect (Echo, Phaser, etc.) to Tape

Limited-Capacity Consoles

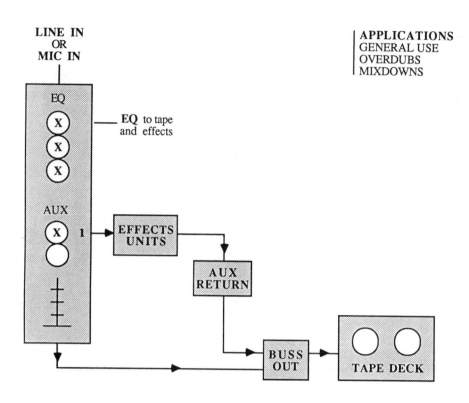

LINE IN
OR
MIC IN

EQ

EQ to tape
and effects

AUX

1

EFFECTS
UNITS

AUX
RETURN

BUSS
OUT

TAPE DECK

APPLICATIONS
GENERAL USE
OVERDUBS
MIXDOWNS

Advantages: By returning the signal to the console before sending it to tape, you will improve the signal-to-noise ratio you would have if you sent it directly to tape.

- Plus, you have better control over the amount of effect placed on the track because through this process you blend the original signal with the effect before it is sent to tape.

Disadvantages: You have very little control over the effect. Using the aux return, you have no EQ capabilities, and you will not be able to provide the musician with a headphone mix that is purely his own.

Procedure:

1. Bring mike or line into a console channel (bring mike into low-impedance input, line into high-impedance input).

2. Patch Aux Send 1 to the input of the effect unit.

3. Patch the output of the effect into the aux return.

4. Balance the two signals to generate the desired blend of instruments.

#11. How to Compress a Signal Being Sent to Tape

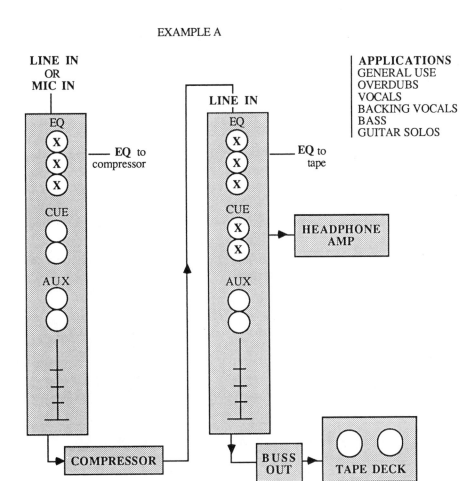

EXAMPLE A

Advantages: With this configuration you can EQ the signal both before and after it is compressed.

- Also, this allows you to add the compressed signal to the headphone mix by pulling it from the return channel.

- Plus, if you want to get elaborate, this setup allows you to send the compressed signal through an effects unit by using the return channel's aux sends.

- And since you're not bringing the signal back in on a buss, you won't have to repatch the buss.

Disadvantages: This process requires a second input channel, which you might not have available.

Procedure:

1. Bring mike or line into a console channel, but *do not* assign it to a buss (bring mike into low-impedance input, line into high-impedance input).

2. Patch the channel output *directly* into the compressor. (Lower fader level so as not to overload input to compressor. If level is still too high, you may need to pad the signal or send it through a direct box and step it down before sending it to the compressor.)

3. Patch the output of the compressor to the input of the return module. Since this signal may or may not be running at line level, be careful not to overload the input.

4. Assign return module to the desired buss in the normal fashion.

#12. How to Compress a Signal Being Sent to Tape

EXAMPLE B

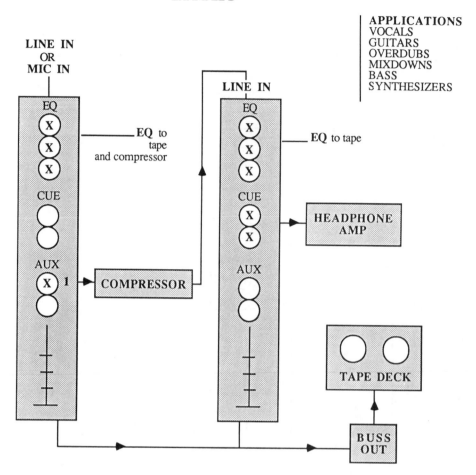

APPLICATIONS
VOCALS
GUITARS
OVERDUBS
MIXDOWNS
BASS
SYNTHESIZERS

Advantages: This technique is useful during vocal recordings in which you want the vocal dynamics retained but the peaks diminished. That's because you're blending the original signal in with the compressed signal, so not everything is being compressed.
- Also, this allows you to EQ the two channels differently in order to eliminate any muddiness the compressor might generate.
- Plus, you can monitor the compressed signal *before* tape and, by blending the two signals, create a more natural sound for problem vocals.

Procedure:

1. Bring mike or line into a console channel (bring mike into low-impedance input, line into high-impedance input).

2. Patch Aux Send 1 to the compressor input.

3. Patch the compressor output to the Line In of the return module. However, since the signal may or may not be running at line level, be careful not to overload the channel circuit.

4. Assign both the input and the return channels to the same buss.

5. Balance the output of both channels as desired.

13. How to Compress and Record a Group of Instruments Using One Compressor

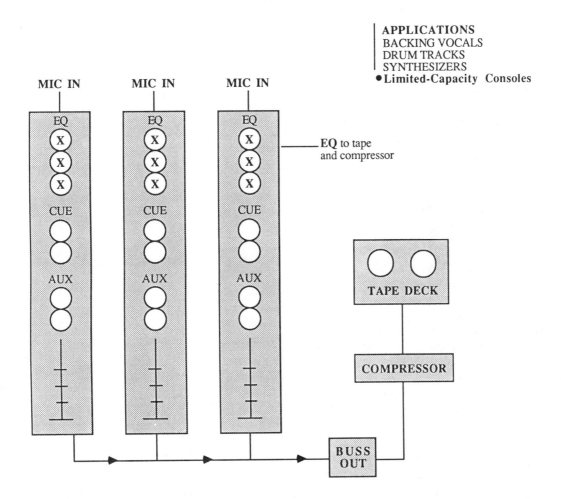

APPLICATIONS
BACKING VOCALS
DRUM TRACKS
SYNTHESIZERS
• Limited-Capacity Consoles

Advantages: This technique is useful for such applications as recording backing vocals, which are all going to the same track.
• Plus, only one compressor is required.
• Compression allows you to smooth out any disparities between the signals you're blending together.
• Also, by EQing the signal *before* it is compressed, it allows greater control over peak limiting.

Disadvantages: When using "group compression," you lack the ability to give each signal its own compression levels.
• Plus, you can't EQ the signal after it's been compressed.
• The only point from which you can monitor the compressed signal is after it's been recorded, so all compression and EQ levels must be set by trial and error.

Procedure:

1. Bring each mike into a separate input channel, using the low-impedance, Mic In jacks.

2. Assign each channel to the same buss.

3. Plug the buss output into the compressor input.

4. Plug the compressor output into the tape deck's input.

5. Monitor the buss and balance the mix of the channels.

6. Set input levels of the compressor and the tape deck.

7. Record some signal.

8. Listen to recorded signal and adjust: (a) the channel balance; and (b) the compression levels.

#14. How to Compress a Signal Being Sent to Tape

Limited-Capacity Consoles

EXAMPLE C

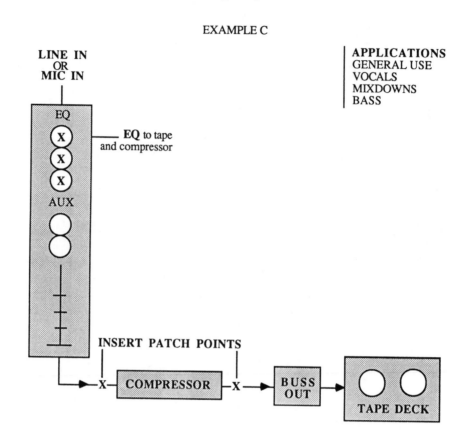

LINE IN
OR
MIC IN

EQ

EQ to tape
and compressor

AUX

INSERT PATCH POINTS

X— COMPRESSOR —X — BUSS OUT → TAPE DECK

APPLICATIONS
GENERAL USE
VOCALS
MIXDOWNS
BASS

Note: In this configuration, compressor can be added using channel-insert or group-insert patch points, depending upon which your console offers. And in the following discussions on EQ, it should be noted that on many consoles, the *channel* inserts are placed *before* the EQ circuits, so the signal is EQed after leaving the compressor (to verify this, check your unit's block diagram).

Advantages: This is a useful configuration if you're using a desk with a limited number of channels or during times when all of your aux and cue sends are being used for other purposes.
- Plus, the advantage of compressing *after* the input channel is that you can EQ before the signal is compressed, which can be useful for peak limiting (especially de-essing), when the compressor is set to react to peaks in specific frequencies.

Disadvantages: Because the compressed signal is sent directly to the buss, you can't re-EQ it before it is recorded.
- Also, when using group inserts, any monitoring of the compressed signal must be done off the stereo buss, which means that it can only be picked up in the head phones after it has been recorded.

Procedure:
1. Bring mike or line into a console channel (bring mik into low-impedance input, line into high-impedanc input).

2. Assign the channel to the desired buss.

3. Patch the buss output to the tape recorder input.

4. Patch the insert output to the compressor input.

5. Patch the compressor output to the insert return.

6. Bring up levels, remembering that for group inserts the channel fader controls the level of the signal going to the compressor (for channel inserts, that level i controlled by the input gain reduction circuits).

7. Set compressor levels.

8. EQ the signal and, if necessary, reset compresso levels.

#15. How to Compress a Signal Being Sent to Tape

Limited-Capacity Consoles

EXAMPLE D

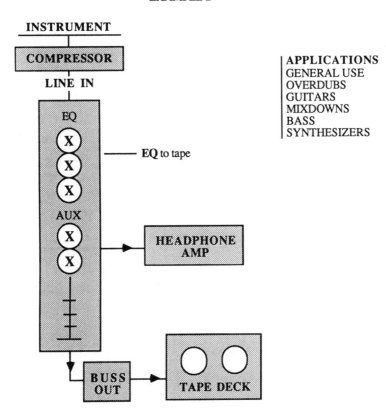

APPLICATIONS
GENERAL USE
OVERDUBS
GUITARS
MIXDOWNS
BASS
SYNTHESIZERS

Advantages: This is a useful configuration if you're using a desk with limited capabilities or during times when either all of your input channels or all of your aux and cue sends are being used for other purposes.

• Since the compressor adds gain to the signal before it enters the mixer, the quality of the bass signal will be improved without having to use a direct box (which you would otherwise be advised to do if your console operates at +4 dB).

Disadvantages: Because the signal is being compressed before it enters the console, you cannot EQ the signal prior to compression.

• Also, you have less control over the amount and quality of compression applied to the signal, since the only control circuits you have are those on the compressor itself.

Procedure:

1. Plug the instrument directly into the compressor.

2. Patch the compressor output to the Line In of a console channel.

3. Assign the channel to the desired buss.

4. Patch buss output to tape input.

5. Use the gain control on the compressor to bring the signal up to level. Be careful not to overload the input into the console.

6. Adjust all levels and set EQ.

ADDITIONAL CONSOLE EQUIPMENT

There is a variety of equipment that you will want to use in conjunction with your mixer. Some of this gear, such as monitor amps and monitor speakers, are vital to console operations, while other pieces, such as direct boxes, simply provide a means to improve the desk's efficiency.

Monitor Amplifiers

Monitor amps are, quite simply, amplifiers that are used to drive studio monitor speakers. They can be anything from standard hi-fi components to specially designed, professional power amplifiers that deliver 400 watts or more per channel.

The truth is that if you have an above-average stereo system, you don't need to buy professional monitor gear. Although you might consider doing so if your tape was going to be heard in a commercial studio, most record companies play demos back on quality hi-fi components. So, if you monitor your tracks and your mixes over a good stereo amp, chances are that if the tracks sounds good on your system, they'll sound just as good on theirs. (Yet, to be safe, you should play the tape at a friend's house before sending it off.)

The major advantage professional monitor amps have over most home stereos is that they produce more power. An amplifier with a high power rating is capable of running a cleaner signal at high volumes. So, for instance, if your home unit only generates 50 watts per channel, it will start distorting at a lower volume than an amp that generates 100 watts per channel. Plus, since the speaker cabinets on the home unit are necessarily matched to a lower power rating, they may not give you the same quality that you'd get from speakers designed for a 100-watt output.

Monitor Speakers

There are many different types of monitor speaker systems available: there are powered and nonpowered speakers, PA speaker cabinets, studio monitor cabinets, and standard hi-fi speaker cabinets.

When you're choosing speakers, the most important thing to remember is that the quality of the speakers should match the quality of your amplifier. For instance, it does no good to spend a lot of money on monitor speakers if you don't have an amp that will drive them. At the same time, if you spend a lot of money on an amp, you'd better get yourself some speakers that will do it justice.

When you go shopping for monitor speakers, you'll find that it's a lot like trying to match the components of a stereo system. In other words, you can't buy your speakers based on what the spec sheets say, because every spec sheet looks impressive, and if cabinets lived up to their specs, each one of them would be a gem. So, when you go looking for a good pair of speakers, you should bring along an album you're very familiar with, so that you can compare the speakers' response to the levels you're used to hearing. You should also bring your amp along, or find one like it in the store, because a speaker cabinet that sounds good through one of their systems may not sound good through yours.

If you have a powered mixer that doubles as a PA, the manufacturer may offer its own line of speakers. Most often, however, these speakers are designed to be used onstage for the PA, and they do not exhibit the same response as a home stereo speaker. Therefore they should not be used as tape monitors, because a mix that sounds good through a PA column may not sound the same when it's run through a home system.

If your home stereo amp is particularly powerful, or if you've purchased a nice slave amplifier, such as those designed for studio use, there are a number of excellent monitor cabinets on the market that we can recommend. In studios, these cabinets are known as "near field monitors," and they are used in conjunction with, or instead of, the "studio monitors" that are mounted in the walls.

One excellent cabinet is Westlake Audio's BBSM-6 (Figure 5j), which uses a three-way speaker system consisting of two 6-inch woofers, a midrange speaker, and a tweeter. Another is Yamaha's NS10-M, which uses a two-way system consisting of a woofer and a combination tweeter/midrange speaker. This is the least expensive of the high-grade cabinets and, like the others, is no bigger than a standard home stereo cabinet.

However, over the years, the most popular professional speaker cabinet has been the JBL 4311 (presently offered as the 4312). In fact, I'd guess that nine out of ten demo tapes played in record company offices are heard either over 4311's or 4312's. So if you want to know how your tape's going to sound to the A&R directors, you can always get yourself a pair of these. That is, if your amp can push a minimum of 100 watts per channel.

Should you decide instead to use your own stereo speakers as monitors, you need to carefully examine the fidelity of their response. Ideally you want a pair of cabinets that will give you a flat, accurate response (they don't favor bass or treble, and the like). However, stereo speakers are often designed more for pleasant listening than for accuracy. So, for instance, you might generate a mix that sounds great on your home speakers, but because they are designed to give you a softer sound, you will have had to push the high end. And if your recording is later monitored on a pair of 4311's, the mix would then seem much too bright, and it would probably include quite a bit of high-frequency hiss.

One way around this is to monitor your recording on a number of different systems before sending it off. Take it over to a friend's house and see how it sounds on his gear. And check the mix out in your car on the way over, because A&R directors often listen to demos while driving to and from work.

gure 5j

onitor speakers.

1. Westlake BBSM-6 *(Courtesy of Westlake Audio, Inc.)*

2. JBL 4312 *(Courtesy of JBL Professionals)*

There are a number of self-powered speaker systems on the market, but in general these monitors are better suited for live stage work. Each cabinet in these systems can generate up to 100 watts of power which would be more than adequate for studio use, but even though they generally include

tone and volume controls, here, too, you probably won't g the same sort of response your home system produces— especially if you're running the speakers at relatively lo volumes.

TAPE TIP #13
Matching Speaker Impedance to Amplifier Output

You can't just hook any set of speakers up to any amplifier. At least not without taking the chance that you'll blow the amp circuits. Amplifiers are designed to generate enough signal to drive a specific load (measured in ohms), and if the speakers are rated *below* the minimum level required by the amp, the circuits will fizzle before your very eyes.

Amplifiers are rated according to the minimum load required (4 ohms, 8 ohms, and so on), while speakers are rated according to the minimum load they will present to the amp (2 ohms, 4 ohms, 8 ohms, and so forth). So when using just one speaker, or speaker cabinet, per output, you simply need to make sure that *the ohm rating of the speaker matches or exceeds the ohm rating of the amp*.

However, when you tie two or more speakers together, the

combined impedance load may change, depending upon how the speakers are connected. In Figure 5k, you'll find the three basic wiring methods used (parallel, series, and series-parallel), and the effect each has on the impedance load. So if you're building your own speaker cabinets, or designing a multicabinet sound system, you may want to refer to this when determining which wiring method is best for your needs.

Note —*If the impedance load from the speakers is greater than what is required by the amplifier, it won't hurt the amp, but the actual volume produced by the speakers will be lower than if the impedance ratings match.*

Figure 5k

PARALLEL:

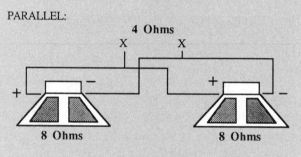

SERIES:

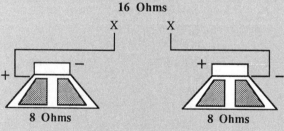

SERIES-PARALLEL:

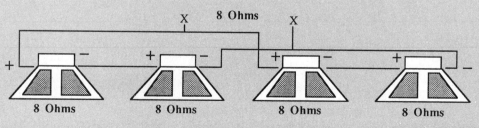

(Courtesy of Carvin Corporation)

Self-Powered Minimonitors

On the other hand, self-powered minimonitor speakers, like the Yamaha MS10 (Figure 5l), can be quite valuable when your only other alternative is to monitor over headphones. For instance, these compact and versatile speakers can drive any line-level source, so they can be used as monitors for a multitrack cassette deck, and they'll give you a better feel for the mix than you would get over a pair of phones. Plus, since these units generally produce only 10 or 20 watts of power, they can be just as useful to someone who likes to work when everyone else in the house is trying to sleep.

The one very important thing you have to keep in mind when you are using these speakers for any serious recording is that they're not going to give you the same response levels as a normal set of hi-fi speakers, and you should make adjustments accordingly. In fact, you should never use these speakers for much other than getting a general blend of instruments or a basic instrumental sound, which you can then adjust by running the signal through your standard monitors before committing anything to tape.

Headphone Amplifiers

Headphone amplifiers pull their signal from the console's cue send outputs, *not* from the headphone jack. As was the case with monitor amps, you can use just about any sort of amplifier as a headphone amp, including the one in your home stereo system. However, if you regularly record more than one musician at a time, you'll also need to use something called a "headphone mixer," which provides multiple headphone outputs. Thus, all the musicians will be able to monitor the music through the phones.

Outboard EQ Units

The amount of EQ control you have is critical to the ultimate recording quality you are able to achieve. So, for example, if your console only provides tone control EQ, or if the range of frequencies it can affect does not reach at least from 10K down to 80 Hz, you'll have a hard time getting your tracks to sound right.

One way around such limitations is to use an outboard EQ device in conjunction with, or in place of, the console's onboard EQ (Figure 5m). These systems can be inserted any-

Figure 5l: Self-powered monitor speakers, such as Yamaha's MS10, provide an alternative to headphone monitoring under restricted conditions. (*Courtesy of Yamaha International Corporation*)

where in the line, such as between the console and the tape deck, so they can be used to add EQ to a signal being sent to tape, to a signal that is being bounced, or to a playback signal that is being used as part of the headphone mix or monitor mix.

These outboard EQ systems are available in parametric, sweepable, click-stop, and graphic formats, and they come in either single-channel or 2-channel (stereo) configurations. Thus, with such a wide variety, you should be able to find something in your price range. And the gear will be worth every penny you spend, because EQ is probably the single most important signal processing tool at your disposal.

Patch Bays

Patch bays (Figure 5n) are basically junction boxes used to route signals to and from the various pieces of gear in your control room. They're much like the early telephone switchboards in that they allow you to plug all of the outputs and inputs from your equipment into one central board. Thus,

Figure 5m: Yamaha's GQ1031 outboard graphic equalizer. (*Courtesy of Yamaha International Corporation*)

Figure 5n: The TASCAM PB-32 is an example of a typical, hard-wired patch bay. (*Courtesy of TEAC Corporation of America*)

you can connect two or more pieces of gear together without having to fumble around looking for the right rear-panel jacks.

There's little reason to run out and buy a patch bay if you're working in a small, home studio setting and you're using a minimal amount of gear to process the signal. However, in professional studios, and in elaborate home setups, where you have a multitude of effects and multiple signal routes, patch bays are essential.

When you set up a patch bay, you use the inner circuits of the unit to establish the normal routing patterns that you use in the studio (Figure 5o). For instance, you might connect the console outputs to one pair of jacks on the patch bay and the tape deck inputs to a second pair of jacks that are wired to form a circuit with the first pair. Thus, unless you alter the signal path—say, by patching in an effect—the signal will follow its normal route from console to patch bay to tape deck.

TAPE TIP #14
Speaker Placement

The quality of your monitors will affect the way your recording sounds outside the studio environment. After all, it's hard to gauge how much bass to add to a recording if you're listening to it through four-inch speakers. But by the same token, the acoustical environment of the room in which you place your console, and the placement of your speakers in relation to your position in front of the console, is also going to affect the final mix.

For example, if the room you're in generates an ambient echo, you'll have a hard time hearing what the true mix sounds like, because you'll set all sorts of frequencies overlapping as they rebound off the walls. Or if the room you're using absorbs much of the high end but makes the low frequencies sound rather boomy, you'll probably overcompensate during the mix, and once outside the room there won't be any bass response in the track at all.

In order to minimize such problems, you should perform your mixes in a room that is large enough to accommodate your equipment, but small enough to give you control over the acoustics. In other words, you don't want to pick a room with fifteen-foot ceilings and hard plaster walls. You want to be able to deaden the sound in the room, yet you also want to be able to sit in the center of the room and still get a good separation from your speakers.

The position of your monitor speakers is also very important. For instance, if you stand the speakers upright in front of you with the woofers at ear level, the tweeters are going to be somewhere over your head and you're not going to hear much of the track's high end. As a consequence, you'll end up overcompensating with generous high-end boosts. On the other hand, if the speakers are too far away, you won't be able to get a good feel for the stereo balance of the mix.

One solution is to place the speakers at eye level, but at least three feet away and about four feet apart. Then lay the cabinets on their sides and angle each so that it is pointing directly at you. Or, if your space is limited, you can move farther back from the cabinets—say, five feet—and stand them upright. If they're at least five feet apart and angled in toward you, it should still be possible to get good separation and balance.

In either case, if you want to check the balance between the low-end and high-end responses, you will have to back away from the speakers. That's because low-frequency waves take longer to form than high-frequency waves, and if you're too close to the speakers, the high end will dominate because it reaches you in a more complete form than the bottom end.

Figure 5o: 1. Wiring the patch bay. In this example, the normal circuit established within the patch bay is as follows: The output from the console is plugged into the jack at point A, and the tape deck input is plugged into the jack at point D. When the jack at point B is not being used, the signal from the console travels from point A to point B, down to point C, and over to point D—where it leaves the patch bay and heads off to the tape recorder. (*Illustration from* Sound Recording *by John Eargle*)

PATCH BAY

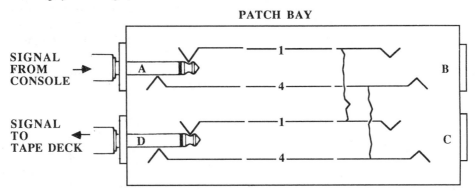

2. Breaking the normal. This close-up of the normaled patch bay jack at point B shows how the normal is broken. When the jack is not being used (left), the signal follows the route previously described. However, when a patch cord is inserted into the jack (right), it lifts metal contacts 1 and 4 and breaks the connection they normally maintain with contact points 2 and 3. This, then, interrupts the signal flow and "breaks the normal." (*Illustration from* Sound Recording *by John Eargle*)

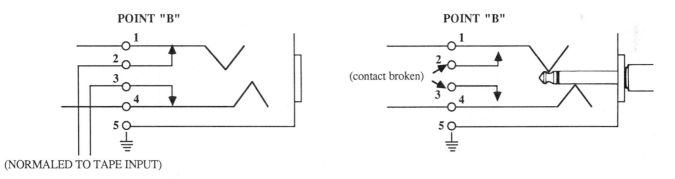

This brings up the concept of normaled inputs, which are the heart and soul of a patch bay. Basically, a normaled input is an input that, when not in use, allows the signal to flow along its normal path. Then, when you plug something into it, you interrupt the flow and "break the normal." There are examples of normaled inputs all around you. For instance, most portable cassette recorders have normaled phone jacks, so that when you plug headphones into the unit, the exterior speakers are cut off.

That is exactly what happens with the normaled inputs of the patch bay: you plug a patch cord in, break the normal, and send the signal somewhere else. For example, let's say that you want to use a limiter on a signal before it goes to tape. And let's say that you want the signal to pass through the limiter somewhere between the console output and the tape deck input. Figure 5p shows just exactly how this is accomplished using the normaled inputs of the patch bay.

As you can see, in the interior of the patch bay, the console output has been normaled to the tape deck input. However, as soon as the plug from the limiter output is patched into the tape deck input jack on the patch bay, this normal is broken (disconnected), and a new signal path is established

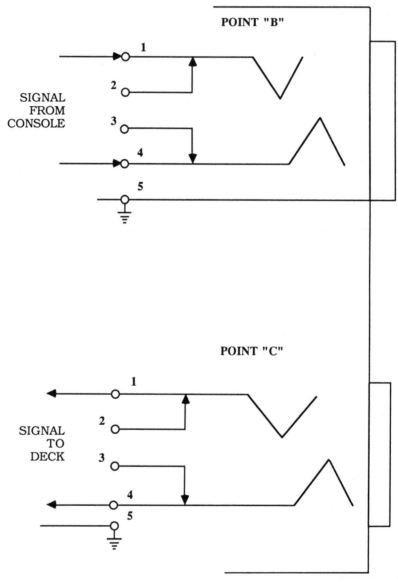

Figure 5p: Inserting a compressor in the line. This close-up of the normaled patch bay jacks at points B and C (of Figure 5o) shows how the patch bay functions when you want to add compression to the signal at a point between the console and the tape deck. In this instance, when the compressor is inserted in the line, the normal signal path (above) is broken (opposite), and the signal exits the patch bay at point B, travels to the compressor, and reenters the patch bay at point C. From there it travels to the plug that is feeding the tape deck input (point D in Figure 5o), from where it heads off for the tape deck. (*Illustration from* Sound Recording *by John Eargle*)

The normal is broken in the tape input jack, rather than in the console output jack, because you cannot send two signals into the same input without first sending them through a mixer. So the circuit is always broken at an input jack to ensure that this doesn't happen.

Preamps

The function of a preamp is to increase the strength of a signal that would otherwise be too weak for a particular piece of equipment to use. For instance, if you don't preamp a signal before sending it to tape, the signal may be very weak relative to the amount of noise it contains, and as a result your recordings will have a lot of hiss.

Since your console actually serves as a preamp, you should never have to boost an incoming signal. However, there are occasions when you might want to preamp the output. For instance, preamps can be used to run a monitor system off the headphone jack. Normally the signal coming from that buss is too weak for the monitor amp, but you can compensate by sending the signal through an amp that has its own preamp circuitry. Your home stereo amp, which has a built-in preamp, can even be used in this way.

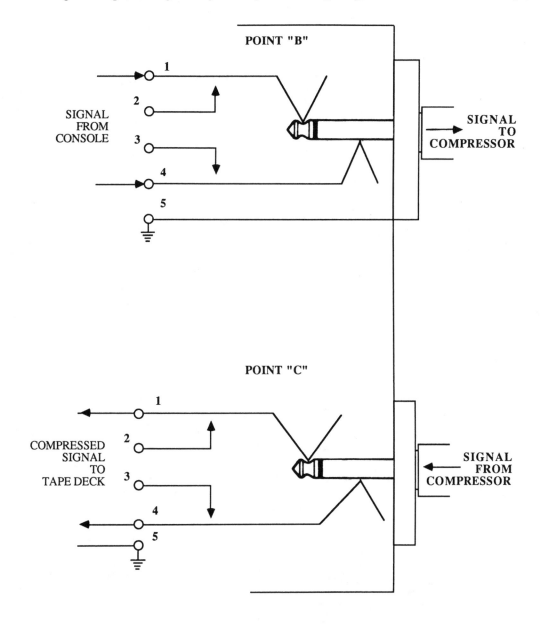

TAPE TIP #15
Direct Box Applications

Many home recording enthusiasts have probably never heard of a direct box, much less used one. Yet a direct box (Figure 5q) can have a very definite effect upon the sound quality of an instrument or an effect that is brought directly into the console.

A direct box is a transformer that is used to alter the impedance level of a signal. For example, an "active" direct box will transform a high-impedance signal to low impedance, while a "passive" direct box will change the impedance level from low to high, or from high to low, depending upon which side of the box you plug into.

There are many reasons you might want to transform a high-impedance signal to low impedance. The first is the instability of a high-impedance signal over distance. The farther a high-impedance signal travels along a cable, the more signal quality it loses. Yet a low-impedance signal is not nearly as susceptible to this type of signal loss, so if you convert a high-impedance signal to low impedance before sending it along cable lengths of fifty feet or more, you'll get a cleaner, more complete signal.

Of greater home studio importance is the effect a direct box has on direct-in recording. By changing the impedance level of an instrument or effect from high impedance to low impedance *before* bringing it into the console, you can enhance the quality of its sound.

For example, it's very difficult to get a guitar to sound good when you plug it directly into the desk. This is partly due to the fact that a guitar is a high-impedance instrument with relatively low gain, which can make for a flat, noisy signal if you have to compensate by cranking the console all the way up. However, if you use a direct box and bring the signal in at low impedance, it has an easier time overcoming the resistance required at the input stage of the console. Plus, the console automatically applies a 60 dB boost to any low-impedance signal upon input, which goes a long way toward making up for any lack of gain.

By the same token, anytime you are bringing an *effect* into a console input channel (as opposed to an effect return chan-

Figure 5q: A custom-made direct box. (*Courtesy of Larry Wichman*)

nel), you will enhance the signal-to-noise ratio if you first convert it from high impedance to low impedance and use a low-impedance input. This applies whether you're treating an instrument with an effect before bringing it directly into a console channel or whether, as we advise, you're returning an effect signal into a console channel during the mix.

The reason this makes such a big difference with effects is that by bringing the effect in at low impedance, you allow the console to give it that 60 dB boost, which means you can avoid using the much noisier amp circuits of the effect. For example, I often use a chorus effect to help the sound of my synth (synthesizer) when I plug it directly into my desk at home. And unless I'm doing something special, I simply insert the chorus between the synth and the desk. Now, if I were to do this without using a direct box, I'd have to plug the signal into the high-impedance inputs of the channel, and as I cranked up the gain, the signal I'd get would be very noisy. Yet by using a direct box and bringing the signal in on a low-impedance input, I'm able to keep the gain low on the chorus unit and use the 60 dB boost from the console to bring the effect up in level.

Although not one of their primary functions, direct boxes can also be used as splitters. Each box has one high-impedance input (usually marked "Instrument In") and one low-impedance output (marked "Low-Impedance Out"). In addition, there is usually a second output (marked "Amplifier Out"), which is hard-wired to the input jack so that it can be used to send a high-impedance signal. This means that you can bring a high-impedance signal into the direct box and split it, sending the low-impedance output to, for instance, the console, while sending the high-impedance output to either an effect or an amplifier. As you'll see in our guitar and bass chapters, this is a very important function.

The necessity of using a direct box will, in some cases, depend upon the level at which your console operates. Some consoles operate at +4 dB, while others operate at −10 dB (check with your owner's manual or retail store to find out which level yours operates at). Without getting into all the technical details, what this means is that for the direct-in recording of instruments, you're less likely to need a direct box if your unit operates at −10 dB. However, when recording direct in on a +4 dB desk, you *will* need to use a direct box to help compensate for the extra gain required.

By the same token, if you were to bring a low-impedance condenser mike into a −10 dB console that does not have a low-impedance mike input, you *would* need a direct box (or an input transformer): in order to get the optimum signal quality from the mike, the signal would have to be changed from low impedance to high impedance.

Note —*For information on the difference between a direct-box transformer and an input transformer, see "Frequently Asked Questions" in chapter 18, pages 283–85.*

MIXING CONSOLE TROUBLESHOOTING GUIDE

Tracking down a problem in the audio chain can be a frustrating experience. There you are with a fresh new musical idea that you know you'll forget if you don't record it right *now,* and you aren't getting any sound through your gear. Well, with a little detective work and a logical approach, you can be back on the air in no time.

The audio chain is aptly named, as each component provides a link to the next, and if any of the links are broken, the signal path is interrupted. The following checklist is designed to help you track down that missing link. However, since in the studio most problems are caused either by a connector that isn't fully connected or by a piece of gear that hasn't been plugged in or turned on, you can save yourself a lot of headaches by paying attention to detail as you set your equipment up.

PROBLEM

No Console Audio at All:

CHECK

1. Make sure all your gear, including the amp, is turned on. If so . . .

then

2. Turn up the amp and make sure you are getting some sort of noise (like hiss) from the speakers. If not, check the speaker wire connections to the amp. However, if you are getting noise from the speakers . . .

then

3. You know the amp and speakers are connected, so turn off all console channels (by deassigning them or by lowering faders), but leave the master faders up. The noise from the speakers should diminish. If it doesn't, then signal isn't getting to the amp, so check the console-to-amp connections. But if it does . . .

then

4. You know the desk is passing signal, so turn the channels back on and check all input connections from mike and patch bays. Also check to see that any effects unit you're using is turned on. If so . . .

No Signal at VU Meter:

then

5. Send some signal through the desired channel and check to see if it is registering on the VU meter. If not, make sure that the channel faders are up and that the module is on. If so . . .

then

6. Check the input trim, and make sure that the phantom power switch is on, should the mike require it. If the meters are still not registering . . .

then

7. Change your mike or line cables. If the meters are still not registering . . .

then

8. Try changing microphones.

Signal at VU,
But No Audio:

9. If you're seeing signal at VU, all the previous checks are unnecessary. The problem, then, is localized between the output of the module and the buss, so check to see if the module has been assigned to a buss. If it has . . .

then

10. Check the settings on your monitor return in order to make sure that you're monitoring "source" rather than "tape." And if you're still not hearing anything . . .

then

11. Try using a different module. And if that fails, the fault may be internal, and you may need to get the desk repaired.

PROBLEM

Distortion When
Using Mike:

CHECK

1. Turn mike input trim down and listen to the signal at a lower volume. If the distortion is still there . . .

then

2. Check to make sure the proper impedance settings are being used and, if you are using a condenser mike, that the phantom power is on. If so . . .

then

3. If you are bringing the mike in from a direct box, check the connections and/or try using a different direct box. If that doesn't work . . .

then

4. Check your EQ settings to make sure that the distortion isn't being caused by an over-boosted band of frequencies. If not . . .

then

5. Check the signal level being sent to any outboard devices you might be using (compressors, echo, and so on) to make sure that they are not being overdriven by too much signal. If not . . .

then

6. Remove the outboard gear from the audio chain. If the mike signal is clear and the outboard device wasn't overloaded at input, either the equipment is faulty or the output level of the device is too high and needs to be padded (or turned down). However, if after removing the device the signal is still distorted . . .

then

7. Check to see if there is a pad on the mike that can be used. If not, then perhaps the sound

pressure level is overloading the diaphragm, and the mike needs to be pulled back from the source. However, if distortion persists . . .

then

8. Check the signal level being sent from the module to the buss by looking at the buss VU meter. If the VU needle is way over in the red, turn down the channel module output. And if the signal still distorts . . .

then

9. Try using a different input module. And if it still distorts . . .

then

10. Try changing mike cables and/or mikes. And if it still distorts . . .

then

11. Try listening to the signal at low monitor levels. If the distortion disappears, it may be that the monitor amp or speakers are distorting because of signal overload. But if distortion persists . . .

then

12. Have your equipment serviced.

PROBLEM

Distortion of a Direct-In Instrument:

CHECK

1. Make the same checks (#1–#12) that you made for mike distortion, but pay special attention to the output level of the instrument relative to the mic-in or line-in setting. The signal

coming from the instrument may be too hot for the console to handle, and balancing the output of the instrument with the console input may require some trial-and-error adjustments.

PROBLEM

Excessive Hiss from Tape:

CHECK

1. Make sure you have calibrated the settings between your console and your tape deck in order to achieve optimum signal-to-noise response. (Calibration procedure is found in Tape Tip #11.) If hiss persists . . .

then

2. Check the impedance settings of the input module to make sure that you are not bringing a low-impedance signal in when using high-impedance settings. If so, correct the settings, but if not . . .

then

3. Check your tone or EQ settings on both the input module and the tape return module, to

make sure that neither has been given an excessive high-end boost. If so, reduce the high end; but if not . . .

then

4. Check the bias switch on the machine and make sure that it is set to the bias level that corresponds to the quality of the tape. Also check to see that you're using the same Dolby settings for playback that you used for record. If both switches are set properly . . .

then

5. Try cleaning the tape heads, and if this doesn't work, take your machine into the shop and have it checked out. The tape bias controls may need adjusting, or the heads may simply be worn out.

PROBLEM

Excessive Hiss from
Outboard Effects Unit:

CHECK

1. Check to see that you are sending the strongest, nondistorting signal possible to the effect device. If so . . .

then

2. Check to see that the input level on the effect is set as high as is possible without distorting the unit. If so . . .

then

3. Make sure that the return signal has not been given any hefty high-end EQ boosts. If so, reduce them; but if not . . .

then

4. Turn down the output level of the device and raise the input level of the return. By doing so, you are able to use the higher-quality console components to raise the gain, and you avoid relying on the noisier output circuitry of the device. However, if the hiss persists . . .

then

5. If you are not already returning the signal on a normal console input channel, try rerouting the effect return to a channel module and adding EQ.

PROBLEM

Excessive Hiss from
Tape Echo

CHECK

6. If the effect you are using is a tape echo, and after having followed Steps #1–#5 you are still getting a lot of hiss, try cleaning the unit's heads and/or installing a fresh tape. You might also have the heads checked for wear at a repair shop. However, if none of this helps . . .

then

7. If you have a Dolby unit available, you can apply it to an effect in the same way it is applied to a normal recording: encoding on input and decoding at the output of the echo unit.

PROBLEM

Distortion from Tape
During Playback

CHECK

1. When most tape decks are placed in a playback or tape monitor mode, the VU meters will register the level of the signal coming off the heads, no matter what you have the output volume set at. So if the machine's meters are constantly pinned (such as all the way over in the red), or the peak light is registering heavily, then the distortion is on the tape, and the track must be rerecorded using different record settings. However, if the meter levels are okay, but you're getting distortion . . .

then

2. Monitor the tape deck directly with a pair of headphones and lower the playback level. If you're not getting distortion here, but you're still hearing it from the console . . .

then

3. Lower the monitor level of the console to see if the distortion is occurring because of amplifier clipping or speaker distortion. And if you still hear distortion . . .

then

4. Since your problem may be the result of an overload of signal at the point of return, search out the source of distortion by following the same problem-solving steps used for mike distortion. If you are using an input channel for the return from tape, this will be particularly valuable.

PROBLEM

Level to Tape at Input Is
Different from Level on
Tape at Return:

CHECK

1. Look at the level of the input signal while recording. Then look at the level of output (of what you've just recorded) on playback. If the level between the two varies dramatically, you need to realign the machine's bias. On some

then

machines this can be done at home using a specially provided alignment tape. However, in most cases you'll need to take your deck in to a qualified repairman. But if, after this, the problem persists . . .

2. Have the tape heads themselves realigned and have them checked for wear.

PROBLEM

Sound of Tape Is Different
from Input Signal:

CHECK

1. If the tape playback sounds different from the signal originally sent to tape, your machine probably needs to be realigned, as described in the previous section. However, the problem

may also lie in the settings you are using for the return. So before you go carting your machine off to the repair shop, check to see that the tape return is not being overly EQed or overly padded.

PROBLEM

While Using Two Mikes
(or a Mike and an Effect),
the Sound Character
Deteriorates Because of
Phase Cancelation When
Both Signals Are Present:

CHECK

1. If either the top end or bottom end of a signal disappears when both mikes are brought up in level, phase cancelation is said to be occurring between the two signal sources. If your console modules have phase polarity switches, flop the polarity on one of the two modules. If not . . .

then

2. Alter the relative physical positions of the microphones by trial and error, until the desired sound is achieved . . .

or

3. Try inserting a reverse-phase patch cord on one of the two signal input patches . . .

however

4. If the phase problem occurs between an effect and a straight signal (see chapter 11 on bass guitars), where no phase switching device is available, try using a delay unit to delay the effect slightly. This is not an ideal solution for rhythm tracks, as you have to be aware of "flamming." However, it is quite acceptable for other applications.

PROBLEM

Everything Sounds Weird!

CHECK

1. This could be occurring because your monitor speakers are out of phase. One way to check their phase relationship is to listen to the playback, then, after reversing the hot and

ground wires on *one* of the cabinets, listen to it again, paying close attention to the bass response. Speaker cabinets that are *in* phase will give you a good, rich bass, while cabinets that are out of phase will not.

PROBLEM

Steady Buzzing Noise:

CHECK

1. Check to see if the buzz is coming from the source or the console by listening to the source (amplifier, drums, and so on) acoustically. If the buzz is due to "cabinet noise," "fret buzz," "loose hardware," or some object in the room, eliminate it.

however

2. If the buzz is in the mike, be sure you're bringing it into the console at low impedance.

or

3. If the buzz is in the amplifier circuitry, make sure the amp is properly grounded, and try lifting the ground with the ground switch on the amp or on the multioutlet plug. If the buzz persists . . .

then

4. Flip the ground switch on the direct box—

if you're using one. And if the buzz persists . . .

then

5. If you're using a powered instrument, such as a synthesizer, try lifting the ground at that point. If you still get a buzz . . .

then

6. Check any outboard devices by eliminating them from the audio chain one by one. And if that doesn't work . . .

then

7. Eliminate the input source from the chain to determine if the buzz is coming from a bad mike cord or a bad line cord. And if that doesn't work . . .

then

8. Eliminate the patches one by one until the buzz is found. Replace the cord with a "ground cable," if available.

PROBLEM

*Signal Not Getting
to Tape:*

CHECK

1. Check to make sure the input module has been assigned to a buss. If so . . .

then

2. Make sure the "target track" of the tape machine is in the input mode and that Sel-Sync is off for that track. If so . . .

then

3. Check the output level of the buss that is

being used to send the signal to tape, and make sure that the signal is registering on the tape deck's VU meters. If not . . .

then

4. Check the input level on the tape machine by raising the track's input volume control. If you still have no signal . . .

then

5. Check the connections between the console and the machine.

PROBLEM

*Signal Is Getting to Tape,
But Not Returning:*

CHECK

1. Make sure that the machine is in the proper monitor mode. In most cases this means taking the deck out of its input status and/or flipping any monitor switches from "Source" to "Tape." If you still don't get signal . . .

then

2. Check to see that the return module's "Line

In" button is engaged, so that the input of the module will be set to accept a line-level source. If so . . .

then

3. Use headphones to check the output of the machine. Make sure that the signal is being made available to the output circuitry and that the level is sufficient. If so . . .

then

4. Go back to Step #1 of "No Console Audio at All" and run through the procedure.

TAPE TIP #16
Pro vs. Semipro Console Channels

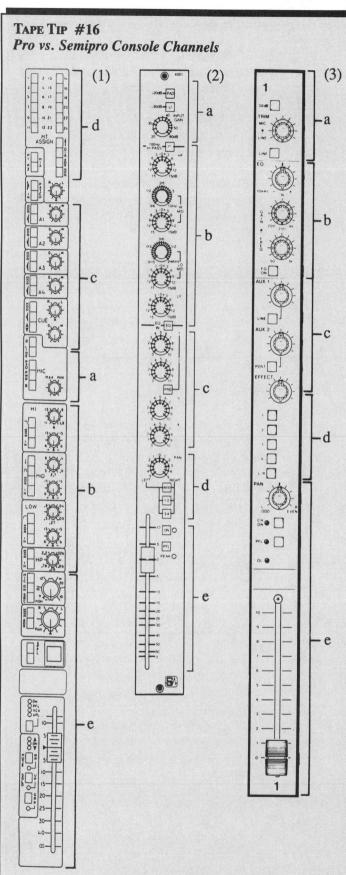

Figure 5r: Comparing pro and semipro consoles.

1. An input channel module on the Harrison MR-4 recording console. (*Courtesy of Harrison Systems, Inc.*)

2. An input channel module on the Soundcraft 400B recording console. (*Courtesy of Soundcraft Electronics, Inc.*)

3. An input channel module on the TASCAM 300 Series (M-308) recording console. (*Courtesy of TEAC Corporation of America*)

KEY

A   Input Controls
B   EQ Controls
C   Effect and Cue Sends
D   Buss Assigns
E   Channel Status

If you already know your way around either a 4-channel or an 8-channel home console, you'd have little trouble moving on to a professional desk. One may have more buttons, lights, meters, and dials than the other, but essentially they do the same thing in the same way.

The easiest way to understand this is to look at how input channels on pro and semipro units compare. In this case, it's not as important to look at the differences as it is to note the similarities, because, for example, while the above Harrison desk has a more elaborate EQ section than the others, the point is that it's still just EQ!

The three console channels we've chosen to compare are from a Harrison MR-4, which is a 24-channel pro studio desk; a Soundcraft 400-B, which is a 16–24-channel pro desk found in homes and studios; and the Tascam M-308, which is a semiprofessional, 8-channel home console.

Harrison MR-4 *(Courtesy of Harrison Systems, Inc.)*

Soundcraft 400B *(Courtesy of Soundcraft Electronics, Inc.)*

TASCAM M-308 *(Courtesy of TEAC Corporation of America)*

Chapter 6

Recording Techniques

As you go through the process of creating a demo, you should approach it as though you are literally *building* a recording—not so much piling one track on top of the next, but integrating them and letting them blend together in much the same way that an artist uses individual colors and brush strokes to create a painting. Among other things, this will require an understanding of the techniques of "bouncing" and "mixdown," through which you can combine individual tracks without losing signal quality or generating hiss.

It is important that you understand how to perform these operations and that you practice them as you would an instrument you were learning how to play, because as you get better at properly executing each procedure, your recordings will sound more professional and more pleasing to the listener. And you'll be faced with fewer "home studio" limitations.

RECORDING AND MONITORING TRACKS

The basic operation of recording a track is relatively simple. You (1) set up the mike, (2) monitor the signals, (3) add effects to the monitor signal, (4) have the musicians play the song at the volume they'll use during the take so that you can set the record and monitor levels, (5) record the track, and then (6) play it back to make sure that it sounds the way you want it to sound. And if it doesn't, you do it over again.

In this section, we're going to cover the first and second steps, as up until now we haven't really had the need to talk about monitor sources or techniques. Yet the way you monitor your material will greatly affect the quality of the finished product.

When you have your engineer cap on, there are two sources you need to monitor: the signal being sent to tape and the signal returning from the tape heads. You monitor

the console output to insure that the signal reaching t[he] heads has the tone, the texture, and the quality you're loo[k]ing for, and you monitor the playback to make sure that t[he] machine was able to capture that quality on tape. Howev[er] as a musician, whose concern is for performance quali[ty] rather than signal quality, you monitor a totally separa[te] "cue" mix that is designed to help you play along with a[n] existing material.

Monitor Mix

When setting the levels of the signal, or signals, being se[nt] to tape, you'll want to monitor the signals in the contr[ol] room monitor speakers. This monitor mix is generated [by] sending the signal to the tape deck and returning it to t[he] console via the line-out jacks on the tape recorder. By mo[ni]toring this mix prior to record, you can adjust each signa[l's] EQ structure and volume level according to the way y[ou] want it to appear on tape and be fairly certain that it w[ill] print exactly as you hear it over the monitors.

While setting your levels, you should consider whether [or] not you want to add any effects to the signal during th[e] initial recording of the track. *As we mentioned in the fi[rst] chapter, it's best to add effects (other than compressio[n]) during some later mixing stage.* However, since that is n[ot] always possible, you may need to add one or more here. [If] so, make sure that you set the levels of the signal before y[ou] add the effect. Then, after adding the effect, you can adju[st] the levels to compensate for any tonal changes that ha[ve] come about.

If you are not adding effects to the signal that is being se[nt] to tape, you will want to add them to the returns from tap[e] so that you'll be able to judge exactly how the track w[ill] sound in its finished form. This can be accomplished [by] ringing the return signals into input channels on the console nd adding effects by using the effect sends. If, during the cording, you need to hear what the track sounds like without the effects, you can solo the console channel that is eing sent to tape (this will let you monitor the output of the hannel module itself).

When you're done recording the track, you will, of ourse, want to monitor the quality of the signal that has een recorded. When you do so, make sure that you've urned off any effects you may have been treating the return ignals with, because such effects may mask a problem that von't be noticed until it's too late to do anything about it.

Headphone Mix

The headphone mix, which is sometimes called the "fold-back mix," is the mix the musician uses to monitor both his performance and the existing tracks. This is an extremely important mix, because it will often determine the extent to which the musician gets into the music. Therefore, you should do everything possible to give the player a blend of tracks he is comfortable with, especially with respect to the relative level of his instrument within the mix.

When you generate the headphone mix, you should be extremely conscious of the use of effects. If you haven't been adding effects to the recorded tracks, make sure you add them to this playback mix, so that the musician can get a feeling for the song as it will sound when it's finished. And make sure you add any effects you'll eventually be giving his instrument, so that he has a feel for the placement his performance will have within the song.

It's very important to work with the musician when creating this mix; you should do your best to provide the player with the blend he requires. For instance, he may need to hear more drums in order to stay on beat, or he may need to hear more bass guitar and less vocal. Also, when you're working with the musician, you should be monitoring the mix through the headphones, if possible, as effects will often seem louder over speakers than they do over the phones. This way you'll better understand the performer's needs.

Monitor Levels

The level at which you listen to music has an effect on the frequency response of the sound. At loud volumes, for example, the high-end and low-end frequencies get louder relative to the midrange. At very low volumes, the highs and lows are softer than the midrange. So if you want to achieve a blend of instruments that will sound right at a normal, living room listening volume, don't mix with the monitors turned all the way up. Instead, turn the monitors down to a reasonable level as you perform the mixes, and you should get good results.

Headphones vs. Monitor Speakers

When the musicians are monitoring their own recording, or listening to other instruments or other previously recorded tracks, they should use headphones to avoid leakage into the microphone. However, headphones do not offer the fidelity that you can get from monitor speakers. So, if possible, you should isolate yourself physically from the musicians and use speakers to monitor everything from the initial tracking to the final mix.

Monitor speakers will give you a truer representation of how the final recording will sound—presuming that it is to be played back over home stereo speakers—because the signal response you'll hear through headphones will be top-end heavy, and you may find that later, when the music is played through speakers, the bass tones are much too strong.

Speakers will also give you a better idea of how well you have utilized stereo imaging (placement of instruments along the stereo plane), because headphones give a distorted view of stereo reality. Speakers transmit sound from in front of you, with the idea that you are standing back from the source—like watching a band perform onstage. Headphones, however, are coming at you from the sides, and the channel separation is exaggerated, as though you're in the midst of the band. And although *you* might like the way the music sounds over the phones, the listener is going to be hearing it over speakers. So, if possible, you should monitor it that way.

However, even if you can't use speakers to monitor each step (some of us *do* have neighbors to think about), at least use them from time to time so you can double-check your progress. There's nothing worse than combining two tracks, for instance, only to later discover that one has too much bass while the other has too little.

TRACK SYNCHRONIZATION

Because of the multitrack capabilities of today's home gear, you don't have to stop recording after one monaural or stereo take. You can add as many tracks as you have left open on the machine, and you can open tracks up by bouncing and by mixing two or more tracks together.

When you add a new track to a recording, it has to play back "in time" with the tracks that are already there. This is called "track synchronization."

Tracks are naturally synchronized if they are all being laid down at the same time. For instance, if you have a 4-track machine and you want to record a quartet, you can mike each instrument separately, give each a separate track, and

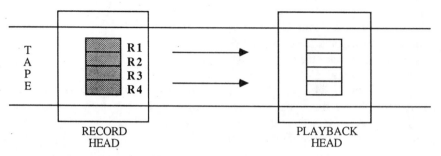

Figure 6a: If all four tracks are recorded simultaneously on the record head, they will play back simultaneously when they reach the playback head.

record them simultaneously. Since the four record heads sit side by side on the head stack (Figure 6a), and the signals all reach the tape at once, they will remain synchronized when they reach the playback heads.

But let's say that you want to record the instruments separately, in four different sessions. That means each musician will need to be able to monitor any tracks that were recorded before his. And that presents a problem.

Normally, you monitor a track through the playback head, but as you can see in Figure 6b, if you struck a note that was to be in time with a signal you were hearing from the playback head, your note would be placed on the tape a good distance behind it, at the point of the record head. That would mean the two tracks would be "out of sync"—not in time with each other. And this is why, when adding fresh tracks to a recording, you must use a "Sel-Sync" mode.

NOTE—*Many newly designed tape recorders utilize a 2-head rather than a 3-head system. This configuration eliminates the need for Sel-Sync, as the record and playback functions are performed on the same head.*

Most manufacturers call this the "sync" mode, but no matter what it's called, it performs the same function: i allows you to monitor a "playback" of existing track through the *record* head, which places them at the same point on the tape that you'll be adding your new signal. This means that if you *now* strike a note that is "in sync" with the playback signal, it will be placed on tape at the same spot from which the playback signal is originating: the record head.

When you use this mode, you may notice that the monitor signal is not as bright or as loud as the signal you get when you monitor the playback head. That is because on some machines, the signal must be "read" at a lower level so that it won't feed back through any adjacent head that has been placed in record. However, on some new decks, you will find that the Sel-Sync signal sounds the same as the playback signal, so you don't have to keep switching back and forth to check the quality of a bounced track against the quality of the original.

To use the Sel-Sync function, all you do is place the monitored tracks in the "sync" mode and set the levels of the new track as you would any other you were recording. Then, if need be, raise the level of the synced channels to a volume at which they can be properly monitored.

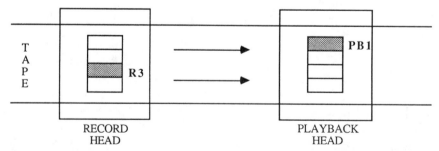

Figure 6b: If you are using the playback heads to monitor a recorded signal on Track 1 while placing an overdub on Track 3, the signals will be out of sync, since the signal recorded on Track 3 will be slightly behind the signal on Track 1. However, Sel-Sync allows you to monitor Track 1 at the point of the record head, so that both signals will exist side by side on the tape. Thus, they will play back simultaneously.

OVERDUBS

Overdubbing is the technique you use to add new tracks to an existing recording. It is a relatively simple process, whereby you place your tape deck in Sel-Sync, send the existing tracks through the musician's headphone mix, and record the new material onto an open track.

The track that is being laid down during an overdub is really no different from the initial track you will have recorded, and it should be treated as such. For instance, you'll want to set the levels and add any effects you want the signal to have on tape, and you'll want to monitor your work over the monitor speakers in the control room—just as we discussed in "Monitor Mix."

Once you have the overdub track prepared, you can turn your attention to the headphone mix the musician is going to use. Again, your concerns here should be the same as those described in "Headphone Mix," and you should be sure to work with the musician so that the mix conforms to his needs.

Once you have all your mixes and levels set, the only thing left to do is place the existing tracks in Sel-Sync, if necessary, and let 'er rip.

BOUNCING AND COMBINING TRACKS

Although it's great to be able to add fresh material to a recording, you need to have an open track to put it on. This can be a problem if your song has more instrumental parts than your machine has tracks. However, one way to increase the number of tracks a recording contains is to mix two or more recorded tracks together and combine them onto a single mixed track.

For instance, you may have already recorded material onto Tracks 1, 2, and 3 of your 4-track machine, when suddenly you realize that you need to record *two* additional tracks in order to polish up the material. Well, you can open up a second track by combining two of the existing tracks, such as Tracks 1 and 2, and recording them onto Track 4, which is still open. You can then record over Tracks 1 and 2 and finish off the song (Figure 6c).

Internal Bounce

This method of combining tracks uses the technique of "internal bouncing," which entails transferring the signals to a track on the same machine. A "bounce" is a transfer of signal from one track to another, and this is termed an internal bounce because there's only one tape machine involved.

Any time you use internal bouncing to combine tracks, you have to remember to place the tracks in the Sel-Sync mode before removing them to the new track location (if your machine so requires). If you don't, and you're only combining *some* of the existing tracks, when you move those tracks they'll be out of sync with the recording. If, on the other hand, you're combining *all* existing tracks, Sel-Sync is unnecessary.

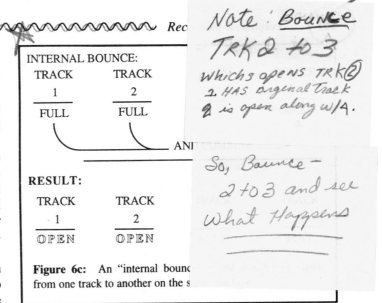

INTERNAL BOUNCE:

TRACK 1	TRACK 2
FULL	FULL

AND

RESULT:

TRACK 1	TRACK 2
OPEN	OPEN

Figure 6c: An "internal bounce" from one track to another on the s...

Handwritten note: Note: Bounce TRK 2 to 3 which opens TRK ②
2. HAS original track ② is open along w/4.

So, Bounce — 2 to 3 and see What Happens

Depending upon the capabilities of your tape deck, one problem you may encounter when you try to combine tracks in the Sel-Sync mode is that if any of the source tracks are adjacent to the track they are to be combined on, the machine won't complete the transfer. That's because Sel-Sync lets you monitor the track from the record head, and the heads are so close together in the head stack that if you were to try to pull a signal from one head and record it on the adjacent head, you'd get feedback within the machine.

To get around this problem, you need to bounce the offending track to a different location, so that it is no longer adjacent to the track you want to combine onto. For instance, if you've recorded on Tracks 1, 2, and 4, and you wanted to combine Tracks 1 and 4, the machine won't perform the operation because Track 3 is adjacent to Track 4.

To rectify the situation, you need to bounce the signal on Track 1 to Track 3 (Figure 6d), then mix the new Track 3

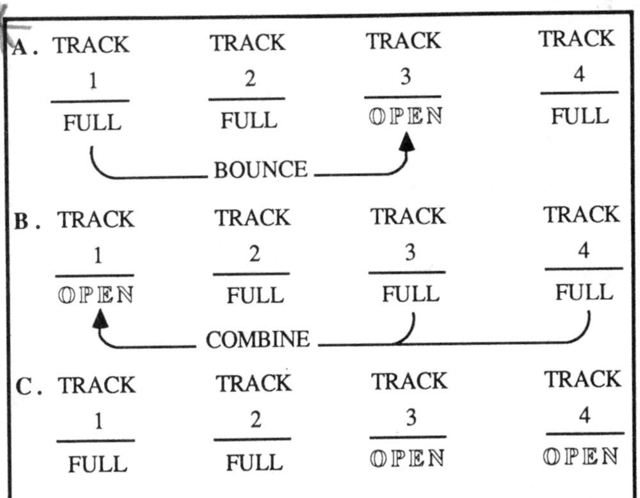

A.

TRACK 1	TRACK 2	TRACK 3	TRACK 4
FULL	FULL	OPEN	FULL

BOUNCE

B.

TRACK 1	TRACK 2	TRACK 3	TRACK 4
OPEN	FULL	FULL	FULL

COMBINE

C.

TRACK 1	TRACK 2	TRACK 3	TRACK 4
FULL	FULL	OPEN	OPEN

Figure 6d: The bounce from Track 1 to Track 3 (A) opens up Track 1, which can then be used to combine Track 3 and Track 4 (B). As a result (C), you now have two tracks open for recording.

with Track 4 and combine them on Track 1. This then places the "original" Track 1 and the "original" Track 4 on Track 1, Track 2 has stayed as it was, and Tracks 3 and 4 are now open for recording.

You should, of course, do your best to figure out a tracking scheme beforehand that will allow you to combine tracks without having to bounce them first. However, that's not always possible. So, as a general rule, just remember that on 4-track machines that won't let you bounce adjacent, you'll only be able to combine either Tracks 1 and 2 or Tracks 3 and 4, and they can only be combined on Track 4 or Track 1 respectively.

External Bounce

There is another combining technique, known as "external bouncing" (Figure 6e), which involves the use of a second machine. In this instance, instead of combining the signals onto one open track on the same machine, you can bounce them to one or *two* tracks of a second machine. If you're using a 4-track, this means that you can record on up to four tracks, bounce them down to a 2-track mix, return that mix to the 4-track, and have two tracks open for recording. Plus, if you have the ability to pan the tracks during the initial bounce, you can give the 2-track mix the stereo image you want it to have in the mixdown.

External bouncing is extremely useful in situations where you've recorded an instrument, like drums, in stereo, and want to preserve its stereo image in the bounce. It's al[so] useful if you want to add a stereo effect to one of the trac[ks] during the transfer. However, unlike internal bouncing, a[ny] time you use an external bounce to combine tracks, eve[ry] existing track will need to be included in the transfer, so, [as] we illustrate in chapter 7, it will require a certain amount [of] preplanning.

Bounce Concerns

One very important thing to remember when combini[ng] tracks is that once they are combined, they can no longer b[e] treated as two individual signals. Therefore, you will have [to] be very careful to create the proper EQ and level balan[ce] between the signals before committing to the mix. This als[o] means thinking ahead and adding any effects that you on[ly] want one of the combining tracks to have.

The procedure for bouncing a track is not all that compl[i]cated. All you have to do is patch the output of the boun[ce] track to an input channel on the console. Then you patch t[he] assigned output (or buss) of the console to the input of t[he] target track and place the bounce track in Sel-Sync. You wi[ll] probably have to boost the level of the bounce track an[d] push the high end up a bit in order to compensate for [a] certain amount of signal loss, but once you have the leve[l] set, all you need to do is put the machine in record and mak[e] a trial bounce. (This procedure has been simplified on mult[i]track cassette decks, as all of the patching is done internall[y.] For further information see chapter 8, "Cassette Portast[u]dios.")

You should always play the bounced track back in order t[o] determine how well it stands up to the original. If it has lo[st] quality, you'll want to make adjustments and record it agai[n.] For instance, you may hear too much bottom end. This is [a] sign that, in fact, there isn't enough *top end,* because th[e] tape heads won't *add* anything to a recording, they'll sub[-]tract from it. So, in this case, you'll want to add some to[p] end. And if the high frequencies sound loud, you need t[o] add some bottom end.

As you can see, if you can move a recording from on[e] track to another without having it suffer an appreciable los[s] of signal quality (such as generation loss), you quite literall[y] increase the track capacity of your machine. Therefore, i[t] would be well worth your time to practice combining an[d] bouncing tracks, especially if you do most of your work on [a] 4-track recorder. After all, it's a shame to spend so muc[h] time recording a track and getting it to sound just right, onl[y] to have the signal lose clarity and gain hiss during a bounc[e] or a mix.

PUNCH-INS/DROP-INS

Sometimes, whether from a poor performance or a technica[l] glitch, a track may be flawed in only one section of th[e]

Figure 6e: An "external bounce" is the transfer of signal to a second tape machine.

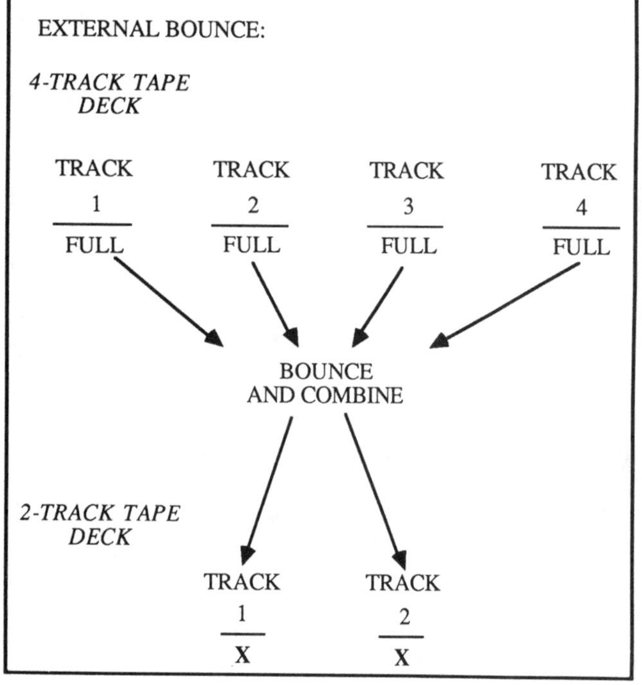

EXTERNAL BOUNCE:

4-TRACK TAPE DECK

TRACK 1	TRACK 2	TRACK 3	TRACK 4
FULL	FULL	FULL	FULL

BOUNCE AND COMBINE

2-TRACK TAPE DECK

TRACK 1	TRACK 2
X	X

cording. The technique most frequently used to repair such substandard tracks is called a "punch-in" or "drop-in." This enables you to correct the problem without having to rerecord the entire performance.

For example, you might want to redo a guitar solo without having to have the guitarist play the entire song. Or you may want to redo a vocal at a point the singer went off key. Or you may just want to erase a drum section laid down to provide tempo for a long, solo-guitar lead-in by "dropping it out" of the track up until the point it (the drum track) is supposed to come in.

The exact mechanisms of dropping in a passage will vary according to the age and head configuration of your machine. Therefore, before attempting any drop-ins, refer to your owner's manual to see what capabilities your machine has.

The basic concept of the punch-in technique is quite simple. All you do is play the tape, and when the flawed section comes up, you kick the machine into record and redo it. Then, when the passage has ended, you immediately stop recording so that you don't erase any material that follows.

If your machine has a Sel-Sync mode, you'll need to place all other existing tracks in Sel-Sync so that the new track will be synchronized with the rest of the recording. However, if your machine has only two tape heads and no Sel-Sync, as is the case with many newer models, then the new track will automatically be in sync.

When determining the exact point at which to begin the punch-in, be aware that there is a slight delay between the time the drop-in point passes over the record head and the time you *hear* it pass over the playback head (see Figure b). There can be quite a delay on some older machines, and this may mean learning to anticipate the drop-in point and practicing until you can get the timing down. Of course, since most older machines do have Sel-Sync, you can always monitor the existing tracks off the record head and use them as a timing reference.

Taking the machine out of the record mode is another important consideration, especially during "tight" punches when there's little room for error), and you should experiment with your gear in order to determine how this can best be accomplished. On some machines, this may mean hitting the rewind function, which is something that I do. This gives you a little added margin of error, as it will take the deck out of record and keep the tape from rolling over the record head should the head be slow to respond.

When performing a punch, you should play a portion of the song leading up to the part that needs to be redone, so that the musician can get his bearings. For instance, if you're inserting a new guitar solo, the tape should be started at least a verse ahead of time. This allows the guitarist to catch the feel and rhythm of the song, and it gives him time to prepare for the solo.

If you have enough tracks on your machine, another way to perform this technique is to record the new section on a separate track. Then, once you have the part down just the way you want it, you can either drop the insertion in from one track to the other, or you can just wait until a mixdown and insert the new part in place of the old one. Since the latter can be done by switching one track monitor on and the other track monitor off at the appropriate times, it can provide a clean, easy form of insertion.

In either case, no matter how you perform the punch-in, the most important thing to remember is that the last thing you want it to sound like is an insertion. Therefore, if you are inserting a passage that appears elsewhere in the song, or if, for instance, you're redoing the vocal in one of the choruses, you must be careful to duplicate the tone and volume of the existing material. If you don't, it's going to be noticeable.

TAPE COMPRESSION

Tape compression is a recording technique that employs the deliberate use of signal distortion in order to limit and compress the sound. However, it is not the sort of recording tool that can be used on every occasion, because the signal distorts in a way that eliminates certain frequencies and causes the sound to flatten out.

Tape compression is the result of tape saturation, which we spoke about in chapter 4. Tape saturation occurs when every particle on the tape is being charged with "signal," and you end up with that totally blackened-in picture. The signal loses definition because at the point of saturation, there is no room on the tape for the high-end frequencies. This also means that the signal cannot get any louder without creating high-end distortion, which is when the signal begins to break down into "noise."

So, for instance, if you're recording a vicious lead guitar part, and you don't want to use a normal compressor, you can "hit the tape" rather hard (record with the peaks far into the red on the VU meter), and it will flatten out some of the highs and take the edge off.

You can also use tape compression on some of the drums, which we discuss in chapter 9, because there are instances when the tone of the drum is not as important as giving it that hard *thwack* sound. But any time you *do* want to hear the harmonics and the complexities of the high frequencies, you should avoid tape compression. For instance, you should never use it on strings or an acoustic piano because it will destroy the tonal qualities of the instrument.

You must be especially careful using this technique if your equipment is fitted with small-gauge heads. For instance, if you try to use tape compression on cassette decks, 1/4-inch 8-tracks or 1/2-inch 16-tracks, when you saturate the low frequencies, you are likely to get crosstalk, which is when the signal from one track bleeds over onto an adjacent track.

TAPE TIP #17
How to Apply Our *EQ Guidelines,* Given Your *EQ Capabilities*

Throughout this book we've included a great deal of specific information about equalization. Yet in each case, unless you understand how our EQ instructions are best carried out on your EQ system, the information will be of little value.

Limitations of Each EQ Format

Each of the four basic EQ formats described on pages 59–60 can be used to alter the tonality of an instrument. However, some give you more control over the process than others, and if you're using an EQ system that has limited capabilities, you'll need to adjust your technique. To illustrate this, we'll look at an example EQ treatment for guitar and see how it would be approached using each of the formats (Figure 6f).

(1)   **EXAMPLE EQ FOR GUITAR:**

Boost: 10K
3K
100 Hz

Parametric EQ:

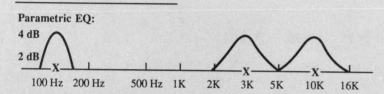

Figure 6f: 1. Parametric equalizers allow you to apply EQ at any point along the frequency spectrum, so that each boost can be placed in the precise location desired. Plus, they enable you to vary the bandwidth of the EQ, as seen in the 100 Hz boost.

(2)   **Sweepable-Band EQ:**

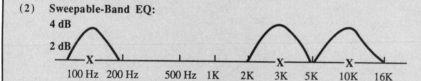

2. Sweepable-band EQ can also be applied at any point you choose. However, this system does not allow you to vary the bandwidth, which means that the 100 Hz boost will be slightly wider than desired and will begin to affect the 200 Hz range.

(3)   **Graphic and Click-Stop EQ:**

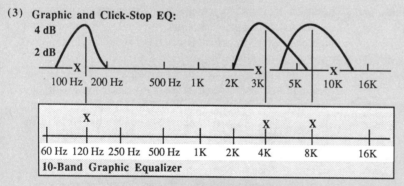

3. Graphic equalizers only allow you to apply EQ at fixed points along the spectrum, which means that you may not always be able to add a boost exactly where you desire. In this example, we had to use the 120 Hz band, the 4K band and the 8K band, as these were closest to the desired frequencies.

(4)   **Graphic EQ Response:**

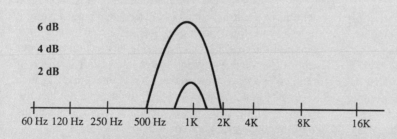

4. On a 10-band graphic equalizer, a 6 dB boost at 1K will affect a band of frequencies stretching from 500 Hz to 2K. However, as seen in the 2 dB boost, the less EQ you add, the narrower the range of affected frequencies.

Note: This same effect is seen with all EQ formats. However, parametric EQs are designed to allow you to enhance extremely narrow bands, in which case the effect of volume will be minimal.

continued . . .

. . . continued

If you're using **parametric** EQ or **sweepable-band** EQ, you should be able to apply each of the three boosts at the precise points we've indicated, because both formats allow you to "sweep" through the frequency spectrum and boost or cut the level at any location you choose. And as long as your system is capable of reaching up to 16K and down to at least 80 Hz, you'll be able to follow any EQ guidelines included in the book.

On the other hand, if you're using a **graphic** EQ or a **click-stop** EQ system, you may not be able to position the boost exactly where we suggest. These systems only allow you to alter the EQ at certain fixed positions along the spectrum (i.e., they are *not* sweepable), and if you need to EQ a frequency that falls somewhere between these fixed positions, the only choice you have is to add EQ at the band closest to the desired frequency.

In our illustration, the low-end boost we're using on the guitar is supposed to be placed at 100 Hz, but since the 10-band graphic EQ device only provides for EQ at 60 Hz and 120 Hz, we've placed the boost in the 120 Hz band, because it's closer to 100 Hz than the 60 Hz band would be. By the same token, since there's no 10K band available, we've used the 8K band for the high-end boost, because it's closer to 10K than the 16K band would be.

The reason you want to do it this way is that when EQ is applied, it affects a wide range of frequencies. For instance, a 6 dB boost at 1K will affect a band of frequencies stretching from 500 Hz up to 2K. However, as you can see in the accompanying graph, the frequencies that are nearest the center frequency in the band are affected the most. So, by boosting or cutting a band that is close to the frequency you originally wanted to EQ, you end up affecting that desired frequency as well.

Unfortunately, this may not always work if your graphic equalizer has fewer than eight or ten bands, because the bands will be spread too far apart, and you may not be able to find a band close enough to the desired frequency to be effective. So check the EQ response graph in your owner's manual to make sure.

Tone control EQ is also unsuitable for our purposes, which is why it hasn't been included in the illustration. These systems affect such broad bands of frequencies, they're ineffective when you need to apply EQ in a specific location. Therefore, if the only EQ you have is tone control, but you still want to be able to use the EQ information we've provided, you'll need to use an outboard EQ system.

Applying EQ in Stages

Another problem you're likely to have concerns the EQ guidelines we've laid down for each of the instruments (chapters 9–15). In many of these instances, we've recommended that you alter the EQ in up to five separate locations. However, most home desks are limited to two-band or three-band systems, which means they're incapable of applying EQ in five separate locations at once.

This may make it seem as though we've given you EQ settings for the home that can only be applied in a commercial studio, but that isn't so. EQ can be applied during the initial recording, as well as during a bounce or during mixdown. So you can make up for your system's limitations by EQing in stages (Figure 6g).

For example, if you need to add three EQ boosts to a signal, such as in our illustration, but you only have two EQ level controls on your console, you can apply two of the boosts as you're recording the track and apply the third during a bounce. What makes this possible is the fact that when

EXAMPLE EQ FOR GUITAR:

Boost: 10K
3K
100 Hz

Figure 6g: Applying EQ in stages. If you have a two-band EQ system, but you need to apply three boosts, you can do so by breaking the EQ treatment down into stages. Thus, the 100 Hz and 10K boosts are applied as the track is being recorded, and the 3K boost is applied during mixdown or during a bounce.

STAGE 1: (EQ During Record)

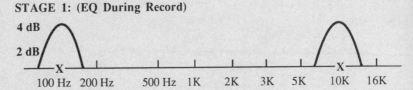

STAGE 2: (EQ During Mixdown or Bounce)

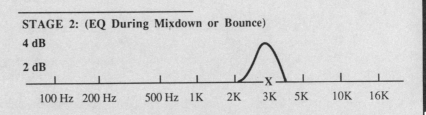

. . . continued

you're adding EQ, you're boosting or lowering specific frequencies that exist within the signal, and since the signal contains the same sets of frequencies during mixdown that it contained as it was recorded, the EQ will be equally effective at either time.

Whenever you do EQ in stages, it's usually best to add the high-end and low-end boosts to the initial track and add the midrange EQ during a bounce. If you wait to add the high-end boost during a bounce, it will increase the level of any tape hiss that was generated during record. And you add the low-end boost at this time in order to get a better overall feel for the balance between the high and low ends.

This also means that you will need to keep a record of what EQ you applied initially, so that when you monitor the signal during overdubs or when you add it to the final mix, you know which frequency bands still need to be treated.

How Not to Apply EQ

If, as in the previous example, you don't have the capability of EQing all the required bands at once, the only choice you really do have is to EQ in stages. Your initial reaction may be to ignore the specific EQ guidelines and to place some sort of compromise boost in between two of the suggested bands (if we, say, boost 4K and 10K, you place a "compromise" boost at 7K instead). However, each EQ boost or cut must be treated independently, because each brings out a different aspect of the instrument's sound, depending upon the frequencies it's affecting. So if you try to replace two separate boosts with one midpoint boost, you'll end up enhancing a totally different part of the sound than you intended.

TAPE TIP #18
Damn, I Wish I Could Remember How I Did That!

No matter what project you're working on, it's always a good idea to maintain detailed records of every setup, setting, and mix level you've used. The logic behind this is simple: since anything *can* and *will* go wrong, if you know what you did the *first* time, it makes it that much easier if, three days later, you discover that you have to do it all again.

Recording engineers often keep such records, because many studios allow other bands to use the room between sessions. And without these records, the engineer could waste hours trying to recapture the sound from just the night before.

Such documentation can be equally beneficial in the home. For example, if you happen to erase something by mistake, it will take only a few minutes to reset the levels so that you can rerecord the part. And if you're EQing in stages (see Tape Tip #17), such records are invaluable.

If you keep records as you go, it makes it easier to experiment with sounds, because once you find a "good" sound, you can copy down your settings and go off in search of a *better* sound. Then, if you don't find one, you've got the original settings to fall back on. And if you ever want to duplicate that sound at some point in the future, all you'll need to do is refer back to these notes.

Recording engineers also maintain something called a "track sheet," which is a running account of the contents of each track. These records can be particularly useful if you're performing a lot of overdubs, because the later the session runs, the easier it is to forget where you've recorded what, and as a result, unless you have a track sheet to refer to, you can end up recording over something you had wanted to keep in the song. (In appendix C you'll find a blank track sheet that you can photocopy.)

The track sheet needs to be updated after each overdub, so that you always know where you stand. However, no matter how carefully you detail your work, it never hurts to solo the track you're going to be recording the overdub onto and listen to the playback so that you can be sure it's empty.

If you're a songwriter, it's also helpful to maintain a "quick-reference" notebook that contains the settings you like to use on instruments you write with frequently. These are particularly handy when all you need is a good, solid recording sound. For instance, if you write on piano, and you suddenly get an idea for a song, you can use these records as a guide and have everything from mike to effects to a drum machine set up and mixed in about five minutes.

Another type of record that is easy to keep, and saves a lot of confusion, is of console channel assignments. In studios, the engineer will place a strip of heavy masking tape across the length of the console just above the channel faders, and on this he'll write the name of the instrument or mike assigned to each individual channel. If necessary, the tape can then be lifted off the console at the close of the session, stored, and placed back down the following day.

As you can see, no matter what level of recording you're at, and no matter how often or how seldom you thread that tape and push record, you will certainly never regret keeping track of your work (Figure 6h). At the very least, it will mean never having to say, "Damn, I wish I could remember how I did that!"

Figure 6h: This is the tracking sheet we used when recording a Men At Work concert for the ABC Radio Network. The recording was made from a mobile, 24-track studio.

RECORD PLANT STUDIOS
321 WEST 44th STREET, NEW YORK, N.Y. 10036 • (212) 581-6505

MEN AT WORK
MERRIWEATHER POST PAVILLIAN
THURS   7·28·83

CLIENT	ENGINEER/ASST.	TAPE	NOISE REDUCTION		DATE 7·28·83
ABC RADIO NET.	PM/PR/DH/BK	☑ AMPEX 456 ☐ AMPEX 406 ☐ SCOTCH 250	☑ NONE ☐ DOLBY ☐ DBX	☑ ORIGINAL ☐ COMP.MAST. ☐ SAFETY ☐ COPY	REEL # ALL
PRODUCER RICK LIEBERT	ORIG. STUDIO/TRUCK BLACK				OF
ARTIST MEN AT WORK	TRACKS 24	IPS 30			

1	2	3	4	5	6	7	8
KICK	SN	HH	TOMS L	R (AUD)	OH L CHIMES	H R	BASS
9 SR GTR	10 SL GTR	11 KB	12 KB	13 VOCODER	14 SAX	15 SPARE MIC	16 LEAD COLLIN VOC
17 KB SREG VOC + FLUTE	18 SL GTR RON VOC	19 BASS JOHN VOC	20 DRUM JERRY VOC	21 STEREO FFX + TAPE L	22 R	23 AUD L	24 R
25	26	27	28	29	30	31	32

RECORDING PROCEDURES

The following is a procedural guide to many of the recording operations you will need to perform in the studio. Each is designed to provide quick-reference assistance for a given situation and to explain the "how's" rather than the "why's" of the procedure. However, if you require further background information, you will find that each has been covered in detail in a previous section of this chapter.

Although we've attempted to use universally accepted recording terminology throughout this section, you may need to refer to your owner's manual from time to time, since different manufacturers will call different controls by different names. There is also a glossary in the back of the book that may be helpful if you really get stuck.

Recording Through a Console
(Without Patch Bay)

1. Calibrate the output levels of the console and the input levels of the tape recorder in order to insure the best possible signal-to-noise response.
2. Mike the instrument.
3. Plug the mike into an input channel on the console.
4. Assign the channel to a buss.
5. Patch the output from the console buss to the input of an open track on the tape recorder.
6. Patch the output of the track into a separate input channel on the console. Assign this channel to the stereo buss (for monitoring *only*).
7. Monitor the signal and prepare it for recording by adding any effects you intend to use on tape.
8. Adjust channel levels and EQ while having the musicians play at their intended volumes.
9. Use the cue sends on the console input channels to generate a headphone mix for the musician.
10. Add any effects you intend to use on this mix and adjust the levels according to the musician's needs. (See Operational Diagram #4, "How to Monitor an Effect on Monitors and Headphones, Without Sending the Effect to Tape," page 20.)
11. Place the tape recorder in record and make a trial run-through of the track.
12. Monitor each channel during the take and "fine-tune" the settings.
13. Monitor the playback of the recording and make any adjustments in level or EQ. Rerecord the track until it is produced and performed to everyone's satisfaction.

How to Overdub

1. Mike the instrument that is to be recorded and send it into an input channel on the console. Add any effects you intend to use on the recorded signal and assign the channel to a buss. (See Operational Diagram #10, "How to Send an Effect to Tape," page 26.)
2. Patch the output from the buss to the input of an open track on the tape recorder, then set all record levels in the normal way.
3. Patch the output of this track to an input channel on the console.
4. Add any effects you intend to use when generating a headphone mix for the musician.
5. Do the same with any previously recorded tracks the musician will need to monitor, making sure to place each on a separate input channel—if you have them available.
6. Place the previously recorded tracks in Sel-Sync, then set the monitor levels for *all* tracks that are being used in the musician's headphone mix (including the monitor mix of the instrument he's playing). This will mean making adjustments in the balance of the tracks and the levels of the effects, according to the musician's needs.
7. Set the monitor levels for the control room mix.
8. Run through the song and make a test recording of the material.
9. Take the previously recorded tracks out of Sel-Sync and slightly reduce their monitor levels to compensate for an increase in gain.
10. Listen to the playback and check the quality of the recording by soloing the recorded track.
11. Make sure that the headphones are not being picked up by the mike. Make whatever adjustments are necessary.
12. Place the previously recorded tracks back in Sel-Sync and go for a take. Continue with #9–#12 until you have a good take.

Note—*When using your console as a return for the previously recorded tracks, make sure that none of these signals is sent back to the tape recorder on a console output channel, or you may get feedback.*

How to Bounce Tracks

1. Patch the output of Track A (the source track) into a console input channel and assign the channel to a buss.
2. Patch the output from the console buss to the "Line In" jack of Track B (the target track) and patch the output of Track B into a separate input channel on the console. Assign this channel to the stereo buss (for monitoring *only*).
3. Place Track A in Sel-Sync and set the EQ and volume levels of the signal in preparation for sending it to tape.
4. Place Track B in record and make a trial bounce. Then monitor the playback of Track B and compare it with the original recording on Track A. Make sure to take Track A out of Sel-Sync when comparing the two tracks, and make sure that the monitor EQ is set the same for both playbacks.

continued . . .

. . . continued

5. Make the necessary adjustments, then try the bounce again. Repeat the process until the bounce sounds as close to the original as possible.

Note —*To adjust for signal generation loss, and for the gain reduction of the Sel-Sync signal, you will probably need to boost the volume level of Track A and slightly increase the high-frequency EQ levels of the signal. For further information, refer to "Bouncing and Combining Tracks," page 101.*

How to Combine Tracks

INTERNAL BOUNCE

1. If your machine won't allow you to bounce to adjacent tracks, make sure that neither of the tracks you intend to combine is adjacent to the track you are going to combine on. (See "Bouncing and Combining Tracks," page 101.)
2. Patch the outputs of Track A and Track B (the two source tracks) into separate input channels on the console.
3. Assign both channels to the same buss.
4. Patch the output of the console buss to the "Line In" jack of Track C (the target track) and patch the output of Track C into a third input channel on the console. Assign this channel to the stereo buss (for monitoring *only*).
5. Place Tracks A and B in Sel-Sync and set the EQ and volume levels of each in preparation for sending them to tape. Pay particular attention to the blending of the EQ levels and to the overall balance of the mix, as you will no longer have individual control over the signals once they have been combined.
6. Place Track C in record and make a trial bounce. Then monitor the playback of Track C and compare it with a blend of the original Tracks A and B. Make sure to take both tracks out of Sel-Sync when making the comparison, and make sure that the monitor EQ is the same for all playbacks.
7. Make the necessary adjustments, then try the bounces again. (See "Note" at the end of "How to Bounce Tracks.") Repeat the process until the bounce sounds as close to the original as possible.

Note —*For information about adding effects to the signals as they are being mixed together, see chapter 16, "Mixdown Techniques."*

EXTERNAL BOUNCE

(In this example we'll combine four tracks from a 4-track onto a 2-track machine, then return that mix to the 4-track.)

1. Patch the outputs of Tracks 1, 2, 3, and 4 into separate input channels on the console, but do not assign them to a buss at this time.
2. Patch the output of console Buss A to the "Line In" jack for Track 1 on the 2-track.
3. Patch the output of console Buss B to the "Line In" jack for Track 2 on the 2-track.
4. Patch the outputs of 2-track Tracks 1 and 2 into separate input channels on the console. Assign these channels to the stereo buss (for monitoring *only*).
5. Pan each of these channels so that they are stereo opposites (one left, one right) and give both the same trim, EQ, and fader levels.
6. Begin monitoring a playback of the 4-track material through the 2-track by assigning the input channels containing those signals to Busses A or B.
7. Establish the stereo image you want the 2-track mix to have by altering these buss assignments and adjusting the panpot. If you want an instrument to appear far left or far right, assign it to only one buss. If you want it to appear in the center, assign it to both busses, but do not pan. If you want it to appear slightly off center, assign it to both busses and adjust the pan.
8. Add any necessary effects to each instrument and adjust the individual EQ. Pay particular attention to the individual treatment each track receives and to the overall balance of the mix, because once the signals have been combined, they will have to be treated as a whole.
9. Make a test bounce and compare the playback with the original blend. Make any necessary adjustments, then repeat the process until the bounce sounds as close to the original as possible.

THE RETURN

10. To return the 2-track mix to the 4-track, clear all buss assignments and repatch the outputs from console Busses A and B to the input jacks for Tracks 1 and 2 (respectively) on the 4-track.
11. Assign the console channels holding these tracks to the stereo buss (for monitoring *only*).
12. Make sure both channels' EQ and fader levels match.
13. Assign the console channel holding Track 1 of the 2-track to Buss A.
14. Assign the console channel holding Track 2 of the 2-track to Buss B.
15. Make sure both channels' EQ and fader levels match and that both busses are set for the same output level.
16. Add any necessary effects by patching them to both Buss A and Buss B.
17. Make a test bounce from the 2-track to the 4-track.
18. Make any necessary adjustments, then try the bounce again. Repeat the process until the bounce sounds as close to the original as possible.

How to Punch In (Insert) a Passage

This is a generalized procedure that is meant to show how a drop-in is accomplished. However, since you can easily de-

continued . . .

. . . continued

stroy an existing track if you don't know what you're doing, be sure to practice the procedure using spare time and tape before trying it out on important material. Plus, the exact mechanics of the procedure will vary according to the age, head configuration, and type of machine you are using, so be certain that you are aware of the specific characteristics of your machine, and read the special section on punch-ins that appears earlier in this chapter.

1. Mike the instrument and prepare for the overdub by setting up the record and monitor mixes as described in #1–#7 in "How to Overdub."
2. Make sure that the overdub matches the tone and volume of the passage you are replacing.
3. Make as many practice passes over the material as it takes for the musician to get the part right.
4. As you will want to hear what precedes the drop-in, set the machine status accordingly. Check your owner's manual to determine which configuration this is. On some machines it will mean placing the tracks in Sel-Sync,

while on two-head machines the method used will be different.

Note—*Some older tape machines do not allow you to change a track from the Sel-Sync mode to the record mode if all tracks are full, so check your owner's manual to see if you need to have at least one track already in record in order to perform this operation.*

5. Begin the playback a verse or so before the passage is to begin, so that the musician can prepare for his performance.
6. When you reach the beginning of the passage that is to be rerecorded, perform the punch-in according to the guidelines in your owner's manual.
7. As soon as the new passage has been inserted, stop recording immediately so that you do not erase over any other material. For a very quick exit, push "rewind."
8. Listen to a playback of the insertion and check it for signal quality and performance quality.
9. If the take is not to your liking, make whatever adjustments are necessary and do it again.

Chapter 7

Track Arrangements for Song Demos

It's important to understand the various methods and techniques of recording, but it's equally vital to understand how each is applied. So in this chapter we're going to take the techniques we talked about in the last chapter and show you, in real-world terms, how they can be used to create the recording.

Of principal importance in this regard is the technique of combining tracks during a bounce. As you'll see, while this increases your capabilities to the point where you can literally produce a one-man, six-part demo, it also increases the need for preproduction planning.

For instance, there's a big difference between the way you would approach a song demo recorded by using internal bouncing and the way you would approach it if you had external bounce capabilities. Each method has its own set of real-world concerns and limitations that directly affect your overdub and mix procedures.

At the end of this chapter, you'll find a set of three examples that illustrate how a song can be recorded using the various bounce techniques. We've also included a separate example of the actual process I used to record a song demo for Pat Benatar, along with a step-by-step explanation of my concerns and my techniques. Although you may wish to refer to these examples as you go through the introductory text, they are designed primarily to give you an idea of the methods available for organizing your production.

A PRACTICAL APPROACH TO BOUNCING

One of Murphy's first laws of recording states that no matter what the format, from 2-track to 24-track, you'll always want to use more sounds than there are tracks to put them on. So in order to avoid a mixdown nightmare where the sousaphone, backing vocals, and lead guitar are all on different sections of the same track, and all must be EQed differently, you need to plan your bounce ahead of time.

In the 4-track and 8-track formats, it's fairly standard procedure to combine tracks during a bounce. However, in order to accomplish this operation efficiently, you need to know from the very beginning what you want the final mix to sound like, and you need to be constantly aware of your options. For example, if you are recording on a 4-track, and you know that there are six musical parts to be laid down, you will either have to combine the instruments as they are being recorded or combine them during a bounce.

If you choose to combine the instruments as they are being laid down, you lose the ability to rebalance them later. In fact, you lose the ability to treat any of the combined tracks individually, whether in terms of EQ, level, or effects. Therefore, unless you're recording a band live, this would not be the technique of choice.

However, there are two other options you can choose between if you're combining the instruments during a bounce. The first, which offers the greatest amount of control, is performed by recording the instruments, without effects, on individual tracks. Then, while adding separate effects to each signal, you balance them, EQ them, and combine them on a new track or tracks (see Examples A and B).

This method offers you the advantage of playing with the mix and experimenting with the balance you've created. It gives you time to think ahead to what the rest of the song is going to sound like, and it gives you a better opportunity to make sure that this mix will fit comfortably into the final mix.

Yet for all the control this method offers, it means performing at least two or three bounces. And if you have trouble with generation loss during transfers, you may want to limit the number of bounces you use and trade off some of that control in order to preserve signal quality. This brings up the second bounce option you have, which is to record a fresh part while the bounce is going down and add this signal to the combination of tracks that are being transferred (see Example C).

Here, too, you lose the ability to alter the blend once it's been recorded, but if performed properly, this technique can be an effective tool. However, since it *is* restrictive, it should be regarded as a method of last resort, used only in instances where it saves you from making a whole set of bounces just to add one more instrument or vocal to the song.

Which Bounce Technique to Use

When planning out the production, most people will be inclined to choose the bounce technique that offers the greatest amount of flexibility—a stereo, external bounce for example. Yet this is not always the best bounce technique to use if, in order to create a stereo transfer mix, you're trading off a significant amount of signal quality.

For example, if you're recording on a standard-gauge, ¼-inch 4-track deck, and you have a standard-gauge 2-track unit available for the bounce, you'll get better quality by bouncing externally, because the heads on a ¼-inch 2-track are twice as large as those on the 4-track. On the other hand, if the only bounce machine you have is a cassette deck, which necessarily uses smaller gauge heads, you'd be better off performing an internal bounce on the 4-track. You'll get much better reproduction, and less noise, bouncing to a second standard-gauge head than you would bouncing to the smaller heads on the cassette. However, if this means using the sync mode, you should compare quality before deciding on the bounce that is best.

Similarly, if you're recording on a 4-track cassette deck, and you have a standard-gauge 2-track machine available for the bounce, you'd most likely get better quality from an external bounce than you would bouncing between tracks on the cassette machine; cassette decks are prone to significant high-frequency loss during internal bounces. Plus, you'd be able to generate a stereo mix.

In the case of 8-track decks, you should have enough track space available to perform a stereo bounce internally, so here your main concern is strictly one of transfer quality. Again, if you're using a standard-gauge, ½-inch 8-track, the quality of an internal bounce will be a bit less than that of an external bounce to a standard-gauge 2-track. However, if you're using a ¼-inch 8-track deck, which has smaller gauge heads, the internal bounce will not be of as high a caliber, and you'll want to bounce externally.

Of course, this all depends upon the needs of your production and the quality of each piece of gear. So before deciding upon one course of action, be sure to test out each technique on your particular equipment. Then, once you've determined which method will give you the best signal, see if you can't arrange your production to make use of that method.

Which Tracks to Record First

The order in which you record the tracks *does* matter and should be given adequate preproduction attention.

For example, you'll always want to lay the rhythm track down first. This will give later musicians a beat to follow and a bass line to play along with during overdubs. By the same token, the lead vocal track should be one of the last to be added, as the quality of the singer's performance often depends upon his being able to hear an instrumentally complete mix of the music.

Another reason to put the vocal off until the end is to avoid having to subject it to a bounce. The vocal is your production's featured track, and it's generally a good idea to keep any key element on its own track, so that you can retain the greatest amount of control over its placement in the final mix. Neither do you want to take the chance of having the vocal lose any signal quality during the transfer. Other such key elements might include a melodic hook played by one instrument, which repeats over and over in the song.

This points out another aspect of tracking order, which is that the earlier a track is recorded, the more likely it is to be involved in a bounce. Of course, each song has its own set of requirements, but it is because of this that preproduction work is so important. You don't want to get trapped into premixing a vocal simply because you recorded it too early in the process and now find that you need to open up tracks in order to complete the song.

Which Instruments to Combine

There are only a few guidelines to follow when deciding which instruments to combine. For the most part, this will be determined by the order of recording and the type of bounce you're performing.

For example, if you're using an external bounce, everything on tape is going to have to be transferred to the 2-track mix, and most likely there will be a few tracks left to add after the bounce. Therefore, your only decision will be in determining which one or two key elements to leave out of the track, so that you can better control them in the final mix.

You will, however, need to take a lot of care with this bounce, because in essence the external bounce is the beginning of a final mix. This means you will have to exercise greater vision over what the final result will be, because the stereo image you are creating at this point is the one you'll be using in the final form.

On the other hand, when performing an internal bounce you're doing so not as a premix function, but as a step meant solely to open up recording space. Still, your choice of source tracks is critical. In general, during an internal bounce, you combine the signals onto just one track, which becomes a monaural component of the final mix. Therefore,

Figure 7a

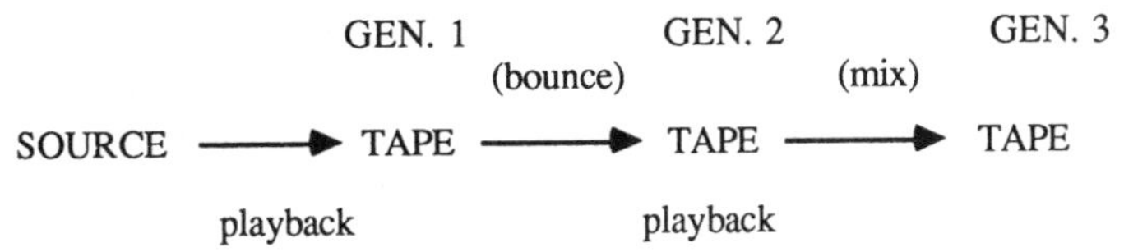

```
                    GEN. 1           GEN. 2          GEN. 3
                         (bounce)         (mix)

     SOURCE  ———▶  TAPE  ———▶  TAPE  ———▶  TAPE

               playback          playback
```

It's a good idea to bounce instruments that share a similar function, as every instrument you include in the bounce is going to image at the same point along the stereo spectrum. So, for instance, you wouldn't want to combine a monaural drum track with an instrument destined for the far left speaker, because you want the drums to image at the stereo center of the recording.

Basically, then, when you plan an internal bounce, you need to think again about the form you want the final mix to have and combine only those instruments that are to share the same stereo location. For instance, bass, kick drum, and snare go well together, because as rhythm tracks they all image in the middle. On the other hand, backing vocals and guitar fills, which are more melodically oriented, often image slightly to the right or left. But again, every song will require a slightly different treatment, so you really have to play it by ear. (See chapter 16, "Mixdown Techniques," for more information on stereo positions of instruments.)

REDUCING GENERATION LOSS

Any time you bounce a track, you subject the recording to "generation loss." This means that the rerecorded signal is one generation removed from the original recording. Each generation results in increased noise and decreased clarity; after the bounce and the final mix, the signal will be *two* generations removed (Figure 7a), so unless you can compensate for generation loss, your recording will suffer accordingly.

One thing you can do to minimize the generation loss effect is to EQ the signal during the bounce. Since the top end of the signal is usually where the greatest loss occurs, the obvious solution is to boost the high-frequency content of the source track during the transfer. However, although this will increase the clarity of the signal, it will also increase the noise.

To get around this situation, you should make a test bounce with 10K boosted about 2 dB. In the playback, listen for the comparison between the original combination of tracks at input and the completed bounce. If the clarity remains diminished but there is no appreciable increase in noise, give 10K another 2 dB boost and try it again. You should continue this process, boosting 10K in 1 dB or 2 dB increments, until you establish a balance between noise and clarity that you can live with.

However, this should all be done in conjunction with any other EQ adjustments you may need to make, such as those that had to be left out of the initial tracking EQ or those needed to compensate for losses the signal may have suffered in other frequency bands during transfer (as discussed in "Bouncing and Combining Tracks," chapter 6).

Another way to limit your losses, so to speak, is to send a good, strong level to tape. Yet you must be careful not to boost the transfer signal too high, or the tape will go into saturation. This balance between a good signal-to-noise ratio and excessive level is a key factor in creating an effective, mixable track.

For further noise reduction, the use of Dolby or similar systems can also be a help. If your machine has Dolby circuitry, and you're using it on an external bounce, simply encode the tracks as they're being bounced to the 2-track and decode them as they are transferred back to the source deck. And if you're using Dolby, the top-end transfer boost can be reduced.

THINGS TO REMEMBER WHEN BOUNCING

All of the above considerations are for the purpose of creating a bounce track that retains, as closely as possible, the characteristics of the source tracks. However, along with the technical quality of the track, you must also be concerned with the aesthetics of the bounce and, in particular, with how the balance of instruments will affect the rest of the recording.

In this regard, you should keep the following factors in mind as you carry out the bounce.

Checklist

Balance Between the Instruments
—Is one instrument more important than the others in terms of its effect on the final mix? If so, the bounce must be performed with this balance in mind.

Placement of the Instruments in the Stereo Spectrum
—Before premixing, establish in your mind a picture of the stereo placement of all instruments to be included in the final mix. Does your premix leave room for placement of later overdubs? Or will the new tracks have to compete for space?

EQ
—The bounce is the time to add any EQ treatment you were unable to apply to a track as it was being recorded, as postbounce EQ will affect *all* the instruments on the track (see Tape Tip #17).

Echoes and Effects
—Any effects applied postbounce will affect all instruments on that track. Therefore, you should decide which instruments require individual treatment and apply the desired effect to those signals during the bounce.

—Harmonizers and delay lines can be used to create a stereo image, or a "mult," which is an electronic double of the signal. (See chapter 16, "Mixdown Techniques.")

—Application of a stereo effect, such as a stereo chorus, during an external stereo bounce, may alter the stereo imaging position of the signal it is being applied to.

—Compressors should be applied prebounce.

—A single effect can be used more than once, and by applying it differently at each stage of recording (such as on each bounce), you can create a variety of effects, with limited resources.

SAMPLE BOUNCE COMPOSITIONS

In the following examples, we've tried to give you an idea of how to plan out your bounces by showing you just what is involved. And although these procedures detail the use of a 4-track machine, the same methods and considerations apply to 8-track, 16-track, and 24-track formats as well.

EXAMPLE A:
Recording a Song Using External Bounce Techniques

(4-TRACK ⟶ 2-TRACK ⟶ 4-TRACK)

This is an example of track organization that uses the technique of bouncing and combining tracks from one machine into another. By bouncing in this manner, you are able to retain the stereo imaging of an instrument such as the drums, or of a mix of instruments, while still opening up new tracks for recording. As you are performing this process, it should be remembered that an external bounce is the beginning of a final mix, and you must be very clear about what the final result will be.

(Note: While Dolby is not a necessary part of this process, we have included details on how it should be applied.)

External Bounce Advantages:
- You have pan control over the bounce.
- Effects and echoes can be panned or reproduced in stereo.
- Stereo imaging of instruments can be retained.
- Dolby can be used.

Disadvantages:
- It requires two machines of roughly equal quality.

Track Capacity: 4-track.

Song Requires: Seven tracks.

STEP #1:
Initial Tracking

TRACKS

1	2	3	4
RECORD DRUMS* AND BASS	RECORD GUITAR #1	RECORD BACKING VOCAL	RECORD BACKING VOCAL

1. Unless you are recording these tracks simultaneously, the drums and the bass guitar should be recorded first, so that when the musicians dub in the guitar and keyboards, they will have a beat to follow and a bass line to play along with.

   *Note: For stereo drum techniques, see "The Reel World, Recording a Four-Track Song Demo," page 125.)

2. This drum part can also be used to time an extended, solo-instrumental lead-in to the song (as a click track, for example), but it *must* be erased before the bounce in Step #2. However, be sure not to erase any count-off used to start the song.

3. Ideally, compression would be the only effect you would want to add during the initial tracking, but only if the instrument needs it. Additional effects should be applied during the bounce in Step #2, as this will give you greater control over the blend of instruments in the bounce.

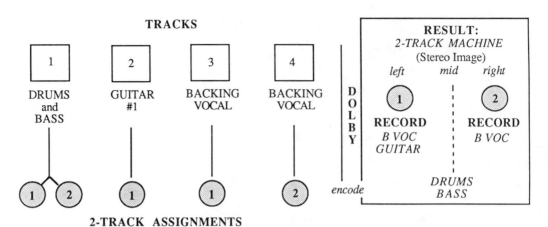

STEP #2a:
External Bounce—Without Panning

TRACKS

1	2	3	4
DRUMS and BASS	GUITAR #1	BACKING VOCAL	BACKING VOCAL

RESULT:
2-TRACK MACHINE
(Stereo Image)

left   mid   right

① RECORD *B VOC GUITAR*   ② RECORD *B VOC*

DRUMS BASS

D O L B Y

encode

2-TRACK ASSIGNMENTS

• Echoes and effects used on bounce should be bussed to Track 1 *or* 2
(or both) for monaural reproduction or Tracks 1 *and* 2 for stereo.

1. Before bouncing Tracks 1, 2, 3, and 4 of the 4-track machine to Tracks 1 and 2 of the 2-track, make sure you have performed any punch-in work the tracks need. This is necessary, because any postbounce punch-ins will affect every instrument on the track.

2. Also, go through the tracks one at a time and delete any material you don't want showing up in the final version of the song—such as stray guitar licks, whispers, and the like.

3. This is the last point at which you will be able to give each instrument its own individual treatment, both in terms of EQ and effects. So be sure to add any EQ boosts you had to leave out of the initial tracking EQ and add all necessary effects.

4. When adding effects, be sure to assign them to the appropriate track or tracks. If it is a monaural effect, such as a phaser you might be adding to guitar, assign it to the same track(s) as the instrument. If it is a stereo effect, such as reverb, assign it to both tracks. (For more effects information, see "Checklist" earlier in chapter.)

5. If using Dolby, make sure you encode the signal that is being sent to the 2-track. You can then decode the signal in a later step.

6. As a result of the bounce, the stereo image on the 2-track machine is as indicated. Note, however, that our diagram does not reflect the position changes that might result from the use of stereo effects.

STEP #2b:
External Bounce—With Panning

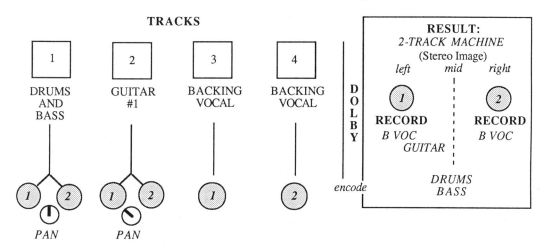

●Echoes and effects used on bounce should be bussed to Track 1 *or* 2
(or both) for monaural reproduction or Tracks 1 *and* 2 for stereo.

1. Essentially, this is the same bounce we performed in Step #2a, and it should be given the same considerations we outlined at that time.

2. The one main difference between the two bounces is that in this version we used the pan function to alter the stereo imaging of the guitar during the transfer, so that it now appears slightly to the left of center on the 2-track.

3. Any time you alter the pan position of an instrument, you should also alter the position of any monaural effects you might be applying to the signal.

STEP #3:
Return Bounce

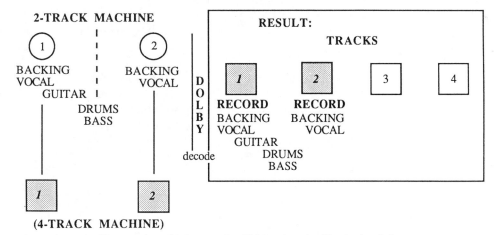

●Any echoes or effects used on this bounce should be assigned to Tracks 1 *and* 2.

1. This is a straight transfer bounce that is used to send the stereo mix back to Tracks 1 and 2 on the 4-track machine.

2. If you need to touch up any EQ levels or add an effect, you can do so, but you will need to apply any change equally to both tracks.

3. Remember to decode the Dolby during this transfer. In other words, if Dolby was used to record Bounce #1, it should also be used during the transfer back to the 4-track.

STEP #4:
Overdubs

TRACKS

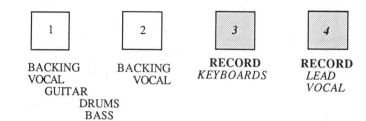

1. When overdubbing on Tracks 3 and 4, apply the same considerations we outlined for the initial tracking in Step #1.

2. During record, be sure to place Tracks 1 and 2 in Sel-Sync if your machine so requires.

STEP #5:
Final Mixdown to 2-Track

TRACKS

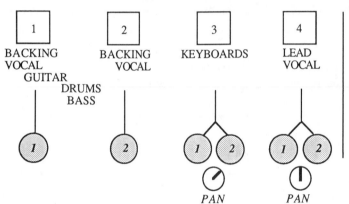

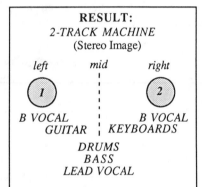

1. By panning the tracks in the above manner during the transfer back to the 2-track, the instruments will be recorded as pictured. You can, of course, alter this pan design according to your needs.

2. Essentially, this final step is a mixdown minus the effects. For more information on mixdowns and adding effects during the mix, see chapter 16, "Mixdown Techniques."

EXAMPLE B:
Recording a Song Using Internal Bounce Techniques

This is an example of track organization that uses the technique of transferring the signals from two or more tracks to another track on the same machine. This is done to open up additional tracks for recording.

Note: In our example, your machine must be capable of bouncing a signal to an adjacent track, so check with your owner's manual before proceeding.)

Internal Bounce Advantages:
- No need for a second machine.

- If your other alternative is bouncing to a cassette deck, you will get a higher-quality bounce from the open-reel machine.

Disadvantages:
- Some machines aren't able to bounce adjacent tracks.
- You lack the ability to pan a track when combining it onto the target track.

Track Capacity: 4-track.

Song Requires: Seven tracks.

STEP #1:
Initial Tracking

TRACKS

1	2	3	4
RECORD DRUMS* BASS	**RECORD** GUITAR #1	**RECORD** KEYBOARDS	

1. Unless you are recording these tracks simultaneously, the drums and bass guitar should be recorded first, so that when the musicians dub in the guitar and keyboards, they will have a beat to follow and a bass line to play along with.

*****Note:** For stereo drum techniques, see "The Reel World, Recording a Four-Track Song Demo," page 125.)

2. This drum part can also be used to time an extended, solo-instrumental lead-in to the song (as a click track, for example), but it *must* be erased before the bounce in Step #2. However, be sure not to erase any count-off used to start the song.

3. Ideally, compression would be the only effect you would want to add during the initial tracking, but only if the instrument needs it. Additional effects should be applied during the bounce in Step #2, as this will give you greater control over the blend of instruments in the bounce.

STEP #2:
Combining Tracks 1, 2, and 3

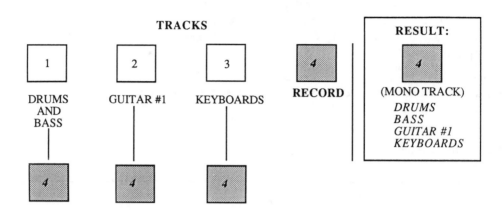

● Echoes and effects used on bounce
should also be bussed to Track 4.

1. Before performing the bounce that combines Tracks 1, 2, and 3 onto Track 4, make sure you have performed any punch-in work the tracks need. This is necessary because any postbounce punch-ins will affect every instrument on the track.

2. Also, go through the tracks one at a time and delete any material you don't want showing up in the final

version of the song—such as stray guitar licks, whispers, and so on.

3. This is the last point at which you will be able to give each instrument its own individual treatment, both in terms of EQ and effects. So be sure to add any EQ boosts you had to leave out of the initial tracking EQ and add all necessary effects. (For more effects information, see "Checklist" earlier in chapter.)

STEP #3:
Overdubs

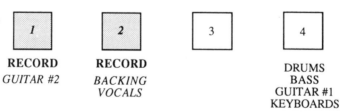

1. When recording Tracks 1 and 2 (which were made available by the previous bounce), apply the same considerations we outlined for the initial tracking in Step #1.

2. During record, be sure to place Track 4 in Sel-Sync if required by your machine.

STEP #4:
Combining Tracks 1 and 2

TRACKS

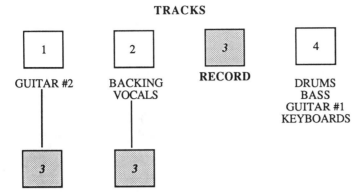

● Echoes and effects used on bounce
should also be bussed to Track 3.

1. When bouncing Tracks 1 and 2 onto Track 3, apply the same considerations we outlined for the bounce in Step #2.

2. Also remember that if your machine has Sel-Sync, Tracks 1 and 2 must be placed in sync during the bounce. If they're not, Track 3 will be out of sync with the rest of the recording.

STEP #5:
Overdubs

TRACKS

				RESULT:	
1	*2*	3	4	*1*	*2*
RECORD *BACKING VOCAL*	RECORD *LEAD VOCAL*	GUITARS #2 BACKING VOCAL	DRUMS BASS GUITAR #1 KEYBOARDS	*BACKING VOCAL*	*LEAD VOCAL*

1. When recording Tracks 1 and 2 (which were made available by the previous bounce), apply the same considerations we outlined for the initial tracking in Step #1.

2. During record, be sure to place Tracks 3 and 4 in Sel-Sync if your machine so requires.

STEP #6:
Final Mixdown

TRACKS

1	2	3	4
PAN LEFT	PAN MIDDLE	PAN RIGHT	PAN MIDDLE

RESULT:		
left	*mid*	*right*
BACKING VOCAL	*DRUMS BASS KEYBOARDS GUITAR#1 LEAD VOCAL*	BACKING VOCAL GUITAR #2

1. By panning the tracks in the above manner, the instruments will play back as pictured. You can, of course, alter this pan design according to your needs.

2. At this point you are ready to begin performing your final mix. For more information on how to add effects in the final mix, see chapter 16, "Mixdown Techniques."

EXAMPLE C:
Recording a Track During a Bounce

If, toward the end of your project, you suddenly realize that there is one more track that needs to be added to the mix, but you haven't the track space to record it and bounce it in the normal fashion, you may want to combine it with an existing track *as* it is being recorded. However, this should be regarded as an emergency measure only, because it requires that both the new part *and* the bounce be performed simultaneously and correctly.

As an example of this process, we refer you back to Ex-

ample A. After completing the initial tracking in Step #
the tracks were filled as follows:

TRACKS

1	2	3	4
DRUMS AND BASS	GUITAR #1	BACKING VOCAL	BACKI VOCA

If, at this time, you realize that you need to add a secon track of guitar fills, you would want to proceed in the fo lowing manner:

STEP #1:
External Bounce with an Overdub

TRACKS

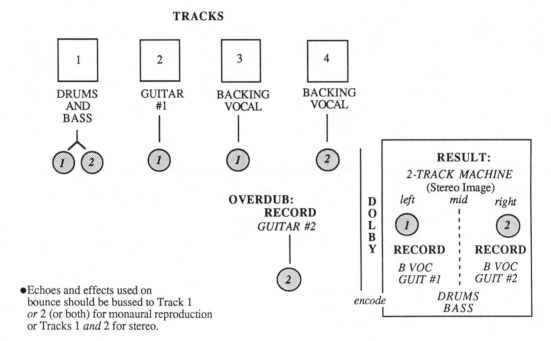

●Echoes and effects used on bounce should be bussed to Track 1 *or* 2 (or both) for monaural reproduction or Tracks 1 *and* 2 for stereo.

1. Prepare Tracks 1, 2, 3, and 4 for the external bounce to the 2-track as described in Step #2a of Example A. Establish a general blend of instruments before proceeding.

2. Prepare to record Guitar #2 directly onto Track 2 of the 2-track during the bounce. However, instead of treating it as an initial track, treat it as if it were an existing track that was being included in the bounce mix. In other words, bring the signal into the console and assign it to Buss 2, making sure to add EQ and to apply any individual effects it should have in the mix.

3. Run through the track a few times with the guitarist

and make sure that he has his part down well. While you're doing so, fine-tune the bounce mix by adding the Guitar #2 part and making any necessary adjustments.

4. When the guitarist is ready, make a test bounce and adjust for the blend you desire.

5. It is very important to get the correct mix at this point, since there will be no going back. But don't wear out the musician's fingers (or patience) by doing test bounce after test bounce. Instead, make two or three separate bounces that each have slight variations and choose between them when your ears are fresh.

STEP #2:
Return Bounce

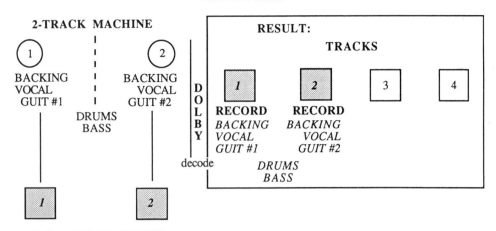

2-TRACK MACHINE

① BACKING VOCAL GUIT #1

DRUMS BASS

② BACKING VOCAL GUIT #2

D O L B Y

decode

RESULT:

TRACKS

1 RECORD *BACKING VOCAL GUIT #1*

2 RECORD *BACKING VOCAL GUIT #2*

3   4

DRUMS BASS

(4-TRACK MACHINE)

● Any echoes or effects used on this bounce should be assigned to Tracks 1 *and* 2.

This is a straight transfer bounce that is used to send the stereo mix back to Tracks 1 and 2 on the 4-track machine.

If you need to touch up any EQ levels, or add an effect, you can do so, but you will need to apply any change equally to both tracks.

3. Remember to decode the Dolby during this transfer. In other words, if Dolby was used to record Bounce #1, it should also be used during the transfer back to the 4-track.

STEP #3:
Overdubs

TRACKS

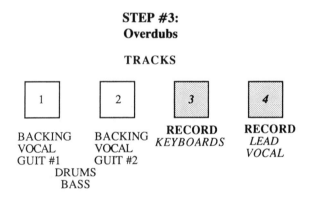

1   2

3 RECORD *KEYBOARDS*

4 RECORD *LEAD VOCAL*

BACKING VOCAL GUIT #1

BACKING VOCAL GUIT #2

DRUMS BASS

When overdubbing on Tracks 3 and 4, apply the same considerations we outlined for the initial tracking in Step #1 of Example A.

2. During record, be sure to place Tracks 1 and 2 in Sel-Sync if your machine so requires.

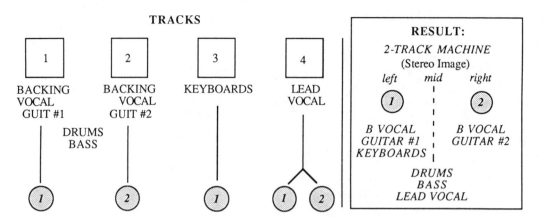

STEP #4:
Final Mixdown

1. By panning the tracks in the above manner during the transfer back to the 2-track, the instruments will be recorded as pictured. You can, of course, alter this pan design according to your needs.

2. Essentially, this final step is a mixdown minus the effects. For more information on mixdowns and adding effects during the mix, see chapter 16, "Mixdown Techniques."

Recording a Four-Track Song Demo

The following is a demonstration of how bounce techniques are used in a real-life situation, with real-life recording concerns.

—Peter McIan

I had written a song that I felt would be right for Pat Benatar, and since she'd recorded one of my songs before, I felt that I knew what kind of demo would best represent the song. Benatar, like many artists and producers, prefers a demo that shows off the material rather than the production, so I wanted to get the point of the song across in a simple but professional manner and give her the opportunity to interpret the material in her own way. Since I didn't need an extravagant production, and since I didn't have much time (she was already in the studio working on a new LP), I decided to do the work at home on my 4-track machine.

I knew there were certain elements of the production that required focus, and, as I had just started to set up my studio, I had a minimal amount of effect gear to work with (no reverb or delay lines). So this meant I had to preplan the production just that much more carefully in order to have control in the final mix. What follows is the chronology of the recording and a list of the devices I used.

Recorded On: TEAC 40-4, (4-track)
External Bounce Machine: Otari 5050, (2-track)
Console: Soundcraft 400-B
Outboard Effects: Roland 555 Space Echo
 DBX Compressor

Instruments:

 Lynn Drum Machine
 PPG Wave Synthesizer
 Bass
 Guitar
 Vocals
 Sax

STEP #1:
Initial Tracking

TRACKS

1	2	3	4
RECORD	RECORD	RECORD	RECORD
DRUMS-L	DRUMS-R	SYNTH	GUITAR
	SNARE		(compressed)
	KICK DRUM		
	BASS (compressed)		

I wanted the drum kit to have stereo toms, so I used Track 1 and Track 2 as a stereo left-right pair. To accomplish this, I assigned the appropriate input channels on the Soundcraft to both Buss 1 and Buss 2 and panned the toms until I had created the stereo image I was after.

The bass player and I then recorded the drums, bass, and synthesizer simultaneously, because I've found that if you record a drum machine first, then overdub all the other instruments, the instrumental tracks often sound rigid. So, by having two people play along with the machine, the tracks had more of a "live band" feel.

The EQ settings I used on the instruments followed the guidelines set down in the instrumental recording chapters (chapters 9–15). Plus, I added compression to the bass at this time, setting the ratio at four to one and the gain reduction at −3 dB. Although I could have applied more compression to the signal, I wanted the bass to have some punch, and the less compression you use on an instrument, the more "life" it has.

Normally I would have recorded the guitar track at the same time as the others, but because of scheduling conflicts with the guitarist, it had to be dubbed in later. And here again, a slight amount of compression was used on the signal as it was recorded.

STEP #2:
Bounce #1

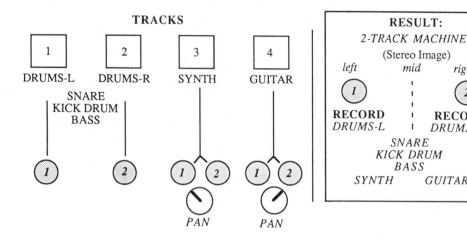

As mentioned in Example A, the mix you create during an external bounce becomes a component of the final mix. Consequently, the planning that goes into the bounce plays an important role in deciding the quality of the end result. When you arrive at the final mix, it often happens that you wish you could go back and redo the bounce and add a little more of this or that. But hindsight is, of course, always twenty-twenty.

In the premix bounce, then, I had to be concerned with the levels of the instruments as they would relate to the tracks that were yet to be recorded—the most important of which was the lead vocal. Frequently, guitars and keyboard will provide melodic "hooks" that support or compleme the vocal, and as a result they are often made a feature component of the mix. However, in this case the bass li provided that hook, so I *over*mixed (boosted) it slightly rel tive to the keyboards and guitar, which were used for bac ground coloration. I also added slap echo to these tw instruments in order to provide further continuity and dept to the mix. And because the song was up-tempo, the drum were also prominently featured.

STEP #3:
Return Bounce

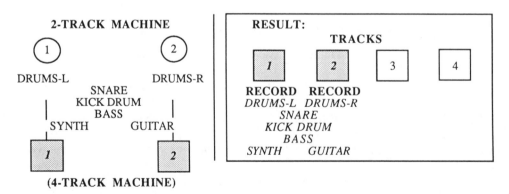

When returning the 2-track mix to the 4-track, I didn't need to add any effects. However, it was still necessary to EQ the bounce tracks in order to insure against any generation los in the signal.

STEP #4:
Overdubs

TRACKS

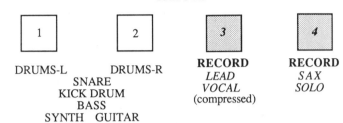

Since this was a *song* demo, as opposed to a performance demo, I knew that the vocal was of key importance. So I waited until after the bounce to record it, and I gave it its own track. This gave me more control over the vocal in the final mix, and it kept the track from being subjected to an unnecessary bounce. I also compressed the vocal slightly during the take in order to reduce the peaks. This allowed me to bring the softer parts of the vocal up in level during the final mix, so that they could be heard above the instrumental tracks.

The sax solo wasn't added until *after* the vocal, as its parts were to weave between the vocal lines.

STEP #5:
Final Mixdown

TRACKS

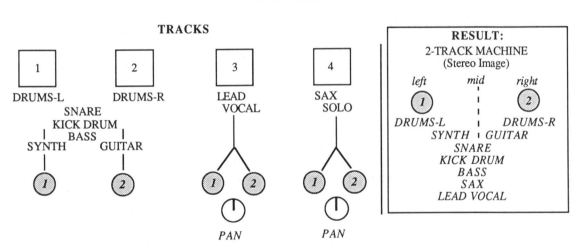

After the final overdub had been recorded, I began to set levels for the final mixdown to 2-track. Again, I didn't have any reverb available, so to keep the vocal and sax from sounding stark and unexciting, I gave them some echo. I had used a relatively quick echo repeat time (set to eighth-note repeats) for the keyboards and guitar, so when treating the vocal and the sax tracks, I lengthened the repeat to half-note triplets. This created a "wash" effect that gave the tracks warmth and enhanced the depth and coherency of the mix.

After that, the final mix was largely a question of riding the vocal and sax levels to achieve the proper blend. And the net result of all the work was that, as of this writing, Chrysalis Records has placed a "hold" (the right of exclusivity) on the song for Pat Benatar's *next* album.

Chapter 8

Cassette Portastudios

When TASCAM introduced the Portastudio 144 in the late 1970s, the unit captured the imagination of every songwriter I know. It offered multitrack cassette capabilities and for the first time combined a mixing console and a tape recorder in one portable package. This made it an ideal songwriting tool. It was lightweight, so it could easily be taken on tour, and although it was sophisticated enough to allow you to do overdubs and add effects using techniques similar to those used in the studio, you didn't have to be a professional engineer to operate it.

While the name "Portastudio" is a registered trademark of TASCAM Corporation, over the years it has become a generic term used to refer to the many multitrack cassette decks that have followed in its footsteps. Some of these units, such as the Fostex 250, use the same basic design, while others, like the Yamaha MT44D, have kept the mixer and tape deck separate and added a patch bay configuration that ties the two together. So, as you read through this chapter, just remember that even though we may not be talking about your unit by name, the information still applies.

THE PORTASTUDIO FORMAT

The first thing that needs to be said about all portable cassette decks is that even though they offer a great deal of recording flexibility, they are not designed to produce the sort of demo tapes that will get a record deal. In a sense, Portastudios are to recording what Instamatic cameras are to photography. They offer a quick, efficient way to capture a sufficiently accurate image. They are a songwriter's tool, a sketch pad upon which a musician can outline his song and experiment with coloration and tone, and to that extent, the Portastudio format is an excellent piece of design work. However, if you expect anything more from your unit, you're going to be disappointed.

Of course there are always exceptions, and Portastudios have, in fact, produced tracks that have made it onto major

albums (such as Springsteen's *Nebraska*). Yet even the manufacturers acknowledge that to get that kind of quality from their decks, you need years and years of professional experience and more than a little luck.

Primarily this is due to the fact that no matter how fancy the hardware is, the machine is still a cassette deck. And, as we discussed in chapter 3, the tape heads on cassette recorders are small and have poor high-frequency response. This makes it very difficult to record a full, strong transient, and it reduces your ability to limit tape noise during a bounce. As a consequence, the sound quality you get from these machines will not meet up to the standards of a 1/4-inch, open-reel 4-track.

To compensate for this, most manufacturers have designed their units to run at 3¾ ips, which is twice the speed of a normal cassette deck. This makes more tape available to the heads and improves the high-frequency response. Plus, most of the machines have built-in DBX or Dolby noise reduction circuits.

Still, I would never recommend that you use these decks for any demo you intend to submit to a record company or a music publisher. If you don't have the experience necessary to overcome the limitations of the gear, in doing so, you risk destroying the effectiveness of a perfectly good song. And that could mean blowing your chance at a perfectly good contract.

APPLICATIONS

These multitrack cassette units may not have been designed for demo work, but they are extremely versatile and have a multitude of other applications.

Bands can make excellent use of these machines. For example, many bands use them to record their gigs. It's a simple matter to plug them directly into a PA board, and once you've set the levels, you probably won't have to touch them again. By the same token, they can also be used to

Figure 8a: Yamaha Producer Series Personal Studio System—MT44D, RM602, and RB353 (*Courtesy of Yamaha International Corporation*)

Figure 8b: TASCAM Portastudio 246 (*Courtesy of TEAC Corporation of America*)

Figure 8c: Fostex 250AV Multitracker (*Courtesy of Fostex Corporation*)

TAPE TIP #19
Portastudio Console Functions

The Portastudio format is designed to give you the capability of performing many, if not all, of the techniques we've discussed regarding tape recorders and consoles. To illustrate this fact, we've broken down the operations of one such unit's channel controls so that they can be compared with the console input channel functions described in chapter 5 ("Recording Consoles").

Although we've chosen to use the channel from a Portastudio 246, which is made by TASCAM, most other units have the same basic configuration.

CHANNEL INPUT SECTION

This section of the module controls the process of bringing a signal into the mixer.

INPUT SELECTOR: This is a routing switch that allows you to bring either an outside signal source or the playback from an existing track into the channel. It will accept anything but extremely low-impedance signals.

INPUT GAIN TRIM: This variable control regulates the strength of the signal as it is brought into the mixer, thus ensuring that it will not cause the console to distort. A separate control (see "Channel Fader") regulates the volume of the signal after it has gained entry.

EQUALIZER SECTION

The controls within this section of the module allow you to regulate the level of specific frequencies within the signal and to enhance the instrument by emphasizing those frequencies that provide its unique character.

HIGH FREQUENCY: This sweepable-band control regulates the level of frequencies between 1K and 8K.

LOW FREQUENCY: This sweepable-band control regulates the level of frequencies between 620 Hz and 1.5K.

AUXILIARY SECTION

This section of the module is used to send the signal to outboard effects units. Each of the sends has its own master buss, which makes it possible to route the signal to as many locations as there are sends.

EFFECTS 1 and 2: These controls regulate the amount of signal sent to Effect Busses 1 and 2. Since each send has its own individual level control, you can send signals from more than one channel through the same effect buss and give each a different amount (intensity) of effect.

ON/OFF SWITCH: This allows you to turn off Effect Send 2.

ROUTING SECTION

This section of the channel module controls which of the mixer's many output points the signal will be sent (routed) to. In this case, either any or all of them can be utilized.

ASSIGN (Group Outputs): These switches allow you to choose which of the outputs you want the signal to go to. Each of the four switches represents a single monophonic output, but they can be paired together in order to provide for stereo output: 1 and 3 being assigned a left channel and 2 and 4 a right channel.

PAN: When engaged in stereo mixing operations, this control is used to route the channel's monaural signal to any point left or right of stereo center. However, to make proper use of the pan, the channel must be assigned to two busses that are being used as a stereo pair.

CHANNEL FADER

This is a sliding volume control that governs the level, or strength, of the signal as it leaves the channel. It is used to balance the level of the signal in one channel against the level of the signal in another.

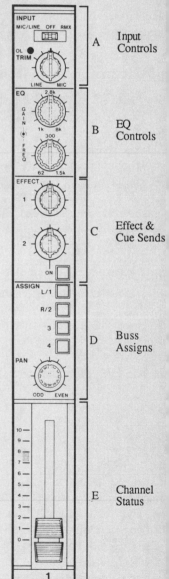

Figure 8d: A channel module from the TASCAM Portastudio 246 (*Courtesy of TEAC Corporation of America*)

record rehearsals, which is something that really comes in handy when you're working on new material.

If you're a songwriter in a band, these decks can make it a lot easier to work out that new material. For example, if you put the material down in a rough form on tape, and overdub the parts you want the other band members to play, you can give everyone a copy of the material a few days before the rehearsal so that they can become familiar with their parts.

And with respect to songwriting, the more sophisticated models have been designed to accommodate drum machines and synthesizers. For example, the Yamaha MT44D system is set up to be used with their entire line of sequencer-oriented hardware. It has a patch point designated for MIDI use, so you can place a time code down on one of the tracks and synchronize the drums and the synths on the others.

Of course, you can do this sort of thing on any multitrack deck, but only the better decks, such as TASCAM's Portastudio 246 or Yamaha's MT44D, will give you enough track isolation to keep the time codes from bleeding over onto the other tracks.

OPERATIONAL TIPS AND TECHNIQUES

If you put your mind to it, you can place some great sounds down on these machines. But it'll take work, and it'll take practice—and it'll take more than just reading this chapter.

You see, basically these units function as normal mixing consoles and tape recorders, so most of the material in this book can be applied directly to their use. For example, if you own one of these decks, you may have skipped the chapter on recording consoles. But if you want to understand how to use the console section of your machine, *that* is where you should look. As you can see in Tape Tip #19, the channel controls on a Portastudio 246 are set up in the same basic configuration as the controls on a professional grade console; and when you read through chapter 5, you'll see that conceptually they share the same functions.

However, the Portastudio format is rather unique, and the machines can be difficult to get a handle on, so in this chapter we've tried to include a few tips and tricks that will help you make the most of your unit.

Owner's Manuals

Believe it or not, most of the questions people have about the operation of their deck are covered in the owner's manual. The problem is that people just don't read them. So, as soon as you take your unit out of the box, go through the manual thoroughly. Then go through it again a few months later, and you'll probably pick up some tips you missed when you were still unfamiliar with its operation.

The TASCAM Portastudio comes with what has to be one of the best manuals I've ever seen for *any* electronics product. The company has done a fine job of explaining all the various functions of the machine, and they've included many excellent features, such as routing diagrams (Figure 8e), which help prepare the owner for its use. So if you happened to buy a used machine, and you didn't get a manual, it would be worth your time to write to TASCAM and get one.

The Console Section

The consoles on these systems operate at a -10 dB level, which makes them ideal for direct-in recording of high-impedance instruments like synths and guitars. It also means that there is no need to use a direct box in conjunction with your gear unless you're either using a low-impedance condenser mike (in which case you'll need to *raise* the impedance level of the signal prior to the console) or using long lengths of cable (in which case you'll need to lower the impedance at one end of the cable and raise it just prior to the console).

It's also important to note that when applying information in chapter 5 ("Recording Consoles") to your unit, you should remember that even though your deck does not immediately appear to have the feature we're talking about, the option may be there in some other form. For example, most of these machines do not provide cue sends, which are normally used to feed an outboard headphone amp, but you can always use the effect sends as cue sends, or you might even be able to use the direct outs from the channels or the headphone buss.

You will also notice that chapter 5 includes a number of diagrams that illustrate the various ways a console can be used to add effects and such. As you apply these to the operation of your gear, you will want to focus on those diagrams that are designated for "limited-capacity consoles." This doesn't mean that you should refer to these diagrams *only*, but they illustrate techniques you should easily be able to perform on your machine.

Recording Levels

As we mentioned, small-gauge cassette heads do not offer the same transient response as standard-gauge heads, and tape saturation occurs at much lower levels. This means that when you record, you will want the VU meters to be registering a little into the red, but you'll never want the transient peaks to push the needle off the scale. And if your unit has "peak lights," which respond much more quickly than the meters, use these to set your levels (making sure that they flicker dimly but never remain brightly lit).

The instrument this most affects is the drums, because, as you'll see in chapter 9, tape compression is an important component of the snare sound. This can also make it difficult to record screaming guitars and cymbal crashes. However, should you be having trouble with the transients, one way to compensate is to use an outboard compressor on the signal and limit the peaks before they reach the heads.

Figure 8e: This is an example of the many excellent operational diagrams provided in TASCAM's Portastudio 246 owner's manual. *(Courtesy of TEAC Corporation of America)*

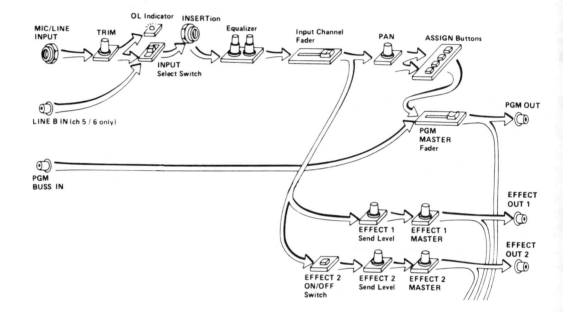

Recording Tape

The type of tape you use will have a telling effect on the quality of reproduction, so you should always refer to your owner's manual to see what is recommended. Most manufacturers will suggest that you use a high-bias tape, since that will effectively increase the high-frequency response and cut down on noise.

The thickness of the tape is also important. The thinner the tape is, the more likely it is to stretch, and in some cases it will cause excess residue to build up on the heads. Plus, if the tape is thin, there will be less material separating the layers of tape on the reel, and heavily transient sounds, such as drums, are more likely to print through onto the next layer.

Outboard Effects

Some of the limitations of the Portastudio format can be overcome by cleverly using outboard devices such as reverb and echo and routing them in one of the ways we illustrated in the Operational Diagrams in chapter 5. However, every unit has a different configuration of sends and returns, and one of the most useful things you can do is experiment with the various alternatives your system offers. And don't be afraid to get creative, because you never know what you'll come up with.

To start with, you might want to investigate ways of using direct outs to feed the outboard effects. This is one way, for instance, to get around the limitations of having only one or two effect sends when you want to add more than two effects during a bounce. Plus, you may be able to use a similar configuration during overdubs, should you want to add an effect to the headphone mix that you don't want printed on tape.

In the latter instance, the Yamaha MT44D provides insert points in their patch bay so that you can break the normal path a signal would take from the tape deck output to the monitor amp input. This, then, allows you to reroute the signal through an effect, which then becomes part of the monitor mix.

The Portastudio 246, on the other hand, provides an insert patch point for each individual channel, which can be used to route the signal through an effect *before* it goes to tape. In essence, this provides an additional send/return circuit, and it means that you can add two effects to a track if you wish, or you can use the direct outs for the effects and the effect sends as a cue system.

There are lots of other ways to use the features we've been describing, and chances are your unit has its own unique set of frills that can be used in some other way. In other words, never assume that a feature has only one application.

EQ Techniques

The upcoming chapters on instruments include suggested EQ settings for particular recording situations, and since the Portastudio format offers limited EQ capabilities, you'll need to make some adjustments.

For example, if your unit only offers "treble" and "bass" tone controls, you won't be able to apply EQ in the manner called for in our guidelines, because each tone control affects a very broad band of frequencies (see Tape Tip #17, pages 104–106). However, you *can* use tone controls to improve the overall sound of a recording, assuming that you're not trying to generate demo-quality tracks. One way to do this is to look in your manual and see where the center of each band is located (treble is usually 8K on these units, and bass is usually 100 Hz). Then, using these center points as reference, experiment with the EQ levels we offer.

Another problem you might have is that in most instances we give you at least three bands to EQ, while even such sophisticated units as the TASCAM and Yamaha desks are limited to a two-band, sweepable system. This means you won't be able to set the EQ properly during record.

There are two ways to get around this. One solution is to EQ two of the ranges as the track is being recorded and add the third during the final mix or during a bounce. The EQ will be just as effective when applied during a bounce as during an initial take, but if you have the option, you should apply the high-frequency boost first, because if you wait until the bounce, it will increase the level of tape hiss that may have been generated during record. The low-end boost should also be applied at this time, as this will give you a better overall feel for the balance between the high and low ends.

The second alternative you have, which can be particularly useful if your EQ control does not extend to the upper or lower limits of the spectrum, or if you only have "tone control" capabilities, is to use an outboard equalizer and insert it in the line either through a patch point or through a direct-out circuit. This is important, because there is a point at which EQ limitations cannot be overcome by making compromises, and unless you have certain EQ capabilities, you won't be able to achieve the recording quality you're after.

When you do add EQ, I would suggest that you EQ mildly, rather than radically, meaning that instead of boosting a band 10 dB, limit your boost to around 2 dB or 4 dB. When EQ is overused, the track can sound very peaky and harsh, and once the signal has been printed on cassette, you'll have a difficult time getting rid of the problem. So the bottom line is that it's better to be safe than sorry.

Bouncing and Combining Tracks

The internal bounce functions of your machine will undoubtedly be explained in your owner's manual. However, what they probably don't explain is that unless you're careful, your bounces will sound noisy and dull. So if you're having this problem, read through the material on bouncing and combining tracks that appears in chapter 5, and pay close attention to the instructions for using EQ to compensate for generation loss.

As an addendum to this information, it should be mentioned that the cassette format is particularly prone to high-frequency loss, and if you try to adjust by boosting the high-end EQ, it may require so much of a boost that you'll end up adding a lot of noise to the track. So, while following the instructions in chapter 5, be very gentle with the top-end EQ and refrain from boosting any frequencies above 10K, because the cassette isn't likely to see the higher frequencies, and you'll just be adding to the noise.

It should also be remembered that these machines are quite capable of performing an external bounce, and if you have a good open-reel machine to bounce to, much of th noise problem can be avoided.

Two-Track Masters

Once you've finished a song, you should always make master copy of the material so that you can use the master make any other copies you might want. This is a lot easi than setting up a 4-track mix every time you need to dupe tape, which becomes unwieldy if you're using a lot of e fects, and it's easier than trying to re-create the mix fro memory should you want to make a copy a year down th road.

Admittedly, a third-generation copy off cassette is n ideal, and for that reason I would suggest making your mas ter on an open-reel machine whenever possible. Of course you *can* master on a second cassette deck, but there will be substantial loss of quality with each generation.

THE REEL WORLD
Pioneering the Portastudio

When it was introduced in 1979, the Portastudio 144 revolutionized the home recording industry. As a compact multi-track system, it offered many of the functions normally found on studio gear, yet it was available at a price virtually any songwriter or hobbyist could afford. This gave the mid-level consumer a "professional" recording tool of his own and opened up a huge new market for home studio electronics.

The Portastudio 144 was designed, manufactured, and marketed by TASCAM, which is the professional audio division of TEAC. There are any number of other manufacturers who have since designed their own multitrack systems, but TASCAM was the Portastudio pioneer. So in order to get some insight into how and why the concept was developed, we went to the source and spoke with David Oren, who, as director of product planning at TASCAM, was intimately involved in the project.

PM/LW: Why did TASCAM decide to develop a product like the Portastudio?

OREN: Well, back about 1974, semipro and pro gear started to become affordable to individuals. For example, when we introduced our ½-inch 8-track, it sold for $3,000, whereas a 1-inch 8-track would have cost $10,000. So 4-track and 8-track home studios were becoming a practical reality for many, many people. But as the musicians got their hands on the equipment, we discovered that many of them just could not come to grips with the complexities of using a console and a patch bay. They wanted a means to *use* the hardware, but they didn't want it to come between themselves and their music.

PM/LW: So, actually, it was in response to the market....

OREN: Yes. "Garage studio" was the buzz word at that time. But this implied large facilities, and before you could record anything, you had to "crank the studi up." There really wasn't anything available for the m sician who just wanted a quick, efficient way to do th job. So what we were really dealing with in those day was a vacuum.

PM/LW: It was also a matter of producing something tha the general public could afford, though, wasn't it?

OREN: Yes, but we wanted to build a product that wou have *universal* acceptance. We wanted to reach the m sicians who couldn't afford pro gear, but the quali had to be there, because we also wanted a product th pros could use. So our feeling was that if we coul apply our manufacturing expertise, we could design good unit, and if we could build and sell enough them, we could hit the price point.

PM/LW: What *did* the original unit sell for?

OREN: When it was introduced, the Portastudio 144 liste for about $1,000.

PM/LW: And today?

OREN: The new Portastudio 246, which is the third gene ation, only lists for $1,395. And to be honest, whe you consider that on the 246 we've added channel a sign and sweepable EQ and insert patching and ever thing else, the machine is probably a better value toda

PM/LW: And to be honest, you have a bit more compet tion today than you did in 1979....

OREN: That's very true. But as a result, the line betwee consumer and semipro and professional gear is blu ring. In fact, these days the difference between semipr and pro quality depends more on who's using the ge than on who made it. And the Portastudio is a perfe example. On a technical level, both the 244 and 24 offer better quality and better performance than the T lefunken machine that the Beatles used for *Sgt. Pepper* So if you've got the chops and you've got years o

...continue

Figure 8f: The Portastudio 144 was the first of its kind. (*Courtesy of TEAC Corporation of America*)

Figure 8g: TASCAM's David Oren displays the original, open-reel prototype of the modern-day Portastudio. (*Courtesy of Larry Wichman*)

. . . continued

experience, you can produce some excellent product. And if you're just starting out, it can be a great learning device that provides an introduction into multichannel recording. You see, the Portastudio is meant to be a creative tool for songwriters, a means for capturing ideas on tape and for developing songs. It may have the potential to be more than that, but it was never designed to compete, on a technical level, with professional gear.

PM/LW: When did the actual design work begin?

OREN: We started tossing ideas around back about 1976, and we built the first prototype here in the back room. It was actually an open-reel model that used an umbilical cord to connect a 4-track with a 4-by-4 mixer. But the thing was just too expensive to build, and it was so big that you needed your own roadie if you wanted to take it anywhere. So we began thinking along the lines of a compact system.

PM/LW: How did you come up with your ideas?

OREN: Well, at about that time our salesman in London had a concept he was noodling with, and we had a few new ideas we were working on over here, and our Canadian rep was involved. . . . It was all what the Japanese call "coffee talk"—you know, bull sessions over drinks and dinner, sketching out ideas on placemats and coasters. Then, in 1977, we finally all got together in one place, and after a few days of meetings and a couple of dinners and lunches, the concept for the Portastudio was born.

PM/LW: So the project didn't originate in Japan?

OREN: No, the ideas were all generated over here and then presented to Japan as a package.

PM/LW: Why is that?

OREN: Well, it's really a cultural thing. You see, the idea of going out and creating music for a living is really a Western phenomenon. And the Japanese couldn't go out and touch it and see it and feel it in the market place. It wasn't until they started coming over here and hanging out with us that they began to understand what we were building. Even the young engineers who were working on the project back in Japan were blown away when they listened to some of the things we were recording on the prototypes. They *themselves* did not realize the quality of the product they were producing.

PM/LW: Did *you* know what you had?

OREN: We knew. We just didn't realize the magnitude of the win.

PM/LW: Did you need to develop any new technology for the unit? Or were all the parts there, waiting for someone to put them together?

OREN: The major challenge that we had at the time was the head section. We already had high-bias tape, and we knew how to build transports that would handle 3¾ ips. We also knew how to build heads, but up until that point nobody had built a head for cassettes that sufficiently reduced crosstalk. So, yes, it did mean developing a new head design, and we had to take some new approaches with the mixer section.

PM/LW: How long did all this take?

OREN: From the time we decided to move in the direction of a compact system until the time the product came out, which would have been the fall of 1979, it was something like three years.

PM/LW: Was it worth it?

OREN: Absolutely! As a company, the one thing we've always been cautious about is not to get too cute. In other words, build quality gear, but keep it simple, and make it friendly, easy to use, and flexible. And I think we succeeded.

PM/LW: Obviously, so do a lot of musicians!

Chapter 9

How to Record Drums

Drums are considered by many people to be the most difficult instrument to mike and record. That's because there are so many variables from one kit to the next and from one room to the next. Not to mention the differences between one *drummer* and the next!

However, I've devised a basic formula that I can count on to produce a good, solid drum sound, and it's that formula we'll be discussing in this chapter. Yet, although we present it here, it is not to be taken as gospel. Rather, it is a basic scheme that you can work from when molding your own drum sound—a sound designed for your own particular preferences.

ROOM ACOUSTICS

The ambience of the room in which you record your drums has a great, perhaps critical, effect on the way the drums sound. So the first choice you have to make pertains to which acoustic environment is most suitable for the sound you're seeking to create.

A room that is heavily carpeted and filled with a lot of soft, sound-absorbent surfaces, will produce what is called a "tight" drum sound. This means that the sound of the drum basically stops right after the initial attack of the stick, so that the room itself doesn't come into play. In other words, you don't *hear* the room the way you would if the walls were reflecting the sound waves and producing reverb.

This drum sound is frequently used in R&B music, but if you're after a hard-rock sound, you'll want to set your drum kit up in a room that is more acoustically "live"—someplace with hard walls and, maybe, a concrete or tiled floor. This enables the sound of the drums to reverberate around the room, and when that is picked up by the mikes, it can make the drums sound *huge!* You can achieve this effect, to varying degrees, in, for instance, a garage, a basement, a school gymnasium, or the Grand Canyon.

GETTING THE DRUM SOUND RIGHT

Drums are an acoustic instrument, and they need to sound good live in order to sound good on tape. No matter how sophisticated the electronic enhancements available during recording, they'll only be improving the level of mediocrity if the kit itself isn't right. Therefore, it is most important that you get your drum kit *sounding* good before you begin to record.

Since every drummer, every producer, and every engineer has his own personal preferences with respect to the sizes of drums, the kinds of heads they favor, and the like, it's quite impossible to cover them all. So I'm going to deal with my own preferences, which are based on extensive studio experience and are also fairly common among drummers.

Kick Drum

I've found that for rock 'n' roll, and for most pop music, a 24-inch kick drum is the most useful and the most versatile. A 26-inch kick will tend to sound "boomy"—particularly if you can't mike and EQ the kick separately. They can become a real problem, since they tend to vibrate the other drums more than a 24-inch kick does, and that creates ringing, which you don't want.

To get a solid kick drum sound, I use a 24-inch Ambassador head with a black dot. Depending upon the feel of the song being recorded, I may have the drummer use a wooden beater, because a wooden beater gives a lot of "pop" to the kick drum. For hard-rock programs, where you want more low-frequency response from the drum, you could go with a hard felt beater.

I always keep the front head off the kick drum, and usually I'll put a couple of sandbags or a pillow or a hunk of foam inside the shell to keep the drum from resonating. Sometimes I'll actually have this padding touch the drumhead, but generally I'll set it a half-inch or so away from the surface.

Tuning the kick drum is important, but it can be a little confusing. Often, in the search for a deeper tone, the drummer will try loosening the kick drum head. But the tone he gets isn't lower, it's *higher*. The reason for this is that the ear doesn't hear low-end frequencies well at all. So when a drum is tuned low, the lowest lows will be inaudible. Whereas when you tune the drum up, suddenly the lowest low the drum can attain comes within the audible frequency range.

So if you're not getting enough sharp attack out of the bass drum, the solution is not to tighten the head but to loosen it a bit, thereby reducing the low end by making it inaudible. Sometimes that can be done by loosening one of the tension rods on the rim, and sometimes it's done by lowering the pitch of the entire head.

So by lowering the tuning, you eliminate some of the boomy quality; by raising it, you get more tonality and more boom. I prefer a lot of attack and very little boom, so I tune the kick drum fairly low.

Tom-Toms

I use a relatively traditional approach to recording the toms. I prefer to have the drummer use one 12-inch or 13-inch mounted tom in conjunction with a 14-inch mounted tom and a 16-inch floor tom (three toms in all). Many people use 18-inch floor toms, but I've found that unless there's a lot of "room" (instrumental space) on the track, they have limited recording value.

Figure 9a: To eliminate excessive ringing from a tom-tom or snare drum, damp the top head by using gaffer's tape and gauze, as shown. (*Courtesy of Laura Marenzi*)

There are also many specialty drums available, such as BuBams, Power Toms, Roto-Toms, and Concert Toms, and though they won't be mentioned specifically, they can usually be tuned in intervals and then miked the way standard toms are.

If a drummer plays the way I like him to play, which is *hard,* then I'll use Remo's Ambassador heads, because they hold up a little bit longer than Diplomats. I keep the bottom heads on the toms, and I tune both the top and bottom heads so that they're at exactly the same pitch. That's so they'll resonate sympathetically—meaning that you'll hear the attack, after which the tone of the drum will gradually fall off evenly.

"Damping" is the practice of artificially reducing any *excess* resonance, or "ringing," a drum may produce after being struck. I try to damp toms as little as possible, and I *never* use internal dampers. When damping is required, I'll tape some Kleenex or a cotton ball against the head (very near the rim) at some point near a tension rod, damping the drum just enough to get rid of whatever buzzes or rattles I'm picking up (Figure 9a).

Tuning drums for studio recording is very different from tuning drums for a live performance. In fact, most drummers don't realize how critical tuning is until they walk into the studio for the first time. In a live situation, drummers tend to tune the drums based on what they're hearing off the top head. But in the studio, you're hearing what comes off both the top and the bottom heads, plus you're hearing the way the shell resonates. So studio drums need to be tuned fairly precisely, and they often need to be tuned differently for each song.

I generally tune drums to the key the song is in, using intervals of thirds, with each tom tuned to a different note in the chord. For instance, if the song is in F major, I'll tune the high tom (12-inch or 13-inch) to an "A" (the A below middle C). I'll tune the tom next to it to the next-lowest note in the chord, which in this case would be an "F." Then, in order to complete the chord, I'll tune the floor tom to the next-lowest "C" (an F chord is made up of F, A, and C notes).

The best way to tune a drum is to take it off the kit and place it on the drum stool or on some other surface that will damp the bottom head. Then, if there's a piano nearby, strike the note you want the head tuned to and wait for the tone to die down (or, if tuning to a guitar, play a harmonic or strike the string lightly). You can then begin tuning the drum to that note by tapping the head at a spot close to one of the tension rods with your drumstick and tightening or loosening that lug until it resolves to the same pitch as the piano. Then, one by one, you put each of the remaining lugs in tune with the first, checking back with the piano from time to time to make sure that the first lug is holding its pitch.

Once you've done that, your drum will be in tune—if, that is, you strike it directly in the center every time. But since most drummers do not strike the head dead center, you have to go back and hit the drum where you *do* generally strike it and check that pitch against the note on the piano. If it's out of tune at that spot, loosen and tighten the nearby lugs until it comes into tune.

In all of these cases, the very last tone you hear coming from the drum should resolve to the same note as the piano. What you're listening for here is the *fundamental* tone the drum produces. When the drum is struck normally, a wealth of overtones is produced by the initial attack. The skin stretches, changing the pitch upward, and then back downward as it begins to vibrate. Gradually, the intensity of these vibrations dies down, and the tone resolves to a note that is the mean average of the tones produced when the head was vibrating violently. This resolution is the one you want to tune.

If the drum is in tune, you can then turn it over and repeat the procedure on the bottom head. Only this time, you can probably get by with just tuning around the tension rods, because you don't *hit* the bottom head.

You might find that when you're done, the drum is resonating in a way you don't want it to. It might be ringing too long, because the heads are resonating sympathetically at the same pitch. Well, what you might do is loosen up one of the tension rods on the bottom rim as an alternative to adding extra damping material.

Snare Drum

For rock 'n' roll songs, I use a chrome-metal snare almost exclusively and fit it with a clear black-dot head. One type of head that I discourage the use of—and never use myself —is a hydraulic head (heads that have a thin layer of oil sandwiched between two outer skins). Hydraulic heads are fine for live play, because they last. But when you record them, they tend to have a damping effect of their own, and that keeps the true tone of the drum from ever properly appearing.

The tuning of the snare drum, unlike the toms, is more a function of what makes the snare sound best in the context of the song's style. In this sense, the pitch of the snare is a function of the tempo. For instance, if the song is very fast, you don't want the snare ringing from one hit to the next (you want to leave some breath between hits), so you'll tune the drum higher. That way the drum won't resonate as long. For ballads, or slower songs, you may want to tune the head lower in order to give it a more serious quality. A brighter pitch will make the snare sound snappier or poppier.

If you want to go for that oh-so-desirable rock 'n' roll *thwackkk,* you should tune the snare as low as you can while still having it "cut through" (be heard above) the track (see the "Mixdown Effects" section in this chapter).

Also, the faster the song, the lighter the drummer is going to be hitting the drum, because the faster he plays, the less time he has to raise his arm and bring the stick down. So it's tough to get the *thwackkk* on a fast song because it requires a hard, solid hit.

To achieve that good, strong snare sound, you must also have control of your snare wires. You don't want the snares buzzing—particularly if they're buzzing in resonance to anything other than the snare drum. So you may find that you need to tighten the snares. Or you may find that you need a different *type* of snare wire set: some are extra broad, with extra snare wires; others are smaller and have fewer wires than the standard sizes. Each drum is different, and you have to listen before deciding which way to go.

TAPE TIP #20
Black Dots

The use of black plastic dots on snare drum and kick drum heads is a highly subjective practice. Some people like them, and some people don't.

I use them because they tend to add a little "crack" of their own to the attack of the drum and give it better definition. Plus, the sound of the stick striking the plastic cuts through the track much better than the sound of the stick striking a standard head. So if all else fails, at least the time-keeping qualities of the kick drum and snare come through.

Black dots come specifically on Remo-brand heads. However, you can also buy the dots by themselves and apply them to any head, which is something I've done in the past as well.

Figure 9b: Remo's CS Black Dot drumheads. (*Courtesy of Remo, Inc.*)

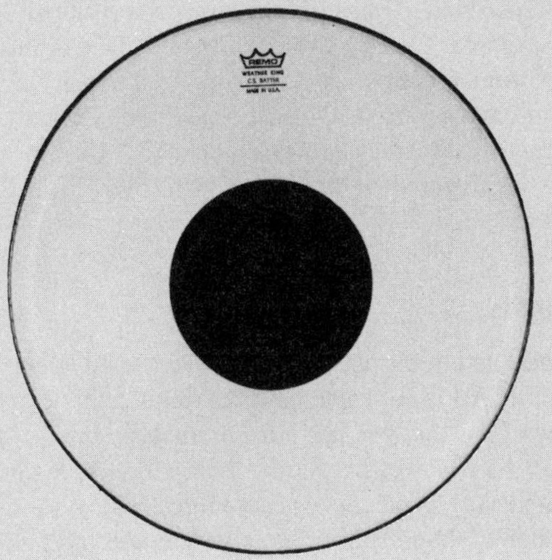

In order to keep the snares from rattling, you might try putting a small piece of half-inch gaffer's tape across the wires somewhere near the outer edge of the drum. This shortens the length of the snares and damps vibration. You can also try changing the tuning of the drum, but since each snare drum resonates differently, it's hard to tell whether you're going to be able to solve your problem by tuning the head up or by tuning it down.

Though it's important to tune the top and the bottom heads of a tom to the same pitch, it's less critical to do so with the snare drum. That's because the snare is used for keeping time, and you don't want to hear all the resonance that's necessary to hear from a tom. In fact, on fast, up-tempo songs, the snare drum decay should be gone before you even realize it was there.

The only time you might want to make sure that you have both heads in synchronized pitch is during an extremely slow song. Slow tempos create a long time interval between hits and demand a thicker snare sound, so it's the one instance when you *do* want to hear the drum decay.

There are a variety of snare drums to choose from when doing a studio session, and though I prefer a chrome metal snare, many rock drummers like to use large wooden snare drums—particularly when the song is slower, and they want to get a deeper, heavier sound.

The disadvantage of a "deep" snare is that there needs to be more room on the track in order for it to have the same impact as one that is brighter and louder. That's because big snare drums emphasize lower frequencies, and those low frequencies simply don't get heard once all the other instruments are playing. So a bigger drum can frequently leave you with a smaller sound.

Another disadvantage of a deep snare is that the bottom of the drum is, by virtue of its physical depth, closer to the kick drum pedal. This can cause the snare mike to pick up low-end rumbling from the kick, which will knock down some of the drum's attack. When that happens, you lose some of the time-keeping effectiveness you want the snare to have.

Another kind of snare that drummers occasionally have in their arsenal is called a "pancake snare." This is an ultrathin snare drum preferred by jazz and R&B musicians. These tend to have a very brittle sound, and they produce a lot of "crack" because they are tuned so high. Usually pancake snares are favored by drummers who, by design, don't hit very hard.

Cymbals

Cymbals are probably the most overlooked element in a drum kit. A lot of people have the attitude that cymbals are just cymbals, that you just put 'em up there and hit 'em. But the fact is, if you're not hitting the right ones, it's not going to sound very good. So when you go looking for cymbals, you should choose those that give you the most versatility for the kind of music you play.

THE REEL WORLD
Jerry Speiser on Cymbal Choice

Rock drummer Jerry Speiser, formerly of Men At Work, is a polished, inventive performer who well understands the melodic components of his instrument—not the least of which are cymbals.

You should never walk into a music store and buy a cymbal without first trying it out. In fact, when you do go to buy a cymbal, try them *all* out! The idea is to walk in knowing the *type* of cymbal you want (ride, crash, whatever), and perhaps even the *size,* give or take a few inches. Then you want to find a quiet part of the shop and have the salesman bring you all the cymbals he has that might be suitable, so that you can test the sound of one against the sound of another, until you find the one you want.

These are a few of the things you should listen for as you go through this process of elimination:

Overtones

The first thing you want to test for is the overall quality of sound, which means that you should listen to all the tones in the cymbal, from high to low.

In some cymbals, the predominant tones are so similar in frequency that they clash, and they give the sound of the cymbal an unpleasant edge. This can best be heard by hitting two cymbals, one after the other, and comparing their sounds. Then, once you compare the first two cymbals, you replace the one that sounds less pleasing and repeat the test.

Eventually you'll be left with two or three cymbals of superior quality, and to narrow the field down, you'll want to test each of these to see which best complements the other cymbals in your kit. So, assuming you've brought your cymbals along, set them up and compare the sounds. What you want to hear is a pleasant tonal interval between cymbals that allows each to ring out individually.

Attack and Decay

Cymbal choice is, of course, a matter of personal taste. I prefer a cymbal that has a fast attack, meaning that it explodes virtually upon impact. Some people prefer cymbals that have a slower attack, so that it takes a fraction of a second for this explosion to peak. In either case, make sure you test the attack of the cymbal before you leave the store.

For crash cymbals, there is another important test. Hit the cymbal twice in quick succession, and, if you intend to use the cymbal in this way, make sure you hear the attack of the second crash. Some cymbals are slow to react, in which case the first crash will muffle the attack of the second.

The decay time of a cymbal is the time it takes the sound to die down once it has peaked. The length of decay will vary from cymbal to cymbal, so when you choose a cymbal, make sure the decay is suitable for the type of music it will be used for. In general, cymbals with quick decay times are

Figure 9c: Former Men At Work drummer Jerry Speiser. *(Courtesy of Laura Marenzi)*

best for fast music, while cymbals with longer decays are best for slow material.

Decay time is also important when you're choosing a ride cymbal. These cymbals are hit continuously, and this creates a natural buildup of sound. However, some ride cymbals have a tendency to build up so much sound that they mask the "sticking." So when you buy a ride, make sure that each tap of the drumstick can be heard clearly.

You should also check to make sure that the bell of the cymbal produces a pleasant, pure ring when hit with the tip of the stick. If you only hear it ring out when you hit it with the shoulder of the stick, move on to the next cymbal.

Hi-Hats

When you test hi-hats, you can use all the above techniques. However, what you're listening for is a sound that cuts through the rest of the kit and does not sound clanky.

My Preferences

As I said, everyone's tastes and needs are different, but I like to have at least the following cymbals in my kit whenever I do studio work. Some I'll use for slow songs, others for fast songs.

Also, I particularly like the sound I get from Sabian cymbals, and I usually use Regal Tip drumsticks by Calato.

My Cymbal Selections

   one 10-inch or 12-inch splash
   one 16-inch hi-hat
   two 16-inch to 18-inch crash (one medium, one medium
      thin)
   one 20-inch ride
   one 20-inch pang, or china

Crash Cymbals

In an ideal circumstance, where a drummer, for instance, is a studio drummer with lots of cymbals, I'll try to find crash cymbals that decay, more or less, in time with the music. If the song is a very fast song, I'll look for a very quick-decaying cymbal that will disappear in a measure or less. That way the cymbal won't still be ringing when the drummer's ready to hit the next crash.

So the first rule of thumb is, don't buy big, gonglike crash cymbals if you play fast music, because they will take *forever* to decay.

In general, I like the drummer to have two crash cymbals that are different enough in pitch to tell when one is hit and when the other is hit—that's for stereo imaging purposes, which we'll discuss shortly. The cymbals should have a nice, smooth decay, so you don't hear a bang and then nothing. Conversely, you don't want a cymbal that, because it was made improperly, shimmers in and out during decay as different frequencies bob up and down in volume.

You must also be careful that the two crash cymbals you choose do not cause acoustic phasing when they're struck simultaneously. This phasing effect, the product of two cymbals that are too similar in pitch, is produced when the sound waves generated by one cymbal cancel out those of the other. So if you stand in front of the kit, you can literally hear the sound rising and falling as the cymbals decay.

Although cymbal phase cancelation is fairly rare, you should check each new addition to your cymbal collection to make sure it can be matched properly with the others.

Ride Cymbals

Of all the cymbals that a drummer buys, the ride cymbal is the most critical. It is also probably the most difficult to choose when you're listening to cymbals in a music store, because the environment makes it hard to pick up the cymbal's subtleties.

I look for ride cymbals to have a very definite "ping," because if the cymbal rings too much relative to the ping, it loses its time-keeping effectiveness. The attack of the drumstick gets buried, and what you hear is a wall of cymbal rather than a series of discrete hits.

Which ride cymbal you choose can also depend on how hard you play, as well as on your ability to control where the stick hits the cymbal. Very good players can get away with using a bad cymbal, while a novice can't.

If you're miking the kit with only a few mikes, the performance of this cymbal is even more critical. You're not going to be able to move a microphone to alter the dynamics of a cymbal without altering the dynamics of everything else. One alternative is to try using sticks that have plastic tips— especially if you've got a big, gonglike ride that you're trying to control. Plastic-tipped sticks will help the attack sound brighter and will allow it to stand out over the excessive ringing.

Figure 9d: This triangular miking technique uses two overheads and a kick drum mike. Note that after miking the kick drum (Figure 9h), it should be covered with a heavy packing blanket. Also note that the overheads in this picture are actually aimed down toward the drums, as the diaphragms in these studio condenser mikes point out to the side. (*Courtesy of Laura Marenzi*)

Hi-Hat

The hi-hat is also extremely important, because it, along with the snare and kick drums, is one of the principal time-keepers for the song. Drummers who play a lot of hard rock often opt for a hard-sounding hi-hat that has a lot of *clank* to it. These cymbals get their "big" sound from the low, mid-range frequencies. For someone who is playing pop-oriented material, particularly R&B, the sibilant, or high-end, quality of the hi-hat is more important. That's because you want each beat to be distinct and to have its own decay time—particularly if you're opening and closing the hi-hat for effect or if you're using it in fills.

MIKING THE DRUMS

There are many ways to mike drums, but the technique you use is going to have to depend upon the number of mikes you have available. For instance, if you have two or three dynamic microphones to use, and that's *all* you have, then your approach is going to be very different from the approach you'd use if you had a roomful of condenser mikes and a studio console.

Triangular Miking

One simple form of miking is called "triangular miking" (Figure 9d). It's easy but effective, and it gives you the broadest coverage three mikes can offer.

In triangular miking, you put two microphones up above the drum kit on boom stands, and you place a third mike inside the kick drum. The overhead mikes, as they're called, will pick up the entire drum kit, while the kick drum mike affords you some discretionary control over the balance between the kick drum and the rest of the kit. You see, the sound from the kick drum travels straight out, while the sound from all the other drums travels up and *then* out. So the overheads, which will be more sensitive to the drums that are aimed directly toward them, exclude a large part of the kick drum signal—which is one reason the kick drum needs to be miked separately.

The overheads themselves must also be balanced relative to the kit as a whole, because otherwise you will end up with a predominance of one drum and the exclusion of another.

So when positioning these mikes, you must be aware of each drum's physical location relative to the microphones.

If the cymbals are too high, for instance, and thus too close to the mike, you'll hear too much cymbal. Or if the cymbals are too low, the toms will be too loud relative to the cymbals. And for that matter, even if the cymbals are perfectly balanced with the toms, they might be physically blocking out the hi-hat.

So try moving the mike in and out, and try rearranging the drums themselves, until you achieve what you consider to be a pleasant balance. As a rule, you want to find a balance that puts the snare at the center of the stereo spectrum, and you want the snare to be *at least* at equal volume with the toms and the crash cymbals. The kick drum volume should also equal that of the snare; however, the hi-hat and ride cymbal can be slightly in the background.

You have to recognize that in triangular miking, you're going to get more of the room sound than you would if you miked each drum individually. But that's not all bad. The technique was used quite successfully by Led Zeppelin. Eddie Cremar, their producer, told me that the *huge* drum sound they were so famous for was a product of triangular technique using three, and in some cases four, mikes. In fact, they recorded one of their albums in a mammoth castle that had stone walls and vaulted ceilings. The ambience of that room literally *made* the drum sound.

Close Miking

"Close miking" is the technique of miking each drum individually (Figure 9e). This is the technique most often used in professional studios today. But since there is such a wide variety of mikes available for close miking, and since each producer or engineer has his own favorites, we will deal primarily with mike positioning.

It should be mentioned, however, that if you have a choice between dynamic and condenser mikes, the latter is preferable, since condensers offer broader and flatter frequency response. The only exceptions to this are in terms of miking the snare and kick drums, which is often best accomplished with dynamic mikes like the Shure SM-57.

When I mike each of the tom-toms (Figure 9f), I come in from the front, mounting the mike on a boom stand and

---

TAPE TIP #21
Stereo Imaging

There are two ways to position the overheads. In England, a format has developed in which the stereo spread of the drums is based on the position of the drummer. This means that as you face your stereo, the drums sound as though you are the drummer and you're facing the audience. Thus, the floor tom is on the right as you face the stereo, and the hi-hat is on the left for a right-handed drummer.

In America it's just the reverse: the stereo spread of the drums is based on the position of the audience, as though you were watching the drummer from out front. So in listening to your stereo, the hi-hat would be on the right and the floor tom on the left.

It doesn't really matter which of the two formats you use, but it *is* something to consider when you're sketching out your track. It's also something to double-check if there's something strange about the sound of the track, and you're unable to figure out what it is.

Figure 9e: In the close-mike technique, each drum is miked individually. (*Courtesy of Laura Marenzi*)

Figure 9f: Miking the tom-toms. (*Courtesy of Laura Marenzi*)

Figure 9g: Miking the snare drum. (*Courtesy of Laura Marenzi*)

angling it down so that it's pointing at the tom but also pointing indirectly at the snare drum. That way I can inject a little ambience into the snare sound.

I position the mike two to three inches above the head and about two inches inside the rim. If you're using a condenser mike, such as a Neumann U-87 (my favorite for this application), you should engage the "Pad" switch to avoid mike distortion. If damping is required, I use a little bit of gauze or cotton, which I apply to the top skin with gaffer's tape, as previously described. And when you're miking drums individually, damping is usually necessary—especially the damping of any resonance created by the attack of the kick drum, which is almost unavoidable.

The mike I normally favor on snare drums is a Shure SM-57, which is a dynamic microphone that's relatively inexpensive. I come in on the snare from an angle, usually from the hi-hat side, but pointing *away* from the hi-hat, using a mike stand and boom (Figure 9g). The mike capsule should be one and a half to two inches off the top of the head but positioned so that the drummer isn't going to hit it when he's playing.

I mike the kick drum with one mike, which I put inside the drum using a boom on a short stand (Figure 9h). I position the mike three inches from the head and point it away from the floor tom, about thirty degrees off axis, so that it's not quite aimed directly at the head. Depending upon the

Figure 9h: After miking the kick drum (left), cover it with a heavy packing blanket (right). (*Courtesy of Laura Marenzi*)

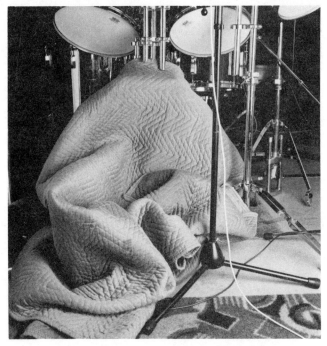

amount of attack that I want, I'll move the mike closer to the beater or farther away; the closer it is, the more initial attack I'll get.

Miking the floor tom (Figure 9i) is slightly different from miking the mounted toms. Unless properly positioned, the floor tom mike will pick up leakage from the kick drum, and this leakage can be very difficult to get rid of, because both drums are in the same frequency range. Therefore, instead of pointing indirectly at the snare, the mike should be positioned in the way that best isolates the floor tom from the rest of the kit—and in particular the kick drum.

With this in mind, I mike the floor tom from the front, using a boom stand, and angle the mike away from the kick drum. I position the mike about three inches above the drum and two to three inches inside the rim. And I pay very close attention to damping.

The hi-hat must be miked differently for every drummer. How it's miked depends on where the drummer plays on the hi-hat and what kind of hi-hat he uses. The different miking options you have really only concern the angle of the mike and how much of the cymbal's edge is picked up. By miking the edge, you'll get more of the sibilants of the hi-hat; by directing the mike more at the center, you get more of the attack of the stick . . . more "clank," if you will.

I personally look for more of the sibilants, with enough attack for definition. So I come in from the top (Figure 9j), facing the mike away from the snare drum in order to keep as much separation between the two as possible. I position the mike about three inches off the top cymbal at an angle of about thirty degrees off the perpendicular and aim the mike slightly at the top, but mostly at the edge, of the cymbal.

Overhead mikes play a dual role in close miking. On one hand they provide definition and clarity for the cymbals, and on the other they provide stereo imaging and ambience for the whole kit. I usually use two overheads, which I come in with from behind the drummer (Figure 9k). Then, listening to the stereo image created by the two overhead mikes together, I use the sound of just the snare and adjust the mike positioning so that I get the snare to image directly on center.

When that's accomplished, then just as you did with the overhead mike in triangular miking, you want to listen for overall drum kit balance and adjust the drums accordingly. What you're looking for here in respect to cymbals, however, is to achieve a louder cymbal sound than tom sound, because these are the only mikes picking up the cymbals, while the toms can be brought up in level through their individual mikes.

I usually use room mikes in conjunction with the overheads. To place them, you first draw two imaginary lines out from the snare drum on an axis that would have them pass through an overhead mike and continue on out into the room to form a giant "V" (Figure 9l). Then you place one room mike on each line, equal distance from the snare. To be most effective, these mikes should also be raised up higher than the overhead mikes.

The room mikes, along with the overheads, hold the key to capturing room ambience. The farther away they are from

Figure 9i: Miking the floor tom. (*Courtesy of Laura Marenzi*)

Figure 9j: When miking the hi-hat, try to avoid aiming it toward the snare drum. (*Courtesy of Laura Marenzi*)

Figure 9k: Overhead mike placement. Note that the overheads in this picture are actually aimed down toward the drums, as the diaphragms in these studio condenser mikes point out to the side. (*Courtesy of Laura Marenzi*)

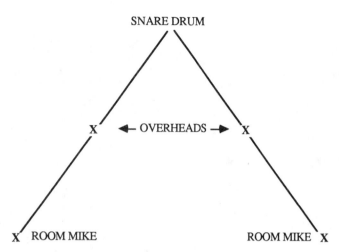

SNARE DRUM

X ← OVERHEADS → X

X ROOM MIKE   ROOM MIKE X

Figure 9l: The room mikes should be placed along a pair of imaginary lines that extend out from the snare drum and pass through each of the overhead mikes to form a "V."

the kit, the more of the room you'll pick up relative to the source. The closer they are to the drums, the *less* room you'll hear.

Once again, when miking and mixing drums, it's terribly important to listen to the sound of the drums themselves. Once you get them sounding good and get the mike coverage balanced, then the tones of the individual drums can be enhanced with EQ.

And while you're trying to establish that balance, remember that you are trying to achieve a rhythmic flow. Imbalance can result in the loss of a critical beat or even the loss of overall dynamic interest.

EQING THE KIT

The next step to take in recording the drum track is to EQ the kit in preparation for putting the drums on tape. There are two points at which EQ can be applied to drums: during the recording of the initial track and during mixdown. So if you only have two bands of EQ, but you need to apply three EQ boosts to get a particular drum to sound right, you may well be able to boost two of the bands during tracking and boost the third during mixdown.

As a general rule, the more EQ you have available to use, the better able you are to solve whatever kinds of acoustical problems arise—whether they have to do with the room environment or with the drums themselves. And in this regard, the use of EQ can mean the difference between the drums being heard clearly or getting lost in the shuffle when other instruments are added.

Stated quite simply, EQ gives you the ability to make your drums sound more natural by increasing or reducing specific frequencies in the drums' tonal spectrum. EQing is made necessary because a microphone, positioned at a fixed point in a room, tends to emphasize some frequencies at the ex-

pense of others. Conflicting overtones, low-end rumble, and the like, can often mask tonal qualities of the drums that you need to hear in order to make them rhythmically effective, and EQ helps you to mute the offending tones and bring out those that need to be accentuated—something that is essential when you find yourself in a room environment that is basically unsuitable for recording.

The first thing you need to know are the frequency ranges that affect the tonal components of drum and cymbal sound. For instance, though we'll go into each element of the kit separately, as a general rule the frequencies generated by the tip of the stick when it first impacts the skin (or, as I call it, the "click") is somewhere between 5K and 7K. The "bang" of the drumhead, depending somewhat upon which drum is struck, can be found somewhere around 1K. And the body of the drums, or the resonance, lies down toward the bottom end of the spectrum, near 250 Hz.

The following discussion of EQ levels and EQing technique will address the effect of altering these frequency-range levels on each drum recorded in the miking configurations previously discussed. However, since there is a great difference between the many types of EQ and the amount of control available from one piece of gear to the next, I will only be able to give you general guidelines from which to work. Once again, the final decision must be made by you after careful listening and by determining for yourself what sounds good.*

NOTE—*See "Drum EQ Reminders" at the end of this chapter.*

TRIANGULAR MIKING EQ

Triangular miking relies primarily on its two overhead mikes to capture the signal from the bulk of the drum kit. So in this mike configuration your EQ is going to have to take into account the ambience surrounding the drums in addition to the drums themselves.

What you're trying to do with EQ in this case is to create colorations of sound by accentuating the hues that serve to distinguish the drums one from the other and, in turn, from the cymbals and, in turn, from the room. So you need to understand how to use EQ to create this "presence."

I'll begin with the high-end frequency range of 9K to 15K, where room ambience and cymbals are located. In the range between 9K and 10K you'll find a lot of the *splash* of the cymbal: the top-end sibilants that we associate with the cymbal "crash." In the range above 10K you'll find the effects of room ambience: the echoes reverberating off the walls and ceiling, and the "air" in and around the kit. The higher you go and the closer to 15K you get, the more "air" you'll hear.

*Don't forget, one way to double-check the effect of EQ is to compare the sound you're getting with the sound you hear on records.

What you'll find in the upper-midrange frequencies between 5K and 7K is the top-end response of the drums—the tick hitting the tom-tom or snare—as well as the snare wires themselves. The one thing you have to be careful about when increasing EQ in this range is not to push it too hard. There is a brittleness in the tone quality that can become unpleasant when overdone.

The frequency range around 1K will give you the transient, which is the "bang" of the drum. The difference between the 1K response and the response of the upper-midrange frequencies is that from 5K to 7K you're getting that initial, brittle attack of the stick's *tip* hitting the skin, whereas at 1K you're hearing the entire *bang* of the stick fully impacting the head. Those frequencies below 1K contain the resonance, or body, of the drum, which is EQed best at around the 100 Hz to 250 Hz range.

Generally speaking, the frequency spectrum can be divided into two basic regions: 1K and above, which is the range for "clarity," and 1K and below, which is the tonal or "body" range. So when you're using triangular miking, you have to be careful of how much boost you give to the lower frequencies, because they have a tendency to mask out all of the clarity that you've gotten by EQing the upper frequencies.

Kick Drum

You can begin EQing the mikes by starting with the kick drum mike—the only mike of the three that is assigned to one individual drum. How you set the upper registers of the kick drum frequency spectrum depends on how much "smack" you want the drum to have. I personally give the upper frequencies a boost at 3K, and sometimes I give it a little push between 6K and 8K, which provides kind of a "click."

The amount I'll boost these frequencies is dependent upon the drum itself. However, the amount is smaller relative to the settings I'll use at 100 Hz, which is where I boost the bottom end. Usually I'll boost 8K one-tenth of the amount I've boosted 100 Hz. So if at 100 Hz I'm adding 10 dB, I'll add 1 dB at 8K. The amount I boost 3K is usually two-thirds of the amount I've boosted 100 Hz, so in this case, 3K would be boosted 6 dB.

When I boost EQ at 3K and at 100 Hz, it's because I want the kick drum to have a "smack" to provide the pulse and a "woof" to provide the tone that feels as if the kick drum sound is hitting you in the chest. The extreme top end, the 8K EQ, simply provides a certain amount of clarity that distinguishes the kick drum beater from, say, the sound of the stick on the tom-tom.

Of course, this is just the way I like to hear a kick drum. You may want yours to have a different sound. In English rock 'n' roll, for instance, they may not include any of the top end at all. They may EQ at 60 Hz, giving it a big boost, because they want a deeper "woof" sound from the drum.

TAPE TIP #22
If It Jingles . . .

It's next to impossible to tell you how to EQ every percussion instrument, because there are just too many. Even the major ones, like conga drums and cow bells, come in many different sizes and have completely different applications.

In general, anything with a skin stretched across it (such as a drum) can be EQed using the basic guidelines laid out in the sections on tom-toms and bass drums. However, we offer the following index for general application to other percussion instruments:

IF IT JINGLES, then the frequency range you want to key in on is 5K and up.
IF IT BANGS, then the frequencies to look for are between 5K and 1K.
IF IT THUMPS, then the key frequencies lie between 100 Hz and 500 Hz.

As a general rule, this will hold true for all percussion instruments. For instance, if you have a tambourine, you know that it jingles, so you should look at 5K and up. But if you want more of the attack of the tambourine hitting the hand, you can hear that it bangs, so you should look to control the frequencies between 5K and 1K.

The Overheads

When you EQ the overhead mike, you are EQing the entire drum kit. Earlier, you positioned the overheads in such a way that there was an acoustical balance between the drums and the cymbals that sounded "natural" in that there wasn't too much of either. What you're trying to accomplish with EQ is roughly the same thing except that now you have to establish that balanced relationship electronically. What you're aiming for is to get the recording to sound as if you're standing in the room, listening to the drum kit live.

To bring out the clarity of the cymbals, you should boost frequencies in the 10K to 12K range. Occasionally, if I want to hear the bang of the stick hitting the cymbal, I'll also boost 3K. In order to capture the snare drum in the overheads, you should try to find, and boost, a frequency that makes the snare a bit more prominent. If you have the capability, you'll want to enhance the sound of the snares, which is in the 5K to 7K region, and the attack of the transient, which is between 1K and 3K. But if you have a limited EQ, then you're going to have to make a compromise and search for a suitable frequency that splits the difference. Then, to enhance the bottom end and bring out some body, you should boost the EQ at 100 Hz.

If you have more EQ available, you might want to reduce the level slightly at 200 Hz (in a narrow band if parametric is available), which will add some clarity to the drum and help out the toms. When you reduce the 200 Hz level, you create a frequency gap between the slap of the stick and the boom of the drum, and that gap will give a little more transparency to the sound of the drums.

Again, in all of these cases, you should make your own judgments based upon listening to the particular drum kit in the context of the particular acoustic environment it's played in. Also be aware that EQ bandwidths vary tremendously from one piece of gear to the next, and that something you do at 200 Hz may actually be affecting the frequencies in a band from 100 Hz to 300 Hz.

Although you use two separate overheads in triangular miking, above all, you want to preserve the symmetry of the stereo image they project. So you want to be sure to EQ both roughly equal. That also applies if you're mixing both mikes together onto the same track, combining them with the kick drum mike to create a monaural recording.

CLOSE MIKING EQ

Although the principles for EQing a close-mike pattern are the same as those for triangular miking—the aim of both being to create a natural-sounding drum kit—close miking necessitates the individual EQing of each drum. This does give you greater control over the drum sound, but it requires that you pay closer attention to detail.

The Overheads

Although we discussed EQing overhead mikes in the last section, the overheads are given slightly different treatment in the close-mike configuration. For one thing, the toms and the snare are individually miked, so the overall EQ pattern of the overheads should serve to enhance the cymbals over anything else. This means making the top end the dominant frequency range, because most of the tonal information for cymbals is up there. Plus, enhancing the cymbal frequencies in this range helps distinguish the cymbals from everything else, because there aren't many other instruments with major frequency response in that area.

So, generally speaking, I will roll back a little EQ at 200 Hz to give clarity and boost the signal somewhere in the 10K to 12K range, depending upon the cymbals. Plus, I'll add a little bit of EQ at 3K if it's a solid rock 'n' roll tune, because that gives a midrange "bang" to the cymbals.

Room Mikes

The room mikes reinforce the same stereo image the overheads generate. They're just farther away from the kit in every dimension: farther up, farther back, and farther out. Here, if the equalizer is capable of it, I emphasize 15K, because what I want to get from these mikes is the "air" that gives the drum kit the impression of being in a room and being some distance away. EQing these mikes like this will give you a "bigger" sound, because with the ambience the drums aren't existing in an acoustic vacuum. But be aware that noise can be a problem in this range, also, and it's easy to start picking up things like air conditioners and the like. You don't want these mikes to be all that loud, anyway.

The room mikes help to establish clarity, so any low-end rumble that appears in either the overhead mikes or the room mikes should be eliminated once the offending frequency is located. In most cases I try to eliminate the kick drum frequencies from the room mikes. An exception to this might be in the case of hard rock or when going for a special effect.

Tom-Toms

The way you EQ the individual toms depends to a large extent on the quality of your microphones. A high-quality condenser mike, such as a Neumann U-87, which many professionals use in the studio, will require quite a different EQ structure from what would be required for a Shure SM-57, which is a dynamic microphone.

Yet when EQing the toms, I'm much more concerned with how the drums sit in the track than with how beautiful they sound on their own. You see, it's the relationship between *all* the instruments on the track that is most important; you can get the greatest drum sound in the world, but if it's sitting in the same frequency ranges as the guitar and synthesizer, all the instruments battle for the same space.

So I EQ the toms' top-end ranges in such a way that the attack of the stick is of paramount importance and the "woof" of the drum is subdued. An important thing to remember is that you can always enhance the body of the drum sound, with effects such as echo, even after it's been recorded, but it's very difficult to remove that body once it's there. So I'm always very cautious when EQing the bottom end, because that is what will give a drum its tonality.

I'll start EQing the toms by boosting the signal at around 7K or 8K, which is the stick-attack frequency area. Then, if I'm recording rock 'n' roll material, I'll add some EQ at 3K (for power) and give it a boost at 100 Hz, which is the bottom end of the toms' register. For colorations, however, some frequency nearer the midrange needs to be boosted.

This frequency should be somewhere around 500 Hz where you find a close relationship existing between pitch, tone, and EQ. Thus, if you want the drum to have an opaque sound, so that when you hit it, it seems to fill the entire stereo spectrum, and you don't intend to use a lot of echo on it, then you might want to bring up the frequencies at around 500 Hz. This brings up the tone and makes the drum a more solid acoustic mass.

Snare Drum

I tend to be a little unorthodox in my treatment of the snare drum. I like a real "bangy," loud snare, so the frequencies I accentuate are in the "bang" range of 1K to 3K.

Usually I'll add a lot of snare EQ at 1.2K, but it's a bit

isky because that frequency can make the snare sound "honky"—as if you were listening to it through a cardboard tube. However, that range also gives you a lot of psycho-acoustic excitement, so proper EQing of the 1K to 2K frequencies can make the bang of the snare drum very effective.

For additional clarity and definition, I'll also add EQ at 5K. Boosting the EQ slightly here will bring out the sound of the snares and the stick hitting the skin, and the resulting "click" will help the listener distinguish between one hit and the next.

For the bottom end of the drum, I'll boost some at 100 Hz. At this frequency the speakers push a lot of air, and consequently the listener can physically feel the pulse of the snare and the kick.

One of EQ's basic functions, in fact, is to enhance the rhythmic qualities of the drums . . . to give them definition. The concept is the same one we applied earlier when choosing a cymbal with the proper decay time: you don't want a drum, especially a snare drum, to ring on into the next beat, because the result, in this case, will be a "wall of snare" with little distinguishable attack. So there can be a certain correlation between the tempo of the song and the EQ of the snare.

To better understand this, it might be helpful to think of the sound of a drumbeat as being like a pyramid. The point of that pyramid represents the attack of the drum: the upper frequencies of the signal. As you move down the pyramid, you reach a section somewhere in the middle that corresponds to the body of the attack—the *thwackkk,* if you will. The bottom end, the broadest part of the pyramid, is what gives you the tone, or the weight of the drum.

If you place a number of these pyramids one after the other in a series, you can see the result of extensive ringing and how it can hurt the drum rhythmically. In Figure 9m the pyramids are properly spaced relative to the breadth of their cone. In Figure 9n, however, because of an increased tempo, the bases of the pyramids begin to overlap, which is what happens when drums ring too long and it becomes difficult to properly distinguish one beat from the next.

Thinking of the sound of a drumbeat in this way, you can get a more concrete grasp of how to alter the pyramid's structure when EQing for the audible duration of the beat. In Figure 9o, for instance, though some of the weight of the drum had to be sacrificed, by cutting back on the low-end frequencies, or "squeezing" the pyramid, the ringing has been reduced, and the drum's rhythmic clarity has been restored.

So, keeping this in mind, you should be relatively careful with the snare drum's low-end response. But at the same time, you can't ignore the low end, because without it your drum sound won't have any strength. So you'll want to boost EQ at about 100 Hz, the amount of the boost depending upon the drum and the song.

If your EQ availability is limited, you might want to make

Figure 9m: Three discrete drumbeats.

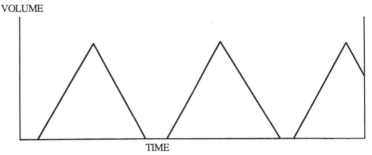

Figure 9n: At a faster tempo, the drumbeats overlap since they don't have enough time to decay.

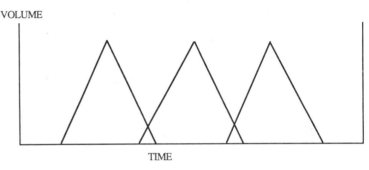

Figure 9o: By altering the EQ of the signal in a way that reduces the decay time of the drumbeats, each is again heard as a single, discrete entity.

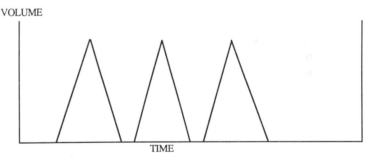

the following adjustments. Instead of EQing tight bands at 5K and 1K, try EQing broader bands at 2K and, to a much lesser degree, 10K. This will cover essentially the same ground as the 1K/5K/10K boosts, though much less precisely—which means that the quality of your 100 Hz boost is going to be more critical.

Though not a large boost, the 10K boost *is* important if you want to capture the texture of the snares. To make sure that I have control over how much of the snare wires get included, I also mike underneath the snare. When I EQ that mike, I accentuate *only* the 5K–10K band, and I try to eliminate most of the other frequencies. I then mix this mike in with the snare mike that's aimed at the top, and balance the mix in with the rest of the kit.

Kick Drum

EQing the kick drum using this mike pattern is basically the same as what was done for triangular miking, except that in this instance you may want to use tighter bandwidths.

Again, what I look for from the kick drum is the "punch" of a very discrete beat each time the beater hits the head. This means that the drum must have "immediacy." For instance, I would never add echo to a kick drum (except for effect), whereas I do add echo or reverb to the toms. So your ear automatically hears the toms as being more removed, more in the background, than the kick—which is in the foreground.

The kick drum provides a low-end pulse that usually doesn't encroach upon the frequency ranges of the other instruments. However, you can EQ the kick so that it complements other elements in the track. For instance, I usually mix the bass guitar and the kick drum so that they each basically become part of the same instrument. In other words, I use the kick drum to provide the rhythmic factor for the bass, and the bass to provide the tone for the kick drum. So when the two instruments play together, they give you the sensation of being hit in the chest, while at the same time providing a tonal center for the song.

Other people do it differently. For instance, in heavy metal music, the bass player follows the lead guitar instead of the kick drum. Since the bass is playing a riff instead of a rhythm pattern, it only occasionally lands when the kick drum hits, so there is less need for rhythmic clarity in the kick. That's generally why heavy metal drums produce a loud boom rather than a discrete smack.

In R&B music, the bass and the kick drum are almost always together, as they are in most pop songs. But in R&B, as with some jazz, the patterns are usually faster than in pop music and more complex, so the kick drum sound is even tighter, and you hear more of the attack than you do of the boom.

Hi-Hat

The hi-hat EQ varies wildly from hi-hat to hi-hat, because a great deal depends upon the size and quality of the cymbals. More than anything, you want to enhance the rhythmic quality of the hi-hat pattern by capturing the sibilants and the sound of the stick as it hits the cymbal.

These sonic qualities are found in the upper frequency ranges. The sibilants are generally brought out in the 7K–10K range. The sound of the tip of the stick hitting the cymbal is at around 5K. But again, that will all have to be determined by listening to *your* particular hi-hat. If you want more of a rock 'n' roll quality to the sound—that "mashing of the oars on the hi-hat"—then you might want a bit more of the "clank." This is found more at around 600 Hz, or between 500 Hz and 1K, depending upon the hi-hat.

Hi-hats are difficult to mike and difficult to EQ. You al-

most need to do them last, so that you can hear what the rest of the kit sounds like. You want the hi-hat to be audible so that you can hear it clearly, yet it should sound natural and take its proper place within the sound of the whole kit.

EQ CONSIDERATIONS

The first thing you need to take into consideration before EQing is how the drums are going to sit in the track. For instance, as was mentioned before, you can spend countless hours getting "the perfect drum sound," only to have it disappear into the track simply because there wasn't enough thought given to the song's overall instrumentation.

So you should always record the initial tracks with a good, basic EQ structure, and once all the instruments are there, *then* go back and fine-tune the drum sound. This way the instruments expand within the parameters that you've allowed and don't have to fight each other for space.

Another good point to remember is that you're better off structuring the EQ of the initial drum recording in a way that keeps the drums from taking up too much room on the track. Although by EQing conservatively the drums may seem a bit small, you'll be able to fill in the gaps and expand the sound with echo or EQ in the final mix. So if possible, listen to the drums with roughly the same echo or reverb levels you intend to mix with.

You can think of the process as being similar to painting a landscape: the initial recording is the sketch, or line drawing, that you start out with, and when you get to the mix you're putting in the colors. It's important that you leave room for those colors. Otherwise the drums are going to end up occupying more than their share of space in order to sound as if they're existing in a natural acoustical environment.

MIXDOWN EFFECTS

The mixdown stage in recording can be used to add tonal colorations to the track through the use of such electronic devices as EQ, noise gates, echoes, and, if need be, compressors. I, for one, rarely add these effects at the time of the original recording, for reasons we'll discuss, and I suggest that you wait until the mixdown as well.

Noise Gates

One of the most useful devices for recording drums is the noise gate, which can be used to eliminate the ringing of an uncooperative drum. Briefly, what the gate does is shut down once the signal strength drops below a certain level, then it opens back up when, and if, the signal strength exceeds that level. Since you can set the gate level at a point greater than the level of the "ring," which means that it takes a signal louder than the drum's ringing to open it back up, you can rid the drums of a lot of unwanted noise.

Unfortunately, good noise gates are usually only available n studios, because units that are technically suitable for the lemands of a drum kit are too expensive for all but the most ophisticated home studios. The problem with the less ex- ensive models, such as those in the guitar foot-pedal for- nat, is that they just don't decay smoothly enough to sound natural.

NOTE—See Tape Tip #23, "Creating an 'Explosive' Snare ound."

Tape Compression and Record Levels

Sometimes producers will use compressors on drums. Al- hough I don't use electronic compressors, I do use the com- ression effect produced by tape saturation. This is often alled "tape compression."

Basically, a compressor makes the lowest, quietest part of he sound equal to the loudest part of the sound. When ap- lied to drums, it brings out a certain quality of opaqueness, while at the same time it can even out the attack volume when a drummer is inconsistent with the force of his hits.

In general, the more opaque the sound of the drum, the ess consistent the drummer needs to be. So if the drummer s very inconsistent, and the snare drum sounds as if it's eing tapped for two beats and then smashed for two, you an salvage the recording by applying compression.

Personally, I use tape compression whether the drummer is inconsistent or not, because this is what gives the snare drum that huge *thwackkk* sound that is used so often in hard rock. I do this by "hitting" the tape machine very hard with the snare drum signal, going into tape saturation at what looks to be about +6 on the VU meter. (Actually, the tran- sient, or attack, is much hotter, causing a distortion that in this case is used positively.) When you do this, you lose some clarity of the attack, but you can recapture it through the overheads.

I use tape compression on the toms, too, which I also record at +6. My reasoning here is the same as for the snare: with the compression, I get a big, opaque bang from the tom, but I still have the high-end accentuation from the overheads, which will provide the decay of the drum.

I do not use tape compression on the kick drum, because if you're not careful, and you hit the tape too hard, you'll lose the attack of the drum—and the attack is critical for the kick. So I usually record kick drums at between −4 and −2 on the VU meter.

I don't use tape compression on the cymbals, either, be- cause I want them to sound as clear as possible. So I record them at a level that peaks at about 0 on the meter (the edge of the red). You don't want them much hotter than that be- cause they'll start distorting.

Unfortunately, in order to record your drums in a way that allows you to apply tape compression selectively, you have to have at least an 8-track tape recorder. These volumes,

---

TAPE TIP #23
Creating an "Explosive" Snare Sound

When Men At Work's *Business As Usual* LP was released, the explosive quality of the snare sound on such songs as "Who Can It Be Now?" caused quite a stir. In order to create this sound, I used what is called a "gated reverb," which is an effect created by "gating the chamber" on a reverb unit—

Figure 9p: Yamaha's Rev-7 digital reverb unit. (*Courtesy of Ya- maha International Corporation.*)

meaning that I used a noise gate to cut short the decay of the reverb. In a very short time, this became a popular studio technique to use on both the snare and the kick drum, and it is an effect you can use at home to enhance the quality of the drum sounds on your machine.

The gated-reverb effect has recently become available among the nonlinear programs included on programmable, digital reverb units like Yamaha's REV-7 and Roland's SRV-2000. Although these units are designed for home use, they provide excellent signal quality and offer a wide selec- tion of effects, which is something we discuss in detail in chapter 16, "Mixdown Techniques."

You can, of course, create a gated reverb from scratch, but unless you have a studio-quality noise gate and a lot of experience with reverb chambers, you'll have a tough time getting it to sound right.

In either case, the important thing to remember when you *do* use this effect is that it will reduce the level of presence of any drum you apply it to. So if you use it on the snare, be sure that you don't overuse it, because you may end up pull- ing the snare back into the track. And if you use it on the kick drum, apply it *very sparingly,* unless you're going for some special effect.

> **TAPE TIP #24**
> *The Better They Come, the Harder They Hit!*
>
> The harder you hit your drums, the better they're going to sound, because the harder you hit, the more tone you get from the drum. And the more tone you get, the better the drums sound.
>
> A good drummer will use his strength to bring out the optimum tonal quality of his drums. The explosive nature of the tom-toms that you hear on rock 'n' roll records, for instance (such as you hear from Mr. Mister's Pat Mastelotto), are due at least in part to the pounding the drums are getting.
>
> However, what makes a good drummer great is his control. You can't just wildly pound the drums, you have to use solid, measured strokes, and you have to be consistent. The toughest drummer to record is one who fails to hit the heads in the same spot with the same force every time: he makes it difficult to keep the levels consistent, and he negates all the work that went into tuning the drums. Consistency is especially critical for the snare drum stroke, where both tone and timing are crucial.
>
> One way to improve your strength and consistency is to change to a heavier stick during practice—something like a 2-B. Then mark a spot on each drumhead, and when you go through your practice drills, concentrate on hitting those spots when you play your fills. And when you're keeping time, really try to nail that spot on the snare with some authority.
>
> If you do this, and then shift back to your lighter sticks for band practices or gigs, you'll see a major improvement in your ability to control your stroke. Remember, there's a big difference between playing live and recording in a studio, and if you want to succeed in the studio, the best thing you can do is work to eliminate the bad habits that lead to sloppy drumming.

don't forget, are record levels, not mixdown levels, and each mike needs its own track if you want to be able to balance the drum sound properly. In other words, if you recorded at these levels and just played the tape back without adjusting the monitor levels, the snares and toms would be too loud, and the bass drum would have faded into the background.

If you're taking your mike from a mixer and recording onto a 2-track machine, you're going to have to bring those levels into balance *before* going to tape. And your drummer will have to be more consistent, because you're not going to be able to use tape compression as fully as you might like to—if at all.

Generally speaking, the less recording gear you have, the better the players and the instruments have to be. So if you want good results, you either have to use more recording equipment or have the musicians play better.

THE DRUMMER VS. THE DRUMS

One thing I always try to keep in mind is that the drummer a human being. So while you're miking and EQing, yo should remember that if you intend to get a track that da it's much better to settle for a drum sound you know you ca enhance later than to tire the drummer out going for one yo don't have to enhance later—although I'm not a great be liever in the "fix it in the mix" approach.

Playing drums is a very special activity, and trackin drums is almost like an athletic event in the sense that th more energy a drummer has left when you finally go record the track, the better his performance is going to be You can conserve his energy by having some idea of th drum sound you want *before* you start and also by realizin that as you go through each stage of the process, unles there's some really horrible problem you need to fix, lik buzzes, you have at least one more opportunity to enhanc the drum sound: the mix.

BUZZES AND SQUEAKS AND WHIRS AND GROANS

The first time a "stage" drummer sets up his gear in recording studio, he's apt to be horrified at all the noises h hears coming from the kit. When you're playing live, yo simply don't hear the squeaky kick drum pedal or the litt buzzes that come from loose hardware or from one dru touching another . . . or the scores of other irritating sound the studio mikes are likely to pick up.

No matter how tiny the noise, you absolutely must inve tigate it, isolate it, and then get rid of it. But since that's n always as easy as it sounds, the following tips might come handy.

In order to locate a buzz or a rattle in a tom or a snar drum, the first thing you should look at is the head. If th head is too old and it's beginning to dimple, it won't vibra evenly. It will leave a little buzz as the vibration stops. Yo should also check the tension rods along the rim, becaus they can come loose and rattle and put the drumhead out tune as well. You might also check to be sure that the tom positioned so that it's not touching any other hardware, a if all else fails, check inside the drum to make sure that th mounting bracket is still securely fastened and that *it* isn causing the buzz.

One way to solve many of the buzz problems with th toms is to get them off the kick drum and onto free-standi tom stands. Unfortunately, I don't see this often enoug With rack-mounted toms, which are connected directly the kick drum, there is more direct vibration to set the dru ringing when not hit and to interfere with the resonance the tom when it is hit. If the kick drum isn't touching th tom or the mount, then all you have to worry about is th acoustic vibration of the kick setting off the toms. Plu there's less likelihood of having tension rods or rack hard ware coming loose from the constant bang of the kick drum

Quite often the foot pedal on the kick drum or hi-hat will squeak. Usually, all it takes to fix that is a little 3-In-One oil. But if you still keep hearing the noise, check the drum stool, because every time a drummer's foot moves, so does the seat of the drum stool.

Sometimes you'll hear a double hit coming from the kick drum. The most likely cause of this is the drummer himself, because many live drummers with scant studio experience will actually keep time with the kick drum on the offbeat by tapping the head and then drawing back and striking it solidly on the downbeat. This subconscious action is the first thing you look for, because you don't want the kick drum foot to be doing anything except kicking the kick drum when it's supposed to.

However, there can also be a technical reason for the sound of a double hit. Sometimes, if the head is old, the beater actually sticks to the head, and when it pulls away it creates what sounds like a second hit. One way to solve this is to put on a new head, because the problem results from a dimple, or indentation, which actually grabs the beater head. As an emergency measure, if it's, say, three A.M. and you don't *have* a new head, you can stick another black dot over the dimple. Sometimes a piece of gaffer's tape will do the job, although that really should be a last resort because some of the glue from the tape can end up on the beater.

DRUM KIT ADJUSTMENTS

If you're getting a lot of kick drum leakage into the snare, or vice versa, it may be due to the height of the snare drum. Some drummers have gotten used to playing their snare drums very low, and it may be that the distance between the snare and the kick drum is not sufficient to isolate the one from the other in a recording studio. If the level of leakage is unacceptable, you may have to ask the drummer to raise his stool and raise the height of the snare drum.

The same applies to the hi-hat. Some drummers have the hi-hat set at almost the same level as the snare drum, which creates a lot of leakage between the two. So, although the drummer may have to make some adjustments, you should move the hi-hat up and out, because the more distant the hi-hat is from the snare, the better the recording will be.

Drummers also have the habit of setting the ride cymbals so that they're practically sitting right on top of the floor tom. So the minute they go to the ride cymbal, you hear it flooding into the floor tom mike. The solution, of course, is to move the ride cymbal, and that may mean the drummer will have to adjust to playing cymbals in the studio that are higher or farther back than he's used to.

ACOUSTICALLY ISOLATING THE DRUMS

If your studio space is limited to your living room, and your recording equipment is only adequate, then chances are

you're going to have to record other instruments at the same time you record the drums. This presents a problem we have not yet discussed: leakage from one instrument into the microphone being used on another.

If I'm in the studio, I prefer to record "live," with as many musicians as possible. But that's in a studio environment, where I can isolate each instrument. If I can't isolate the instruments, then I might choose to record the drums and bass first and add the other elements later.

If your recording capabilities are limited, and you want to include the bass with the drums, you can either mike the base amp or record the bass direct to tape. The latter can be done by using a direct box or, if necessary, plugging directly into your mixer. You're certain to avoid leakage this way, and if the drums have a tendency to rattle when certain bass notes are hit, you get a cleaner drum track. If you must use the bass amp, get it as far away from the drums as possible and mike the amp up close.

If you're restricted to the use of one large-to-average-size room and can't separate instruments by placing some in different rooms (which you can sometimes do in a house), the only choice you have is to limit, rather than eliminate, leakage.

What you should do, then, is place the instruments carefully around the room in such a way that the microphones are not pointed at other instruments. In other words, if you have a guitar playing with the drums, what you'd want to do is put the guitar amp as far across the room as you can get it, aim it so that it faces the drums directly, and place the guitar mike in front of it. That way the *back* of the guitar mike is facing the drum kit, and the *back* of the drum mikes are facing the amp. Then, if have the guitarist play at a mid-to-low volume and mike the amp up very close, you'll reduce leakage to all mikes concerned

This is the most efficient way to reduce leakage without using baffles and blankets, but if you can get your hands on similar sound-absorbent materials, you'll find them very useful. For instance, I use lots of packing blankets over and around the drum kit, whether the kit is recorded solo or not. That's because I want to keep as much of the kick drum as possible out of the room and out of the other mikes. If the kick starts reflecting off the walls, and the other mikes pick it up, the kick drum will sound more distant—and you want that rhythm pulse right up in your face if it is to be effective.

The thing to remember in any of these cases is that the more ambience you include, the more depth the sound of the instrument will have, and the farther away it will seem to be. So if you want an instrument to appear to be right in front of you, close mike or damp it, and don't use echo.

NOTE—*For more information on baffles and on isolating instruments in separate rooms, see chapter 17, "Studio Acoustics."*

MELODIC DRUMS

It seems amazing that a drummer can go through many years of lessons and never be taught the simple art of tuning a drum, but it happens. And then the drummer wonders, once he gets into the studio, why his drums don't sound very good.

The drums don't sound good because they aren't tuned in a way that enhances the natural quality of the drum. It's an easy thing to learn, but it's something that is simply overlooked.

The fact is, many drummers are unaware of the musical quality of their instrument. They don't realize that they can play melodies as well as rhythmic patterns on their tom-toms. However, with this awareness, the drummer adds a new dimension to his drumming. For instance, Jer Speiser's tom fill to start Men At Work's "Down Under" is prime example of melodic thinking.

In the studio, tuning is critical. If the drums are tuned the key of the song, they will resonate with the overtones all the other instruments, and that makes for a bigger dru sound. It also makes the drums fit more neatly into the trac

Almost without exception, every drummer I've ev worked with initially tuned his drums to the pitch th sounded best with that particular drum—not to the pitch th sounded best with the *whole* kit in the context of the son That's only natural, because in a live situation you can't tu each tom differently for each song. But in the studio y can, and it really does make a big difference.

DRUM EQ REMINDERS

Suggestions

Read "Triangular Miking EQ" and "Close Miking EQ" in chapter.

Be careful with low-end boosts in the overheads.

Read Tape Tip #13, chapter 6.

General EQ

The Overheads

To hear more room REVERBERATIONS:
boost 10K–15K

To hear more CYMBAL:
boost 9K–10K

To hear more CRACK from the heads:
boost 5K–7K

To hear more of the SNARE WIRES:
boost 5K–7K

To hear more BANG from the drums:
boost 1K

To hear more drum RESONANCE:
boost 250 Hz–300 Hz

To hear more BODY from the drums:
boost 100 Hz *or* 250 Hz

Triangular Miking

The Kick Drum:

BOOSTS
3K
6K–8K—lightly
100 Hz

The Overheads:

BOOSTS
10K–12K
5K–7K or 1K–3K

CUT
200 Hz

Close Miking

The Overheads:

BOOSTS
10K–12K
3K–5K

CUT
200 Hz

Room Mikes:

BOOST
15K

CUT
200 Hz

Tom-Toms:

BOOSTS
7K–8K
3K—for "transparent" toms

or

500 Hz—for "opaque" toms
100 Hz

Snare Drum:

BOOSTS
10K—lightly
5K
1K—2K
100 Hz

Kick Drum:

BOOSTS
3K
6K–8K—lightly
100 Hz

Hi-Hat (varies according to cymbals):

BOOSTS
7K–10K
5K
500 Hz

RECORDING DIAGRAMS
DRUMS
Triangular Miking Technique

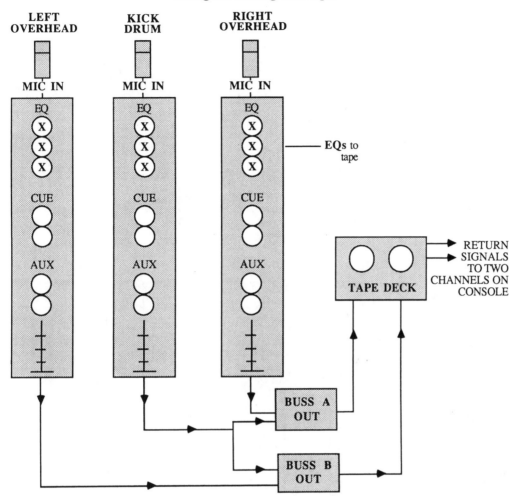

Procedure:

1. Tune and adjust drums until they sound right for the song. Damp heads that ring too much, get rid of squeaks, and so on.

2. Mike drums with three mikes: one inside the kick drum and two on overhead booms that are positioned slightly in front, and to either side, of the kit.

3. Bring the right overhead mike into the low-impedance input on a console channel, and assign the channel to Buss A.

4. Bring the left overhead mike into the low-impedance input on a separate console channel, and assign the channel to Buss B.

5. Bring the kick drum mike into the low-impedance input on a console channel, and assign the channel to Buss A and Buss B, remembering that any channel assigned to two sides of a stereo pair will image in the middle (as long as both sides have the same output level).

6. Patch Busses A and B to separate input channels on the tape recorder.

7. Patch the outputs of the two tape recorder channels to separate console input channels.

8. Pan the left overhead return channel left and the other right. Give each the same trim and volume levels, and use them as the monitor source for establishing the desired stereo image.

9. Bring up the level on the bass drum, and set EQ.

10. Bring up the level on the two overheads, and adjust both the position of the mike relative to the drums and the EQ, remembering to EQ for the best overall blend of drums.

11. Fine-tune the levels and record a test track. Make any necessary adjustments, then go for a take.

DRUMS
Close Miking
with Limited Console Space

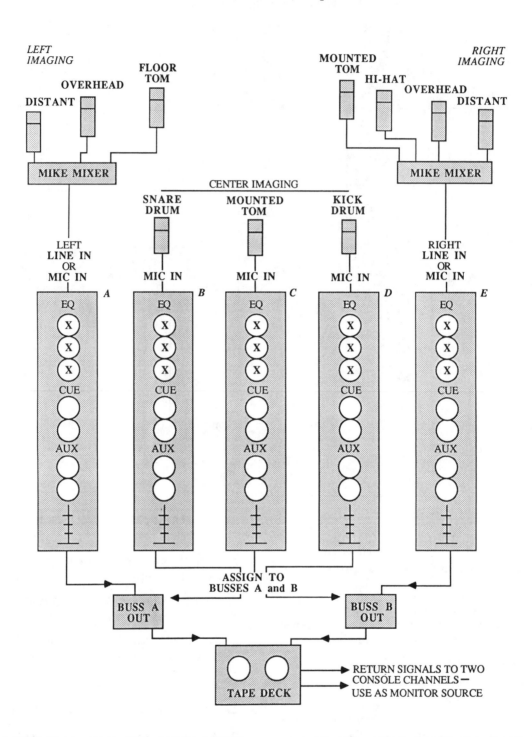

To have optimum control over the recording, drums should be close miked in the same "one-mike/one-input-channel" configuration we show in the triangular miking example. However, this may require that you have eleven separate console channels available, which is not always possible. In such cases, the following example can provide an acceptable alternative. However, one very important factor to keep in mind is that in the following configuration, the mikes that are sent through the mixers must be EQed as a group rather than individually, and with a "problem" drum kit you may not achieve the best possible results.

Procedure:

1. Tune and adjust drums according to needs of the song. Damp heads that ring too much, get rid of squeaks, and so on.

2. Mike each drum (and hi-hat) individually, adding two overhead mikes and two distant room mikes as described in text.

3. Plug the left-distant mike, the left-overhead mike, and the floor tom mike into a mike mixer.

4. Patch the mike mixer into console Channel A, and assign Channel A to Buss A. (Use the Mic In if the mike mixer operates at low impedance.)

5. Plug the right-distant mike, the right-overhead mike, the hi-hat mike, and the right-mounted-tom mike into a second mike mixer.

6. Patch this mike mixer into console Channel E, and assign Channel E to Buss B. (Use the Mic In if the mike mixer operates at low impedance.)

7. Bring the snare drum mike into the low-impedance input on console Channel B, and assign the channel to Busses A and B, remembering that any channel assigned to two sides of a stereo pair will image in the center.

8. Bring the kick drum mike into the low-impedance input on console Channel C, and assign the channel to Busses A and B.

9. Bring the left-mounted-tom mike into the low-impedance input on console Channel D, and assign the channel to Busses A and B.

10. Patch the outputs of Busses A and B to separate inputs on the tape recorder.

11. Patch the outputs of the two tape recorder channels to separate input channels on the console.

12. Pan the return channel that corresponds to the left side of the drum kit left, and pan the other right. Then give each return channel the same trim level and volume level and use them as the monitor source for establishing the desired stereo image.

13. Bring up the level on the kick drum and set EQ.

14. Bring up the level on the snare drum and set EQ.

15. Bring up the level on the two mike mixers and set the relative volume levels for each mike.

16. EQ each mike mixer output separately. EQing for the overall blend of instruments, as with the overheads in the triangular miking example.

17. Go back to the kick drum and begin fine-tuning the mix.

18. Make a test recording, and after listening to the playback, make any necessary adjustments and go for a take.

Chapter 10

Electronic Drum Machines and Drum Kits

Like most of today's working songwriters, I use a digital electronic drum machine on all of my song demos. The units are convenient, reliable, and programmable, and if you add the right effects, they're capable of generating some great sounds. They're also a great help when I sit down to write because, unlike the days when I'd needed to get a band together just to hear what a new song of mine really sounded like, I can get a feel for the arrangement right from the very beginning.

THE ADVANTAGES OF USING A DRUM MACHINE

Many musicians are under the impression that drum machines are just a poor substitute for acoustic drums, while in fact they offer the songwriter several advantages. For one thing, the performance of the drum machine remains consistent time after time after time, so in effect the drum track requires only one take. Plus, drum machines don't require microphones. So if you're on a tight budget, a drum machine can be cost-effective, because even though a new unit can run anywhere from $700 to $6,000, you can easily spend that much on all the microphones required to properly mike a drum kit.

Yet one of the biggest advantages drum machines offer is that they can be used to trigger and synchronize all sorts of programmable gear. This gives the songwriter an enormous amount of flexibility when both writing and recording his material. During the writing stage, a songwriter can use this feature to lock the drum machine up with a synthesizer, so that as he creates various instrumental parts on the synth, they can be mixed in automatically with other elements of the song. And during the recording stage, this feature effectively increases the number of tracks he has available to

record on, since both drums and synths can be placed on tape together during the final mix (see "MIDI/SMPTE/'Sync Pulse' Recording Techniques").

There are, of course, certain disadvantages to using a drum machine, and many of those are discussed throughout this chapter. But if you're a songwriter, and you want to be able to record song demos at home, a drum machine is one piece of gear you should not be without.

GENERAL RECORDING TECHNIQUES

The first digital, programmable drum machine was developed by Roger Linn. His unit, which was appropriately called the "Linn Drum Machine," enabled you to create patterns drum by drum, so that, much like a real drummer, you could include tom fills and cymbal crashes. You could also alter the sound of the drums by inserting one of many interchangeable microchip programs into the machine. These chips were programmed to mimic anything from strange tom effects to hand claps to something as simple as a different drum kit sound.

Then, as other manufacturers began developing their own drum machines, a second format emerged that utilized digital "sampling" technology. These machines, such as EM-U Systems' SP-12 (Figure 10a), enabled you to make a digital recording of any audible sound, be it a car horn or the snare drum sound from a record, and the machine would then include that sound in the kit. So, for instance, if you wanted to use the clang of a trash can lid in place of a hi-hat, you'd simply record the sound of the lid and insert it in place of the hi-hat.

However, no matter how sophisticated digital drum machines have become over the years, you can't just plug them in and expect them to sound like the real thing. They in fact

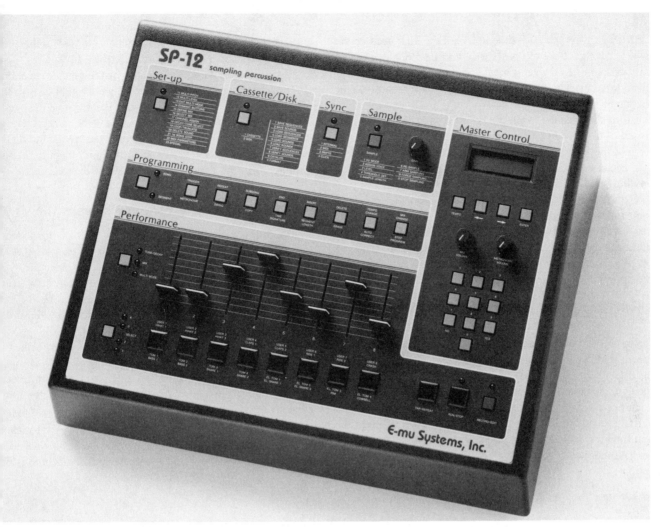

Figure 10a: E-MU Systems SP-12 (*Courtesy of E-MU Systems, Inc.*)

require the same sort of care and attention you would give to acoustic drums, yet because they're *not* acoustic, they also need to be given certain special considerations.

EQ Techniques

With a drum machine, as with a drum kit, in order to have as much control over the total drum sound as possible, you should try to EQ each drum and/or set of cymbals individually. This, of course, is not a problem if your drum machine has direct-outs for each of the sounds and your console has enough input channels. However, not all drum units have individual direct-outs, and there may be times when there aren't enough channels available on your console. So in these cases you need to come up with a compromise.

There are a number of alternatives available to you, depending upon your situation, but basically what you want to try to do is group together sounds with similar EQ needs. For example, you may want to group all the cymbals together and send them into one console channel and group all the toms together on another, as we've illustrated in a recording diagram at the end of the chapter. This way you

can give all the cymbals and toms the same basic EQ treatment they would have received individually, but instead of using five or six console channels for these sounds, you've used two.

The one compromise you *don't* want to make is with respect to the snare drum and kick drum. These sounds require special attention, as they are two very key components of the rhythm track. So if at all possible, they should be given their own individual channels and their own specific EQ treatment. This is also necessary if you intend to add any effects to either of the drum sounds, because, as we mentioned last chapter, you don't use the same type of effects on the kick drum that you use on the snare.

"Real Drum Sound" EQ

It's difficult to be specific about EQing a drum machine, because so many different sounds are available. But as a general rule, if you want the drums to sound like real drums, and your drum machine offers these sounds, you can apply the EQ specifications from the last chapter.

However, as you experiment with EQ, you need to be aware that the effect of boosting certain frequencies may be very different from what it would be if you were using a real drum kit. For example, in order to get a good snare sound, the manufacturer must include a certain amount of white noise in the signal ("white noise" is a signal that is comprised of all audible frequencies). So you must be careful not to give the snare too much of a boost in frequencies above 5K, because you'll be adding as much noise to the signal as anything else.

Cymbals also contain elements of white noise, and since their range of frequency response reaches from 5K *up*, they can be even trickier to EQ. So if they're really sounding dull, you can try giving them a boost in the 8K–10K range, but it's futile to add EQ above 10K, because that's usually the upper limit of a drum machine's frequency response.

"Electronic Drum Sound" EQ

If you want to use the drum machine to produce a percussive effect you wouldn't find in a traditional drum kit, you'll need to refer to the more general guidelines we included in the last chapter. So if the effect is derived from the basic sound of a drum, the bang area will still be found at about 1K, the "tip of the stick" sound will still be up around 8K, and the kick drum will still be present at around 100 Hz. If, on the other hand, you're trying to EQ something like a hand

clap or a totally nontraditional sound, you can follow the guidelines set down in Tape Tip #22 (page 149).

In any case, molding the tonality of the percussive sound is going to take quite a bit of experimentation both with the sounds you have available and with the EQ treatment you can give those sounds. But you must at all times keep in mind that the drums and bass are going to provide the rhythmic foundation for the demo, and you don't want to let any gimmicks destroy the drum track's effectiveness.

Combining a Blend of Percussive Sounds

If your drum machine has the capability of changing sounds such as we discussed earlier in the case of the Emulator or the Linn, there may come a time when, for example, you want to use one drum sound for the toms and a different drum sound for the rest of the kit. This is done by first recording a "sync code" track and then recording the drum parts in a series of overdubs.

This technique in itself does not present any particular EQ problems. However, if, in the overdubs, you start adding a lot of cowbells and whistles and such, you need to realize that the more complex you make the drum track, the more concerned you need to be about the blend of percussive sounds you create. This blend is as important as any other blend of instruments in the mix (such as the blend of guitar and keyboards), and to establish the proper balance, you

Figure 10b: Yamaha RX-5 (*Courtesy of Valley Arts Guitar*)

ay have to treat the drums as a group of instruments rather
an as one specific instrument.

The mixdown chapter contains some general guidelines
or balancing combinations of instruments, and it should
elp you decide such issues as which registers you want to
mphasize and which percussive elements you should fea-
ure and which should be used for background coloration.
owever, the more complex you make the track, the more
replanning you're going to have to do. So before you
egin, make sure you have a clear picture in your mind of
ow you want each of the various elements to fit.

And above all, *don't get carried away*! As you go along,
y to decide what constitutes clutter and what constitutes
nythmic pulse, because it's that clear, strong pulse that's
oing to drive the track, not a bunch of little doodads.

itting the Drum Track into the Mix

f you try applying traditional EQ settings to a particular
ercussion sound, be it "realistic" or "electronic," and the
rums just don't seem to fit in properly with the rest of the
nstruments, you'll need to adjust your approach and treat
ne drums as you would any other key musical component of
ne mix. So if you want the drums (particularly the snare) to
e dominant in the track, you should try boosting EQ in the
K range, as this will accentuate the fundamental tones that
re produced by the instrument. Basically, however, this is
ist a matter of trial and error.

Vhen to EQ

Jnless you're recording the drums on five or six separate
racks, you'll want to EQ the drum sounds as they're being
ecorded. If you were to wait until a later stage of the pro-
ess, any EQ treatment you apply is going to affect *all* of the
rack instead of just the one or two elements it's intended
or. Besides, the frequency response of drum machines is
uch that EQ will have a very limited effect on decay times
nd transients, so make sure you've got the drums sounding
he way you want them to *before* they go to tape. One way
o do this is to check the sound against the drum sounds on
our favorite albums as you go.

VHEN TO RECORD THE DRUM TRACK

s we told you in chapter 7, when you're using acoustic
rums on a song, the drum track and the bass track should
e the first tracks you record, because the musicians need
hese rhythm tracks for reference during overdubs. However,
vhen you're using programmable electronic drums, you
ave the option of either recording them as one of the initial
racks, which is the way we've been treating them thus far,
r adding them to the recording during mixdown, which is
ccomplished by using a prerecorded "sync" track that keeps
he drums synchronized with the other instruments through-
ut the entire recording process (see next section).

The reason you might want to record the drums directly
onto the master is that it gives you more control over the
way each of the drum sounds fits into the mix. In a professional studio, the drums are each given a separate track, and
they're added to the final mix as individual elements, rather
than as a premixed, 2-track stereo package. So the producer
can adjust the level of the snare drum and kick drum, for
example, without affecting the cymbals. Thus, each individual drum and cymbal can be made a balanced component of
the mix.

You have the same degree of control in a 4-track studio if
you give each drum sound its own console input channel,
then record the drum track during the final mix. By doing
so, you are able to mix each drum sound individually, just as
if each had been recorded on a separate track, which gives
you more flexibility than if you had recorded the drums as
one of the initial tracks and guessed at the blend of cymbals
and drums you'd need during mixdown.

So, basically, although you can record the drums at either
time and still get a good drum sound in the final mix, if the
drum track is fairly complex, or if you're not good at judg-
ing the blend you'll need for the final mix, it would be advisable for you to record them last.

MIDI/SMPTE/"SYNC PULSE"
RECORDING TECHNIQUES

One of the most useful features of today's drum machines is
their ability to generate a "sync code," which is an electronic
signal that can be used to trigger and synchronize a group of
programmable instruments. What makes this feature so important in terms of this chapter is that if you record the sync
code on tape, it can be used to trigger the drum machine
itself. And, as a result, you are able to build a song around a
drum pattern without having to record the drum sounds until
mixdown, which, as we just told you, is the ideal time to
record an electronic drum track.

Over the years, a number of different sync code formats
have been developed. Most of the early machines use what
was called a "sync pulse," and while virtually all of the new
units use MIDI, the next generation of drum machines will
begin offering SMPTE *along with* MIDI so that the units can
be synchronized to videotape. (SMPTE is used to synchronize audio recordings with video recordings, as well as to
establish audio-to-audio and video-to-video linkups. MIDI,
on the other hand, can be used only for interaudio synchronization.)

Although it's beyond the scope of this book to provide a
specific, technological explanation of how each of these systems works, when the code is being used to trigger the drum
machine off tape, the process is basically the same in all
cases. You begin by creating the drum program you want to
use for the song, and then you record the sync code onto an
empty track on the tape recorder. This recorded signal is

then used to trigger the machine during playback, so that you can build the song around the drum track, even though the drum sounds haven't yet been recorded. Then, when you reach the mixdown stage, you use the code to trigger the machine one last time so that you can record the drums, which are still perfectly in sync with the existing tracks, directly onto the final 2-track mix.

Recording the Code Track

There's nothing complicated about generating the code, because the machine does that automatically. So after you've created the drum pattern for the song, you simply send the sync output of the drum machine into an input channel on the console (so that you can control the level to tape), and you record the sync code onto an open track by playing the song program through *once* from beginning to end.

It's best to record the code on one of the "edge" tracks (Tracks 1 or 4 on a 4-track, Tracks 1 or 8 on an 8-track, and so on). This will limit any problems you might encounter with crosstalk, as you'll only have *one* adjacent track to worry about.

You see, if the signal from the code track leaks onto the adjacent track, the sync code will be audible in the background noise of anything that is eventually recorded on that track. And if the signal from that adjacent track is so strong that it leaks onto the code track, the drum machine will start trying to read *it* as part of the sync code, with disastrous results. To insure the integrity of both the code track and the

adjacent track, record the sync code at the levels we sugge in the next paragraph and avoid recording any strong signa —particularly transients—on the adjacent track.

In order to make sure that this "code track" comes o clear and sharp, you should record it *without* noise redu tion, and you should set the level so that the VU mete register at between −5 dB and −7 dB. This level will re main constant throughout the entire song, as the signal tha is being placed on tape is not the actual sound of the drum (in fact, it sounds more like a speeded-up recording of pack of screaming turkeys). However, if you also have th drum machine's channel outputs plugged into the conso during this process (see "Overdub Procedures"), you will b able to monitor the drum sounds as the code track is bein recorded.

Triggering the Machine

Once you've recorded the code track, you patch the outp of the track into the sync input of the drum machine, so tha when you place the tape deck in the playback mode, th code track will start and stop the drum unit automaticall and keep the tempo constant. Thus, the unit will always pla the same pattern at the same tempo, and the drums will b perfectly synchronized with anything you record on the othe tracks.

The best way to test the accuracy of the synchronization to record the kick drum once, using the code track to trigge the drum machine, then check it against the kick drum signa

---

There are a great many brand-name drum machines on the market, and each offers a unique set of features. Some give you the ability to alter the decay of the drums and cymbals and to alter the pitch of each drum; others do not. Some offer individual direct-out circuits for each drum sound, while others offer only a simple, 2-channel stereo output. Some allow you to completely change the sound of the kit by inserting interchangeable microchip programs, others offer the option of using either presets or acoustic sounds from the environment—and still others offer little or no control over the sound at all.

This means that before you buy a drum machine, you need to consider how you're going to use it and how much you can afford, because you don't want to invest in a unit that won't meet your needs. For example, if you want to use the unit for song demos, but you don't have a lot of money, then you should buy a unit that offers you the best *sound* quality for your money rather than the one that has the most features. But if you do have the money for a quality piece of gear, then you need to focus on the features you want the machine to have—two of the most important being pitch control and individual direct-out jacks for each drum.

If, however, you expect to run synthesizers and program-

mable effects off your unit, then the feature at the top of that list should be the sync code function. As we mentioned, there are three different time codes currently in use—"sync pulse," MIDI, and SMPTE—and none of the three is compatible with the others. So if you want to be able to lock your existing gear up with the drum machine, you either need to buy a unit that utilizes the same type of code, or you need to buy a sync code conversion unit that provides an interface for the two conflicting code formats.

If your existing gear uses MIDI, chances are good that *any* new machine you buy will be compatible, because MIDI is presently being used by virtually every manufacturer of programmable gear. And as SMPTE makes its way into the market, it's being made available *along with* MIDI, so you shouldn't worry that any MIDI-compatible device will become obsolete in a few years. On the other hand, if you plan to synchronize your recordings to video, then you may *need* a unit that generates SMPTE code, since SMPTE is used to lock up audio gear to video.

Basically, if you're just starting to assemble your studio, or if you only have one other piece of programmable gear, you should talk with your music dealer or with friends who have drum machines and research the advantages and disadvantages of the different code systems. This will give you a better point of reference should you need to find a compromise between your needs and your budget.

enerated when the code track triggers the drum machine uring playback. Since the drum machine was triggered by he code track in both cases, the kick drums should be perectly synchronized. Thus, if you solo the two signals and an them both to the center, you should hear phase cancelaon (a loss of bass response).

If the signals are *not* synchronized, make sure that (1) the ode track was placed in the tape deck's "sync" mode during oth run-throughs, and (2) the kick drum track was in the sync" mode during playback.

Overdub Procedures

Once you've determined that the drum machine will be in ync with anything you might add to the tape, you can begin verdubbing instruments onto the surrounding tracks.

Conceptually, these overdubs are performed just as they would be had you actually recorded the drum track, the diference being that instead of monitoring the playback of an xisting track, you use the code to trigger the drum machine o that it plays "live," and you use that as your monitor ource. Therefore, there are only a few special consideraions, over and above those included in chapters 6 and 7, hat you need to give to these overdubs.

For example, if your tape recorder utilizes Sel-Sync, then whenever you record an overdub, the code track must be placed in the tape deck's "sync" mode. Otherwise, when you each the mixdown stage and you place the deck in "repro" ather than "sync," the drum track will, in fact, be *out of* ync with the rest of the recording.

In addition, as with any other overdub situation, the perormers need to be able to monitor the drums. So you need o patch the channel outputs from the drum machine into nput channels on the console, and you'll want to add some everb or effect. However, since you also need to use the nput channels for various other overdub functions (tape reurns, effect returns, and so on), you may not want to use he individual direct-out channels on the drum machine. You an, however, generate an adequate monitor mix using the tereo "group" outputs on the drum unit, which will only equire the use of two input channels.

Bounce Techniques

In order to perform a bounce using this method, you have to bounce *internally*. If you were to bounce to an external machine, you would have no way of syncing the bounce tracks with the already printed code, which should always remain in a first-generation state. Therefore, if you're unfamiliar with the process of bouncing tracks, you should follow the procedures in chapters 6 and 7 regarding internal bounce techniques.

Mixdowns

If you intend to record the drum track during the final mix, then at this point you need to alter whatever monitor config-

uration you were using for overdubs and set the console and the tape deck up for the mix. This means (1) switching the tape deck from the "sync" mode to the "repro" mode, so that all of the tracks (including the code track) are being read off the playback heads, and (2) giving each of the existing tracks (excluding the code track) its own console input channel. Then, any channels that are left can be used as inputs for the drum machine.

If the drum machine provides direct-outs for each drum sound, and if there is an input channel available for each direct-out signal, then as you set up the mix you can use the pan controls on the console to create a stereo image for the drums that is similar to the imaging we talked about in the last chapter. However, if there aren't enough input channels available, or your drum machine doesn't offer direct-outs, you can plug the stereo outputs from the unit into individual console channels and use the drum machine's internal pan mechanism to create the stereo image.

Then all you need to do is set the mix levels and record the 2-track master.

TRICKS AND TIPS

No matter how "wonderful" electronic drum machines are, they're still machines, and they do have their limitations. However, there are lots of little tricks you can use to enhance the sound of the drum track.

Cymbals

If you don't like the sound of the cymbals on your machine, you might consider using real cymbals and either adding them to the drum track as it's being recorded, or dubbing them in. This can be a particularly useful technique to apply to any cymbal crashes you may want in the track, as the crash cymbal sounds available on most drum machines have very poor decay. However, this technique can be applied to any and all cymbal sounds, and if you have enough confidence in your time-keeping abilities, or if you are, in fact, a competent drummer, you may want to go so far as to provide the ride cymbal or hi-hat portion of the program.

By adding such "live" percussive elements to the track, you also help disguise the fact that you're using a drum machine—which, by its very nature, keeps perfect time. So if you have the track space, you may find it advantageous to "fill in" for the drum machine whenever something like a tambourine or cowbell is required. Ultimately, however, your final decision on such matters should be based on which sounds better, the drum machine's tambourine or yours.

Effects

If you're not going after a "traditional" drum sound, there are many interesting effects you can use to alter certain elements in the track. For example, you can use a phase shifter on the hi-hat or on the crash cymbals in order to create a swirling effect. Or you can use a chorus on the snare drum, which will give it a fatter sound. In fact, your choices in this regard are limited only to your imagination and to the effect gear you have available.

To enhance the "traditional" drum kit sound, you should look to those effects mentioned in last chapter's "Mixdown Effects" and in Tape Tip #23.

"ELECTRONIC" DRUM KITS

Electronic drums are playing an increasingly greater role in modern music. An "electronic" drum kit is a set of non-acoustic drums, such as the Pearl "DRUM-X" or the Simmons "SDS" kits (Figure 10c), which utilizes touch-sensitive pads instead of drumheads. When these pads are struck by the drumstick, they trigger a "brain" in which the drum sounds are stored and sampled, and the brain, in turn, generates a signal that is sent directly into the console.

Advantages

Unlike drum machines, these electronic kits need to be played by a drummer, so they have the advantage of providing the feel of real drums. Plus, the pads on the truly good kits are quite sensitive, so the drummer can alter the dynamics of the sound by striking them harder or softer.

These drum kits also offer many of the advantages of a drum machine. For example, each of the drums has its own direct-out, so it can be treated independently. And since these kits are electronic, you'll only need to mike the cymbals, which, again, can save you money. Also, they can be monitored over headphones during the takes, so the only sound your neighbors will hear is the occasional cymbal crash. Last, although you can alter the pitch of each drum once you've tuned the kit, you don't have to worry that one of the drums will drop in pitch.

Disadvantages

The one disadvantage to using an electronic drum kit is that there is no ambience to the sound. So in order to get a big "room" sound, you really need to know what you're doing with echoes, because the only way to create ambience is to generate it electronically.

EQ Techniques

The problems you face EQing an electronic drum kit are similar to those you face with a drum machine. They offer a wide variety of sounds and effects, and many of them give you the ability to change the decay time, the tonality, and the pitch of the drum. So when you set about establishing the EQ levels, the only thing you can do is refer back to the general guidelines we laid out for you in the last chapter and use them as a basis for experimentation.

Figure 10c: "Drum-X"—Model "DRX-1" (*Courtesy of Pearl International, Inc.*)

RECORDING DIAGRAMS

ELECTRONIC DRUM MACHINES
Recording the Code Track

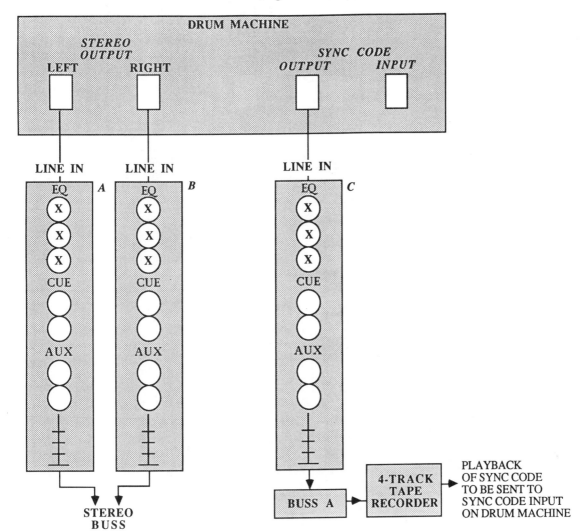

Note: Your drum machine may use a sync code system that requires outboard gear not included in these general procedures (as with MIDI converters or sequencers), so refer to your owner's manual before you begin.

Procedure:

1. Patch the stereo output from the drum machine into the line-level inputs of console Channels A and B.

2. Assign console Channels A and B to the stereo buss and use this as your monitor source.

3. Create the entire drum pattern for the song.

4. Patch the sync code output from the drum machine into console Channel C.

5. Assign console Channel C to Buss A.

6. Patch the output of Buss A into the input of tape recorder Channel 4 (Track 4).

7. Place the tape recorder in "record" and play the drum program through from beginning to end. Do not use noise reduction on the track, and set the levels so that the VU meters on the "code track" register at between -5 dB and -7 dB.

8. Patch the output of Track 4 into the sync code input of the drum machine (this signal does not usually need to be sent through the console).

9. Place Track 4 in the "sync" mode (if your tape deck uses Sel-Sync).

10. Place the tape recorder in playback and make sure that the code track triggers the drum machine.

ELECTRONIC DRUM MACHINES
Monitoring the Drum Track Off Sync
Code During Overdubs

To have optimum control over the drum track, each drum sound should be given its own console input channel. However, should you be short on channels during overdubs, the following example can provide an acceptable alternative. In this case, the individual drum sounds are split between direct-outs (snare and kick) and the "group" stereo output (cymbals and toms). So to get a good mix of elements, you will need to remove the kick and snare from the machine internal stereo mix (or drastically lower their volumes in the mix) and internally pan the toms to the left channel and the cymbals to the right channel.

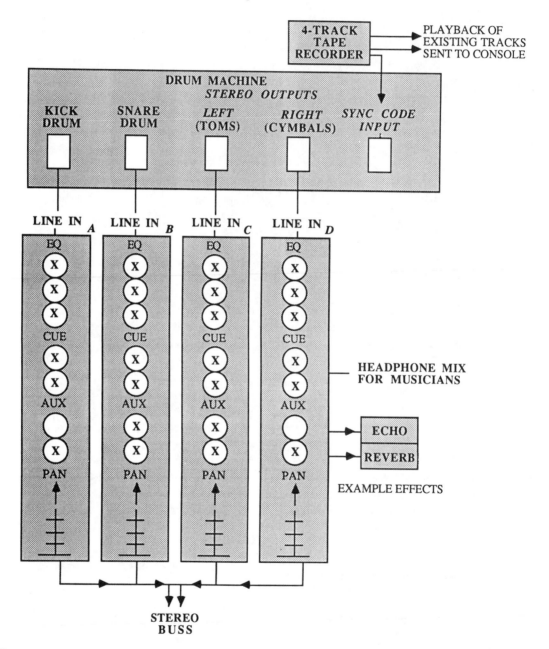

Procedure:

1. Patch the output of the code track (Track 4) on the tape recorder into the sync code input on the drum machine (this signal does not usually need to be sent through the console).

2. Patch the kick drum's direct-out channel into console Channel A.

3. Patch the snare drum's direct-out channel into console Channel B.

4. Patch the drum machine's stereo outputs into console Channels C and D respectively.

5. Assign all four console channels to the stereo buss so that you can monitor the signal, then center the pan controls on each channel.

6. Place the code track in the tape recorder's "sync" mode (if your tape deck uses Sel-Sync).

7. Place the tape deck in playback so that the code track triggers the drum pattern.

8. Adjust the internal levels and pans on the drum machine so that all the toms are sent to the left "stereo" output and all the cymbals are sent to the right "stereo" output.

9. Eliminate the kick drum and snare drum from the drum machine's stereo mix. On some machines, you may only be able to reduce the levels of these drums relative to the levels of the toms and cymbals. On others, the kick and snare can be eliminated entirely.

10. Add any desired effects to the drum sounds and add EQ.

11. Remix the sounds for the desired blend.

12. Patch the output from any existing instrumental tracks into individual console channels and assign those channels to the stereo buss.

13. Place the tape recorder in playback and blend these tracks in with the drum mix.

14. Set the record levels for the tracks to be overdubbed and generate the headphone mix for the musicians.

ELECTRONIC DRUM MACHINES
Recording the Drums as an Initial Track

This example offers one alternative for recording the drums as an initial track when you do not have enough console channels available to treat each sound individually. In this case, you will need to make the same internal adjust-ments on the drum machine that we outlined in the previou[s] recording diagram on overdubs. *Note:* A recording diagra[m] detailing the procedures for recording drums during the fin[al] mix is included in chapter 16, "Mixdown Techniques."

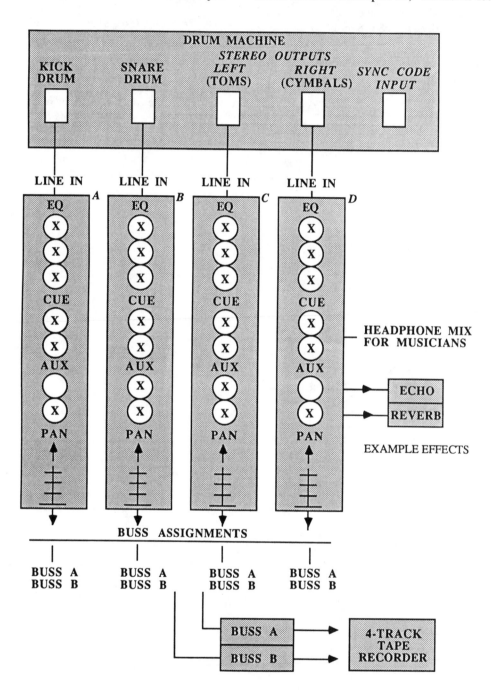

Note: If you *are* able to give each drum sound its own console channel, *all* channels should be assigned to Buss A and Buss B, and the pan controls on the console should be used to create the desired stereo image.

Procedure:

1. Create the drum pattern for the song.

2. Patch the output of the code track (Track 4) on th[e]

tape recorder into the sync code input on the drum machine.

3. Patch the kick drum's direct-out channel into console Channel A.

4. Patch the snare drum's direct-out channel into console Channel B.

5. Patch the drum machine's stereo outputs into console Channels C and D respectively.

6. Assign all four console channels to both Buss A and Buss B and center the pan controls.

7. Patch Buss A into tape recorder Channel 1 (Track 1).

8. Patch Buss B into tape recorder Channel 2 (Track 2).

9. Adjust the internal levels and pans on the drum machine so that all the toms are sent to the left "stereo" output and all the cymbals are sent to the right "stereo" output.

10. Eliminate the kick drum and snare drum from the drum machine's stereo mix (i.e., "stereo" output). On some machines, you may only be able to reduce the levels of these drums relative to the levels of the toms and cymbals. On others, the kick and snare can be eliminated entirely.

11. Add any desired effects to the drum sounds and add EQ.

12. Make any necessary adjustments in the levels of the mix and record the track.

Chapter 11

How to Record Bass Guitar and Stand-up Bass

The bass guitar track is an extremely important part of any recording, because the bass, along with the drums, provides the foundation upon which the song is built. Therefore, without a strong, effective bass track, it is very difficult to produce a strong, effective recording.

The bass combines with the kick drum to produce the heartbeat of the track—the former providing the melodic and rhythmic punch that propels the song, the latter providing the pulse. In fact, the two are so closely tied that in contemporary music the kick drum is often treated as the rhythmic component of the bass, and the bass as the melodic component of the kick drum.

During the fifties and sixties, you could barely distinguish the bass from the other instruments, as it usually appeared as some low-end rumble that was used to provide a tonal foundation for the song. Today, however, the bass plays a much more important role, and more attention needs to be given to providing it with the clarity and substance it requires in order to do its job effectively.

ELECTRIC BASS GUITARS

Before discussing the variety of techniques used in recording a bass guitar track, it is necessary to discuss various aspects of the electric bass that will affect the sound of the track in any and all cases.

Intonation

Although it's important for any string instrument to have accurate intonation, for a bass guitar it is critical. A bass that isn't properly intonated will cause some notes to "speak" louder than others, so that while the first few notes of a passage may register at the proper recording level, the next few may be louder, or boomier, and the following few may be considerably quieter. This occurs because the harmonic series of each string becomes unbalanced, and as a result some frequencies cancel each other out while others reinforce the tone and create a boost in level.

If you're having problems with the intonation, you should take the bass in to a local guitar shop and have the neck and bridge adjusted. Also have the pickups looked at, since they can create a similar response problem. If you don't, you're going to have to use excessive amounts of compression on the track just to maintain a consistent level.

Strings

It is not necessary to place a new set of strings on a bass guitar every time you sit down to record. But the age of a bass string *will* affect the sound of the instrument, as bassist Erik Scott points out in this chapter's "Reel World."

There are three different types of bass strings—round-wound, flat-wound, and half-round-wound—and each has its own unique sound.

Round-wound strings have bright tonal characteristics and sound somewhat like the lower strings on a piano. This makes them ideal for hard-driving songs that require brilliance and clarity. However, round-wound strings are strung with round strands of wire, and the surface is very bumpy, which makes them prone to fret buzz and finger noise.

On the other hand, flat-wound strings are strung with thin strips of wire. This makes them smooth to the touch and very quiet. And although they do not have as much clarity as the round-wounds, they produce a softer, more mellow tone, which can be very useful for jazz tunes and gentle, slow-moving ballads. In fact, if you play flat-wound strings with your fingers instead of a pick, you can get a sound approximating that of a stand-up bass.

Half-round-wound strings are useful for getting a wide variety of sounds. They offer a brilliance approaching that of the round-wounds, so they can be suitable for rock 'n' roll as well as R&B, and they often prove more complementary to rock ballads than the flat-wounds. Plus, the ridges on the half-rounds are somewhat flattened out, so they will not create as much noise as the round-wound strings.

Pickups

When the electric bass was first introduced to rock music, the guitars were all equipped with standard pickups. Today, however, bass guitars are also available with "active" pickups, which are driven by internal preamp circuitry and generate a much stronger signal.

The difference in signal strength between the active and passive pickups can have an effect upon the approach you take in recording the bass track. For instance, an active pickup will boost the signal as much as 8 dB higher than the signal you'd get from a standard, passive pickup. This means that if you're recording the guitar direct into the console, or sending it through an effects pedal, you have to be acutely aware of distortion. Plus, because the signal is so much hotter, if you're not careful, you could conceivably overload and blow out the console channel's input transformer. So before you begin to record the bass, be sure to find out what type of pickups you're dealing with.

One easy way to determine whether the pickups are active or passive is to find out if they use batteries. Active pickups use them to drive the preamp circuits within the guitar, while passive pickups do not. If you are using active pickups, have the guitarist replace the batteries before each session so that you don't start losing level or generating internal distortion halfway through the track.

The tonal difference between active and passive pickups is relatively minor. Active pickups will generate a bit more high-end response simply because they preamp the signal, but more important, this added signal strength often makes active pickups more suitable for direct-in recording. Ultimately, however, if you have a choice between these two pickups, the only way to determine which is better for your particular recording is to try each of them out—running them both direct in and amplified—and choose the one that sounds best to you.

Playing Techniques

As with the standard guitar, the musical ability of the bass player can make or break the overall sound of the recording. Of particular importance is the guitarist's "touch control," because any combination of erratic intonation and erratic technique will create a situation that makes the bass a very difficult instrument to record.

The better the player's touch, and the better the intonation, the less compression you'll need to apply to the signal in order to even out the level. This is important, because if you overcompress, you end up boosting some of the muddy, low-end frequencies that are normally deemphasized. And this will mar the clarity of the track.

If the player is having difficulty maintaining a consistent level, and the problem is not intonation, the only solution is proper practice. Erik Scott, who has played with acts as diverse as Alice Cooper and Kim Carnes, is in my opinion one of the premier bass players in rock music today. He has practiced with a VU meter and a metronome for years, varying the speeds at which he plays a passage, while making sure that the level on the VU meter, no matter how fast he's playing and no matter what note he's playing, remains at roughly +2 dB.

Another thing to make the bass player aware of is the recording relationship between the kick drum and the bass. Since the bass is often the melodic component of the kick drum, the guitarist should try to control the duration of the notes so that they complement the pulse of the kick. So when you're recording a bass player—or just recording the bass track yourself—it's a good idea to run through the song a few times, then listen to the track together to see if the notes are ringing too long, in which case they need to be muted, or if they're not ringing long enough.

BASS GUITAR RECORDING TECHNIQUES

There are four basic methods you can use to record a bass guitar track: close mike the amplifier; record direct in; combine close mike with direct in; or combine two direct signals, one of which carries a flanger, chorus, or similar effect.

Recording an Amplified Signal

Recording an amplified bass guitar is similar to recording a standard amplified guitar (chapter 12), and in each case the first matter you want to concern yourself with is the state of the speaker cabinet.

The bass signal can be very powerful, and the vibrations it produces may cause the cabinet to buzz or rattle. So the first order of the day will be to check the cabinet for unwanted noise and tighten any loose screws. Once this is done, you'll want to listen closely to each speaker and mike the one that is in the best shape.

Unlike the dual miking technique used on standard guitars, you never want to use a room mike when you record the bass. The distant mike is used primarily to pick up room echoes, which gives added depth to the signal. However, when you're recording the bass, you want to give it as much presence as possible, and that is accomplished by eliminating such echoes.

In order to damp the signal properly, you'll want to raise the speaker cabinet one or two feet off the floor and sur-

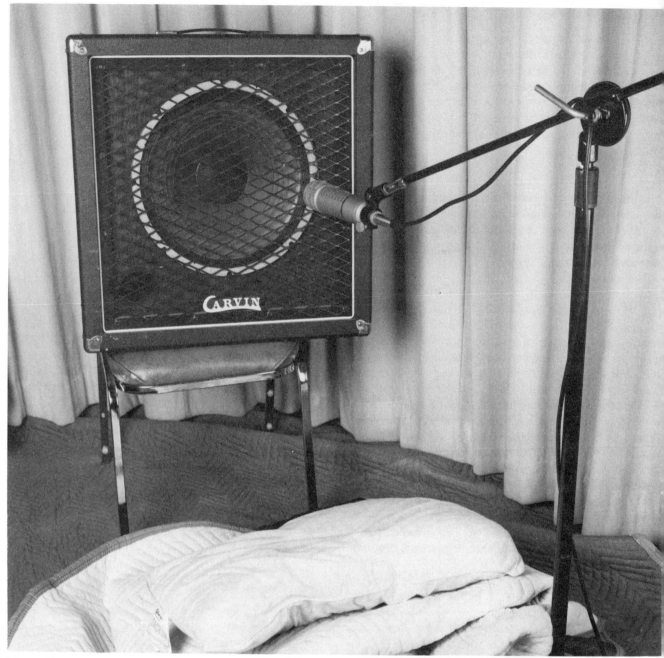

Figure 11a: When recording the bass through an amp, raise the bass up off the floor and use a close-mike configuration. For additional acoustic damping, build a tent around the amp using blankets or baffles. (*Courtesy of Laura Marenzi*)

round it with baffles. You may even want to build a little tent around the cabinet (Figure 11a), leaving about three feet of space in front of the speakers and facing them toward a soft surface. In either case, you should pad the floor directly in front of the amp, so that the signal does not reflect back up into the mike.

When you mike a bass amp, you'll get the best results by close miking the speaker cabinet and playing at relatively low volumes. As we discussed in chapter 2, by recording at high volumes, you'll simply distort the microphone. When you keep the volume at a reasonable level, any possible loss

in the tonal quality of the amp will be offset by the broader frequency response the mike will exhibit.

To close mike the amp, you place the microphone about three inches out from the cabinet, facing the speaker, but at an angle of about thirty degrees off center. At this angle, the mike should be pointing at a spot about halfway between the outer edge of the speaker and the central cone.

Although any number of different mikes are suitable for bass recordings, my favorite studio mike, which is actually not often used for bass, is an Electro-Voice RE-20. A Sennheiser 421 will also prove quite satisfactory.

Recording Direct In

Direct-in recording is the technique of plugging the guitar directly into the console and forgoing all use of the bass amplifier.

If you're using a guitar fitted with passive pickups, the technique is performed exactly the same as with a standard electric guitar. As we discuss in the next chapter, all you have to do is send the guitar into a direct box, if you have one, and send that signal into the low-impedance input on the console. If you don't have a direct box available, the bass can be plugged directly into the console using the ¼-inch high-impedance inputs. And if the guitar produces enough level for your desk, the quality of the signal should not suffer.

At the same time, if you are using a guitar with active pickups, you may want to eliminate the use of a direct box altogether, since the preamp circuitry within the guitar should produce enough level for any console.

Direct-In Combinations

By itself, direct-in recording is not always the most desirable technique to use. Often the bass will sound flat and lifeless. If this is the case, you may want to combine the direct-in signal with that of the close-miked amplifier or even combine it with a second direct-in signal, to which you can add flanger or chorus effects.

Each of these alternatives is widely used in professional studios, and both are easily accomplished at home. In the case of combining amplified and direct-in signals, all you have to do is split the signal coming from the guitar, run one line to the amplifier, which has been miked and sent into one channel on the console, and run the second line directly into a second channel. If you are using a direct box, the split can be made there, and the low-impedance output of the box can be sent to the console. If you're not using a direct box, you may have to use a Y-cord (see "Recording Diagrams" at the end of the chapter).

Depending upon the number of tracks you have available, you can either combine the two signals at the point of the console and place them on the same track, or you can record the signals on separate tracks and wait until later to decide how you want to mix them together.

When you do finally mix the two, the process is one that can only be done by ear. There's no way to tell you how much of each signal to add, except to say that you should balance the sound in respect to what you find pleasing. As a guide, you should use the direct-in signal to provide the deep, fundamental tone of the instrument, while the amplifier signal should be used to provide clarity. As we'll see in the EQ section, this can serve to give the track some life.

A similar relationship exists when you combine the direct-in signal with a signal that has been treated with chorus or flanging. The effect signal is used to add brightness to the track and to provide the melodic component of the overall sound, while the direct-in signal is used to provide the fundamental tone or body.

There is, however, a slight difference in approach when you combine the direct-in signal with a second direct signal, but only in terms of how you send the signal into the console. In this case, you treat the affected signal as if it were an additional bass instrument, meaning that after you split the signal at the direct box and send the low-impedance line into the console, you send the second line (high impedance) to the pedal effect and from there to a second direct box, so that the effect signal can be converted to low impedance before you bring it into the channel. If your console runs at a +4 dB level, using direct boxes in this way will help to cut down on any signal noise the effect might generate (see "Recording Diagrams" at the end of the chapter).

However, if you're not using a direct box, and you need to cut down on pedal effect noise, you do have a second alternative. Just run two direct lines into separate channels on the console and use the effects' loop circuitry ("effect send/receive") to add the effect to one of the signals. This circuitry is designed to accept signals with a strength as low as −10 dB, so there's much less noise.

Compression

No matter how hard you try to avoid using compression, you'll probably need to compress the signal to some degree in order to get the uniformity you desire. When doing so, you may want to send the signal through the compressor before it enters the console. However, this usually adds a certain amount of noise to the signal, which can be eliminated if you send the signal into a channel on the console first, then send that signal to the compressor before bringing it back into the console on a second channel (see "Recording Diagrams" at the end of the chapter).

No matter what recording technique you're using, the compression settings remain the same. A compression ratio of 4:1 is normally sufficient, and since you want to use as little compression as possible, you should try to limit the gain reduction to about 3 dB. If the guitarist is very erratic, and the gain reduction has to go above that level, you should still be able to live with the results. But be aware that if you overcompress the signal, there will be an increase in the level of the extremely low frequencies, and that will make the bass sound muddy.

EQ TECHNIQUES

The EQ settings for the bass track are going to vary, depending upon which recording technique you use. If you are recording a single signal, whether from a miked amp or a direct box direct in to the console, you will want it to have as complete a response pattern as possible. So you'll EQ it in a way that balances low-end strength with midrange clarity. However, if you are blending a direct signal with a secondary signal, the direct signal will be EQed to provide the low-end punch, while the secondary signal will be EQed to provide clarity.

The exact treatment you give the bass will also vary based upon the player's technique (each is different) and the sound you're going for. For example, if you want to get a funky R&B sound from the bass, you'll need to emphasize the midrange frequencies. For a Paul McCartney–type throbbing bass sound, you'll need to emphasize the low-end EQ.

The one thing that remains the same in all cases is that as a whole, the bass track should be EQed to provide a strong, fundamental tone center for the song. You must remember that it will carry the lowest pitch you'll hear in the song, which means you will need to boost the low end; yet if you forget about the upper ranges of the signal, you'll lose the definition that allows you to distinguish one note from the next.

If you're using a parametric EQ, you'll want to keep the bandwidths of the boosts relatively narrow. This is especially important when you're EQing your low-end boosts, because you want to be certain to avoid boosting any frequencies in the 200 Hz range. In fact, no matter what type of EQ you're using, if you push a frequency too close to 200 Hz, which is that "proximity effect" range, the track is going to sound dull and muddy.

On the other hand, one of the nice things about recording a bass track is that when you EQ for clarity, you never get much higher than the midrange frequencies. This means that you can place some serious EQ reductions in the frequencies above 8K, because the only part of the signal that's up there is the hiss! So if you're generally having problems with signal noise, you're going to love the clean sound you'll get recording the bass.

Single-Signal EQ

If you're only bringing one bass signal into the console, which would be the case if, for instance, you're simply miking the bass amp or using a single direct line, you want to give that signal as complete a response pattern as possible. It is, after all, the only bass signal being sent to tape.

When you begin EQing the signal, you should start by giving it a low-end boost at about 100 Hz. This will help enhance the lower frequencies, which is important because the bass does include the lowest pitch you'll hear in the recording.

Some engineers might think that 100 Hz is too high a frequency for the low-end boost and instead would boost more in the 40 Hz to 60 Hz range. However, unless you're in a pro studio, with 300 watts' worth of signal blasting from each monitor, low, low-end frequency response does you lit-

tle good. If you include those superlow frequencies in the signal, it can hurt you when you go to make tape copies. Very low frequencies require a great deal of "energy" space on the tape, and that leaves less room for the weaker, higher frequencies. As a result, you get a less-than-optimum response pattern for the overall recording.

Another reason to ignore these low frequencies is the fact that very few home systems can accurately reproduce anything below 60 Hz, and most car stereos only go as low as about 100 Hz. So if you EQ those superlow boosts and set the volume level according to what you're hearing on your gear, the bass may disappear when the tape is played on a system that can't read those low signals. You do, of course, want to give the impression that the bass contains those extremely low frequencies, but you want to do so without having to boost them.

If you try boosting the EQ at 100 Hz, and the instrument just doesn't give you the frequency depth you want, try boosting at 80 Hz instead. Still, this is a bit risky, because you have to remember that the point at which you place the boost is actually the center point for the band of frequencies being boosted. So if you give it a boost at 80 Hz, you're also boosting frequencies that are lower down the line, and as we just mentioned, that can get you into trouble.

The next boost you will want to make should be placed at the 800 Hz level. This will bring out the harmonics of the low notes, which will make it easier for the listener to detect pitch. You see, it's very difficult for the human ear to determine low-frequency pitch, so by enhancing the response range of the harmonics, you'll bring out the frequencies in which pitch can be detected. For instance, when the bass plays an "A" two octaves below middle C (A-110), it sets off harmonics in the higher octaves. One of these harmonics is A-880, and by boosting the signal at 800 Hz, you're boosting the response level of that harmonic.

The midrange and high-end boosts should be placed at 3K and 5K respectively. This will help bring out the rhythmic qualities you want the bass to have, as you'll be able to hear more attack when the pick (or the finger) plucks the string. And if you're letting the notes ring, this will increase the amount of high end you will hear during the decay.

EQing Combined Signals

When more than one bass signal is being recorded, the direct-in signal should be treated as the fundamental bass signal—the one that will provide the tonal center of the song and will contain the lowest pitch. The secondary signal is then used to enhance the first by providing upper-end clarity.

Since the direct signal is the dominant signal, it should be EQed first. This is done by placing boosts at 100 Hz, 800 Hz, 3K, and 5K, as we discussed in the previous section. However, since in this case there will be more than one signal, you should hold back on the amount of boost you

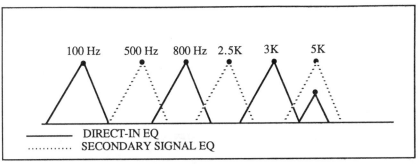

Figure 11b: EQ treatment for bass guitar when using a direct-in signal and a secondary signal.

give to 3K and 5K, because you're going to use the secondary signal to enhance those upper frequencies.

When you begin EQing the secondary signal, you want to make sure that you place the boosts in different locations. That way you don't get an overabundance of response in any one frequency range. So instead of giving the secondary signal a boost at 100 Hz, you'll want to try a boost closer to 500 Hz (Figure 11b). Instead of an 800 Hz boost, you'll want to give it a significant push closer to 2.5K. And while the direct signal is given only the slightest nudge at 5K, here the secondary signal should be given special attention.

When using a flanger or chorus in conjunction with the direct-in signal, you may want to skip the 100 Hz and 500 Hz boosts altogether, opting instead to give the signal a push somewhere near 800 Hz. You want to steer clear of a 100 Hz boost because as the pedal effect moves in and out of phase, it has a particularly telling effect on the phase relationships of the slow-moving waves in the lower frequencies. So if you boost EQ at 100 Hz, you give more attention to the effect the phasing has on those low frequencies, and as a result the bass will begin to sound muddy.

Again, the most important thing to keep in mind as you're EQing this secondary signal is that its whole purpose is to provide clarity and brightness to the overall sound of the track.

RECORDING A STAND-UP BASS

The use of a stand-up bass for rock 'n' roll was something of a lost art until the emergence of the Stray Cats in the early eighties. Of course, it's not as if the instrument is exactly making a big comeback, but since you may wish to perform acoustically oriented music that makes use of a double bass, we thought we'd add a few words about the techniques you might want to apply.

Before the electric bass came along, the stand-up bass was the only bass available. It's fretless, so you don't have to worry as much about the strings buzzing, and it's played by plucking the strings with your fingers, so you don't have to concern yourself with the sound of a pick. However, because this somewhat limits the strength of the attack you

---

TAPE TIP #26
Out of Phase, Out of Mind

Whenever you're combining two signals that are coming from the same instrument simultaneously, you stand a chance of running into problems with phase cancelation. With the bass, this can cause certain notes to appear muted, so that the instrument seems to disappear in the middle of a passage. Or it can simply cause the whole track to fade into the background.

To determine whether or not such fluctuations are, in fact, due to phase cancelation, you should listen to the direct signal alone, paying particular attention to the amount of bottom end the signal contains. Then bring up the level of the secondary signal. If the bottom end begins to disappear, chances are the two signals are out of phase with each other.

This can happen for any number of reasons. If the second-

ary signal is coming from a miked amp, it could be that the mike is wired out of phase. Or it could be that either the cable or the console input is out of phase. In such cases, if your console is equipped with a phase switch, you can just reverse the phase. If you don't have that option, but you're using a patch bay, you can reverse the phase with something called a "phase cord," which is actually an out-of-phase cable. If you use this cord to send the secondary signal into the console, it should bring it back into phase with the direct signal.

So remember to check the phase relationship of the two signals before you begin to record—especially if you're placing them on separate tracks and waiting until later to combine them. After all, there's nothing worse than getting a great performance and then discovering that no matter how much you boost the bottom end, you're completely unable to hear the instrument.

normally hear when the pick strikes a bass string, when you record a stand-up bass, you have to be particularly careful to give the signal as much clarity as possible.

One way to increase the amount of attack you hear is to work with the player on his technique. The harder he plucks the string, the louder the attack will be, and the more likely it is the string will vibrate violently enough to create a bit of string buzz. And in this case, a slight buzz will help provide each note with a sense of high-end separation.

Miking Techniques

When you record a stand-up bass, you want to place it in a room with dead acoustics. You may even want to build a small tent for it, as we described earlier when discussing the miking of a bass amp. If the room has a wood floor that resonates, you will want to pad the surface directly beneath and around the bass in order to avoid having the mike pick up any reflections.

When you close mike the bass, you should place the microphone farther away from the instrument than normal so that you capture the full resonance of its rather large shell. Usually, a distance of twenty to thirty inches is good. However, if you find that you're picking up too much of the resonance and not enough of the individual strings, and all the notes seems to run together, you can try bringing the mike in as close as fourteen inches and pointing it directly at where the player's fingers strike the strings.

As was the case with the miking of a bass amp, you never want to add a distant mike to the configuration, because the last thing you want is to have any room echoes show up in the signal. You want the stand-up bass to have as much presence as an electric bass.

Compression

Compression should be avoided at all cost. However, you may need to use compression if the bass player is at all erratic. If this is the case, the levels of compression you use would be the same as those we outlined for the electric bass.

EQ

The EQ settings for a stand-up bass may vary from instrument to instrument. However, in general, you can use those settings previously discussed in "Single-Signal EQ" as a guide.

For instance, if you're not getting enough clarity from the instrument, you'll want to turn your attention to the 3K–5K range. Or if the instrument sounds boomy, you may need to forget about the 100 Hz boost and try boosting the level in the 500 Hz–800 Hz range.

The stand-up bass is a versatile instrument, however, and it should not take very long to EQ.

THE REEL WORLD
Erik Scott on Studio Bass Techniques

(Erik Scott is a highly respected bass guitarist who has recorded with such acts as Kim Carnes, Alice Cooper, Bill Conti, Jack Douglas [producer], Peter McIan, and Carl Palmer [of Emerson, Lake & Palmer], to name but a few.)

Figure 11c: Erik Scott onstage. (*Courtesy of Eric Scott*)

In the studio, the sound of the bass guitar is most affected by three things: the strings, the pickups, and the player. Yet at home the effect the strings have is too often overlooked.

The type, gauge, and age of a string will make a vast difference in its tonal quality. For instance, there are three types of strings, and each sounds quite different. Round-wounds are the brightest and have the most high end, half-rounds have less brightness, and flat-wounds have even less. Sustain will also vary, though only slightly, with round-wounds having the most and flat-wounds the least. So when picking the type of string to use, make sure the sound fits well with the style and instrumentation of the music.

The gauge of the strings will also make a difference in the tonal quality of the instrument, and they, too, should be chosen carefully. You may want to avoid prepackaged sets so that you can handpick the gauge of each string. For instance, you may want the E and A strings to be a medium-light gauge, while using slightly heavier-gauged high strings. Yet since each instrument and each song is different, you should experiment with the gauges to see which works best.

The age of a string is something that is often oversimplified. Bass strings are not merely "live" or "dead." They go through three distinctly different sonic stages before they finally die and have to be buried. When brand new, they sound very bright and have a great deal of sustain. They also produce a wealth of harmonic overtones, which gives the sound a transparency that keeps it from obscuring other instruments in the track.

This first stage, which lasts for one or two days of regular playing, is followed by a period during which the strings are, according to some bass players, at their best. They still have all the sustain you can use, and though they've lost some of their metallic brittleness, they still have plenty of high end. Plus, the harmonic overtones have calmed down, so you can get more of the *punch* that complements the kick drum. Unfortunately, however, this stage only lasts two or three days, after which the strings lose sustain and brightness and tend to just *thud* along.

Some players can do wonderful things with dead strings, particularly in fat-back R&B, but they make the bass sound too dull for most other applications. One way to bring dead strings back to life is to boil them in water for about three minutes. Then, once you take them out of the pot, you dry them off with a hand towel and carefully blow-dry each of the ends, which should keep them from breaking prematurely. When you put them back on the bass, they'll sound as good as new, although they will go through each stage of aging a bit more rapidly.

As you can see, with so many different variables involved, it's important to keep track of your strings. However, that doesn't mean just being aware of the strings you're using at the time, because if you do enough recording work, you'll have numerous sets of strings around, and each will have been subjected to a slightly different amount of wear.

For example, I might be working a session with strings that are in the second stage of wear, but the producer wants to hear a brighter sound from the instrument. That means putting on a new set of strings. But instead of just throwing the old set, which is still in an ideal condition for certain sounds, into the garbage, I'll label them and put them away, so that the next time a track calls for the punchier sound of slightly used strings, I can just put these strings back on.

Another reason I catalog strings according to age is that it makes it easier to replace a broken string in the middle of a session. For example, if I'm using a three-day-old set of strings, and one of them breaks, I can't just stick on a brand-new string, because there would be a noticeable difference every time I played a note on it. However, by cataloging my strings, I'm usually able to pull out a replacement string that is as old or as new as the rest of the set.

Another useful aspect of studio technique is muting, or "choking," the strings as you play. This can be done either with the heel of the right hand, which allows you to vary the amount of muting you give to each note in the pattern, or with a piece of foam, placed under the strings by the bridge, which mutes each note evenly.

The muting technique you choose should depend upon the style of music being played. For instance, when recording the power-type rock of Alice Cooper, I would choke the strings with the heel of my right hand, while attacking the notes with a fair degree of force. By doing so, I was able to create a punchy rock rhythm while avoiding the sustained rumble of unmuted strings. When recording for Kim Carnes, whose music is more open and less influenced by guitar, a track would occasionally call for the *slight* but even muting produced by placing foam under the strings.

Of course, the other alternative is to play with a wide-open, totally unmuted string sound, which offers an unlimited amount of sustain. You should be careful when applying this technique, however, because the recording will need to have plenty of room for the expanded bottom-end response.

BASS EQ REMINDERS

Suggestions

Use narrow-band boosts

Avoid boosting 200 Hz

See Tape Tip #17, chapter 6

When Recording One Bass Signal

BOOSTS

100 Hz (no lower than 80 Hz)

800 Hz

3K

5K

When Recording Two Bass Signals

Direct-in Signal:

BOOSTS

100 Hz

800 Hz

3K—lightly

5K—lightly

Secondary Signal:

BOOSTS

500 Hz

2.5K–3K

5K—lightly

Secondary Signal (If Treated with an Effect):

BOOSTS

800 Hz

2.5K–3K

5K—lightly

Stand-up Bass

BOOSTS

100 Hz

800 Hz

3K

5K

RECORDING DIAGRAMS

BASS GUITAR
Combining an Amplified Signal and a Direct Line

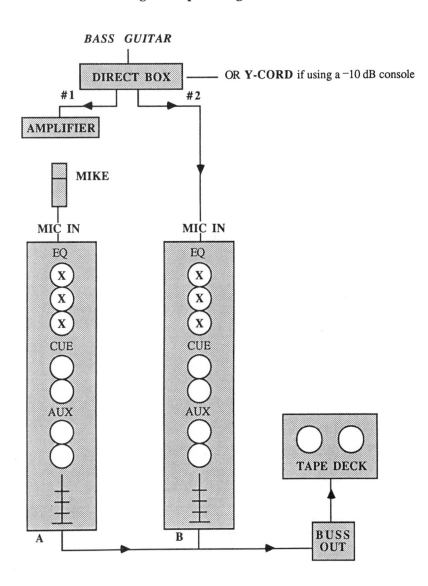

Note: This particular procedure applies when using a console that operates at a +4 dB level. Some home consoles operate at −10 dB, in which case a direct box need not be used to enhance the signal quality.

Procedure:

1. Plug the bass into the high-impedance input of the direct box ("DI").

2. Plug the DI high-impedance output (#1) into the bass amp, and plug the low-impedance output (#2) into the low-impedance input ("Mic In") on console Channel B.

3. Close mike the bass amp and bring the signal into the low-impedance input on console Channel A.

4. Adjust input gain on Channels A and B and solo each in order to set EQ.

5. Assign Channels A and B to the same buss—unless you have enough tracks to record each separately.

6. Blend signal as desired.

BASS GUITAR
Combining a Direct Line and an Effect

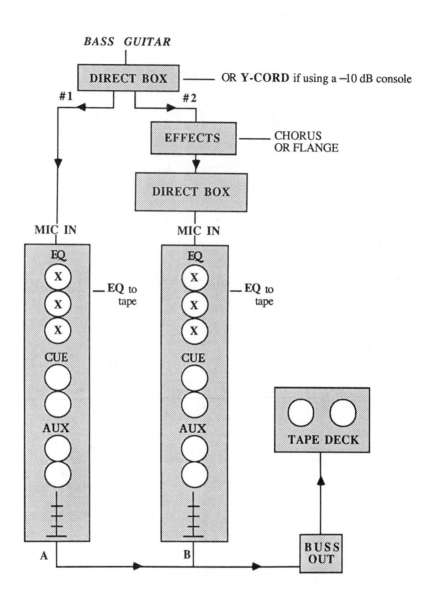

Note: This particular procedure applies when using a console that operates at a +4 dB level. Some home consoles operate at −10 dB, in which case a direct box need not be used to enhance the signal quality.

Procedure:

1. Plug the bass into the high-impedance input of the direct box ("DI").

2. Plug DI low-impedance output (#1) into the low-impedance input ("Mic In") of console Channel A, and plug the high-impedance output (#2) into the effects unit.

3. Plug the output from the effects unit into the high-impedance input of a second direct box.

4. Plug the low-impedance output of this DI into the low-impedance input of console Channel B.

5. Adjust input gain on Channels A and B and solo each in order to set EQ.

6. Assign Channels A and B to the same buss—unless you have enough tracks to record each separately.

7. Blend signal as desired.

BASS GUITAR
Adding Compression to the Signal
(Under Limited Conditions)

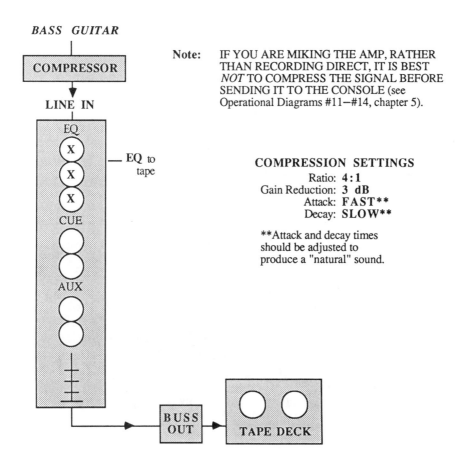

Note: IF YOU ARE MIKING THE AMP, RATHER THAN RECORDING DIRECT, IT IS BEST *NOT* TO COMPRESS THE SIGNAL BEFORE SENDING IT TO THE CONSOLE (see Operational Diagrams #11–#14, chapter 5).

COMPRESSION SETTINGS

Ratio: **4:1**
Gain Reduction: **3 dB**
Attack: **FAST****
Decay: **SLOW****

**Attack and decay times should be adjusted to produce a "natural" sound.

Note: Used in this manner, the compressor should supply enough gain to the bass signal to insure the quality of the sound. However, if the compressor output is *too* hot, you may need to step it down by sending it through a direct box and bringing it in on the low-impedance Mic In of the console channel.

Procedure:

1. Plug the bass into the compressor.

2. Patch the compressor output to the Line In input of a console channel.

3. Assign the channel to the desired buss.

4. Patch the buss output to a tape deck input.

5. Use the gain control of the compressor to bring the signal up to level. Be careful not to overload the input into the console.

6. Adjust all levels and set EQ.

Chapter 12

How to Record Guitars

You can make the argument that were it not for the electric guitar, there would be no rock 'n' roll. The advent of the electric guitar did more to change the face of modern music than any other musical development in recent history.

In the music of the 1940s, tonal "excitement" was provided by the sound of trumpets and saxophones, which gave big bands their high-end punch. Then the electric guitar came along, and suddenly one man could create the excitement that it had taken an entire brass section to provide. Plus, the instrument was easier to control in the studio, and it offered greater tonal flexibility.

THE GUITAR IN RECORDING

In this chapter we're going to deal with three basic recording techniques for guitar: recording an amplified electric guitar, recording a nonamplified electric guitar direct into the mixing console, and recording an acoustic guitar. With very few exceptions, every guitar sound you hear on a record is recorded in one of these three ways.

Experienced guitar players may find some elements of this chapter to be redundant—especially those sections relating to guitar mechanics and the interaction of guitars and amplifiers. However, it's important for nonguitarists to understand how a guitar works before diving into the track.

Guitars are primarily acoustic instruments that produce sound when their strings are plucked or strummed. This causes the strings to vibrate, which, in turn, sets the air around the strings (and the body of the guitar) in motion and creates sound waves.

These principles apply whether the sound waves reach your ears through the aid of an amplifier or directly from the sound hole of a six-string acoustic. When the strings on an acoustic guitar vibrate, for instance, they transfer most of their energy to the shell, or body of the guitar. In a sense this is their "amplifier," because the shells are designed to resonate, which means that they act like a soundboard and increase the strength of the signal that is projected out from the round hole beneath the strings.

On the other hand, electric guitars do not rely on resonating shells for their acoustic projection and tonal enhancement. Instead, they have pickups, which act like little microphones. The pickups turn the sound waves into electronic signals, which are then passed along to the amplifier for boosting.

However, strings do not just produce the sound of a single note when they are struck. As they vibrate, they also produce tones that are sympathetic to the fundamental. These tones are called "harmonics" and "overtones."

Overtones are notes of different pitches that are created along with the fundamental. As the string vibrates, it stretches and contracts at varying rates, creating certain sympathetic tones at frequencies other than the primary. Each note has its own particular series of overtones, and each overtone has its own specific volume relative to the others in the series.

Harmonics are part of an overtone series but specifically represent octaves of the fundamental. For instance, if you were to play an open D string, it would cause octaves of the D, in both higher and lower registers, to ring as the string vibrated.

The reason why overtone series are so important is that they add timbre to the instrument. They "fill out" the sound, as it were, and give it a certain character. This will become important when you begin to mike a guitar, and later when you begin to EQ it, because at both of these points you can very easily lose the overtones and mar the quality of the guitar sound.

The harmonic and overtone structure of guitar acoustics

also makes it necessary for you to consider how the guitar is going to interact with other instrumental elements of the song *before* you begin to record. This is important, because as each instrumental track is added to the song, it has an effect on those already recorded, and, as well, it will be affected by those yet to come. So in order to record a guitar that is going to complement the track, you have to know how you want it to sound and, thus, how you want it to affect the other musical elements.

For instance, you may go for a heavily distorted guitar sound, only to find later that the guitar fills up so much of the musical room on the track that your vocalist, who happens to be singing in the same register, is competing for space and can barely be heard. As a result, you're faced with the choices of either mixing the guitar down or the vocal up, which, in either case, diminishes the effectiveness of both. In this example, if the track had been planned out beforehand, the trouble could have been avoided. So the first thing you need to do when you sit down to record a guitar is figure out how you want it to fit into the track. That, in turn, will dictate the techniques you'll want to use in order to get it to sound that way.

The recording options discussed in this chapter will produce different kinds of guitar sounds. The decision to use one as opposed to another will hinge upon the desired effect you wish the guitar to have on your particular track. The understanding of how to make that decision can only be achieved by becoming a better "listener," as we discussed in chapter 1, and by recognizing that recording is not just the process of getting *a* good sound on tape, but the process of combining a *variety of different* sounds on tape in a way that is complimentary to all of them.

If, however, you're not sure of exactly what kind of guitar sound you need, you may find some answers in the "Guitar Special Effects" section toward the end of this chapter.

RECORDING AN AMPLIFIED ELECTRIC GUITAR

There are a great many variables that enter into the process of recording an amplified electric guitar. There are, of course, such determining factors as the way you mike the amp, the room that the amp is in, and the recording equipment you have available to use. But there are also the myriad variables determined solely by what particular combination of guitar and amplifier you've got.

For this reason, it is impossible to approach the process of recording an amplified guitar as specifically as one would approach, say, cooking a pot roast. So you won't find many set-the-oven-to-350-degrees recipes here. Instead, we'll try to give you a conceptual understanding of how you might use your particular equipment to achieve certain sounds, as well as what combinations of equipment and which techniques are best suited for specific effects.

Nondistorted vs. Distorted

The two very broad and basic choices we'll discuss are clean amplifier sounds and distorted amplifier sounds. There are, of course, any number of gradations that lie between the two extremes, but they depend entirely on the guitarist, the specific equipment being used, the number of outboard devices being used, and the acoustics of the room.

In this case, a "clean amplifier sound" does not refer to a sound that is soft, or bodiless, but one that has as little circuit noise and distortion as possible. In other words, a clean sound is the sound closest to the pure tone the instrument itself produces. The instrument begins to lose that clean quality when it gets amplified, and noise from the amplifier circuitry creeps in.

On the other hand, a "distorted amplifier sound," in an extreme state, would be a sound lacking all tonal characteristics. For example, if you think of sound as being the surface of a lake, and tone as being your reflection on the surface, a clean sound would be represented by the lake when it was perfectly calm and your reflection was crystal-line clear. However, a distorted sound would be represented by the lake as the surface would appear in the middle of a rainstorm, in which case there are so many ripples on the surface that it's impossible to make out any of the characteristics of your reflection.

Now, this illustration is an exaggeration, of course, but it gives you an idea of the difference between a clean and a distorted sound. Again, this is not to say that a clean sound can't be gutsy or full-bodied, or that you can't get a slightly distorted sound to fade back into the track, as you'll see later in the chapter. These two terms refer strictly to the tonal *quality* of sound, not the quantity.

Choosing the Guitar Sound

Again, the first thing you need to do when you sit down to record a guitar is determine where you want the instrument to appear on the track. This will determine the sound you'll want the guitar to have on the recording.

Unfortunately, you may not always have much choice in the matter, as many bands prefer to stay with the sound that they have—in which case you're going to pretty much have to work with (or around) what you've got. However, when you do have the option of choosing the guitar sound, there are four things you need to take into consideration: the player's technique, the type of guitar he's using, the type of amplifier he's using, and the type of song being recorded.

For instance, it's very difficult to produce a nondistorted sound when you're using an amplifier with speakers that have been beaten to the point of terminal fatigue by years of touring and abuse. So if you're going to be recording a demo that requires a clean sound, you'll have to find some way to work around it—such as by going direct into the mixing desk or by doing some prerecording work on the gear and playing in those registers that create the least amount of distortion.

Getting the Sound Right

The process of creating the guitar sound is one of trial and error and should never be approached with the preconception that since you don't have such-and-such equipment, you won't be able to get this or that sound, because it's simply not true. Almost any guitar/amp combination can provide a sound that works in the context of the song. It may take more time fooling around with the settings and the miking, and the sound may not be ideal, but then few ever are.

In fact, I can honestly say that I've never gotten the exact guitar sound I wanted in the beginning, and the same holds true for virtually every producer and engineer in the business. Often, I've gotten something *better* than what I thought I wanted, yet more often I've gotten something that was good, and worked in the context of the song, but wasn't exactly what I'd gone for.

The fact of the matter is, whether you're in a professional studio or recording at home, there's only so much time you can spend going through the process of trial and error in an attempt to create the sound exactly as you perceive it in your mind's eye. So if you're not totally successful in your endeavors to get the "perfect" sound, there's nothing wrong with settling for one that's less than perfect. You definitely won't be the first on your block to have done so.

What Amplifier to Use

The two major components of any amplified guitar sound are, of course, the amplifier and the guitar. Certain guitars tend to perform better in a given situation than others, and the same holds true for amplifiers. For instance, guitars with Humbucker pickups, which are more tightly wound than most other pickups, will send more gain to the amp, so they tend to perform better when you want a lot of sustain or distortion.

In the case of amplifiers, the important thing is how well they perform at high and low volumes. For instance, if you want a relatively clean sound, you want to use an amp that can sound warm and full at relatively low levels. You don't want to have to run the amplifier so loud that the volume level causes the speakers to distort—and if the only way you can get the amp to sound right is by running it at that level, then you won't be able to get a clean sound.

Increased volume levels also have an effect on the various nonelectronic noises that amps are prone to generate—things like buzzes and rattles in the cabinet or the tubes. These are discussed thoroughly in the next section, but they need to be mentioned here, because the louder the amp is run, the more buzzes and rattles you are likely to get. And you don't want noises like that to interfere with the sound.

There are many amplifiers that will perform well at low volumes, but my personal favorite is a Roland JC120. It sounds fairly warm and full at low levels, and it maintains its tonal quality over a relatively wide range of volumes.

If, on the other hand, you're trying to get that take-no-prisoners power guitar sound, you're going to want an amplifier that operates warmly at a louder volume. You may think this is a characteristic shared by all amplifiers, but it's not—many will sound terribly shrill when pushed too hard. And that's one reason why Marshall amps are overwhelmingly preferred by performers who desire really hard guitar sounds. Even at loud volumes, Marshalls still sound warm, and they retain a certain bottom end "grunt," which a lot of amplifiers lose when they're run at high volumes.

Of course, not everyone has access to a Marshall, and even fewer of us live in an area where you can crank one up and not have the neighbors on the warpath. So in that case you might want to try using something like a Fender Princeton amp or a Roland Cube amp, or even a small Studio-15 Marshall. When set so that they run slightly distorted, these can be very effective in terms of creating a heavier rock 'n' roll sound than the size of the amp would indicate.

This brings up the question of whether or not to use built-in preamp circuitry. Many amps, such as the Fender Princeton or the Fender Twin Reverb, have both master volume controls and channel volume controls. This allows the guitarist to electronically simulate speaker distortion by overloading the channel circuitry (cranking it full up), while regulating the overall volume to the speakers with the master control. When run like this, the amp can sound as if the speakers are being terribly overloaded, while in fact the amp is barely louder than your TV set.

Some people try to use this circuit distortion in their home studios in an attempt to give the guitar sound some guts. And if you have the right amp/guitar combination, and you only use a hint of distortion, you may even be successful with it yourself—especially in situations where you're literally going to be burying the guitar under a ton of reverb anyway. But in general, success with this technique is the exception, not the rule, because electronic distortion just doesn't sound the same as speaker distortion.

Another question that is often raised is whether the amplifier should be open-backed or closed-backed. In all honesty, it really doesn't make that much difference. Closed-back amplifiers will project more sound forward, but that isn't necessarily desirable. In fact, in some cases, this gives the amp a tendency to sound a little harsh.

There *are,* however, some important differences between the sound generated by a tube amplifier and the sound you get from a solid-state amp. Tube amplifiers tend to sound warmer, because their range of signal response includes cer-

Figure 12b: Roland JC-120. (*Courtesy of Roland Corporation*)

Figure 12a: Marshall Studio 15. (*Courtesy of Marshall*)

Figure 12c: Fender Twin Reverb II. (*Courtesy of Fender Musical Instruments Corporation*)

tain low-end frequencies that solid-state amplifiers, for whatever reason, are unable to generate. There are all sorts of theories as to *why* this is—one being that in tube amps, the tubes themselves provide a low level of distortion at all times, whereas the solid-state amplifiers, because they pass signal in a more efficient way, do not. But the bottom line is that the "tube" sound is preferred by guitarists who play hard, driving rock 'n' roll because it gives their guitar sound substance at louder volumes.

Finally, there is the amplifier's speaker size to consider. In general, for most applications, a 12-inch speaker or a 10-inch speaker are the most versatile. Fifteen-inch speakers, which some lead guitarists add on when they're playing live, tend to produce too much bottom end to be suitable in a studio environment. The 12-inch speakers have a little more bottom end than 10-inch speakers, but the amount of bottom end is at least manageable.

Amplifier Noise and Rattle

One of the biggest problems with amplifiers is that they tend to vibrate right along with the speaker cones. So when you get around to bringing the amp up to level, you'll more than likely have to deal with a number of buzzes, squeaks, and rattles that result when the cabinet starts to vibrate.

You probably won't begin to hear the noises until you've miked the amp. Theoretically, if the cabinet sounds good live, it should sound good through the monitors or on tape. But when you're in the same room with the amplifier, the volume of the guitar overshadows any rattles that might be generated, and anyway, you will probably be listening for the tonal sound that is being created, not the buzzes.

In fact, many times you may not even hear the noise until the third or fourth run-through of the passage. Or you'll get everything set up just right, and the guitarist will be halfway through the song and everything's sounding great, when suddenly he hits a chord and you hear something that sounds like a snare drum coming from the speaker.

These problems can be minimized if you get into the habit of taking good care of your equipment.

What Guitar to Use

There are many styles of guitar available, and each has a different tonal quality. There are hollow-body electrics like an Ovation electric-acoustic, semihollow-body instruments like the Gibson 335, and solid-body models like the Fender Stratocaster. Each style varies from manufacturer to manufacturer.

As you would expect, the tonal differences between the three basic styles relate directly to the body of the guitar. A hollow body, for instance, produces a semiacoustic guitar sound—in fact, some hollow-bodies are just acoustic guitars with built-in pickups. On the other hand, semihollow-body guitars have quite definitely what you would think of as an "electric guitar" sound, except that they'll give you slightly fatter sound than you'd get from a solid-body instrument, which has more "edge."

The type of guitar you'll want to use on a particular song is strictly a question of the type of guitarist you're working with, what his preferences are, and what kind of sound you're going for on the track.

Gibson and Fender are the two major manufacturers of "classic" electric guitars, and you'll find the majority of rock guitarists using instruments modeled after their basic design or sounds. However, there are many components companies that sell replacement pickups for Fenders and Gibsons that will change the guitar's performance, and there are custom manufacturers, such as Schecter, who literally allow you to create your own instrument.

The point is, there is no clear-cut answer to exactly which guitar to use in a given situation. Guitar sounds vary from make to make, model to model, and even model year! So when you're considering what type of guitar to use, just as when you're choosing an amplifier, try whatever guitars are available and use the one that creates the sound that goes best with what you're trying to achieve as a final result.

For example, if you're recording a very melodic guitar part, and you need to have it cut through the track (be heard above the other instruments), you would want to use a guitar that has a thinner sound than one you would use if the guitar were appearing on its own. Again, when making your guitar choice, you *must* take into consideration how you want the instrument to appear on the track. This at least gives you some parameters within which to work.

And remember, you can alter the sound of the guitar by using a different gauge of strings, by changing the volume and tone of the amp, by changing the volume and tone of the guitar, by changing the room the guitar is in and the way it is miked, and by adding effects. But if you don't have a clear idea of where you're headed, you can commit to something on tape that you may later have to fight.

Room Acoustics

When an instrument produces sound by vibrating the air around it, the environment in which the sound is produced becomes an important component of that sound. So the acoustical conditions of the room in which you record will have a great deal of effect on the sound of the instrument.

In the case of an amplified guitar, room acoustics become very important, because the amount of ambience (room echoes) you allow the microphone to pick up during the recording will determine how close or how distant the guitar will sound on tape.

The amount of ambience you have available in a given room is determined by the size of the room and the texture of the walls and floor. You hear ambience as echoes and reverb, which are created when sound waves reflect of

Figure 12d: Fender's Elite Telecaster and Elite Stratocaster. (*Courtesy of Fender Musical Instruments Corporation*)

Figure 12e: A custom-made guitar from Schecter. (*Courtesy of Schecter Corporation*)

acoustically nonabsorbent surfaces. So the harder the room's floor, ceiling, and walls, the more prominent the ambience. As well, the larger the room is, the longer it will take the sound waves to travel to and from the reflective surfaces, so the delay time of the echoes will be longer, and, psycho-acoustically, the environment in which the instrument is playing will seem larger on tape.

Of course, as you'll see, there are instances when you definitely do not want the sound of the room to be a part of the overall sound of the guitar. For example, if you're trying to get a clean amplified sound, you won't want to include a lot of ambience in the signal because it can cloud the clarity. In those instances you would want to place your amplifier in a room filled with soft, absorbent material that "deadens" the sound by keeping the sound waves from reflecting.

The amount of ambience in the signal is also determined by the way you choose to mike the amp, which is something we'll get to in a little while. However, without the proper room acoustics, you have nothing to work with when you reach that point.

Clean Guitar Ambience

The first acoustical environment we'll look at is the one you'll want to use when going for a relatively clean, ampli-fied electric guitar sound—like what you might hear on a record by Dire Straits or Men At Work.

In the case of Men At Work, the guitar sound was created by running the amplifier at a relatively low volume in a relatively dead space. To accomplish this, we surrounded the amplifiers with baffles, which are made of soft material, and miked the amps up close. In this way, most of the sound from the amp was absorbed before it had a chance to reach the walls or ceiling.

When you're going for this kind of sound at home, you may find that you don't need baffles—that is, if you can find a room, like a bedroom, perhaps, that is packed with soft surfaces and furniture. However, if you can't find a room that's dead enough, you can construct your own baf-fles out of blankets, foam, or just a heap of pillows (see chapter 17, "Studio Acoustics").

Power Guitar and "Live" Guitar Ambience

If you're going for the sound of a power guitar, like you might find in a heavy metal band like Mötley Crüe, or for the feel of a "live" guitar, a rockabilly sound such as the Stray Cats used, you will want to include a lot of ambience in the signal.

In this case, you're going to want to set the amp up in a room that has a lot of hard surfaces so that the sound waves can bounce back and forth off the walls and ceiling. One of the best rooms in the house for this sort of effect is the bathroom, where there's literally nothing that absorbs sound waves but toilet paper.

However, if your bathroom is exceptionally small, you might try using the basement or the garage—especially if either of these rooms has brick walls or hardwood paneling. These areas are larger, which extends the delay time of the echoes and gives the ambience more of a live quality.

If you're using a hallway or a small room in order to get that "live" effect, you need to test the acoustics to see if they are really suitable for your needs. To do this, you should stand in the middle of the space you're thinking about using and clap your hands. If, when you do this, you hear a sharp slap or hollow ringing, chances are the acoustics are going to make the guitar sound brittle.

You want to find a space that produces a clear reflection or a distinct echo. When this is not the case, and the room is too small, the sheer volume of the amplifier is going to send the sound waves bouncing around the space at such a high rate that, instead of a deep echo, they create an irritating "ping."

AMPLIFIER MIKING TECHNIQUES

There are dozens of ways to mike a guitar amplifier, but each is a variation of the basic techniques of close miking and room miking. These are the two principle forms of mike placement, and each produces a different result, as we will see. However, before we begin to discuss where to put the mikes, a few words need to be said about how mikes work and the effect that volume has on their efficiency.

Microphone Distortion

Microphones "hear" differently from the human ear, an they respond better to certain frequencies. However, on thing microphones and ears do have in common is that nei ther responds well to very loud volumes.

Microphones work off a similar principle as ears: the have a receiving device of one kind or another that vibrate in response to sound waves. These waves travel through th air, and when they strike this device they set it in motion This motion is then transformed into an electronic signal which can be sent to an amplifier. In the case of our ears this signal is sent off to the brain.

What the mike capsule is really responding to when it i set in motion is the pressure created by the air molecules a they're pushed along by the sound waves—and if you don' understand what is meant by "pressure," just put your han in front of a bass speaker when it's in use and feel the breez blowing between your fingers.

In fact, when you're talking about microphone distortion it's actually helpful to think of the sound wave output of speaker as "wind." You see, a microphone can only take s much sound pressure (volume) before it distorts. What hap pens is that the surface of the mike's "eardrum" is hit b such a gust of pressure that, like the sail of a ship when it' filled with air, it becomes so taut that for all intents an purposes it's rigid. Since in this condition its ability to re spond to any subtle vibrations is diminished, the signal i sends out along the wires is a severely distorted image of th sound.

Therefore, if you're looking for clarity and sparkle from the guitar, you're not going to get it by running the amplifie flat out if you have a microphone that can't take the pres sure. The mike is going to distort, and as a result you'll en up with a low midrange distortion that is anything bu pleasant.

The Guitarist Factor

When you're faced with using equipment that is not top o the line, the guitarist's playing technique becomes just tha

---

TAPE TIP #27
Where You Can Stick Your Amp

Whether you're recording a guitar at home or in a professional studio, you'll get the best results if you isolate the amplifier by placing it in a different room from that of the console.

Many people who record at home simply set the amp up in the control room area and monitor the signal over a set of headphones. There are a number of disadvantages to this. The biggest is that unless the acoustics of the room are suitable to the guitar sound you're trying to achieve (see "Room Acoustics"), you are going to be hindering the track. Plus,

having the amp in the same room makes it virtually impossible to tell what the guitar part will sound like on tape, because some of the amp sound in the room is going to leak into your headphones.

The best thing to do is to find a room or a hallway with suitable acoustics and set the amp up in there. Then run your mikes back to the console and create the guitar sound from there. If you're working alone, this may mean running back and forth to adjust volume and tone controls, but in the end you'll be glad you expended that little extra energy, because you're going to have much more control over the sound of the recording.

much more important. Any peculiarities of his play that have the effect of muddying the sound, creating excess finger noise on the strings, or producing inconsistencies in level from one note to the next, will be made more obvious on tape and will lessen the quality of the track.

Some players believe that "more is more," meaning that the harder, the louder, and the more frantically they play, the better it sounds. But in fact, when it comes down to recording a guitar, even a heavy metal guitar, exactly the opposite is true: *less* is very definitely more.

"Controlled playing" should be the cornerstone of every guitarist's studio technique. Not soft playing, not hesitant playing, but authoritative, controlled playing.

There's a real misconception about power guitar techniques. You don't have to pound a guitar to get power out of it. A power chord does not sound powerful because the strings are struck hard, but because the player strikes them in such a way as to make them resonate powerfully.

A lot of guitar players I've worked with in the studio feel that if they don't "wind up" like Pete Townshend, they're not playing a power chord properly. Their technique may look wonderful onstage, but in the recording studio the result is a blast of noise, roughly in the same key the rest of the band is playing in.

When you thrash the strings like that, the pick passes across them so quickly that the overtones and the harmonics literally don't have a chance to be heard. They interact at such rapid rates that they wash together, and you lose all the definition of the individual strings. What you end up with is a blast of noise.

Sometimes that's great, but usually what we think of as power chords—chords that sustain in the background or add punch to powerful passages in the chorus—are performed with controlled strokes, with a lot of care and detail being given to voicing (chord position). They are not, as you might think, played with a mallet.

Close-Miking Techniques

Close miking can be used alone or in conjunction with one or more distant mikes. By itself, close miking is used when you want to capture only the sound of the amplifier, and you want very little of the room ambience to leak into the mike.

In order to help isolate the sound and prevent the sound waves from bouncing around the room, you'll want to surround the amp with an environment of soft materials, such as baffles. You'll also want to cut down any reflections you might get off the floor by raising the amp up two or three feet and placing some foam down in front of it.

The first thing you'll need to do when you place your microphone is to find the one speaker in the cabinet that sounds the cleanest, shows the least amount of fatigue, and has the fewest buzzes and rattles. Whether it's a four-speaker or a two-speaker cabinet, if the speaker that you choose is on the bottom, turn it over so that you stay as far away from floor reflections as possible. If you can't turn the cabinet over, at least make sure it's a few feet off the floor.

The microphone should be placed six or seven inches out from the amp, aimed at the speaker on an axis about thirty degrees off center—meaning that you first point the microphone at the center of the speaker, then swivel it about three inches in any direction, so that it's pointing roughly at the edge of the speaker. This should approximately give you your thirty-degree swing (Figure 12f).

Figure 12f: To reduce the effect of room ambience, close mike the amplifier and surround it with baffles. (*Courtesy of Laura Marenzi*)

Figure 12g: By using a distant mike i[n] conjunction with the close mike, you ca[n] add room ambience to the signal. (Note tha[t] the diaphragm in the condenser mike at to[p] points out to the front side, so that the mik[e] is directly aimed at the speaker.) (*Courtes[y] of Laura Marenzi*)

The reason you don't want the mike aimed directly at the center of the speaker is that you don't want it to have to confront the signal straight on and risk any potential distortion or an overload of any one frequency. You're trying to get a relatively clean sound with close miking, and you want the amplifier to interact as little as possible with the mike as well as the guitar. All you're trying to do is provide the guitar with a little body and have the microphone capture the sound while creating as little noise as possible.

Close-Mike/Distant-Mike Combination

This is the miking technique used when you're going after a power guitar sound, but it can also be used to give any guitar track the effect of being a live recording. It combines both close and distant miking and adds room ambience to the sound of the track.

In creating a power guitar track, you really have to treat the guitar and amplifier as one instrument. Unlike the way an amplifier is used only to boost the signal during the recording of a clean guitar track, a power guitar amp is used to change the signal through distortion, feedback, and sustain.

Jimi Hendrix was the master at using an amplifier as an instrument. Though the complexion of the power guitar's role has changed since the late sixties, the fact remains that in order to generate feedback and get those massive guitar sounds, you need an acoustically active environment. Over the years, every acoustic technique you can think of has been tried in this respect, including placing amplifiers in elevator shafts, long corridors, and school gymnasiums—and, in one case, miking a stairwell and kicking the amplifier down the stairs.

To set up for a power guitar or "live" track, you must first find a room with suitable acoustics—generally this will be an area, be it a bathroom or a hallway, with acoustically reflective properties. Then you'll want to set up two mikes in the room and run them into the console on *separate channels*.

The first mike should be set up in a close-mike configuration, exactly as described in the previous section, except that in this case there is no need to deaden the acoustics of the room.

The second mike is your distant mike, or "room mike." This is the mike that is used to pick up the acoustics of the room and can only really be positioned by listening to what kind of signal it's picking up. However, in general, you can begin by placing the mike about six feet back from the amplifier (less, of course, if you're in a small room), about one or two feet above the plane of the close mike and aimed directly back at the speakers (Figure 12g).

You'll want to place some foam down on the floor immediately around the microphone, and between the microphone and the amplifier, in order to avoid any problems with clarity. Floor reflections from immediately in front of the microphone often cause either acoustic phase cancelation, which will reduce the signal's low-end response, or a buildup of bass wave forms, which will cloud the signal.

Once you've positioned the microphones, you can then begin to balance the amount of signal from the close mike with that of the room mike. (This is why you put the two mikes in separate channels.) The amount of room ambience you include in the signal, via the distant mike, will depend entirely on the position you want the guitar to have on the track. The more ambience you give the overall signal, the more distant it will appear.

ELECTRIC GUITAR EQ

Setting the EQ levels for your guitar is as important as remembering to plug the mike cables into the desk. Proper EQ will bring out the best frequencies of the guitar and enable you to more easily position it within the track.

Here again, you need to have a good idea of the sound you want the guitar to have, so that by EQing it, you can keep its dominant frequencies from clashing with those of the other instruments.

Effective EQ Ranges

In general, the important frequency ranges of any amplified guitar are the same, whether the overall sound is dirty, distorted, or clean. The bottom end, or the "grunt" of the guitar, is usually around 100 Hz. However, while you're definitely going to want to make sure that the guitar has plenty of bottom end (which gives the guitar warmth), you have to be careful of any boost in this range. That's because a short distance away, at 200 Hz, you run into a frequency that, when present in large amounts, has the effect of throwing a blanket over the sound and destroying all clarity.

The frequencies that comprise the "body" of the guitar sound generally fall between 500 Hz and 600 Hz. However,

the frequency range that gives the most psychoacoustic excitement to the sound lies between 3K and 4K. These are the frequencies that give the guitar its "edge"—but these are also the frequencies that can give *you* a headache, because if you hit them too hard, the result can be piercing.

The 5K to 8K frequency range brings out the sibilants of the strings. These are the same frequencies that regulate the snares on the snare drum, and with distorted guitars a boost here will produce a sort of buzzing sound. For clean-sounding guitars, by boosting the EQ in this range you'll add a little sparkle to the sound, as this is the area that will bring out the sound of the pick striking the strings. However, in either case you need to be careful of how much boost you apply, because when overused, these frequencies can become very unpleasant.

The frequencies at around 10K will bring out the high-frequency clarity you want a clean-sounding guitar to have. These are the frequencies that will help separate the guitar from any other instruments, such as a piano, that might be playing in the same register. You'll bring out the upper-register harmonics and overtones in this area, which will give the guitar a more complete sound.

When you add EQ at 10K for a power guitar that is distorting, you give the sound a bit more "splash." This is the frequency that is used to bring out the sound of crash cymbals, so if your guitar is playing over cymbal crashes that are punctuating the power chords, you might want to accentuate the 10K frequency in order to make sure that the cymbal and guitar blend together well.

Distant-Mike EQ

When EQing the distant mike, whether for a clean, "live" guitar or for a power guitar, the object is to bring out as much clarity of sound as possible. That's because the more clarity there is to the signal, the more ambience you'll be able to distinguish coming from the mike. So to begin with, you're going to want to boost the EQ in the range of 10K and up, because those are the "clarity" frequencies.

Another frequency you're definitely going to want to affect is at 200 Hz. As we previously mentioned, the effect 200 Hz has on the clarity of the signal is devastating, so you're going to want to drop the level at 200 Hz and possibly compensate by giving the frequencies at 100 Hz a slight boost.

Aside from the upper-register and 200 Hz frequencies, the frequencies that you choose to emphasize or reduce will depend upon the fundamental sound of the signal and the effect that room echo has when added to it. In order to determine what really sounds best, you're going to have to experiment with each of the frequency ranges we previously listed and create the sound yourself.

And this brings us back to planning ahead so that you know exactly how you want the instrument to fit in with the others.

ELECTRIC GUITARS RECORDED DIRECT IN

One alternative to miking and recording an amplified guitar is to record the guitar directly onto tape via a mixing console.

There are a number of advantages to recording a guitar this way. For one thing, you avoid any noise problems with the neighbors. But more important, "direct-in" recording eliminates all the variables with respect to room size, amplifier cabinet noise, mike quality, guitar/amp pairings, and all the rest, because it gives you the pure, electronic tone of the instrument and nothing more.

In direct recording, you are, in effect, using your console as an amplifier. Instead of getting the signal from a speaker, via a microphone, the mixing desk gets it directly from the guitar pickups, so the console alone processes the sound that goes onto tape.

However, this recording technique is not without its problems, as the level that a normal guitar pickup produces quite low—usually somewhere between −10 dB and −2 dB, depending upon the instrument. And many mixing consoles operate at +4 dB. This means that if yours is one these desks, the level of the guitar into the console is going to be relatively low, and you'll have to crank up the level the input channel. This, in turn, can create an unacceptable amount of signal noise.

Of course, if your mixer happens to operate at a −10 d level, as many home mixers do, then you should be able get plenty of level from the guitar (especially if it has Hum bucker pickups), and your concern will be more one of balancing the output levels of the guitar against the input gain control on the mixer.

However, if the gain of the guitar signal *is* low, your fir alternative is to use a direct box and send the signal into th low-impedance inputs of the console. Direct boxes act a

---

Tape Tip #28
High-to-Low Impedance Via Direct Box

Whether you're recording in a studio or at home, chances are your amplifier is going to be in another room, since you'll need to be listening to the monitor speakers in order to set EQ and effects levels. Chances are also good, particularly when overdubbing, that the guitarist is going to be in the room with you, just so it's easier to communicate.

Should this be the case, the guitarist is going to need an extra-long cord, which can present a problem. You see, a guitar is a high-impedance instrument, and high-impedance signals will lose a certain amount of high-frequency response when they have to travel through long lengths of cable. So if you're forced to use forty or fifty feet of cable, the sound quality of the instrument is going to suffer.

The best way to avoid signal loss is to use a direct box,

which converts high-impedance signals to low impedance. A low-impedance signal is transmitted at a slower velocity, and for reasons that really don't matter here, this translates into less signal decay, which means that you end up with a more complete signal at the other end of the cable.

Most studio players will use two direct boxes: one, placed in the control room, to transform the signal from high impedance to low impedance, and a second, out by the amplifier, to convert the signal from low impedance back to high impedance. That way, rather than run all that high-impedance cable length, all he has to do is plug the guitar into the first direct box, run a low-impedance cable (which uses a three-prong XLR plug) to the second direct box and on to the amplifier, which accepts high-impedance signals. That way, the longest section of the cable, which runs between the two direct boxes, is low impedance, where less signal is lost.

Figure 12h

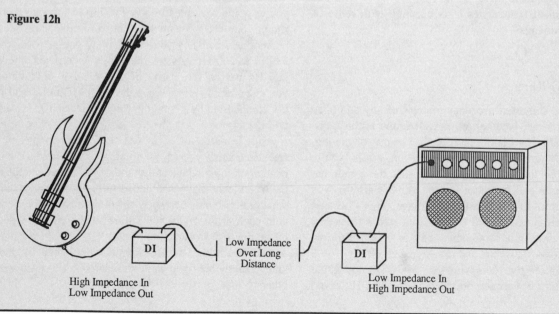

High Impedance In
Low Impedance Out

Low Impedance
Over Long
Distance

Low Impedance In
High Impedance Out

ansformers that convert signals either from high impedance low impedance or vice versa, and by altering the impednce level of the guitar from high to low impedance, you ill effectively enhance its signal-to-noise ratio.

The basic reason for this improvement is that when you ring the guitar signal in at low impedance, it has an easier me overcoming the resistance required at the input stage of ne console. Plus, the console automatically applies a 60 dB oost to a low-impedance signal upon input, which means nat you're using a much cleaner source of amplification. his is particularly important in cases when you are adding n effect to the signal, as the amp circuitry in an effect can e relatively dirty.

If you don't have a direct box, a second alternative for ncreasing the quality of the sound is to plug the guitar into ome sort of preamp device. Preamping raises the level of ne signal before it enters the desk and compensates for the ow level of the signal from the guitar itself.

Many different pieces of outboard gear, such as compresors or reverb units, can be used quite successfully as reamps, though as we mentioned, they do not provide the leanest source of amplification. But if your guitar amplifier appens to have a "preamp out" circuit, you can preamp the ignal that way and send it directly into the high-impedance nput on the console.

One of the most versatile preamp guitar devices *ever* to ome along is Scholz Research's Rockman, which was deigned by Tom Scholz, former leader of the band Boston. he Rockman, which is about the size of a Sony Walkman, an serve as a practice amp (monitored through headphones) nd a preamp, and it can add echo, stereo chorus, sustain, nd overdrive (all in varying amounts) to synthesizers, keyoards, and guitar.

Uses of Direct-In Recording

As we mentioned, one advantage of recording direct is the limination of recording variables. However, a second adantage is the tremendous "presence" this recording techique gives to the sound of the guitar. There is literally no mbience, or "air," to the signal and no discrete echoes, so he guitar seems to be sitting right in your face.

This makes direct-in recording particularly useful when he guitar is being used for rhythmic purposes. For instance, he guitars on many R&B records are recorded this way, vith effects being added later, during the mixing stage, or ometimes while the track is going down.

The advantage of presence is that it emphasizes such ounds as the pick hitting the string, which helps to bring out he rhythm. However, the disadvantage of recording direct n is that the sound that is created can be very thin, because t lacks both the tonal characteristics of the amplifier and the mbience of the room. For this reason, direct-in signals are isually enhanced by effects of various types.

One way to give the guitar more body during direct recording is to combine the direct signal with a twin, amplified signal. This can be done by splitting the signal at a direct box, sending one line directly to the console and the other to an amplifier—which is then miked and brought into the console on a separate channel.

This technique offers you the best of both worlds. You get all the clarity and rhythmic enhancements you had using direct-in by itself, while adding some body and sustain to the guitar, which you couldn't get only by recording direct.

There are two ways to control how much of each signal you include in the overall sound. One is to place the two inputs on adjacent tracks on the mixer and blend them together onto one track on the tape. However, if you have enough tracks available, you also have the option of placing the signals on separate tracks and combining them later, when you're closer to the final mix and you have a better idea of the context of the song. In either case, the choice you're making when you do combine them is how much clarity the signal should have versus how much body.

Direct-In EQ

Once you're happy with the signal level going into the console, the next step is to EQ the sound. The EQ parameters of the guitar remain the same whether you're recording direct in or off an amplifier, so those effective frequency ranges we discussed in EQing amplified guitars also apply here.

When EQing direct-in guitar signals, your major concern is going to be adding sparkle and clarity to the sound. Therefore, the frequency ranges you'll be concentrating on are probably from 3K upward.

Beginning with the upper registers, you'll add some sparkle to the guitar if you give the signal a boost at 10K. A boost in the range of 3K to 6K will give the guitar some upper-midrange "edge," and a nudge in the frequencies between 1K and 3K will bring out the attack of the pick striking the strings. About the only body or tone you'll find in the signal will be somewhere around 500 Hz.

When you're combining direct-in and amplified signals, you should begin by EQing the latter, using the same guidelines we laid out in the previous section on EQing amplified guitars. Then you'll want to EQ the direct-in signal so that it fills in any frequencies that might not have been emphasized in—or may have been totally missing from—the amplified signal.

In other words, if you're boosting the amplifier EQ at 3K and 500 Hz, and you're dipping it a little at 6K, then you'll want to boost the EQ of the direct-in signal slightly at 6K, and again at 10K, in order to fill in the gaps. By doing this, you're emphasizing the body of the guitar with the EQ settings of the amplified signal, and with the direct-in signal you're bringing out clarity and rhythmic presence without also bringing out noise—as would be the case if you had boosted the amplifier at 10K.

TAPE TIP #29
Slick Licks

Any time you're recording an electric guitar direct, or miking the neck of an acoustic guitar, there's a good chance you're going to pick up the noise of the guitarist's fingers as they move across the strings. Normally you don't hear this noise because it is generally masked by the volume of the signal coming through the amplifier, but when you have a signal coming directly into the desk that is EQed for high-end clarity, the noise becomes apparent because there's very little midrange and low-end signal for it to hide behind.

In some instances, finger noise is the result of sloppy guitar playing, in which case you can try to get the musician to be more careful. But more likely than not, it's going to be due to the fact that the passages being played require such quick movement along the neck that there's no way such noise can be avoided.

If this is the case, one way to reduce at least some of the noise is to coat the strings with a very fine layer of vegetable oil (Wesson Oil, Crisco Oil, and so on). All you do is apply a small amount of oil to a rag—just enough so that it almost still feels dry—and rub the rag along the strings. You have to be careful not to apply too much oil (the fingers shouldn't feel greasy after playing), but just enough to do the job.

The oil literally greases the strings, so that the fingers create much less friction when they slip from one to the next. The effect, in my opinion, is better than what you'll get using something like Finger Eeze, which you'll find in any music store, and the cost is a whole lot less.

The only problem with coating the strings like this is that after a short period of time the strings will tend to lose their brightness, so they may need to be changed before the next session.

ACOUSTIC GUITARS

Like any acoustic instrument, acoustic guitars rely on the movement of air to produce their sound. However, acoustic guitars are not amplified, so unlike an electric guitar, the quality of the sound you get from an acoustic depends solely on the quality of the instrument and the ability of the musician.

The tone quality of an acoustic guitar is dependent upon many factors, such as the brand of the instrument, its age, the number of strings, the size of the shell, the gauge and makeup of the strings, and the quality of the wood used in its construction. For instance, a very small, wide-necked Martin that is strung with steel strings will produce a clear, bright tone, while a great big, jumbo Ovation will tend toward a deeper, more full-bodied sound.

The musician's effect on tone quality is a little simpler. A good musician, using proper techniques, can generally make even a mediocre acoustic guitar sound good, while a mediocre musician, using improper techniques, will sound mediocre on any guitar. Certainly there are many different styles a guitarist can use on an acoustic guitar, but playing like an electric guitar is not one of them. By that I mean that an acoustic is not the sort of guitar to bang on if you want to get the full acoustic effect. Neither is it the kind of guitar you want to use if the music demands that particular playing style.

Room Acoustics

Before you mike an acoustic guitar, you have to decide on the type of acoustical environment you want to record it in. This will primarily be determined by the type of music you're doing and where the guitar is going to sit on the track.

If you're recording a solo acoustic guitar, which is going to provide the sole accompaniment for a vocal, then you want the guitar to sound as big as possible. That is accomplished by placing the guitarist in a room that is acoustically "live"—meaning that its walls and ceiling will reflect, rather than absorb, the sound, thus providing a certain ambience to the recording.

If the guitar you're recording is going to appear in the midst of a lot of other instruments, then you might consider using a relatively dead space. This will give the guitar more presence, which can then later be altered, if the need arises, by adding echo or reverb. More often than not, it's better to have this flexibility, because, as we said earlier, whatever you record on the track stays on the track. So including too much ambience in the signal early on can sometimes be a risky proposition.

Miking Techniques

The two primary miking techniques used to record acoustic guitars are, once again, close and distant miking.

To capture the full sound of an acoustic guitar, the close mike should be placed no closer than seven inches from the strings, pointing at the sound hole, on about a thirty-degree axis off center (Figure 12i). Depending upon the guitar, you might place it as far away as twelve or fourteen inches, as there's no hard and fast rule about this. However, large, very full-bodied guitars will project a more powerful sound and will require a greater distance between itself and the mike.

Miking the sound hole will give the guitar a full, rich tone. However, you can achieve different effects with the close mike by aiming it at different parts of the guitar (or by similarly using two close mikes). For instance, if you mike the guitar closer to the bridge, you will get a shorter duration of the tone and a crisper, more metallic, high-end sound from the strings. If you mike it along the neck, you will get a light, mellow sort of sound.

Any time you're miking away from the sound hole, you have to be aware of the guitarist's idiosyncrasies and techniques. For instance, if you're miking the neck, there is the chance of picking up the noise of fingers moving along the

Figure 12i: Close miking an acoustic guitar. (*Courtesy of Leita Purvis*)

strings. And if the guitarist happens to bang his thumb against the body of the guitar to keep time, you don't want the mike picking that up, either.

Another miking technique you might want to try involves using a distant mike in conjunction with the close mike, just as we did with an amplified guitar in order to give it that "live," concert-hall sound. This can be particularly effective when the guitar is providing the sole accompaniment for a vocal and needs to sound huge, and it is often used when recording classical, gut-string guitars.

In this case, you begin by setting up and leveling the close mike. Then, depending upon how loud the player plays, and

how much of the room ambience you want, you place a second microphone anywhere from three to four feet past the close mike and about two feet higher. Then you point the microphone at the sound hole, but in exactly the opposite direction as the close mike. In other words, if you have the close mike pointing back toward the bridge at thirty degrees off center, you want the room mike pointing toward the neck at thirty degrees off center (Figure 12j). However, you may want to alter these angles somewhat if you run into phase cancelation from the mikes.

By using this configuration, you are trying to capture more of the room ambience. But sometimes it can also be an

Figure 12j: Using a close mike and a distant mike on the acoustic. (*Courtesy of Leita Purvis*)

effective tool for capturing the realism of the performance—particularly during the recording of a guitar solo. Often, the movement of the player provides a subliminal air of realism—the sound of his foot tapping, his fingers on the strings, or his clothes moving . . . these things provide a sense of experiencing the solo firsthand.

The amount of ambience you include in the signal is something that can only be determined by listening to the product. Sometimes it can be a function of the way a guitarist plays. For instance, if the guitarist plays very loud, the distance the microphone will have to be from the guitar would be greater than what would be necessary in the case of a classical guitarist, who plays very softly with his fingers.

Again, mike positioning all comes down to listening. For instance, if you're trying to record a track, and you're using the standard approach you'd use on any of a dozen other acoustic guitars, but for some reason it isn't working, chances are it's not your standard approach that is wrong. More than likely the problem is that you're dealing with a different guitar player, and you need to adjust what you're doing to suit his style.

Acoustics with Pickups

If your acoustic guitar has built-in pickups, you can plug the guitar into the console and record direct. In this case, the treatment you'd give the signal would be the same as that outlined in the electric guitar sections. However, acoustic guitar tracks sound much better when they're recorded with microphones rather than pickups, so I would recommend that you avoid using this technique unless it's absolutely necessary.

Acoustic Guitar EQ

When you EQ an acoustic guitar, you almost have to treat it like a piano. The sound of the guitar is a product of its resonating shell, and each shell, like each piano, is going to have its own individual sound. Plus, you're going to have to take into account such variables as the guitarist's technique, the number of strings on the guitar, the gauge of the strings being used, the size of the body, the age of the wood, and all those other indefinable characteristics that go into making up the tone.

As if that weren't enough, the EQ levels are also going to depend upon the role the guitar is supposed to play in the song. For instance, if it is to be the sole support for a vocal, you're going to want to bring out different qualities of its tone than if it were being used as a lead instrument or for rhythmic fill.

If you want to enhance the guitar's rhythmic qualities, then you will want to bring out the sound of the pick striking the strings. This can be accomplished by boosting the EQ in the upper registers of 5K and up. If, for instance, the guitar player is finger picking, then it's more important to hear the sound of the pick (or the finger) hitting each individual string, which would instead mean boosting the level somewhere in the range of from 1K to 3K.

If, however, you're looking for the big, full-bodied choral sound, then you would want to give the signal a boost in the area of 250 Hz and 500 Hz, remembering that any boost in the area of 200 Hz should be avoided since this will destroy the clarity of the sound. In fact, if the guitarist is using a guitar with a large shell, and he's playing rather "vigorously," you might even want to lower the signal level at 200 Hz to increase the clarity of the individual strings.

When you boost the very top end of the spectrum, at around 10K, you'll be adding some sparkle to the sound. This is a particularly useful boost when you're recording a 12-string guitar or when the guitar passage includes material in the upper registers of the instrument. The higher frequencies control the ambient quality of the sound, and when boosted they provide a little extra sustain and some additional body to any extremely high-pitched notes.

When you're using the combination of close and distant miking to record a classical guitar, or to provide more of that concert-hall sound to a standard acoustic instrument, you will want to EQ the signal from the room mike so that it emphasizes ambience rather than guitar tone. The latter is a function of the close mike, while the distant mike's sole purpose is to capture the sound of the room.

You should begin by exploring the effects of boosting upper-frequency ranges between 10K and 15K, which control the amount of "air," or high-end reflections, in the signal. You may then want to give the signal a boost somewhere between 7K and 10K in order to give the guitar some sparkle. However, you don't want to increase the level of any frequencies much below 5K, because you will begin to get some conflict between the high frequencies and those produced by lower notes. As a result, the ambience begins to sound muddy.

USING COMPRESSION ON GUITAR

Signal compression is a means of controlling the level of sound a signal produces. In other words, when you com

Figure 12k: Compression has the effect of rounding off and limiting the peaks in a signal, while bringing the quieter "valleys" up in level.

Noncompressed Signal

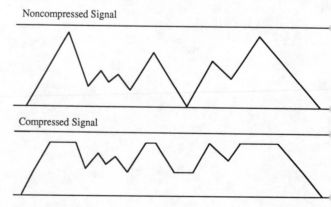

Compressed Signal

ress a signal, you create a limit to its dynamic range, so that it doesn't sound loud and overbearing one minute and then disappear the next.

In classical recordings, guitar compression is taboo, because you *want* the effect of unbridled dynamics. Classical artists use extreme shifts in volume as a tool. However, in the case of pop music, compression is generally desired, because by limiting the dynamic range of the guitar, you can insure that no matter how many other instruments are playing, you will always be able to hear the guitar in the same spot and at the same level.

Over the course of a song, the dynamic range of the recording will fluctuate. As more instruments are added, the dynamics increase; when instruments are removed, the dynamics recede. This is different from classical music, where the dynamics vary with the way an instrument is played. For instance, a horn player may play very quietly during the first four bars of a piece, then play very boldly in the succeeding passage, and the dynamic range may jump a good 80 dB in the process—which is a much greater increase than pop music could effectively handle.

So in order to keep the guitar—particularly a rhythm guitar—contained within a dynamic package that is suitable to the song, you use a compressor/limiter. These devices compress the signal, more or less squeezing down on it from the top (Figure 12k), so that the level of the quietest frequencies in the signal and the loudest frequencies in the signal draw closer together. In other words, if you visualize the signal as being a series of peaks and valleys, compression squashes the peaks and raises the floor of the valleys so that the terrain looks more like a landscape of rolling hills than the Rocky Mountains.

Compressors can be used for many purposes. They're effective as limiters during guitar solos, for instance, and as a general rule they can help compensate for the inability of a guitarist to play at a consistent volume. In some instances, signal compression can be accomplished within the tape recorder itself through tape saturation, as we talked about in chapter 3 ("How Signal Is Placed on Tape"). This has the advantage of allowing you to avoid any trouble you might have reducing the noise a compressor is prone to generate. However, when properly set up, compressors will certainly do the job.

Compressor Settings

When I set compression levels for recording, I usually use a compression ratio of 4:1, and I limit the amount of gain reduction to a level of about −3 dB or −4 dB on the meter (on some compressors the amount of gain reduction is indicated by a series of LED lights). If the guitarist is relatively consistent in his play, I know that with these settings, the loudest notes are only going to reduce the gain 3 dB or so, and the quietest notes should be at a suitable level for recording.

On the other hand, if the gain reduction remains at zero on the meter during the loudest passages, chances are the quieter parts of the recording are going to disappear. This is because when setting the level of the guitar track in relation to other instruments, you'll have to turn the track down as a whole so that the loudest sections aren't too loud. As a result, the subdued notes will just drop out.

Acoustic guitars and lead guitar solos often lend themselves to slightly different compression levels. When compressing a lead guitar, you might want to lower the compression ratio and limit the gain reduction to −2 dB or so. In this way, the lead, which is after all one of the focal points in the song, will maintain some dynamic flexibility, while basically remaining within the dynamic range parameters.

There are also times when you might want to use compression on an acoustic guitar in order to get the body of the guitar sound to ring as long as possible. In this case, you'll perform a technique that is called "squashing" the signal.

In order to squash the signal and extend the ringing effect of the guitar, you want to set the compressor so that it lets through the attack of the pick striking the strings, but compresses the body of the sound that follows immediately afterward. Depending upon your particular compressor, you may have to increase the time of attack (the time it takes the compressor to "kick in" and begin compressing the signal) so that the initial attack of the pick doesn't get compressed. Then you'll want to establish a compression ratio that produces a consistent, relatively high level of gain reduction (−5 dB to −6 dB) for the body of the signal.

Compressor EQ

There's some debate over how to equalize a compressed signal. Some people EQ the sound of the instrument before it is compressed, and others, like myself, compress the signal first and then EQ it. By using the latter technique, you're sometimes able to recapture parts of the signal (usually in the high end, at 3K and above) that are muted during compression and reduce some of the unwanted frequencies (such as 200 Hz) that were brought up in level.

There are advantages and disadvantages to both methods. For instance, if you EQ before compression and boost the frequencies that are going to be lost during compression, there is a chance that the compressor is going to compress those frequencies even farther because of their dominance. By the same token, if you EQ after compression, you have to be careful not to boost the muted frequencies too much or you'll simply "undo" the job the compressor just did.

Ultimately, either method will work, and neither one is easier than the other. Though I feel that I have more control over the amount of noise contained in the signal when I EQ it after it's compressed, the determining factor for you should be whether the sound you get on tape is the sound you want.

USING GUITAR EFFECTS EFFECTIVELY

If you're anything like the rest of us, the first thing you do when you get your hands on a new piece of effects gear is grab it out of the box, toss the instruction manual on some pile of magazines somewhere, and proceed to try your new gadget out on every piece of equipment you've got. And what do you do when the sound you get is really exciting? You go through a period during which you use it every way you can imagine, on every track you lay down.

This sort of reaction is only natural, and it can be healthy in the sense that at least it will get you familiar with the way the effect is operated and the types of sounds it can produce. But when you sit down to do serious recording, the "effects binge" syndrome can get you into a lot of trouble.

When you use effects with such unbridled enthusiasm, you can too easily lose your perspective. Instead of using an effect because it creates a particular sound that allows the guitar to sit in a certain spot on the track, you just begin using the effect for effect's sake. And the result can often be that instead of being able to slip your guitar into a comfortable niche on the track, you have to jam it in at the expense of the other instruments.

So we return again to the concept of planning out your recording strategy before you begin to record, because even though you work on a recording one track at a time, all the tracks have to fit together when you're done. And when you begin adding in the variations of sound you get from today's guitar effects, if you're not careful, your recording can fall into the category of "best laid plans."

The problem is that when you sit down to plan out the sort of guitar sound you're going to want, your mind can often trick you. You may think that you want a great big sound for the guitar, but by the time you get it recorded, you discover that there isn't enough room available on the track for you to let all the characteristics of that big sound come through.

That isn't necessarily the fault of your guitar planning, but rather an overall miscalculation—because you can, of course, use a huge guitar sound as the focal point of a song. You just have to treat the other instruments on the track in such a way that you leave enough room for the guitar to fit in.

Many times, among those "other instruments" will be a second or even a third guitar (not including bass). When this is the case, you should try in some way to treat each guitar differently so that the listener can distinguish one from the other (that is, unless you're layering a guitar part by having the guitarist repeat a passage note for note on a separate track, in which case you want the guitar sounds to be as similar as possible).

Layering is one technique you can use to emphasize a passage by making it sound bigger. But it's not the only technique you can use, and it may not always be the best. For instance, returning to the concept of "less is more," you are likely to find that you're able to get a bigger and more complete guitar sound using one guitar track than you are using two. You may think that you're going to get a big guitar sound by layering, but when you layer, you run the risk of having the two tracks cancel out certain of each other's frequencies, which has the net effect of making the sound appear smaller than if you'd used one guitar and simply enhanced and broadened its sound.

So when thinking in terms of effects, you should consider the various alternatives available for achieving a particular sound, then go with the one that gives you the most control over the signal. Of course, this will depend somewhat upon the equipment you have available, because if you don't have very many alternatives, you have to work with those you have.

And if you are in fact going to be repeating a guitar passage for effect, one of the nicest ways to do it is to send one guitar through the left channel and one guitar through the right channel. Though not essential, if each channel is panned slightly toward center during mixdown (or to opposite left-right positions), this can have a very full, rich effect—certainly a much more pleasing sound than when the two signals are just lying on top of each other.

Another important consideration to be made while you're planning out your track, or even as you're going along, is how the voicing given to the guitar parts is going to affect the overall blend of material. In other words, chords can be played at various locations along the neck, and sometimes the register in which you place a chord can put the instrument in direct conflict with other elements of the song.

This means that if you're using the guitar to provide vocal support, as opposed to, say, providing a solo lead passage, you'll want the guitarist to avoid playing any chords that are in the same register as the lead vocal. Instead, you might want the guitarist to play the chord either lower down the neck or higher up the neck. Or, instead of using a voicing that includes the playing of all six strings, you may want to have the guitarist play only the two bass notes from the chord, which will also effectively place the two components in different registers.

The necessity of keeping a distance in range between the guitar and vocal may seem obvious, but when I first started recording, it was something I never considered. So for the longest time I'd find that I would get a guitar part that sounded really exciting, and a lead vocal that sounded equally as great, but when I put the two of them together, they never sounded quite as good. It took a while before I realized that, more often than not, the guitar and vocal had been sitting in the same register, battling for psychoacoustic attention—and in such cases there are no winners.

Guitar Special Effects

The five basic guitar effects we'll be discussing in this chapter are chorusing, tape echoes, distortion, phasing, and flanging. However, before we begin, a word needs to be said about the signal noise that many of these devices generate.

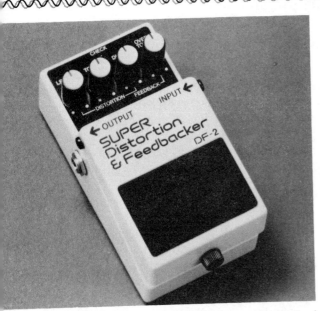

Figure 12l: The Boss DF-2 distortion pedal. (*Courtesy of Roland Corporation*)

As they say, you get what you pay for, and in terms of effects pedals, this is certainly true. In general, the more expensive the gear, the better it's going to perform and the less noise it's going to generate in the process (a good example of which are the expensive, "no-noise" digital effects pedals which have hit the market). So when you buy a bargain pedal, you're going to be buying a little extra noise as well.

Unfortunately, there's really very little you can do to get rid of the noise. You may find that you can reduce the level of noise by running the effect through your console's auxiliary send/receive circuits, and you can also reduce the noise somewhat through EQ. Another possibility is to step the signal down in level by sending it through a direct box and then on to the console, where you plug it in through the low-impedance circuit.

Then again, your only alternative may just be learning to live with it.

Chorusing

In general, the purpose of a chorus pedal is to add dimension to your guitar signal and make it sound as though more than one performer is playing—in other words, to give you a chorale effect.

The effect itself is created by taking one, unaffected signal feed from the guitar and combining it with one or more slightly different versions of the signal, each of which has been treated with variable-pitch modulation. This creates very slight variations in timing and pitch, which are similar to what you might hear from a group of well-schooled musicians.

You might think of chorus as being the electronic equivalent of a group of violinists who are all playing the same

part: they won't all be perfectly in tune with each other; they won't all be playing the finger vibrato at the same rate; and no two violins are going to produce the exact same sound, even when played by the same musician. And this is what gives the violin section in an orchestra such a broad sound.

Well, chorus provides that same broad, orchestral effect through fluctuations in the very, very, *extremely* small delay times produced by the pitch modulation. This causes the pitch of the affected portion of the signal to drift in and out of tune with the original, just as you would hear happening among the violinists. In fact, the concept of chorus was first used on early synthesizers and keyboards in an attempt to imitate the sound of a string ensemble.

There are two basic types of chorus pedals available: standard chorus, which layers the affected and unaffected signals and generates a monaural output, and stereo chorus, which produces a "stereo" chorus feed, which can be sent to two channels of the console for stereo effect. Both basic formats offer variable control over the amount of affected signal you want added to the original ("depth") and the rate at which you want the phase effect to fluctuate, or sweep ("rate").

There are a number of stereo chorus formats available on the market. One has a single stereo output plug, which sends a separately phased signal (along with the original) through each of the two output circuits. This produces an extremely broad chorusing effect.

However, there is a second stereo format that allows a greater number of options. These pedals include a mono output, like those on standard chorus pedals, along with an output for the affected portion of the signal and an output for the unaffected portion. By sending these two latter outputs to separate channels on the mixer, and panning them to opposite sides, you get a slightly more dynamic stereo effect than you do with the other format.

In either case, a stereo chorus really only creates a stereo-like effect. It isn't a true stereo sound, because to achieve that, there must be a slight delay in one of the two "stereo" signals. In this case, neither side is really delayed—one is simply treated differently from the other.

Police was one of the first bands to help popularize the use of chorusing on guitars. They used the effect on both rhythm patterns and leads, and because it gave them such a "big" guitar sound, they were able to perform live as a three-piece band without losing any of the depth they had achieved on records.

Chorus can be a very helpful effect to use when recording. For one thing, it helps disguise any tuning problems that might occur during the course of a track. It's very frustrating to finish laying down a great take only to find that the guitar was ever so slightly out of tune with the other instruments. In certain cases like this, the chorus can help smooth over the problem, because its function is to make part of that signal appear to drift in and out of tune. You just have to be careful not to overuse the chorus in this way, or you can make *everything* seem out of tune.

Figure 12m: The Roland RE-501 is a tape echo unit that also offers chorusing. (*Courtesy of Roland Corporation*)

Chorus also has the effect of softening the sound of a guitar. For instance, you'll lose some of the crispness you normally get from the attack of the pick, because instead of hearing just one clearly defined attack, you'll also hear the slight variation contained in the altered signal, which makes the sound somewhat fuzzier.

You can also use chorus to create an effect we'll call "splash chords." These are brightly voiced chords that are played in conjunction with a cymbal crash in order to create a burst of color within the music. There is no set guide as to the amount of chorus you should use for these chords, since that will depend upon the amount of coloration you want to produce.

There are also a few specialized ways a chorus pedal can be used. For instance, you can "double chorus" a lead guitar by plugging the chorus into a second chorus. This creates a sort of "underwater" effect, where the out-of-tune characteristics of the chorus are deliberately emphasized.

Chorus can also be used effectively on an acoustic guitar. This can be done by recording the acoustic and sending the recorded track through a chorus pedal. Then you can either rerecord that chorused signal onto another track or wait until the mixdown and record it onto the final mix.

When you do this you have to be careful, because the level coming off the console may be too hot for the chorus pedal to handle. If this is the case, you may have to use a direct box to step the level down so that the chorus pedal doesn't distort.

Tape Echoes

When discussing the use of echo, a distinction has to be made between the rapidly repeating room echoes we spoke about in previous acoustic sections and the delay echoes we'll be covering here. While the concept of echo is certainly the same in both cases, the delays you'll want to create electronically will generally be of a longer duration and will remain relatively separate and distinct from each other, as their numbers will be few.

Probably the most important "trick" to using delay echoes properly is to make sure that the speed of the delay corresponds in some way to the tempo of the song. In some instances, this is just a nice way to keep all of the elements balanced temporally as well as harmonically. However, in other instances it is critical to the effect.

For example, if your echo device is calibrated to maintain very consistent speeds, it can be used to double-time rhythm parts on extremely fast songs. Say, for instance, that you want the rhythm guitar to play eighth notes throughout certain sections of a song, but the song is so fast that playing the part with any consistency is a nearly impossible task. Well, all you have to do is set the echo device so that it produces a single repeat and set the delay time to correspond to the duration of an eighth note. Then all the guitarist has to do is play consistently timed quarter notes, and the echo machine will fill in the eighth notes. This way, even though the guitarist is only playing four times per beat, the echo is making it sound like eight.

Of course, this is not the only way echo can be used on a rhythm track. Usually it is used simply to enhance and broaden the sound of the guitar. Under these circumstances, I set the echo to repeat in quarter-note durations, so that it falls either on a kick drum beat, a snare beat, or in a triplet of the tempo. This helps the echo vanish into the track but still allows it to expand the sound of the guitar.

In the case of lead guitars, your options are a little more varied. You may want the guitar to have a deeper, more distant effect, in which case you would want to extend the delay time and/or increase the number of repeats. As a general rule, when I use echo on a lead guitar, I like to set the delay so that it creates a quarter-note triplet—meaning that I use three repeats in the duration of a half note. This gives the echo an appearance of existing in three-quarter time, so that it almost seems slower than the rest of the elements in the song.

By using very long periods of delay on lead passages, you can create a melodic, cascading guitar effect. Long, well-timed delays allow the guitarist to play a six-note or eight-note lead line, and as it repeats it can be made to harmonize with the next six-note or eight-note line in the solo. While Led Zeppelin's Jimmy Page may not have been the first guitarist to use echo in this way, he was certainly one who mastered the technique, and many of his solo guitar pieces remain classics to this day.

In order to achieve this effect, you must first work out the precise guitar lead that you're going to use. Then you set the echo by determining how far into the passage you want the harmony to begin—meaning that if the first melodic passage takes two beats to complete, the delay time should be set to two beats; if it takes a half beat to complete, the delay time should be set to a half beat.

In other words, if the guitar part is constructed so that after a four-note passage is completed, the guitar begins playing a second four-note passage that is intended to harmonize with the first, you want to set the delay time so that it equals the duration of the first four-note passage. That way, when the second four-note passage begins, the notes will fall directly on top of the repeat of the first passage.

Distortion Pedals

Distortion pedals are very much in demand these days—particularly the Boss Heavy Metal pedal. In fact, it's so popular that its name is being used generically by other manufacturers.

Basically, distortion pedals are designed to create the sound of a distorted amplifier, so that you can re-create the sound no matter what level your amp is running at. Of course, at low volume the sound you get is not the same as a Marshall, but used in certain contexts it can be very effective. In fact, a lot of heavy metal bands use the heavy metal pedal *and* the distortion of the amplifier in order to get their sound.

The amount of distortion you use is something you have to be very careful about, because, again, when you're recording a guitar, you have to be concerned with where the vocal is going to fit relative to that distortion. A lot of the overtones created by a distorted guitar will mix with the overtone series of the human voice. And the voice is very rich in overtones, so you have to be particularly careful voicing the guitar so that it does not appear in the same register as the vocal.

Phasing and Flanging

Phasing and flanging are two closely related effects. In fact, these were among the first pedal effects to hit the market.

The effect of phasing can perhaps best be described as sounding like wind—that sort of *swishhhhhhh* of air, rising and falling with the fluctuations of the breeze. As was the case with chorus, you are able to vary the amount of phase applied to the guitar signal, and you are able to alter the sweep rate (the speed at which the phase undulates).

Phasing can be used to give rhythm passages an enhanced quality that makes them appear to be more than just ordinary rhythm fills. To use the phase effectively, you have to make sure that the sweep rate is roughly in time with the tempo of the song. In other words, you may want to set the rate so that one full sweep cycle corresponds to one four-beat bar. Or you may want to slow the sweep rate in half so that one full sweep is completed every two bars, and so on.

One of the most effective rhythmic uses for phasing is when it's applied to repetitive chains of eighth notes or quarter notes, such as were used for rhythm on old rock 'n' roll songs. The phasing makes the pitch of the notes appear to rise and fall slowly almost like the Doppler-effect sound of a train whistle, which rises as the train comes toward you and falls as the train speeds away.

When used by itself, phasing is not a very complimentary effect to use on lead guitars. It has a tendency to dull the definition of the sound, and there are so many frequencies washing together in the phase that it becomes difficult to keep the guitar from dropping back into the track—which is not what you want a lead passage to do.

The difference between a phase pedal and a flange pedal is that the flange pedal, which also uses phasing to create the effect, gives the musician more control over the effect. In the early days of recording, phase was created by more or less combining two versions of a recorded signal, sent by two separate tape recorders. Flanging came about when some studio technician decided to hold his finger on the flange of one of the two tape recorders, and by pressing down, or letting up pressure, the phase sweep could be altered to better match the music.

Thus, in essence, flanging is simply a more musical approach to phasing and as such offers greater control over the phased signal. For instance, some flangers allow you to slow the sweep rate down to the point where it takes twenty seconds to complete a full cycle. Plus, they allow you to delay the phase, and by manually altering the delay time, you can produce pitch-bending effects.

General Effects Treatment

There are many effects, such as guitar synths and wah-wah pedals, which we've not touched on here for one reason or another. But if any of these pieces of gear happen to be your favorite, just remember that no matter what effect you're using, make sure you know how it's going to affect the overall sound of your song before you place it on a track—because any effect you apply to an instrument during recording is going to stay there.

GUITAR EQ REMINDERS

Suggestions

EQ settings will vary according to the style of music and the guitar/amp combinations, so use these suggested settings as guidelines from which to work.

Read Tape Tip #17, chapter 6.

Amplified Electric Guitar

Close-Mike EQ

For more low-end GRUNT or WARMTH, boost 100 Hz

For more BODY, boost 500 Hz–600 Hz

For more EDGE, boost 3K–4K—carefully

For more STRING, boost 5K–8K—carefully

For more CLARITY or SPLASH, boost 10K

Distant-Mike EQ

BOOST
10K

CUT
200 Hz

(Upper-register settings will depend upon the fundamental sound of the guitar.)

Direct-in EQ

BOOSTS
10K
3K–6K
1K–3K
500 Hz

Direct-in Signal and Amped Combined

Direct-in EQ
(EQ for clarity)

BOOSTS
10K
6K

Amplified EQ
(EQ for body)

BOOSTS
3K
500 Hz
100 Hz

CUT
6K

Acoustic Guitar EQ

Close-Mike EQ

For more SPARKLE, boost 10K

For more STRINGS, boost 5K–8K

For more PICK hitting strings, boost 1K–3K

For more BODY, boost 300 Hz–500 Hz

To remove MUDDINESS, reduce 200 Hz

Distant Mike EQ

BOOSTS
10K–15K
7K–9K

RECORDING DIAGRAMS

GUITAR
Adding Stereo Chorus to the Signal

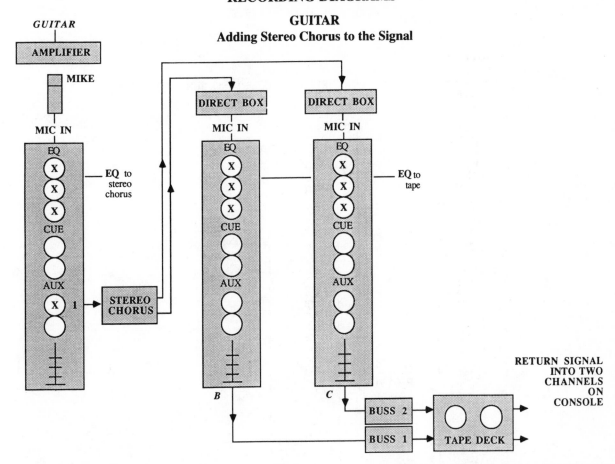

Note: 1. For optimum results on a +4 dB console, the effect should be routed through direct boxes (as shown) before being returned to the console channels. However, many home consoles operate at −10 dB, in which case direct boxes need not be used to enhance signal quality, and the signal can be brought into the console through the high-impedance inputs.

2. In this procedure, you will be recording only the output of the stereo chorus effect. If, however, your chorus pedal does not include the unaffected signal in either of the two sends, you may want to include it in the mix by assigning Channel A to both Buss 1 and Buss 2.

PROCEDURE:

1. Plug the guitar into the amplifier and close mike the amp.

2. Bring the mike into the low-impedance input of console Channel A, but do not assign the channel to a buss.

3. Bring up level on the channel and set EQ. Then, if you don't want to include the original signal in the mix (see **Note**), mute the channel by pulling the fader all the way down and set Aux Send 1 to prefader. If your auxiliary sends are only capable of postfader

operation, you will need to keep the level up on the channel fader in order to send signal to the effect.

4. Patch Aux Send 1 to the input of the stereo chorus.

5. Patch the left and right outputs of the chorus into separate direct boxes, using the high-impedance inputs.

6. Patch the low-impedance output of one direct box into the low-impedance input ("Mic In") of Channel B.

7. Assign Channel B to Buss 1.

8. Patch the low-impedance output of the second direct box into the low-impedance input of console Channel C.

9. Assign Channel C to Buss 2.

10. Patch Busses 1 and 2 to separate input channels on the tape recorder so that they will record on separate tracks.

11. Send level to the chorus unit by turning up the Aux Send 1 pot on Channel A.

12. Bring up levels on console Channels B and C using the channel faders and set both EQ and chorus effect levels.

GUITAR
Adding a Phase Pedal Effect

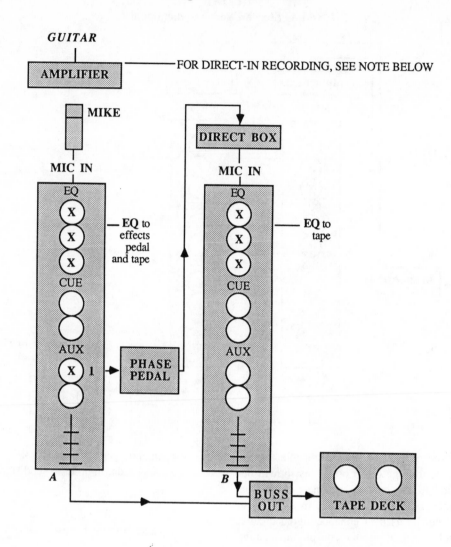

Note: 1. If your console operates at − 10 dB, the post-effect direct box need not be used to enhance the signal quality of the effect.

2. If using a +4 dB console and recording direct (instead of using an amplifier), the guitar should be plugged into a direct box, and the device's low-impedance output should be plugged into the low-impedance input of the console.

Procedure:

1. Plug the guitar into the amplifier and close mike the amp.

2. Bring the mike into the low-impedance input ("Mic In") of console Channel A.

3. Patch the console's Aux Send 1 into the input of the phase pedal.

4. Patch the output of the effect to the high-impedance input of a direct box.

5. Patch the low-impedance output of the direct box into the low-impedance input of console Channel B.

6. Assign Channels A and B to the same buss.

7. Patch the buss into an input channel of the tape recorder.

8. Bring up level on Channel A and set the preeffect EQ.

9. Bring up level on the effect by turning up the Aux Send 1 pot on Channel A and by bringing up the fader on Channel B.

10. Solo Channel B in order to set the posteffect EQ.

11. Blend the signals as desired.

Chapter 13

How to Record an Acoustic Piano

Before the advent of the synthesizer, the piano was by far the most versatile instrument available. Not only has it been used to play everything from classical to country, but it's safe to say that more music has been composed and arranged on a piano than on any other ten instruments combined.

ROCK 'N' ROLL PIANO

In dealing with the piano, we're primarily going to be looking at how the instrument is used in contemporary rock music, both as a vehicle for ballads and as a support instrument for rock 'n' roll. However, with very little difficulty these same principles can be applied to such piano styles as jazz, classical, and honky-tonk.

In order to determine the best way to record the instrument, it's necessary first to decide how you intend to use the piano in the song. As you'll see, miking techniques and EQ will vary with each particular application.

In rock music, the piano is normally used in one of two ways. It can provide the principal accompaniment to vocal, as in the case of Elton John, where the piano is used as the melodic component of the song and other instruments provide the rhythm. Or it can be used as just another "fill" instrument in the band, providing additional melodies, color, and support rhythms.

THE INSTRUMENT

The piano is capable of producing a very full sound, for unlike other instruments, it offers the possibility of playing ten notes at once. Unfortunately, this "asset" can quickly become a liability in the studio, because if you're not careful with your recording techniques and musical arrangements, the full, rich accompaniments you wrote in your living room may leave little acoustic room on the track for other instruments.

There are many variables involved in getting the piano track to sound right—not the least of which is the tonality of the instrument itself. So once you've decided how you want to use the piano in the song, you then have to put a critical ear to the instrument you're playing, in order to determine what adjustments you need to make in order to give it the appropriate sound.

Like violins, no two pianos sound alike. For example, the sound of an upright piano is very different from the sound of a grand, and if you put three uprights next to each other in the same room, each will have its own, distinct tonal characteristics.

These characteristics are known as the piano's voice, and they represent the overall tonal response of the instrument. A "well-voiced" piano is one that has a smooth, even response, both in terms of volume and pitch, from the lowest note to the highest note. By the same token, poor voicing can make one piano sound boomy and another sound hard and brittle.

Most pianos in recording studios are voiced and tuned fairly regularly, so the tonal response of the instrument should be relatively smooth and even. However, few living room pianos are maintained to those same strict studio standards, and you'll undoubtedly need to compensate for flaws in the piano's voicing by altering EQ and adjusting the positions of the microphones.

In order to determine just where you stand with your piano's voicing, the first thing you'll want to do is mike the piano and have a listen to how it sounds.

MIKING AN UPRIGHT PIANO

In most situations, you should use two microphones to record the piano. You can get away with using one mike if, for instance, there's a shortage of microphones or if you're recording an entire band and there's a shortage of console inputs. However, with one mike, you're much less likely to pick up the whole spectrum of octaves being played, and you're less able to compensate for the particular tonal characteristics of the piano.

To mike an upright, the first thing you do is remove the top front panel (the one above the keyboard), so that your mikes have direct access to the strings. You'll notice that once you've opened up the piano, the instrument will have a lot more presence, because the sound will pass directly out into the room instead of first bouncing around in an enclosed box. If you have a boomy or dull piano, this will enhance its tonal response by making the higher registers crisper and the lower registers cleaner and less dominant.

Microphone Positioning

The exact mike placement will vary according to the specific tonal characteristics of the piano. Unfortunately, since every piano is different, finding the proper position for the mike is going to be a trial-and-error process. Therefore, you should begin with a basic mike configuration and make adjustments according to how the piano sounds on playback.

When you're recording with two mikes, as in Figure 13a, one will be used for the bass strings, and the other will be used for the treble strings. You should begin by positioning the mike about six inches out from the strings, aimed a few inches up from the hammers. Then angle them thirty degrees off center so that they point toward the strings at either end of the keyboard. When using six- to eight-inch microphones in the configuration, the butt ends of the mikes should just about be touching, and you should have coverage of all but the extreme top and bottom ends of the instrument—which few people play anyway.

Adjusting for Tone

At this point, you'll want to record a little of the piano, keeping the EQ flat, and listen to the playback. This will give you a better idea of the piano's inherent sound characteristics, and from this point you can begin to make the necessary adjustments.

For instance, if you find that the bottom strings are substantially louder than the top strings, you may want to compensate for this by raising the volume of the mike you've assigned to the treble strings. However, it's often more efficient just to move the two mikes so that they don't have exactly the same relationship to the strings.

On the other hand, if you find that the bottom end is both loud and muddy, then you're not going to solve the problem simply by boosting the level of the treble strings. You will

Figure 13a: When miking an upright, first remove the front panel. Mikes should then be positioned about six inches out from the strings and angled thirty degrees off center, so that they point slightly toward opposite ends of the keyboard. Adjustments can then be made, depending upon how the piano sounds on playback. (*Courtesy of Larry Wichman*)

also have to EQ the bottom strings in order to establish a balance between the two.

If you're only using one microphone, you're going to have a difficult time balancing the bass and treble strings. However, you can make it a bit easier on yourself if, when placing the mike, you favor the strings above middle C. This placement is still going to be subject to trial and error, but since the bottom end of most pianos is louder than the high end, you should at least be in the ball park.

Adjusting for Effect

When you begin to move the microphones, you will want to keep the piano's musical role in mind. For instance, the farther the mike is from the piano, the less hammer noise it will pick up. So on certain types of music, like ballads, in which you don't want to hear much of the hammer, you'll want to keep the mike back. However, don't forget that there's a human being playing the keyboard, and the closer the mikes get to him, the more of his noise you're going to pick up.

There are other times, such as on straight rock songs, when you'll want the piano to have a punchy, percussive sound. This is accomplished by moving the mike closer to the strings so that the sound of the hammers becomes more prominent.

Unfortunately, if your hammers are worn—meaning that the felt is soft and full of string indentations—the only hammer noise you're going to hear will be in the form of squeaks and clicks from the hammer mechanisms themselves. That's because in order to get a good punch from the hammers, they have to have a firm surface. So before you go too far with the close-in miking, check the condition of the hammers to make sure it's worthwhile.

In this regard, you may have been told that one way to toughen up the hammers is to coat them with fingernail polish. Or you may have been told to try sticking a thumbtack on the head to brighten the sound. Well, before you try *any* home remedy, just remember that if you screw up the hammers, they cost a lot of money to replace. So unless you know what you're doing, *don't do it*.

Adjusting for the Player

As you listen to the playback, you will also have to keep the pianist's playing style in mind. For instance, certain players place more emphasis on the left hand, while others place more emphasis on the right. And you have to make a decision in the musical format as to whether you want one of the two to dominate or whether you want to hear an even blend between the two. Again, this can be effected either by adjusting the microphones or by raising the level on one of the two channels.

Phase Cancelation

Any time you are using more than one microphone to record an instrument, you run the risk of phase cancelation. Therefore, another thing to check is whether or not the mikes are out of phase.

If you're sending each mike into a separate console channel, one way to check the phase relationship is to monitor a monaural mix of the two channels, paying particular attention to low-end response. If the bottom end of the instrument seems to disappear, chances are that the microphones are out of phase.

The best way to solve phase problems is by physically moving one of the microphones. This may mean moving it in or out, or it may just mean adjusting its angle to the strings. And since it's rare that the two mikes will be completely 180 degrees out of phase, any "phase flop" switch you might have on your console will be of little help.

Piano and Vocal

Unfortunately, if you're going to be singing while you play an upright, there's no real way to keep the vocals from being picked up by the piano mikes. Obviously this is a disadvantage, so generally speaking, you should try to record each separately. However, if it's essential to add a vocal, one way you might be able to get around the problem is to remove the lower front panel and mike the piano from below the keyboard. This will minimize the amount of vocal reaching the mikes. However, in this position the mikes are liable to pick up a great deal of noise from the sustain pedal mechanisms, so it's best if the pianist doesn't use the pedals.

RECORDING A GRAND PIANO

The techniques used to mike a grand piano are virtually the same as those you would use to mike an upright—the main difference being that the microphones are brought in from above the strings rather than from the front (Figure 13b). The only two additional considerations you would give a grand concern the amount of ambience you want the track to have and the degree of isolation its mikes need during the recording process.

With an upright, if the piano is the only instrument on the track, and you want to increase the amount of ambience in the signal, you move the mikes back from the strings so that they pick up some of the sound reflections in the room. However, with a grand piano, you have a further option, which is to fully open up the lid. In fact, for a very open sound, you may just want to remove the lid completely— that is, if you aren't at all concerned with isolating these mikes from other instruments or vocals.

If, however, you do want to isolate these mikes, you can't do it by just clamping down the lid. Instead, after you've

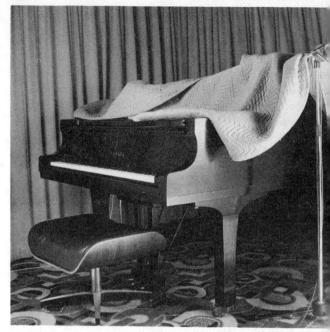

Figure 13b: Mike placement for a grand piano (left) is the same whether you want to isolate the instrument or include room ambience. To isolate the instrument, you cover the shell with blankets (right) after adjusting the mikes. For an ambient sound, blankets need not be used, as the lid is to remain fully or partially open (left). (*Courtesy of Laura Marenzi*)

positioned the mikes inside the shell, you lower the lid to its lowest support position (most lids have two such positions) and use packing blankets to cover any open space between the lid and the case of the piano. This allows you to leave a little distance between the mikes and strings while insuring that very little outside noise enters the shell.

Adjusting for Tone and Effect

As with the upright, phase cancelation must be checked, and the mike positions will need to be adjusted according to the particular voicing of the instrument. Here, too, the process will basically be one of trial and error.

PIANO EQ SETTINGS

The piano is capable of generating a truly full range of frequencies. To begin with, the keyboard itself covers over five full octaves, which means that a single note can generate a great number of harmonics. And when you begin to consider the complexity of the harmonic response in a ten-note chord, and the frequency ranges that are effected, you can understand why a piano can sound so full.

Add to this that the frequency response of every piano is different, and you can see why it is impossible to tell you exactly how to EQ a particular piano in a specific musical situation. So much depends on the quality of the instrument, the condition of the hammers, the resonance of the casing, the tuning of the strings, and so on that for the most part, you're going to have to EQ by trial and error. However, there are some guidelines we can give you to work from, so that you have some understanding of the general ranges you can look to EQ.

As a rule, if the lower end of the piano sounds muddy, and you don't hear a nice, clear tonality when you play a chord in the lower registers, you might find it helpful to reduce a narrow band of frequencies at, or around, 200 Hz. Again, this is the frequency range that has the effect of blurring a signal's definition and giving it that mucky pea-soup sound. So by reducing level in this range, you enhance the piano's tonal clarity.

You can also use EQ to enhance the piano's musical role. For instance, when it's being used as an ensemble instrument in a rock 'n' roll band, you'll want to EQ the piano so that it complements the recording and fits neatly in among the other instruments. Generally, then, you'll want to try boosting the signal at around 100 Hz, which will enhance the lower registers, at around 3K, which will blend the piano in with the guitars, and at around 10K, which will bring out the brilliance of the strings.

On the other hand, when you're using the piano for vocal accompaniment, and the instrument is literally providing the vocal with its sole means of support, you'll want to structure the EQ so that it complements the voice rather than a bunch of instruments.

One range that can be boosted rather successfully, assuming that the piano is not too muddy to begin with, is the 250 Hz range. This band of frequencies is in the lower spectrum of the human voice, and by boosting it you create a sense of ambience and warmth that provides low-end support for the vocal. By the same token, by boosting EQ in narrow bands around 5K and 10K, you provide top-end vocal support by enhancing the fundamental tones of the notes and bringing out the brilliance of the strings.

If you have more than three bands of EQ available (or if you're using a graphic EQ), you might want to reduce level in the 300 Hz–500 Hz frequency range. This can be particularly helpful if you notice that the piano and the vocal are fighting for space, because these are among the dominant tone frequencies of the human voice. Therefore, cutting the piano back in this range will open it up for the vocal.

COMPRESSING THE PIANO

Compression can help the piano track in a number of ways. For instance, it can be used to even out the tonal response of the instrument and to compensate for flawed voicing. However, you have to be careful when you compress the piano, because with compression you run the risk of changing the instrument's tonal decay.

Compressors are frequently used on guitars for the express purpose of increasing the instrument's sustain. However, this is not something you want to do with the piano, because if you increase the decay time of each note, once the piano part is mixed in with other instruments, you find that notes from the piano will start ringing over into the next notes the other instruments are playing. And this can make for a very messy mix.

So if you are compressing the signal, you'll want to listen to how the instrument sounds by itself, and you'll want to listen to the effect compression has when the piano is being played at tempo with other instruments. That way you can make sure that the compressor isn't holding the note longer than you really want it to.

The compressor can also be used to enhance the percussive qualities of the piano. For instance, if you're recording a rock 'n' roll track, and you only have a big-sounding grand piano at your disposal, you will probably want to combine the previously mentioned "ensemble" EQ settings with a fairly heavy dose of compression. In this case you'd want to keep the compressor's threshold very low, so that the compressor is almost always engaged, but you'd also want to keep the ratio of compression low as well, so that the unit doesn't overcompress the signal and make it sound too dull. Basically, you just want the unit to compress the signal constantly and evenly.

PLAYING TECHNIQUES

As with all the other instruments we've talked about, there are a variety of musical considerations that need to be given to the piano track.

Arrangements

Usually, when you're composing in the living room and accompanying yourself on piano, you want the instrument to sound as full as possible in order to provide support for the vocal. However, when you sit down to record that track, more than likely you'll be adding other instruments, and these instruments are going to be playing those extra notes

you were adding to the piano part in order to make it sound so full. So when you're creating the arrangement, you will automatically want to reduce the complexity of the piano part and the number of notes being played, so that the piano will be a balanced part of the recording.

If you're not careful in this regard, your recording will have all of the makings of the dreaded "war of the mix," in which instrument is pitted against instrument for space on the track—and the engineer always loses.

Sustain Pedals

Sustain pedals can be damaging to a recording. Although piano sustain may sound great in the living room, when you use the pedals excessively in the studio, you get one note ringing into the next, and as a result you reduce the clarity of the attack. This, in turn, reduces any of the punch you might want the instrument to have and gives it a reverb effect that pulls it back from the surface plane of the track.

Sustain pedals can also screw up the EQ. For instance, until I discovered "the sustain pedal factor," I couldn't figure out why a piano would be sounding great on its own but when added to the track would sound muddy. What was happening was that while the player wasn't using the sustain pedal as I was setting EQ, the minute the song started, he put the pedal down, thus creating a reverb that altered the piano's tonal response.

So whenever you EQ the instrument, make sure that the pianist plays the part exactly as he's going to play it during the take—sustain pedals and all. And if he insists on using the pedals, listen to the playback and make sure that the track isn't going to interfere with the clarity of the recording.

STEREO PIANO TRACKS

When two mikes are being used on the piano, you have the option of recording in mono or in stereo. However, about the only time it would make sense to record the piano in a stereo format would be when it is used as sole accompaniment for a single vocal, and you want to give the recording the fullest sound possible.

Normally pianos aren't recorded in pure stereo because it sounds unnatural when you have the bass strings coming out of one speaker and the treble strings coming out of the other. Only someone actually sitting on the piano bench hears the instrument this way. So unless it is your intention to make the listener feel as though he's sitting right next to the performer, it's best to keep the piano tracks monaural.

There are, however, many times when you will want to give the piano a stereo image in the final mix. As you'll see in the chapter on mixdown techniques, this can be accomplished by sending a single track through a harmonizer and splitting the signal. By "creating" the stereo image in this fashion, you are able to make the piano sound full while maintaining the naturalness of its sound.

PIANO EQ REMINDERS
(For All Piano Types)

Suggestions:

Every piano has different tonal characteristics, so use these settings as a general guide and make adjustments where necessary.

Read "Piano EQ Settings" in this chapter.

Read Tape Tip #17, chapter 6.

Problem:

If your piano sounds MUDDY,

BOOST

10K

CUT

200 Hz

Rock Piano EQ:

BOOSTS

10K

3K

100 Hz

Piano as Sole Vocal Accompaniment:

BOOSTS

10K

5K

250 Hz

CUT

300 Hz–500 Hz

RECORDING DIAGRAM

PIANO
Recording Through Two Console Channels

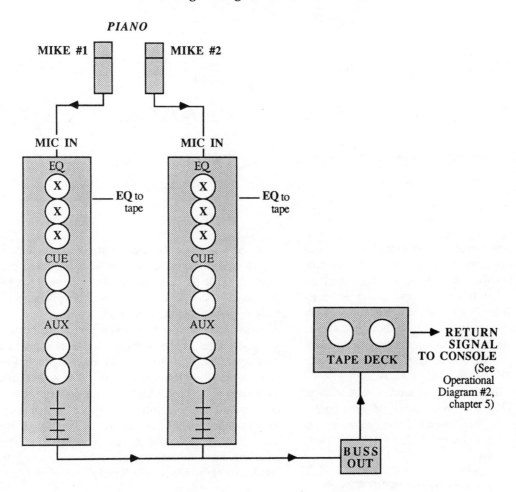

Note: To add compression, see Operational Diagrams #12–#15, chapter 5.

Procedure:

1. Position microphones six inches out from strings, as shown in Figure 13a.

2. Bring mikes #1 & #2 into the low-impedance inputs on separate console channels and adjust volume levels.

3. Assign both channels to the same buss. (Note: If recording stereo, assign each channel to a separate buss.)

4. Check for mike-induced phase cancelation by monitoring a monaural mix of the channels.

5. Record piano with flat EQ and listen to the playback.

6. Adjust positions of mikes and EQ settings until you achieve the sound you desire.

Chapter 14

How to Record Synthesizers

The first synthesizer was developed in the mid-sixties by Robert Moog. At the time, the instrument was seen as being little more than an in-studio novelty, though an expensive one, and only a few of the most farsighted musicians ever expected that it would one day become such an integral part of the music industry. In fact, those first synths were so large and unwieldy that live performances were out of the question. So for the most part they were used to make records like Walter Carlos's *Switched-on Bach*.

In those days, a synth player was as much a technician as he was a musician. The early devices required patch cords, and the patch bay of the early Moogs, for instance, resembled the patch bay of a commercial studio (Figure 14a).

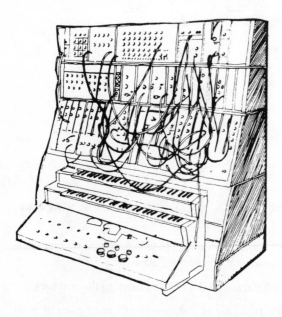

Figure 14a: Depiction of an early studio synthesizer. (*Courtesy of TOA Electronics, Inc.*)

However, thanks to the availability of microchips, the size and complexity of today's synthesizer has been drastically reduced, while the capability of the instrument has increased enormously. As a result, synthesizers are playing an increasingly greater role in modern music.

Synths are having a huge impact on home recording. As synthesizers get smaller, cheaper, and more sophisticated, an increasing number of songwriters are using them to provide most, if not all, of the music on their demos. It's not unusual for a musician to connect a group of synthesizers and a drum machine and run them off a sequencer, so that once all the parts have been written on the synths, they can all be played back simultaneously and placed on tape. Thus, instead of recording three or four initial tracks and mixing them together during a bounce, the "tracks" are placed in memory and mixed as they're being laid down.

This technique has been made possible by the introduction of MIDI (Musical Instrument Digital Interface) technology, which takes the musical output of a device and translates it into a digital readout. This information can then be stored in the memory banks of a sequencer or a computer, and when it's recalled and sent back to the instrument, the synth repeats the part note for note.

However, how and why synths do what they do is a subject for another time and place, because there are many different types of synthesizers and many different brands, and each has its own peculiarities. So to talk in specifics about one synthesizer would be very misleading if you were to try to apply that information to another synth.

For this reason, instead of focusing on the various methods used to generate synthesized sounds, we're going to be talking about the treatment you'll need to give those sounds as they're being recorded. This is an important consideration, because you can spend hours creating just the right texture and coloration for a part, only to have it lose its effectiveness once it's been translated to tape.

SYNTHESIZER ARRANGEMENTS

No instrument offers as much control over raw sound as a synthesizer. Yet this can be as much a curse as it is a blessing. When you have so many sounds available, you tend to want to use them all, and in doing so you run the risk of filling up so much space with these tracks that there's little room left in the production for other instruments.

Therefore, the most important thing to remember when you're dealing with synthesizers is that *less* is definitely *more*. In other words, to use the instrument effectively you must be selective about its application and learn not to overuse it. This doesn't mean that the synth can't play a variety of roles in a song, but unless you're careful, the instrumental part that was to be the focus of the arrangement will just fall back in amidst a lot of musical sound.

EQ TECHNIQUES

As with any instrument, the EQ treatment a synthesizer receives will have a significant effect upon the success of the track. Yet when you're talking about EQing a synth, you're literally talking about EQing an orchestra, which means that there are no simple formulas, and each case must be treated individually. It also means that you'll be forced to do a lot of your EQ work by trial and error.

Essentially, there are two broad approaches you can take to synth use, and each requires a different EQ technique. The first is to use the synthesizer to mimic the sound of existing instruments, like strings or brass, in which case the idea is to disguise the source of the sound in order to make it appear as though you're listening to the actual instruments. The second approach is to use the synth to create a purely electronic sound that has no acoustical equivalent, in which case you'll want to enhance its synthetic qualities.

Re-creating Existing Sounds

Many synthesizers come with factory presets for strings, brass, and the like, which, when treated with a little bit of reverb, are very difficult to distinguish from the real thing.

Figure 14b: Yamaha DX7-II (*Courtesy of Valley Arts Guitar*)

Figure 14c: E-MU Emulator II (*Courtesy of E-MU Systems, Inc.*)

These programs utilize the same frequency ranges and the same overtones and harmonics as the instrument the synth is mimicking, which is one reason they sound so authentic. Consequently, when you EQ one of these sounds, you should EQ those ranges that are most closely linked to the original acoustic instrument.

If you're using the synth to produce the sound of one of the instruments we discussed in chapters 11–13, all you need to do is look through the EQ material pertaining to that instrument and apply it to suit your needs. Yet there are many instruments, such as strings and brass, that were not discussed, and to EQ these you'll need to refer to the frequency chart in Tape Tip #4 (chapter 1). For instance, if the synth is emulating the sound of a flute, the frequency chart will tell you what the dominant frequency range is for the flute and how high up the harmonics go. Then you run through these frequencies and adjust the EQ by trial and error until you find an appealing sound that fits appropriately into the song.

One thing to keep in mind as you set the EQ is that the programs on all but the most expensive synthesizers lack the upper harmonics normally produced by the acoustic instrument. Or, if they are included, more often than not the harmonics won't remain true. So any boosts above 8K or 9K will be of very limited use and, in fact, will probably just add noise to the signal.

TAPE TIP #30
Recording Brass and Strings "Live"

Should you have a particularly important brass or string track to lay down, instead of using a synthesizer, you may want to record the acoustic instruments themselves. For example, while I use a synth for most noncritical brass or string parts, whenever I want to include something like a sax solo in the arrangement, I have a sax player come in and perform the part live. This gives the solo a more dynamic feel, and since an acoustic sax has a broader range of frequency response than the sax sound you find on a synth, the upper harmonics of the instrument can be included in the signal.

On the other hand, synthesizers do an excellent job of mimicking the sounds of acoustic instruments, and many of the techniques included in this chapter can be applied directly to the process of recording a live brass or string track. So even if you don't have a synthesizer, you'll want to refer to "EQ Techniques" and "Synthesizer Arrangements" in this chapter when deciding how best to treat the instrument during record and mixdown.

As you'll see, these tracks are relatively easy to generate if you use a commonsense approach. Basically, it's a process of listening to what you've got and experimenting with EQ and mike placement until you find a sound you like.

EQ Treatment

Much of what you need to know about EQing a brass or string instrument can be found in "EQing for Clarity" and "Re-creating Existing Sounds" in this chapter. For example, the EQ treatment you give the instrument should be based upon the role the instrument plays in the song, as was the case with synthesized sounds. And in order to know which frequency ranges to experiment with, you'll need to refer to the frequency response chart in Tape Tip #4 (chapter 1).

However, although we warn against applying high-end EQ to a synthesized sound, you *should* explore the ranges above 8K when EQing an acoustic brass or string track. This is where the upper harmonics of the instruments are found, and by enhancing these frequencies, you give clarity to the sound. This is particularly important if you want to hear the sound of the bow being drawn across the strings, or if you want to bring out some of the breathy quality of a saxophone.

Room Acoustics

When you record one of these instruments, the ambient environment is quite important. If you're looking for a concert-hall sound, you may, in fact, try recording the instrument in an auditorium. Normally, however, you can simply set up the mike in an acoustically dead environment and wait until the mix to add whatever reverb effects you want the track to have.

Miking Techniques

In most cases, you'll only need to use one microphone when you record brass or strings—that is, unless you're recording a brass or string *section,* in which case you can either give each musician his own mike, or you can break up the musicians into groups of two or three and have each group share a mike. In the latter case, in order to create a balanced blend of instruments, you will need to adjust the distance each member of a group is from the mike, using the same technique we outline in chapter 15, "Backing Vocals" (page 228).

One important thing to remember when you're recording brass is that if you place the mike too close to the source, it may distort. However, you don't want the mike to be too far from the source, either, because then it will start picking up the reflections in the room. So begin by placing the mike about a foot from the source and move it in or out according to what you hear on the monitors.

A word also needs to be said concerning the use of electronic pickups. Under live stage conditions, electronic pickups are fantastic, as they allow you to isolate the instrument from all the noise around it. However, under studio conditions it's much better to mike the instrument, as this allows you to capture the sound in the air *around* the horn— not just the sound coming out from the bell.

TAPE TIP #31
Recording Organs and Small Synths

Although organs *are not* synthesizers, the techniques used to record organs (other than those using a Leslie) are similar to those used for synths. Organs, after all, are electronic keyboards. They may not generate sound in quite the same way synthesizers do, or have the flexibility of one, but they do offer a (small) variety of sounds and settings, and they have the capability of being recorded direct.

Unless you're in a church recording a pipe organ, or unless you're going for some special "live" effect using a Leslie (in which case you'd mike it like an amplified guitar), the best way to record an organ is to use the direct-in technique covered in this chapter. This will give you the least amount of noise and the greatest signal clarity.

If, however, you get a lot of signal noise going direct, try listening to the signal through a guitar amp. If the device is still noisy, and it's an old instrument, the problem is likely to be an internal one—in which case there's little you can do. But if it's not as noisy going through the amp, and you're using a +4 dB console, try running the organ through a direct box and bringing it into the desk at low-impedance. This should reduce a lot of the noise.

The same holds true for very small synths and many Casios. Here, however, you may also be generating excess noise by using AC adapters rather than batteries. Such adapters add signal noise because the equipment being powered simply isn't designed for serious studio work. So this should be one of your first checks.

In general, the synth EQ procedures outlined in this chapter (particularly "EQing for Clarity") can also be applied to organ EQ. In fact, most synthesizers have at least one or two "organ" presets. However, with cheaper gear you may find that the higher octaves generate a weaker signal than the lower octaves, in which case you will have to use your EQ to balance the two.

For instance, if the upper octaves are weak, try applying some high-end boosts. Start off with boosts at 4K or 8K, and experiment to see how this affects the sound. Or if this generates too much signal noise, you may want to try *reducing* low-end EQ instead. Start at 100 Hz or 200 Hz—or maybe go as high as 500 Hz—and experiment until you find a tonal texture that you like.

Ultimately, the EQ settings you choose will depend upon the organ (or synth) sound you're after, as well as its placement within the context of the song. If you're having problems, try arranging the musical parts so that you're only using the high-end, mid, or low-end octaves. This way you only have to worry about EQing for sound quality and not balance. But if that's not possible, EQ experimentation is the only answer.

It should also be noted that electric pianos can be EQed using the same guidelines set out in the chapter on acoustic pianos. However, as with synth EQ, many of these instruments generate little, if any, signal above 10K. So extreme high-end boosts will be ineffective and noisy.

Creating Electronic Sounds

When you're using the synthesizer to create an electronic sound that has no acoustic counterpart, you'll want to be just as concerned over the effectiveness of the EQ treatment. Yet since the sound has no acoustical equivalent, it won't be represented on the frequency chart, and you're going to have to adjust the EQ by ear.

The best way to do this is, again, by trial and error. In other words, after you create a sound you like, you use the equalizer to find out what its frequency components are. Then, when you're ready to mix the track in with the other instruments, you'll have some idea of which frequency ranges you want to enhance.

There's nothing terribly technical about all this. To analyze a sound, all you do (basically) is boost the EQ level, sweep through the frequencies, and listen to the effect each has on the sound. And when you hit one you like, or when you find the upper end or lower end of the spectrum, you make note of it.

After you've analyzed a number of different sounds, you should begin to recognize the basic effect certain frequency ranges have, and as a result you'll know where to look when you want to bring out a certain quality or texture. For example, you'll hear a buzzy quality in the 5K–7K range that gives the sound presence, while the 3K–5K band gives the sound midrange authority and excitement. And if you want to give the sound warmth, you'll know to look in the 100 Hz–800 Hz range.

This is, in fact, an excellent method of ear training, because with an electronic instrument like a synth, you can create a sound that's relatively complex but doesn't exist in the acoustic world. This gives you the opportunity to work with an unfamiliar sound, and unlike EQing something like a violin, in which you would always be hearing a violin in your mind and EQing the sound to fit the image, with a purely electronic sound you'd have no such expectations. Thus, as you apply EQ, you can analyze the tonal colorations of each frequency range more objectively. In other words, you're able to treat the sound as an object, not as an instrument.

EQing for Clarity

As with any instrument, the synth should be EQed based upon the role the track plays within the context of the song.

If it's used for lead material, you may want to accentuate the instrument's fundamental pitch (usually between 500 Hz and 800 Hz), so that the melodic tones stand out. If it's used for fill, you'll probably want to deemphasize the fundamental pitch and concentrate instead upon EQing the harmonics, so that you capture the color and timbre of the instrument. Yet in all cases your goal is to maintain clarity within the mix of tracks, and your use of EQ should reflect this.

Clarity is particularly important when you're using the synth to create what's called a "pad," which is a nondistracting background coloration of music that adds atmosphere and mood to the composition. If you don't use discretion when you EQ a pad, it can take up so much room in the recording that the other instruments will have to fight just to remain out in front of it.

The same type of thing can happen if you're using one synthesizer to generate a variety of sounds on many tracks. Each synthesizer tends to have its own tonal signature, so that the overtone characteristics remain the same, even though the sounds vary. As a result, if you use the same synth over and over to build up the tracks on a song, you're liable to lose the clarity that normally allows you to distinguish one track from the next. And in such cases the use of EQ can make all the difference in the world.

As a general rule, when you're EQing for background atmosphere, the upper frequencies will give you clarity and the lower frequencies will give you warmth. However, you may find that the upper registers of the program you're using include wave forms that sound buzzy. This is often the case, for instance, on string programs, where the upper-range oscillator creates a buzz that is meant to simulate the sound the bow makes as it's drawn across the strings. If this is the case, you have to be very careful with the high-end EQ (5K–7K), because if the buzz gets too much play, it can interfere with the lead vocal or create a distracting background in which the pitch of the strings is overshadowed by the buzz.

When to EQ

The sounds generated by a synth can be so complex that it is usually best to EQ the instrument during a bounce or during mixdown, so that you can hear it in the context of all the other instruments. This is particularly true when the synth is being used for "atmosphere," because then you can make the synth fit in with the other instruments instead of trying to build everything else around it.

When I approach a synth part, I always try to generate the desired sound on the instrument itself, so that I can record it *flat* (without adding any EQ embellishments). Then, once it goes to tape and I'm in the mixdown mode, I EQ the track according to its function. If it's an orchestral pad, I'll EQ it so that it fits unobtrusively into the song, and if it's a lead of some sort, or if it provides a melodic hook, I'll treat it as I would any lead instrument and EQ it so that it stands out.

RECORDING TECHNIQUES

From a recording standpoint, synthesizers are like any other electronic instrument, meaning that the same rules apply to synths as apply to any other direct-in recording situation. In fact, because of the complexity of the instrument, and the enormous amount of control it gives you over the signal, you'll probably spend more time in the trial-and-error process of creating the right sound than you will recording the track.

Producing a Clean Track

A synthesizer generates its own output level, so to reduce signal noise and avoid distortion, you'll want to adjust the output level of the synth and the input level of the console until you achieve the optimum signal-to-noise response. In most cases, this means keeping the output of the synth loud but not distorting, and using gain reduction on the signal as it enters the console.

I always use a direct box in conjunction with a synth, but since the instrument produces a high-impedance signal, most synthesizers sound just fine when they're brought into a channel at line level. However, from time to time you may run across a program that generates a lot of high-frequency activity, and if the instrument doesn't have enough gain to provide a good signal-to-noise ratio in the upper registers, the synth will sound very noisy. In such cases, you can often compensate for this by sending the signal through a direct box and then bringing it into the console through a low-impedance input circuit. Note, though, that this only applies when you're using a console that operates at +4 dB.

Adding Outboard Effects

Outboard effect devices like phase shifters and chorus pedals can often be used to enhance the sound of a synthesizer. For example, I always apply a chorus effect to string tracks that record at home, because it makes them sound full and more orchestral. By the same token, reverb can be used to give depth to a track, and echo can be used in dozens of imaginative ways. In fact, as with everything else about synths, the creative applications of effects are virtually limitless.

Yet adding an effect to a synth is like adding it to any other instrument. Any effect that can be used on a guitar, for example, can be used on a synth, and the direct-in recording techniques are the same as those we've been discussing throughout the book. You have the same options for routing the signal through the console, and you have the same option of adding the effect to the initial track or waiting until a bounce.

And, again, if your console operates at +4 dB and the effects unit is generating a lot of signal noise, you'll want to plug the synth into the effect and the effect into a direct box, so that you can bring the signal into the console through a low-impedance input circuit.

RECORDING DIAGRAM

SYNTHESIZERS
Adding a Chorus Effect

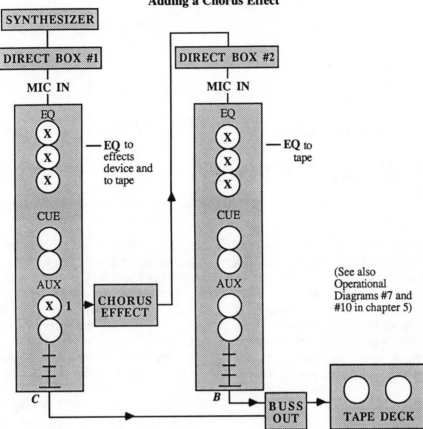

(See also
Operational
Diagrams #7 and
#10 in chapter 5)

Note: 1. When using a stereo chorus, each output from the device should be sent to a separate console channel, and each channel should be assigned to a separate buss. The channel containing the preeffect signal, in this case Channel A, may then need to be assigned to both busses if your chorus does not include the unaffected signal in one of the two sends. (See also the Recording Diagram in chapter 12, "Adding Stereo Chorus to the Signal," page 205.)

2. This particular procedure applies when using a console that operates at a +4 dB level. Many home consoles operate at −10 dB, in which case direct boxes need not be used to enhance signal quality. When using a −10 dB console, both the synth and the effect can be plugged directly into high-impedance inputs.

3. In either case, Direct Box #2 can be eliminated if you send the output of the effect to an effect return buss (see Operational Diagram #10 on page 76). However, when doing so, you are unable to provide separate EQ control over the effect.

Procedure:

1. Plug the synth into the high-impedance input of the direct box.

2. Plug the low-impedance output from the direct box into the low-impedance input ("Mic In") of console Channel A.

3. Patch the console's Aux Send 1 into the input of the chorus device.

4. Patch the output of the effect to the high-impedance input of a second direct box.

5. Patch the low-impedance output of this direct box into the low-impedance input of console Channel B.

6. Assign Channels A and B to the same buss.

7. Patch the buss into an input channel of the tape recorder.

8. Bring up level on Channel A and set the preeffect EQ.

9. Bring up level on the effect by turning up the Aux Send 1 pot on Channel A and by bringing up the fader on Channel B.

10. Solo Channel B in order to set the posteffect EQ.

11. Blend the signals as desired.

Chapter 15

How to Record Vocals

The two most important elements of any hit record are the song and the singer. If either element falls short, so will the recording. Therefore a great deal of care has to be taken anytime you put vocals on tape.

Throughout the last few chapters, we've been harping on the necessity of preplanning all your tracks so that you can be sure every instrument will fit properly into the recording. Although the vocal may be one of the last tracks you record, it should be the first one you consider when you sit down to work out the song.

LEAD VOCALS

One of the most difficult "instruments" to record is the human voice. It is acoustical in nature and particularly rich in overtones, which are the elements of the signal that give each voice its unique tonal characteristics. Consequently, when you record a vocal you want to do everything you can to preserve the overtones. They will give clarity to the sound of the voice and add breadth and spirit—and this is one time you don't want to skimp on *either*. After all, the vocal *is* the song.

Room Acoustics

As with other acoustic instruments, the environment in which the vocal is recorded affects the sound it has on tape. In this case, the more ambience a vocal track includes when you record it, the more difficult it becomes to control its placement within the song, and the more likely it is to lose clarity. So although it's fine to add ambience to the vocal during the mixdown (see chapter 16, "Mixdown Techniques"), you want to keep it as dry as possible when it's being laid down.

In keeping with this, you should record your vocals in an acoustically "dead" space. This, as we discuss in the studio acoustics chapter, can be an existing room, where the walls are soft and the floor is carpeted. Or it can be artificially created by constructing a five-by-five, three-sided booth out of baffles or blankets. You should place your microphone in the center of this alcove, about three feet out from the back wall (Figure 15a). Then, if you point the microphone *away* from that wall, when the vocalist faces the mike and sings, the sound of his voice will be absorbed by the baffles.

Creating the proper acoustical environment is particularly important if you are going to be putting any compression on the vocal. If the acoustics are at all ambient, the compressor will hear the echoes and work to bring them up in level. As a consequence, you'll have even more ambience in the signal, and the vocal will appear farther away (the more echo you hear in the vocal, the more distant it will appear).

So if you're hearing too much ambience in the vocal, it may be one of two things: either the acoustics are too "live," or the compression is set too high.

Creature Comforts

Although the acoustics of the environment are important, so is the convenience factor. Thus, you will want to create a comfortable space in which the vocalist can perform to his fullest potential.

This means providing the singer with a comfortable stool to sit on, whether between takes or while performing. It might mean getting a music stand for his lyric sheets, so that he doesn't have to fumble with papers as he sings. And you should definitely see to it that the vocalist has everything he needs nearby, like water or an ashtray, because nothing should distract the singer from his performance.

In this regard, you have to remember that even something that seems trivial to you may be very important to the overall quality of the vocal. For instance, a performance may be affected by something as simple as the way the room is lit: one singer may find it difficult to sing a slow love song in a room that's lit like a gymnasium, while another may have a

Figure 15a: To cut down on room reflections, the vocal mike should be placed in a deadened alcove or tent baffle. (*Courtesy of Larry Wichman*)

tendency to feel sleepy if the lights are too dim. The temperature of the room may also be important, because some singers are sensitive to the cold, so if the room is too chilly, their throats close up and their voices sound strained.

When you're recording your own vocals, it becomes even more important to create an environment that helps you avoid distractions. You already have your hands full just operating the equipment and worrying about how the vocal is going to sound on tape; the last thing you need is to run out of cigarettes or develop a backache because the stool you're using is too high off the floor.

Microphones

In previous chapters, we avoided the issue of microphone selection, because there are so many variables involved—finances being principal among them. However, vocal recordings can be greatly affected by your choice of microphone, so in this chapter we'll try to give you a general idea of which mikes the pros use and which mikes you can use given the more limited budget of a home studio.

When I'm in the studio and I have a selection of mikes at my disposal, the microphone I'll use will depend on the particular characteristics of the singer's voice. As a general rule, if the singer has a harsh voice, I'll use a tube microphone, like the Neumann U-49. Tube mikes will warm up the vocal a little bit and reduce any strident qualities the voice may have. On the other hand, if the singer tends to mumble, I'll use a brighter-sounding mike, such as the Neumann U-89, which is a favorite of mine.

Other mikes that are often used for vocals in pro studios include the Telefunken 251, the AKG C-12A and 414, and the Shure SM-7.

Unfortunately, microphones of this quality can cost as much as $1,000 or more, which essentially prices them right out of the home studio market. So if you're looking for more moderately priced microphones that can still do the job, you should try out some dynamic microphones, like the Shure SM-57 or the AKG D-330. If EQed properly, either of these two mikes is capable of giving you a high-quality vocal sound, and neither should cost more than $200.

If you do have a number of mikes from which to choose, one way to determine which is best suited to the singer's voice is to run each into a different console channel and have the singer try them all. Your choice should become apparent fairly quickly this way. (See also chapter 18, "Buyer's Guide to Studio Gear.")

Figure 15b: Excellent mikes to use when recording vocals.

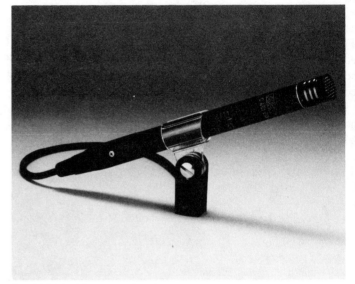

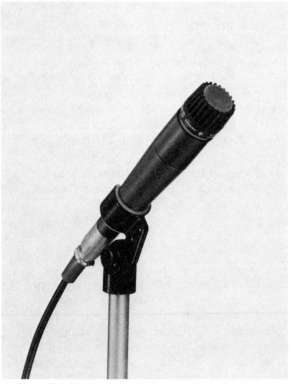

1. AKG 414 (*Courtesy of AKG Acoustics, Inc.*)

2. AKG 451 (*Courtesy of AKG Acoustics, Inc.*)

3. Neumann U-89 & U-87 (*Courtesy of Gotham Audio Corporation*)

4. Shure SM-57 (*Courtesy of Shure Brothers, Inc.*)

Miking Techniques

The vocal can often be affected by the position of the mike in relation to the singer. It is usually better to have the vocalist sing up to a microphone rather than down into it. By hanging the microphone one or two inches above the singer's mouth, the singer has to lean back, which tends to open his throat. This makes it easier to press for those high notes and gives the voice more clarity.

The microphone should be positioned so that it's approximately eight to twelve inches away from the singer's mouth (Figure 15c). This will avoid what is called "proximity effect," and in the case of vocals, it's particularly important. If the singer is too close to the microphone, the proximity effect will make the vocal sound dull and muddy.

However, even though you've put some distance between the singer and the mike, occasionally a singer will sneak back up on the mike, and you'll find that while you've gotten a great vocal performance on tape, it sounds a bit louded. Should this happen, you may be able to alleviate the problem with EQ. If you have parametric EQ capabilities, you can reduce the level in a very narrow band at 200 Hz, and that will usually help clear up the signal.

Vocal EQ Levels

EQing the human voice is always an interesting proposition, because each and every vocalist is unique. Luckily, however, vocals do fall into various categories, which makes it possible to give you a general idea of how certain voices should be approached.

For instance, you'll find that some vocalists who sing very hard in high registers will hit certain very piercing notes. The source of this unpleasantness usually lies in the range between 900 Hz and 3K and will need to be located and reduced.

In the case of my own voice, for instance, a moderate reduction (2 dB or so) at 900 Hz helps smooth out such tones. In the case of certain other singers I've worked with, and particularly with female vocalists, a reduction in the area around 3K seems to be more effective. You have to be careful, though, because if you reduce that frequency range too much, you can lose a lot of vocal excitement.

In fact, when EQing a vocal, if you have parametric capabilities, you will want to use narrow bandwidths in all but the extreme high frequencies. By doing this, you allow the vocal to remain separate from the rest of the instruments, as there will be less chance that you will be enhancing the exact same frequencies as, for example, the guitar. You should also EQ fairly gently so that you do not create any frequency spikes.

If your equalizer is not parametric, applying EQ requires a bit more ingenuity. Graphic equalizers have relatively wide bandwidths, so they're not as effective on vocals as you might like them to be, although sweepable-band systems can provide at least adequate control (see Tape Tip #17, chapter 6).

The fundamental pitch, or body, of a male singer's voice

Figure 15c: The vocal mike should be positioned so that the singer must sing *up* into it. Unlike hand-held mikes, the diaphragm in this condenser mike points out to the side, so although it may appear that this studio mike is aimed straight down, it is actually aimed directly at Peter's mouth. (*Courtesy of Laura Marenzi*)

(unless he's Frankie Valli), lies somewhere between 500 Hz and 800 Hz. This is the range where the bulk of the signal can be found, and because it's so dominant, you'll probably never have to boost it. If anything, you may occasionally have to cut it slightly in order to give the overtones a bit more prominence.

Whatever warm qualities the voice contains are found in the range between 250 Hz and 500 Hz. However, that's also very close to the proximity effect frequencies of 180 Hz–200 Hz, and as we mentioned in previous chapters, any boost there will cause a drastic reduction in signal clarity. So you have to be careful not to muddy the sound when you're EQing for warmth.

The 5K–7K range is the area where sibilants occur. So if the singer has a tendency to swallow *S*'s, and they sound a bit more like *F*'s, you might want to carefully boost EQ in a narrow band somewhere around 7K. On the other hand, if the singer has a tendency to whistle his or her *S*'s, you will need to make a narrow band reduction in this area in order to make the sound less piercing. You should never use a broad band boost in this range, because then when the vocal is added to the track, it mixes in with the sibilants of *all* of the instruments—cymbals, the top end of guitars, synthesizers, and so on—and creates what sounds like a musical lisp.

The 10K–15K frequency range, which contains many of the characteristic overtones and upper harmonics of the human voice, is frequently ignored in home recording. You can do a great deal to enhance the vocal's position on a track by paying particular attention to this area. It will provide the feeling that the vocal is surrounded by air and will bring out any breathiness in the voice.

When I EQ this section of the spectrum, I generally use shelving to produce a very broad band boost all the way from 12K through 15K. Some people like to begin this boost down around 10K, but I find that area to be a bit risky. It's awfully close to the sibilants range, and a boost here could create that harsh musical lisp.

Don't forget that when you're mixing, the vocal becomes the dominant feature of the track, and if you get the vocal sounding great, then everything else just seems to fall into place.

Optional Miking Techniques

When you're miking vocals in a home studio situation, you may not be looking for the same standard of quality necessary for a record. And if that is the case, the single-mike technique should serve you well. However, if you have the time and the equipment, there is an interesting method of miking you might want to try, which makes use of two, separately EQed microphones.

This is the technique I used with Men At Work's Colin Hay, whose voice is very strong, yet very rich in overtones. In fact, the sheer strength of Colin's delivery can overpower

the more delicate, throaty characteristics of his voice, and when I tried miking Colin's vocals in a normal fashion, the fundamental pitch of his voice tended to dominate the track. As a consequence, the compressor was being activated in a way that was unflattering to his voice, and a lot of the dynamics were getting lost.

In order to capture both the strength of Colin's voice and the more delicate overtones it contained, I placed two microphones in the room. The first mike, a Neumann U-89, was positioned in a standard fashion, approximately twelve to fourteen inches from the vocalist. Then I placed a second, brighter-sounding mike—an AKG-414—three or four feet behind the first and about two feet above it (Figure 15d).

The close microphone was used to capture the body of Colin's voice, so the signal from that mike was compressed slightly, and the frequencies in the lower registers, from 250 Hz through 3K, were emphasized.

The distant mike was used to capture the overtones, so it was EQed to enhance the frequencies above 5K—the range that had not been included in the close-mike EQ. This also meant rolling back all those frequencies that had been boosted on the other mike, such as the 200 Hz–400 Hz range and the bottom-end register of 100 Hz and below. And

Figure 15d: This dual-mike configuration is similar to that used for the Men At Work vocals mentioned in text. (*Courtesy of Larry Wichman*)

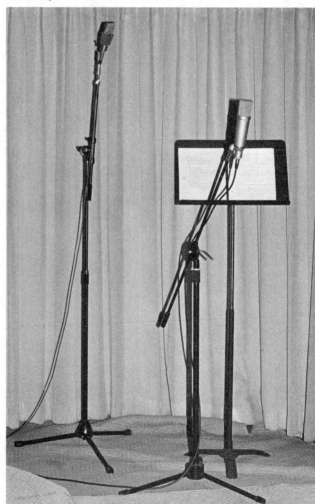

because I didn't want to compress the signal from this microphone, I had to dip the level at 3K, so that if Colin really let loose, the signal wouldn't contain any of the stridency (harshness) that might be generated.

By not compressing this signal, I was able to retain a lot of the dynamics of Colin's voice and at the same time capture the subtle vocal qualities that make it so pleasant to listen to.

If you want to try this technique out at home using microphones of lesser quality, it may require slightly different EQ settings. However, as long as your console has individual EQ capabilities of one sort or another, you should be okay. The approach is basically the same as the one you would take when setting up distant room mikes to record drums, but with a different result. Here, the goal isn't to capture more ambience, but to capture the overtones.

There is no set formula for the distance between the two microphones because that will vary according to the strength of the singer's voice and the amount of overtones you want to capture. However, there is a way to determine if the distances are wrong, and that is to listen for phase cancelation.

When the vocal is phasing in this recording setup, the overtone range is eliminated, so it sounds as if the singer is singing through a cardboard tube. The only way to get rid of the effect is by physically moving the second mike and finding a place where you're able to capture the overtones yet not interfere with the phase relationship in the vocal.

All in all, it may take some work getting used to this miking technique, but it can do a lot to improve the quality of the vocal.

Headphone Mix

There are many effects that can be applied to a vocal, such as reverb, echo, phasing, phased echo, delayed echo, slap echo, and more, but none of these should be added to the vocal when it is first put down on tape. That is a process better suited to the mixdown stage of recording. However, it is essential that you *do* add the effects to the signal being monitored by the vocalist.

One of the most critical elements of recording any vocal, or any overdub, is the headphone mix (AKA foldback mix). This is the particular blend of instruments the musician hears as he plays, or in this case sings, and it has a significant effect upon the quality of the performance.

As any musician knows, the more exciting the track sounds, the more inspired the musician becomes. So even though the mix in the headphones will be different from the track as it's going on tape, you want it to sound as much like the finished product as possible.

As far as the singer is concerned, the most important part of the mix will be the volume of his voice in relation to the surrounding instruments. Some singers like their vocal to appear loud, with the track just audible enough to be used for pitch reference, while others are intimidated by volume,

and if the vocal's too loud, they'll hold back. Still others like the feeling of being surrounded by the track and need to have all the elements included in the mix in order to become inspired.

Whatever the singer's preference happens to be, the important thing is to give him what he needs for his performance. There are times when you may think that you know the singer's needs better than he does, but that's not always the case, so work with the vocalist and remember that the key to making everybody happy is communication.

As you're going through the track, you may run into some problems that can be rectified by altering the mix. For instance, if you feel the singer is singing behind the beat, you can raise the level of the drums. Or if he complains of hearing too much of his own vocal, you can raise the level of a rhythm guitar line or a synthesizer part, in order to provide him with a musical security blanket. And if the singer is having pitch problems, it may be very helpful to boost the bass track. On the surface, a bass guitar doesn't seem like an easy instrument to use for pitch reference, but it appears to help most singers.

After you've been tracking for a while, the singer may begin complaining that he's no longer hearing enough of the mix. This is inevitable, because after a number of passes, the singer will become used to what he's hearing, and he'll want something new to propel him into his performance.

It often helps to anticipate this, and to monitor the singer through headphones yourself. Then, as you begin to lose that sense of excitement, you can enhance the track a bit as you go. For instance, if there's a guitar solo at one point, you may want to boost it a little. You may also give the rhythm section a little boost while lowering some of the other overdub instruments—which will make the singer feel more surrounded by the sound.

The quality of the sound you send through the headphones is also important. In this case, you should EQ all of the previously recorded instruments and add the effects you plan to give them during mixdown. You should also give the singer an idea of the way you plan to treat his vocal, so that he can gain inspiration from that as well.

For examples that illustrate this technique, you can refer to Operational Diagrams #4–#7 in chapter 5.

Headphone Mix for Two or More Singers

If, when recording backing vocals or duets, you have limited control over the vocal mix the singers hear, one of the artists may have difficulty picking up his own voice. This is particularly true in cases where all the singers are using one microphone, because it's then impossible to bring up the level on just one vocalist.

If this is the case, you might want to have the singer listen to the track with one ear and remove the headphone from the other, so that he can hear the other singers. Just make sure that he holds the unused phone tightly against his head, or the signal might leak into the mike.

Leakage can occur for any number of reasons, so every time you finish a vocal track, you should solo the vocal up and check the track to make sure that the level of leakage is acceptable. If it's not, you'll have to retake the track, because leakage will make the recording sound muddy once all the tracks are added together.

To avoid leakage problems, make sure that anyone who is using a set of headphones in the studio doesn't leave them lying around without first unplugging them. Plus, you should never use monitor speakers when you're doing overdubs, because they'll definitely leak into the mike. And make sure that the headphone mix is not so loud that every time the compressor kicks in, it detects the signal and brings it up in level.

TAPE TIP #32
Snap, Crackle, Pop Filters

Everybody's got a theory on what makes the best pop filter (a device that reduces the "puuh" effect created by the burst of air that enters the mike every time you pronounce a *P*).

In vocal recording applications, very few people use the pop filters that come with the microphone. Those are the spongy things that fit over the capsule end of the mike. These screens are designed basically to filter out wind, and as a consequence they filter out a lot of the high frequencies you want to have appear in the signal. Since these are generally unsatisfactory, a variety of pop filters have been developed, usually out of whatever was lying around the studio.

One very effective method of eliminating pop is to tape a pencil to the front of the microphone, dividing the capsule in half (Figure 15e). This creates a barrier that will spread any explosive bursts of air to either side, which keeps the full

force of the gust from directly affecting the mike. Better still, this does not inhibit the mike's ability to pick up the top end.

Unfortunately, unless you can get very ingenious with a roll of Scotch tape, it's very difficult to use this technique on a ball mike. So you might want to stretch a nylon stocking across the open expanse of a coat hanger (Figure 15f) and place it a few inches in front of the mike. It helps if you mold the hanger into the shape of a loop—a professional-looking variation of which appears in the studio on the *USA for Africa* video—but it's not essential.

And if you can't get your hands on some panty hose, you can use the pop filter that came with the mike once you cut perpendicular slits in the material. However, this is not your most effective alternative.

Figure 15e: An example of a pop filter made by taping a pencil to the mike screen. Note that on this studio condenser mike, the diaphragm points out to the side, meaning that in this picture, the mike is actually aimed at the camera. Therefore, to use this technique on a ball mike, the pencil would need to be taped to the very end of the microphone, making it look like a propeller. (*Courtesy of Laura Marenzi*)

Figure 15f: An example of a pop filter made by stretching nylons (or panty hose) over a coat hanger. Such filters are often used in the studio, and they are extremely effective. (*Courtesy of Laura Marenzi*)

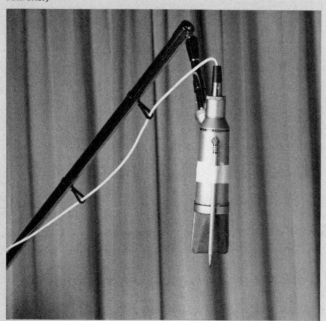

Compressor Settings

When you record a lead vocal, you want to make it appear to be as real as possible. Thus, you want the signal to be as transparent as possible—meaning that it retains its complete dynamic and frequency range response. Therefore, you want to keep the record levels low enough so that the tape does not go into saturation, and you want to use as little compression as is necessary. You never want to overcompress the vocal, because compression removes much of the vocal's character and limits its dynamics.

Some people who home-record use compression as a vocal crutch. Instead of learning how to properly use a mike and how to control their voice so that there are no giant leaps in level when they belt out a loud note, they have the compressor control the level *for* them. This is something you should never do, because it hurts the vocal track a lot more than it helps.

If anything, you should take exactly the reverse approach and work on your mike technique as described in the next section. And if you don't want to take voice lessons, talk to anyone you know who has a controlled vocal technique and try to pick up some pointers. You'll be amazed at the difference it will make.

Of course, small doses of compression are advisable on vocal tracks as a means of taking care of any dynamic slips that might be made. So when I compress a vocal, I generally set the compression ratio at about 4:1, and I set the levels controlling gain reduction so that when the compressor is hit the hardest, it doesn't reduce the gain by more than 2 dB or 3 dB. If the gain is reduced any farther, the signal can take on the sucking quality that vocals played on the radio sometimes have (radio stations severely compress their signals).

Vocal Technique

One major component of recording any vocal is the singer's vocal technique. As we've mentioned before, you can't make a bad instrument sound great, no matter what you do, and that's particularly true with lead vocals.

For instance, if the vocalist is singing at the same volume all of the time, never varying the dynamics of the vocal, it's going to be very difficult to create an interesting vocal track. And if the singer has no mike technique, and goes from a whisper to a shout without pulling back from the microphone, you're either going to end up with a very compressed vocal, or you're going to drive yourself crazy during the mix trying to limit it manually with the fader.

When you're working with a singer, you may have to make him or her mindful of studio mike techniques, because the technique a singer must use onstage, where he or she literally has to eat the microphone, is totally different. It's particularly important to let the singer know that when he's belting out a loud note, he should back his head away from the mike so that he doesn't trip the compressor unnecessar-

ily. The only alternative you would have would be to turn the mike level down and let the singer lean closer to the mike during the softer parts—but that is something you *don't* want to do because of the potential for developing proximity effect problems. So make sure he knows that when he's singing the softest, he should be twelve to fourteen inches away from the mike, and during the loud sections he should pull his head farther away.

Many singers will approach a song with the attitude that the louder and stronger they sing, the more powerful and emotive their voice will sound on tape. And then they're mystified when the vocal sounds whimpy on the playback. This happens because the vocal is being overcompressed.

The compressor is a great "neutralizer," and the louder somebody sings, the more likely it is that the vocal is going to get squashed. So the first thing you have to make a singer aware of is that a compressor will limit his voice if it gets too loud, and that a much more powerful performance can be had if he uses vocal "technique" to limit the volume. For instance, Michael McDonald sings very softly, yet his vocals sound huge.

Some singers may respond by saying that it doesn't seem natural doing it that way, and that they feel like they should be "going for it," as they do live. Well, the reality for vocalists is that what they do live isn't necessarily what works best in the studio, where mike technique probably becomes the single most important component of a good vocal sound.

Mike Booth Noise

When you record a vocal, you have to make sure that the singer isn't wearing a lot of noisy jewelry, and that when he's singing, he's not thumping his foot or jumping up and down. Such idiosyncrasies may be fine live, but it's not so fine at the mixdown stage, when the signals are EQed for clarity, and you suddenly start to hear weird jingles and rumbles that must then be eliminated.

It's also important to mount the mike on a mike stand or a boom, because the singer is apt to generate quite a bit of noise if he or she handles the mike during the performance.

Vocal Fatigue

The voice is a delicate instrument, and a vocalist suffers fatigue much more quickly than a guitarist or a drummer. Therefore, you want to spend as little time as possible setting the levels and getting the vocal sound.

One approach is to rough in the sound while the singer is singing solo (warming up)—make sure there's no distortion on the microphone and set the compressor. Then, if you feel the singer is ready, immediately begin recording the vocals as you put on the final EQ touches. Doing this, you just have to take the chance that the singer isn't going to come up with his ultimate performance on the first few takes.

Another thing to consider is placing performance ahead of perfect track sound. In other words, if the performance is

TAPE TIP #33
Getting It Right the Second Time: Overdubs

Overdubbing and punching in vocal parts can be a very effective way to cleanse your track of those unflattering mistakes every singer seems to make. The miscue may be something as subtle as a bad vocal inflection or as obvious as a sour note, but if the overall performance is a solid one, then it's senseless, and fatiguing, to have the singer do the whole track again. Besides, there is no such thing as a perfect performance from start to finish. So what you do is move the tape ahead to the offensive passage and simply drop in a new vocal.

There are two ways to do this: the easy way and the hard way. If you have twenty-four tracks to work with, you can just have the vocalist sing the new passages on an open track. Then these overdubs can be inserted in place of the bad vocal lines, either during the mix or by combining the two tracks onto a third and dropping the new vocal parts in as you go. Or if you do have the three tracks open, you can lay complete vocal tracks down on two of them and combine the best parts from each onto the third track, which then becomes your master vocal.

This technique is used on almost every recording that comes out of a professional studio, and its advantage is that it breaks the process down into two separate steps. So you can concentrate first on getting the vocal to sound right and *then* deal with dropping it into the track.

Unfortunately, you don't have this luxury when you only have a few tracks to work with, and more than likely you're going to have to perform both steps at the same time—a detailed account of which can be found in "Punch-Ins/Drop-Ins," chapter 6.

However, when using this technique on vocals, the main thing you have to remember is that unless you can recapture the sound of the vocal exactly as it was during the first take, the inserts are going to be obvious to the listener.

So when you're dropping in lines, it's important that the singer sing along, even while you're not recording. This will help him keep the dynamics of the vocal consistent. Lots of times the singer will wait quietly for the line he's going to sing and then jump in—at the wrong volume. And if the level of the line you're dropping in is radically different from the level of the original vocal, you're defeating the whole purpose of compression.

If you're not using a 24-track machine, and you have to place the overdubs directly onto the original track because no other track is available, you won't have the luxury of altering the sound of the overdub during playback. Therefore, you should try to do your overdubbing as soon after the original tracking as possible, and make sure that the vocalist tries his best to match the original dynamics.

In some cases this may well be impossible, and you may have to rerecord the vocal for an entire verse, or chorus, in order to avoid making the insertion obvious. But at least that's better than having to redo the whole song. And since each machine is slightly different in its drop-in timing characteristics, you should practice on the machine before having the singer waste his voice through miscalculation.

---

there, but there are minor sound problems that can be corrected in the mix or through overdubs, keep the track. I've always felt that the quality of an exciting performance far outweighs any slight sound problems.

In fact, overdubbing is a very useful tool when you don't want to wear out the singer's voice. There are many ways to overdub vocals—everything from punching in a phrase to mixing phrases from two or more complete vocals together—and they're all covered in Tape Tip #33: "Getting It Right the Second Time: Overdubs."

BACKING VOCALS

There are probably as many different theories on recording backing vocals as there are record producers. For instance, some producers believe that the simpler something sounds the better, so they will only record one track of backing vocals using one or two harmony parts. Other producers prefer them to sound huge, so they multitrack their backing vocals in order to achieve a chorale effect.

The backing vocal sound of the Eagles would be a good example of the first technique. In their case, the individual-

ity of each voice is of prime importance, and you can almost pick out which Eagle is singing which harmony part. This produces a very intimate blend of voices, which is a feeling the band reinforces by limiting the harmonies to one or two parts.

The second technique is evident on Roy Thomas Baker productions of bands like Queen and Foreigner, where instead of hearing a few isolated harmonies, the listener is treated to a wall of vocals. An excellent example of this is Queen's "Bohemian Rhapsody," which is packed with them.

This chorale effect is achieved by tracking the backing vocals over and over and having each singer repeat his part. This creates layer upon layer of voices, and along with producing a truly huge sound, it tends to smooth out any pitch or timing indiscretions committed by the vocalists and gives the vocals a glossy quality.

It's a question of judgment as to which technique you will want to use. On the one hand, the chorale effect will give you a big sound; on the other hand, it lacks a certain sense of realism. And with the first technique, although you may preserve a sense of intimacy, a much higher degree of precision is required to carry off the track.

Miking and Acoustics

The mechanics of recording backing vocals are roughly the same as they are for lead vocals, with one exception. Depending on the number of singers, you might have to alter the response pattern of the microphone. The microphone used to record lead vocals should exhibit a cardioid, or kidney-shaped, response pattern, but when you're recording a larger group of backing vocalists, that pattern is too narrow. So you will either have to use multiple microphones or pull out a mike that exhibits an omnidirectional (circular) or bidirectional (semicircular) pattern.

When using multiple microphones, mike positioning becomes important, because you have to be careful of the same phasing problems we discussed earlier. However, the advantage of having multiple microphones is that you have greater control over the voices of the individual singers.

For instance, if there's a group of six singers using three microphones, you can control each group of two singers. But if you're only using one mike, to get the right blend of voices you're going to have to move the vocalists in and out of the pattern until their physical relationship produces the right blend. That's because if you have one singer who, because of the note he's singing, is singing very hard and loud, in order to create a blend he would have to be farther away from the microphone than the vocalist who is singing lower and softer.

This blend of voices is probably *the* critical element in recording backing vocals. The object is to create the correct acoustic blend, so that the harmony structure resembles a chord and each note appears with equal importance.

Frankly, creating a successful backing vocal track has less to do with recording the material than it does with creating a blend in the room before it ever goes to tape. This is particularly true if all of the backing vocals are being put onto one track, because once they have been recorded, there's little you can do to alter them. This is one reason a producer will use the layering technique. Instead of having to be exact about the blend, he can create a mean average of a number of recordings of the same parts.

EQ and Compression

You can EQ backing vocals the same as you would a lead vocal; however, you may not want to enhance the upper-frequency, overtone portion of the signal to the same degree. If you remember, these overtones are what give each voice its individuality, so since you want the lead vocal to remain dominant, you want it to have more overtone response than the other voices.

The amount of compression you use on the backing vocals will depend on the singers. There are some people who don't compress these vocals at all until the mix, because the parts don't have the dynamics of a lead vocal. Although this is probably your best bet as well, if you do need compression during the take, use the same guidelines as for lead vocals, trying for as little compression as possible.

VOCAL EQ REMINDERS

Suggestions:
Use narrow bandwidths and EQ gently.
Read "Vocal EQ Levels" in chapter.
Read Tape Tip #17, chapter 6.

Problem:
If the singer's high notes are piercing,
   MALE vocal, reduce at 900 Hz
   FEMALE vocal, reduce at 3K

If the singer's S's produce a piercing whistle, reduce at 7K

General EQ:
BOOSTS
   12K–15K—shelving
   5K
   250 Hz–500 Hz—lightly

CUT
   500 Hz–800 Hz—if necessary

Double-Mike Technique:
Close Mike
   BOOSTS
   5K
   250 Hz–500 Hz

   CUT
   3K—slightly

Distant Mike
   BOOSTS
   12K–15K
   7K
   3K

   CUT
   100 Hz
   200 Hz–400 Hz

RECORDING DIAGRAMS

VOCALS
Adding Compression to a Vocal

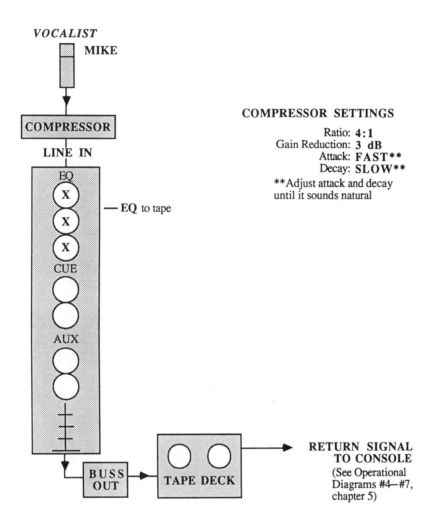

COMPRESSOR SETTINGS

Ratio: **4:1**
Gain Reduction: **3 dB**
Attack: **FAST****
Decay: **SLOW****

**Adjust attack and decay
until it sounds natural

Procedure:

1. Prepare the singer's recording environment: check stool for squeaks, make sure there is a place for lyric sheets and a stand for the mike, make liquid refreshments available, and so forth. Also, prepare a general headphone mix of the music.

2. Plug the microphone directly into the compressor.

3. Patch the compressor output to the Line In of a console channel.

4. Assign the channel to the desired buss.

5. Patch buss output to tape input.

6. Use the gain control on the compressor to bring the signal up to level. Be careful not to overload the input into the console.

7. Fine-tune the headphone mix and adjust vocal EQ and compression settings. Try not to waste time doing so, as you don't want to wear out the singer's voice.

VOCALS
Generating the Headphone Mix

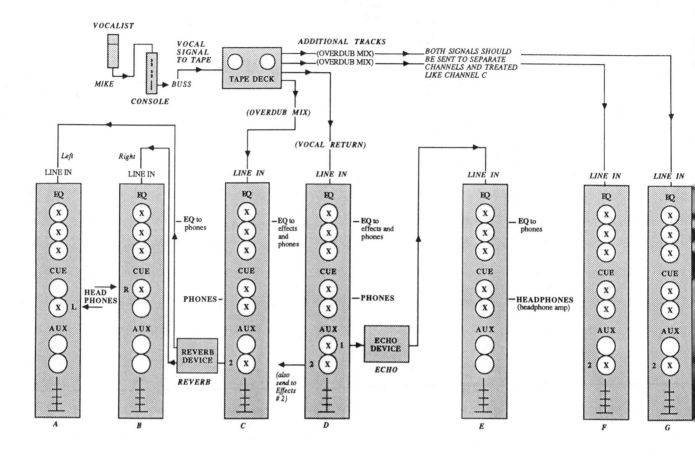

In order to aid the vocalist's performance, the headphone mix should be made to sound as much like the finished product as possible. This means that you should try to treat the mix with any effect you intend to add during mixdown. In this case, we'll be applying echo to the vocal and stereo reverb to both the vocal and the overdub mix.

Note: 1. The cue mix is generated by blending the preeffect and posteffect signals from the appropriate channels (as indicated).

2. If you don't have any input channels available to use as effect returns, you can return the effect signals via the aux returns, as illustrated in the next diagram.

Procedure:

1. Send the vocal signal to tape in the normal fashion: bring the mike into the low-impedance input on a console channel, assign the channel to a buss, and patch the output of the buss to an input on the tape deck.

2. Return the vocal to console Channel D by patching the appropriate tape deck output to the channel's line input.

3. Return any existing tracks, which are part of the overdub mix, to separate console channels. (In this example, patch the output of the first of those tracks to the line input of console Channel C, with the understanding that any procedures that apply to this signal also apply to the two other overdub-mix tracks.)

4. Patch the console cue sends to the inputs of the headphone amplifier.

5. Patch Aux Send 1 to the input of the echo device.

6. Return the echo output to console Channel E.

7. Patch Aux Send 2 to the input of the reverb device.

8. Return the *left* reverb output to console Channel A and the *right* reverb output to console Channel B.

9. Use your own set of headphones to monitor the mix and work with the singer, adjusting levels to his needs.

10. Bring up level on the overdub mix using Channel C fader and cue sends. EQ the signal.

11. Bring up level on Channel C's Aux Send 2.

12. Bring up level on Channels A and B by using the faders and the cue sends (left cue for Channel A, right cue for Channel B).

13. Isolate Channels A and B by turning down the cues on Channel C. Then balance and EQ the reverb signal.

14. Bring up level on Channel C cues and regulate the amount of reverb applied to the mix by adjusting the level of Channel C's Aux Send 2. (Do same with Channels F and G.)

15. Bring up level on the vocal using Channel D fader and cue sends. EQ the signal.

16. Apply reverb to vocal by bringing up level on Channel D Aux Send 2.

17. Balance the amount of reverb applied to the vocal and re-EQ the reverb mix on Channels A and B if necessary.

18. Bring up level on Channel D's Aux Send 1 to add echo.

19. Solo Channel E and bring up level on echo using fader and cue sends. Adjust echo delay time and EQ the signal.

20. Adjust the amount of echo contained in mix by using the Channel D Aux Send 1.

21. Rebalance the vocal level and the overdub mix level according to the singer's needs.

VOCALS
Generating the Headphone Mix
(For Limited-Capacity Consoles)

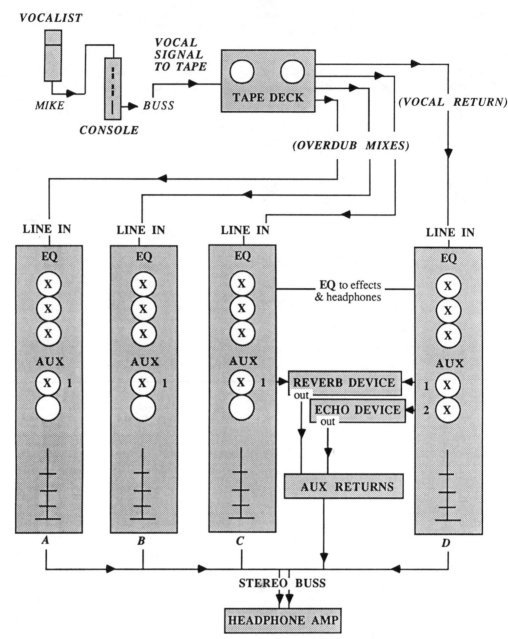

If you have a limited number of channels to work with, or a limited number of aux sends, the following diagram can provide a means of creating an acceptable headphone mix for the vocalist.

Note: Since the effect signals are being routed through the monaural effects send/return circuitry, you lose the capability of returning a stereo effect signal—such as that from the stereo reverb we used in the last diagram.

Procedure:

1. Send the vocal signal to tape in the normal fashion: bring the mike into the low-impedance input on a console channel, assign the channel to a buss, and patch the output of the buss to an input on the tape deck.

2. Return the vocal to console Channel D by patching the appropriate tape deck output to the channel's line input.

3. Assign Channel D to the stereo buss.

4. Return any existing tracks, which are part of the overdub mix, to separate console channels by patching the tape output for each track into a separate input channel. (In this example, these signals are returned on Channels A, B, and C.)

5. Assign all channels to the stereo buss.

6. Patch Aux Send 1 to the input of the reverb device.

7. Patch the reverb unit's output to the Aux Return 1 input on the console.

8. Patch Aux Send 2 to the input of the echo device.

9. Patch the echo unit's output to the Aux Return 2 input on the console.

10. Patch the stereo buss sends to the inputs of the headphone amplifier.

11. Use your own set of headphones to monitor the mix and work with the singer, adjusting levels to his needs.

12. Bring up level on each overdub mix, using the channel faders. EQ the signal.

13. Add reverb to these mixes one at a time by bringing up level on each input channel's Aux Send 1 pot.

14. Re-EQ the mixes.

15. Bring up level on the vocal using the Channel D fader. EQ the signal.

16. Apply reverb to the vocal by bringing up level on Channel D's Aux Send 1 pot.

17. Apply echo to the vocal by bringing up level on Channel D's Aux Send 2 pot.

18. Adjust levels of reverb and echo to suit the singer's tastes. Re-EQ the signal.

19. Rebalance the vocal level and the overdub mix level according to the singer's needs.

Chapter 16

Mixdown Techniques

Now we come to the point in the recording process called the mix, or mixdown, which is when all of the recorded elements are placed within the stereo spectrum.

In the first chapter, we defined the stereo spectrum as a three-dimensional space emanating from two sources: the speakers. And in this sense, a mix is similar to a sketch or a painting, in which a three-dimensional image is created on a two-dimensional plane through the use of "perspective." So what we're going to be talking about in this chapter are ways in which you can create that perspective electronically, taking the "dry" tracks of the initial recordings, applying effects and EQ, and blending it all together in a way that complements the tone of the music and provides a focal point for the listener.

Mixdown is the most subjective part of the recording process, and you'll need to make aesthetic judgments about the quality of the blend every step of the way. So to make the process easier to understand, we're going to structure an imaginary 8-track mix (bouncing eight tracks down to two tracks, which gives us a master copy) and lead you through it step-by-step. Although we've chosen an 8-track format, fundamentally the same considerations will apply to everything from 4-track mixes to 24-track mixes, with minor variations.

We've chosen to perform an 8-track mix, because with eight initial tracks (drums on four tracks, bass, keyboards, guitar, and vocal), we would not have had to combine any of the original tracks during a premix bounce, which is a technique outlined in chapter 7. So in terms of EQ, effects, and levels, each of the elements we're combining can be treated individually (don't forget, each of the tracks is, at this point, still dry, as you've been waiting until now to add the effects).

However, it should be noted that much of the information included in this chapter can, and should, be applied to all premix bounces, because at that time you'll need to be adding effects and EQ to the bounce tracks, just as you would

during mixdown. In fact, you'll virtually be setting up your final mix in the process, so you'll need to plan carefully and keep all of these mixdown considerations in mind.

HOW TO APPROACH THE MIX

Mixdown is not just the mechanical process of combining tracks. In fact, it is different from anything we've done so far, and it needs to be approached from an entirely new angle. For example, all of the elements of the mix are interrelated, and what you do to the sound of one instrument will affect all of the others. Therefore, you need to forget everything you learned in the instrument chapters, because you can no longer treat the instruments as individual entities. You have to look at them as being part of "the big picture."

This also means that you will constantly need to reevaluate the effectiveness of what you are creating, because each step you take will alter the balance of the mix. And balance is the key to a successful mix.

What you're trying to do via the mix is give the blend of instruments a cohesive structure, so that the listener has a point of focus. In essence, you're creating a musical painting, and you need the structure to reflect this. Thus, some elements will be made to play support roles and provide background shading, while the more important elements, such as the vocal and the drums, will be made to stand out, so that they're the focus of attention.

In each instance, the decision of how you structure the mix, and which instruments you use for the key roles, will be a matter of personal taste. Therefore, while we can lay out the basic concepts, and give you an idea of what you need to shoot for, we can't provide you with a specific recipe for success. Nor should you consider our aesthetic preferences to be gospel, and if you prefer the sound you get when you do something *your* way, and it works, then go with it.

And remember, to a large extent mixdown is a matter of

controlled experimentation. So above all, don't be afraid to play around with it!

CREATING THE STEREO IMAGE

In order to give a three-dimensional perspective to the music, you need to apply panning in combination with ambient effects like echo and reverb. Panning allows you to place the signal at any point along the linear surface of the stereo plane. Reverb and echo are used to give depth and to move the signal back from the foreground.

Panning

There's nothing mysterious about panning. Every channel is monaural, and when two output channels are used as a stereo pair, the panning function allows you to alter the percentage of the signal that is sent through each (Figure 16a). This, in turn, determines where the signal will image.

For example, when the pan is centered, the volume of the left channel and the right channel are equal, and the instrument will image in the center. If you move the pan slightly to the left, you increase the volume of the left channel and

decrease the volume of the right channel, and the instrument images farther to the left. Finally, if you position the pan "hard left," meaning all the way to the left side, you maximize the volume of the left channel and completely cut off the right channel, and the instrument images to the far left.

For a simple demonstration of how the pan control utilizes volume, all you need to do is assign a console input channel to two busses and solo one of them so that the other can't be heard. Then, move the pan from one side to the other. As you do so, you'll hear the volume drop, and eventually the signal disappears altogether.

Depth

Depth is accomplished by applying reverb or echo to the signal, and the more you add, relative to the source, the more distant the instrument sounds.

It may be easier to understand the concept if you imagine standing in a cave. If someone is standing next to you and talking, the ambience of the cave has very little effect on the sound of his voice because it's much louder than the echo. But if he moves to the back of the cave and speaks to you,

Figure 16a: Depth and panning.

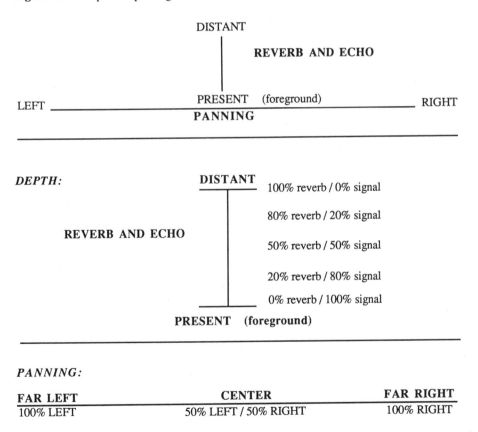

DISTANT

REVERB AND ECHO

LEFT ———————— PRESENT (foreground) ———— RIGHT
PANNING

DEPTH: **DISTANT**

REVERB AND ECHO

100% reverb / 0% signal

80% reverb / 20% signal

50% reverb / 50% signal

20% reverb / 80% signal

0% reverb / 100% signal

PRESENT (foreground)

PANNING:

FAR LEFT	**CENTER**	**FAR RIGHT**
100% LEFT	50% LEFT / 50% RIGHT	100% RIGHT

LEFT-CENTER	**RIGHT-CENTER**
80% LEFT / 20% RIGHT	20% LEFT / 80% RIGHT

the echo will be more pronounced, and thus it will influence your perception of how far away he is.

In everyday life, if you were to walk through the world with your eyes closed, or sit in a marble room completely in the dark, the relationship between room echoes and distance would be quite obvious, because subconsciously you use this relationship as one means of determining distance in your physical environment. So by applying this concept to a stereo recording, you are able to use a two-dimensional medium to make your mind "hear" in three dimensions.

PREPARING THE MIX

Before you begin adding effects, you first need to set up a "dry" mix that includes all of the musical elements you're going to be working with. After all, each instrument is a separate part of the musical picture, and you need to assemble all the parts before you can begin to put them in their proper relationship.

The procedures for generating this initial blend are as follows:

1. Return each recorded track on the tape recorder into a separate input channel.

2. Assign each channel to the stereo buss (frequently labelled "Mix").

3. Place the tape recorder in "repro."

4. If the tracks were encoded (recorded) with noise reduction, be sure they are set to decode on playback.

5. Bring up the level on each fader and set the pan position for each particular instrument.

6. Patch the console's stereo buss into the 2-track tape machine you'll be using to record the master copy.

SETTING THE PAN POSITIONS

When you set the pan positions for each of the instruments, you always want to begin with the most important elements. Then, once they have been positioned, the instruments that play support roles can be placed around them.

In our example, we'll use placements that are fairly standard (Figure 16b). However, you may want to vary these according to taste. (For example, while we place the drums and vocals in the center, the Beatles, for instance, would occasionally put drums on one side and vocals on the other, just for effect.)

Figure 16b: Stereo imaging of instruments.

1. Low-frequency instruments, primary rhythm elements, guitar solos and lead vocals should image in the center:

LEFT	CENTER	RIGHT
	BASS GUITAR	
	KICK DRUM	
	SNARE DRUM	
	VOCAL	

2. Adding pre-mixed, stereo drum tracks to mix:

LEFT	CENTER	RIGHT
TOM #3 TOM #2	TOM #1	HI-HAT
CRASH CYMBAL		CRASH CYMBAL

RESULT:

LEFT	CENTER	RIGHT
DRUMS AND CYMBALS	BASS GUITAR	DRUMS AND CYMBALS
	KICK DRUM	
	SNARE DRUM	
	VOCAL	

3. Final panning configuration:

LEFT	CENTER	RIGHT
DRUM AND CYMBALS		DRUMS AND CYMBALS
GUITAR	KEYBOARDS	
	BASS GUITAR	
	KICK DRUM	
	SNARE DRUM	
	VOCAL	

The Center Position

It is important to understand that one of the functions of the mix is to create focal points for the listener so that he has something to grab on to. This is accomplished by taking certain key elements of the song, such as the lead vocal, the guitar solo, and the snare and kick drums, and giving them dominant positions in the mix.

One way to do this is to pan them to the center of the stereo spectrum, as this is where the listener's attention is naturally drawn. However, the center position can be beneficial in other ways as well.

For example, I generally reserve the center for low-frequency information, as lows create a monaural image anyway, due to the length of the wave. Thus, I always place the bass guitar in the center.

I've also found that the principal rhythm components of the mix have much more punch when they're in the center of the spectrum. So I also place the snare drum and kick drum there.

Finally, since the lead vocal virtually carries the song, it too should be placed in the center, as you want to make it as dominant as possible.

There is an additional advantage to this configuration, which is that the vocal is the only melodic element occupying this space, and as you'll see when we begin to add EQ, this reduces the chance that the vocal will conflict with other instruments in the same frequency ranges. In other words, this helps set it apart from the rest of the mix.

Far-Left/Far-Right Positions

Once you've placed these basic components in the center of the spectrum, you'll want to add the rest of the drums to mix.

In our imaginary song, we premixed the toms and cymbals into a stereo pair as they were recorded, which allowed us to save tracks. And at that time, we panned the drums so that they would image at specific points across the spectrum (Figure 16b). Now, when we add these tracks to the mix, we need to pan them hard left and hard right respectively, so that the toms and cymbals will remain in their original stereo configuration.

There are, of course, many other uses for far-left and far-right panning. As you'll see later in this chapter, they're used for doubling tracks, and they're used in conjunction with stereo choruses and harmonizers, when you want to create a false stereo image. You can also use far-left and far-right placement for such elements as backing vocals (particularly if you want to create a choral effect), as well as for guitar solos—if it produces the effect you're looking for.

However, you have to be careful with this, because if you pan everything hard left and hard right, and place the vocal up the middle, it can sound very unnatural. Unfortunately, this is a trap many musicians fall into when they're unfamiliar with mixdowns.

Left-Center/Right-Center Positions

With this in mind, you now want to add the rest of the instruments to the mix, and in our case this means adding keyboards and guitars.

These instruments supply the melodic support for the vocal, and for this reason I usually place each in a left-center or a right-center position (Figure 16b). As a general rule, the more important an element is to the song, the closer it should be to the center. This is particularly true for instruments that are providing vocal support, as you want them to image relatively close to the vocal.

Remember, you want to use panning to create a blend of elements that fills in the entire spectrum, from one side to the other. However, you want to avoid positioning an instrument in a way that makes it stick out and appear unnatural —which is what would happen if you placed the vocal in the center and placed its melodic support out in the boondocks.

PRE-EQ PLANNING

Once you've brought up the levels on the instruments and panned them to their desired positions (and *before* you've added any effects or any EQ), step back and have a noncritical listen. That is, don't think as the producer, but as the audience.

After you've become familiar with the overall sound of the song in this raw stage, begin to think in terms of the dynamics of the mix and ask yourself (a) what's missing, (b) what are you hearing too much of, and (c) where is the focus. Then, using this as a guideline, begin planning out the structure you want the mix to have.

This really consists of two considerations: making sure that the key elements in the mix stand out and making sure that the song builds in terms of its level of excitement.

In the first instance, your focus should be on the instruments that play important roles throughout the song. For example, if you have a guitar solo in the middle of the song, you will want to be sure that it's as dominant as the lead vocal it's replacing. If there's a melodic hook on the keyboards that comes in and out during the choruses, you will want it to have some degree of dominance as well. So as you listen, you want to make note of these key elements and begin planning how to treat them.

Your second concern is in how well the song builds, which also must be planned for. You want the recording to be exciting, but to be truly exciting it has to have movement. It has to build up to something. An obvious example of this would be the Beatles' "Hey Jude," which begins with piano and vocal and swells to an outchorus that sounds as if it includes every musician in the free world. And Yoko. Of course, you don't need to go to that extreme, but you do need to create some low points if you want the high points to be effective.

Unfortunately, many people approach a mix with the idea that they'll take one particularly exciting element of the song, like a hot guitar lick, and use it all the way through, because they figure it will make the whole song sound exciting. This is a mistake, because it leaves them nowhere to go. The human ear will only perceive something as being exciting if it's in relation to something that is less exciting. So a song that begins and ends on the same emotional pitch will ultimately become boring or annoying.

SETTING THE EQ

Once you've had a noncritical listen, you can then begin to use equalization to fine-tune the placement of each instrument, according to its importance.

However, before we go any further, it's extremely important for you to understand that when you EQ an instrument during mixdown, you must EQ it in the context of its role within the mix and *not* as an individual entity. What counts is how well it fits into the mix, not how great it sounds on its own.

Many musicians, and for that matter many studio engineers, make the mistake of treating mixdown EQ as if they were recording an initial track. In fact, what frequently happens is that they'll solo up a guitar, for example, and when they've EQed it, they'll be sure they've got the greatest guitar sound ever in life. But then, when they place it back in the mix, they find that it upsets the balance and loses its effect.

This is partially due to the fact that when you EQ one component of the mix, you automatically affect all the other components. For example, if at this point you add a load of 3K to the guitar, it will take on a dominant role in the mix, because 3K is psychoacoustically exciting. You haven't moved the fader or made the guitar itself louder; you've simply increased the volume of a particularly exciting frequency. Yet by making the guitar more prominent, everything else seems to recede into the background.

So when you EQ an instrument in the context of the mix, you can't really go by the EQ guidelines you used for the initial track. The guidelines are still important, as they were designed to make it easier to fit each of the instruments into the mix, and you can, at this time, add any EQ you had to leave out of the initial track (a technique we discussed in Tape Tip #17, chapter 6). However, you will probably need to make some additional EQ adjustments as well. In fact, you may find that in order to get an instrument to fit properly into the mix, you'll end up EQing frequencies that normally are not even associated with the instrument!

EQ Considerations

At this point equalization becomes a question of aesthetic judgment, because you want to apply EQ according to the role each instrument is going to play in the mix!

For example, in our mix the keyboards (synth) provide a string sound and a piano sound, and we want to EQ them so that they will provide melodic support for the vocal. Also, since the song is a rock 'n' roll number, the kick, snare, and bass are very important, and they'll need to be made dominant. And of course the vocal is always of critical importance, so it should stand out above everything.

Actually, the entire mix should center around the relationship between the rhythmic pulse and the vocal. Everything else should then be used to fill in the spaces, so that while you end up with a nice, full blend, you're able to hear the drums and vocal quite clearly throughout the song.

When I EQ a mix, I always begin with the most important elements, because those are the ones that people focus on as individual sounds, and I want to be sure to get them right. The support instruments are generally heard as "coloration," and it's rare that a listener will focus on something like a string part and say, "God, what a great sound." Instead, he'll be listening to the vocal and the drums, which should be placed right up front.

It should be mentioned that the relative levels of the vocal and the drums are very important to the success of your mix. However, the relationship you establish between these two elements is purely a judgment call on your part. In modern rock music, for example, the trend has been to make the kick and snare almost as loud as the vocal, so that, together with the bass guitar, they become the dominant instrumental components of the song. Still, it's up to you to establish the exact relationship, and about all we can suggest is that you listen to some of your favorite records, and when you hear a particular blend that you like, use it as a starting point and build from there.

Once you've gotten the vocal and drums to sound the way you want them to, you can move on to the other instruments and set their EQ. However, one thing you don't want to be doing at this point is "riding the faders," which is a technique we talk about at the end of the chapter. The whole idea behind EQing the mix is to reduce frequency conflicts between instruments so that they're not fighting each other for space, and if you constantly have to raise and lower the volume of instruments in order to adjust their relationship within the mix, there's something wrong.

You'll go a long way toward avoiding this situation if you plan out your recording as you go (which is something we harped on in the instrumental chapters), because as you're laying down the tracks, you need to do everything you can to insure that the musical components won't end up competing with each other in the mix. This is where we talked about working out the arrangement so that the guitar part, for instance, isn't in the same register as the vocal, which is in the same register as the piano, which is in the same register as the strings, and so on.

What you want to do is create a musical "hole" for each instrument (particularly the vocal) to fit into, so that they don't end up fighting for dominance when you get to the mixdown stage. This is really where mistakes in the initial recordings will show up, because chances are that if instruments are fighting each other in a mix, it's because you haven't recorded the instruments in the proper registers to begin with.

Where to Place EQ

Figure 16c illustrates the interrelationships we'll be establishing with our example mix EQ (which itself is represented in Figures 16d and 16e). By using this sort of a structure, you can see that you create very little conflict in the EQ. The instruments that are EQed in the same range tend to perform different functions. For example, even though we've boosted the vocal and the snare wires at 5K, the vocal is a constant, melodic component of the mix, while the snares are rhythmic and intermittent. Thus, one doesn't really get in the way of the other.

At 10K and above there's no conflict, because the only part of the mix that's affected are the cymbals, although you may occasionally want to give the vocal a boost in that range in order to bring out some of the breathiness.

The 7K boosts bring out the sibilants of the strings and enhance the top end of the piano. They also let you hear more of the attack of the toms, which is rhythmic so it's not going to get in the way of either the strings or the piano.

Then at 5K you have the snares, which are also intermittent, and you have the vocal, which is constant. And if you want to bring out any bell-type qualities on the synth, you can also give it a boost here.

As we mentioned, 3K brings out the dominant characteristics of the guitar, and since you want it to cut through the mix, it should receive a 3K boost, as should the kick drum, as this will enhance the top end and give it some punch.

By the same token, in order to bring out the snare drum, it should be given a boost at 1K, which is the range that will also enhance the percussive quality of the piano.

You might want to add a little EQ to the vocal at 500 Hz in order to give it some body, but I rarely do this, because there's usually plenty of body in the vocal as is. However, if I'm replacing the vocal with a guitar solo in the middle of the song, I usually give the guitar a boost at 500 Hz, just to make sure that it has the necessary punch. After all, the last thing you want is to have a strong vocal bridge followed by a wimpy lead guitar.

Figure 16c: Example EQ treatment during mixdown. While the left-hand column represents the specific EQ boosts used on our "imaginary" mix, the keywords in the right-hand column can be applied to all mixes. So if you're performing a mixdown, and you're not sure where to place a boost in order to enhance a particular feature of an instrument, these keywords should help.

"IMAGINARY" MIX EQ		KEYWORDS	
10K and above	cymbals	**10K and above:** DECAY RANGE— "separation"	
7 K	synth (string sounds) top end of tom-toms (stick) top end of piano	**7K:** SIBILANTS	
5 K	snare wires vocal synths (bell-type sound)	**5K:** PRESENCE— "brightness"	
3 K	guitar top end of kick drum	**3K:** EXCITEMENT— "punch"	
1 K	snare drum piano (percussion of hammers)	**1K:** BANG	
500 Hz	vocal (if necessary) midrange of guitar solo	**500 Hz – 250 Hz:** WARMTH	
250 Hz	vocal warmth string warmth		
100 Hz	kick drum bass guitar rhythm guitar (low strings)	**100 Hz:** THUMP	

LEFT	CENTER	RIGHT
DRUMS AND CYMBALS		*DRUMS AND CYMBALS*
+10K		+10K
+7K		+7K
+250 HZ		+250 HZ

	GUITAR	*KEYBOARDS*	
	+3K	+7K	
	+500 Hz	+1K	

BASS GUITAR
+6K
+800 Hz
+100 Hz

KICK DRUM
+3K
+100 Hz

SNARE DRUM
+5K
+1.2K
+100 Hz

VOCAL
+250 Hz

Figure 16d: EQ application for example mix. All EQ boosts should be performed in 2 dB increments. For example, if, after a boost of 2 dB, you find that more EQ is required, continue boosting in 2dB increments until you achieve the desired sound (in other words, don't use a 10 dB boost as a starting point). However, you will need to reevaluate these EQ levels after each step in the mixdown process, as you may need to boost or reduce some of these levels after effects have been added. In fact, coloration effects like chorus and phasing may alter the frequency location of a required boost.

Below 500 Hz, you find the range of frequencies that add warmth to vocals and strings. Generally, 250 Hz is a good spot to place this boost, although you have to be careful if you're not using parametric EQ (with parametric, you want to use a narrow bandwidth), because, as we've often mentioned, you want to avoid boosting any frequencies close to 200 Hz.

Plus, if you're boosting the vocal here, it should be a gentle boost, because 250 Hz is a nonarticulated frequency —meaning that it will blur the percussive quality of a sound. So if your singer has any problems with enunciation, you may want to avoid this boost altogether.

Finally, I prefer my mixes to have a good, solid bottom end, so I pay special attention to the low-end EQ. By adding EQ in the 100 Hz range, you provide foundational support for the vocal, and again, since these frequencies fall below the vocal range, there's no conflict.

In our example mix, we've applied 100 Hz boosts to the kick drum and the bass. You'd also want to add the guitar to this group if it's being used to provide a rhythm pattern, as this will bring out the sound of the lower strings.

General EQ Treatments

You'll notice that Figure 16c also includes keywords that refer to each of the frequency ranges we've included in our EQ treatment. You can apply these keywords, in a general way, when you're setting up the EQ for your own mixdowns.

For example, we've referred to 10K and above as the "decay range," because this is where you hear the upper harmonics of an instrument, and these harmonics become more prominent during the decay. So 10K and above tends to separate one instrument from another, because you're better able to distinguish among the individual decays.

By the same token, the 3K range is referred to as the "excitement range" because it is psychoacoustically exciting and will add punch to such string instruments as guitar and piano.

Each of the keywords is meant to be self-explanatory, so if you want to bring out the "bang" of an instrument, you'd look to 1K, and for warmth you'd look in the 250 Hz–500 Hz region, and so on.

BOLD — added during mixdown
ITALIC — applied during initial recording

	PIANO	BASS	GUITAR	VOCAL	KICK	SNARE	DRUMS
12-15K				*12-15K*			
							10-12K
10K	*10K*		*10K*			*10K*	**10K**
7K	*7K*			*(-7K)*	*7K*		*7K*
5K		*5K*	*5K*	*5K*		*5K*	
				5K	**5K**		
3K	*3K*	*3K*	*3K*		*3K*		*3K*
1K	*1K*					*1K*	
				(-900 Hz)		**1K**	
800 Hz		*800 Hz*					
500 Hz			*500 Hz*	**500 Hz**			*500 Hz*
			500 Hz	*250-500 Hz*			
250 Hz				**250 Hz**			
100 Hz	*100 Hz*	*100 Hz*	**100 Hz**		*100 Hz*	*100 Hz*	*100 Hz*
		100 Hz			**100 Hz**		

Figure 16e: EQ Treatment applied before and during mixdown. When EQing the mixdown, you may find that you need to boost some of the same frequencies you originally EQed during the initial tracking (such as the 500 Hz boosts given to the guitar). Also, if you have limited EQ capabilities, this is the time to add any EQ boosts you could not add earlier (see Tape Tip #17, chapter 6).

CREATING DEPTH WITH ECHO AND REVERB

Once you've EQed the mix, you need to give it a sense of depth. This will help open up more room, so the instruments won't appear as crowded, and along with creating atmosphere for the listener, it will enable you to make each instrument audible, so that none get buried in the background.

As we said earlier, you create depth by adding reverb or echo to the source. The more reverb you add, the farther back the instrument appears. In actual fact, what you're creating with these effects is an artificial environment or a psychological "room" the listener can envision the band playing in. In other words, along with everything else, echo and reverb are used to add a sense of realism to the recording and to tie all the elements together so that they appear to be originating in the same ambient space. Thus, recorded music sounds much more natural with reverb.

Reverb Chambers

There are many different electronic reverbs and echoes available, but the most basic is the "reverb chamber." The term itself originated in the days when recording studios all had rooms, called reverb chambers, which generated a natural reverb (see Tape Tip #34). Yet while many still do to this day, the term is now used to refer to any device, from a spring reverb to a digital unit, which creates a simple "room" reverb.

Spring reverb provides only the most fundamental level of control over the effect, meaning that it has a fixed decay time, and it only allows you to vary the amount of reverb used. However, professional reverb units, which are called "echo plates," and the new digital reverb devices, such as Yamaha's Rev-7, allow you to vary the volume of the reverb as well as the decay time.

Decay time is the length of time it takes the reverb to die out after the initial impact, and what this represents is the period of time that sound would be reflecting around the "room" (much the same way a ball bounces back and forth within the confines of a racquetball court).

In this respect, the length of the decay time is directly related to the size of the room. Generally, the longer the reverb, the bigger the room and the more elegant the sound.

The longer decay times (three seconds and up) have traditionally been used for things like orchestral tracks and ballads and for songs in which the piano needs to sound as big as it would in a concert hall. On the other hand, short decay times (anywhere from .5 seconds to 1.5 seconds) are more common in modern rock and R&B music, just as they were in fifties' rock.

Thus, if you are using a unit that allows you to vary the decay time, you are given a great deal of flexibility in terms of the environment you wish to create. On the other hand, if you have a spring reverb, which can still be quite effective as long as it offers stereo reverb capabilities, about the only thing you'll be able to do is vary the depth of the effect, which is accomplished by altering the amount of reverb applied to the signal. And in this regard, let me offer a suggestion you may not have considered.

Most spring reverbs operate like rudimentary mixers in that they allow you to control the volume of the source as well as the amount of effect applied to the source. Well, the tendency most people have is to set the source (input) level as high as possible, then use the depth control to add the amount of reverb they want the signal to have. Yet if you think about it, this is silly, because your mixing console operates much more efficiently than the reverb chamber, and you'd be better off using *it* to blend the reverb with the source. So in most cases you'll get much better quality if you crank the depth control all the way up and keep the source relatively low. Then you can use the mixer to establish the blend.

Echo Effects

The next type of reverberant effect is the echo. A lot of people make the mistake of using the terms "echo" and "reverb" interchangeably. I frequently do it myself. But they're two very different things.

Unlike natural reverb, which is comprised of multitudes of individual echoes that have their own individual delay times, echo is comprised of one or more discrete repeats of the original sound, and each repeat has the same delay time as the one that preceded it. This is akin to the old comedy gag where somebody's in the Alps, yells, "Hello," and then a few seconds later hears "Hello" answer back.

Slap Echoes

In fact, this most basic type of echo is known as a slap echo. It can have one repeat (*Hello . . . hello*) or multiple repeats

---

TAPE TIP #34
How to Build a Reverb/Echo Chamber . . . Without Taking a Bath

Ever wonder why you sound so terrific singing in the shower? No, it's not because the running water drowns out your voice. It's because your bathroom is a natural reverb chamber!

Most bathrooms make great reverb chambers, because with the exception of the toilet paper, there's nothing in there that absorbs sound. All the surfaces are either tile, linoleum, glass, Sheetrock, or porcelain. So, generate a sound wave in a bathroom, and it will bounce from tiled wall to tiled wall, off the porcelain fixtures, up to the shower stall, over to the mirror, down to the linoleum . . . You get the picture.

Unfortunately, very small bathrooms do *not* create a usable reverb, because the delay time of the room echoes is too short, and the signal can sound rather brittle. In order to determine whether or not the acoustics of your bathroom are acceptable, just stand in the middle of the room and clap your hands. If the sound you hear come back from the room is *boing*y or hollow sounding, then the ambience is no good. What you want to hear when you clap your hands is a clear, distinct reflection.

Reverb chambers are really quite easy to set up and use: it's just a matter of positioning the amplifier and miking the room. The basic layout is illustrated in Figure 16f. After placing the amp in the center of the room, you place the mikes at the opposite end of the chamber and point them away from the source. Although you may need to alter the direction they're aimed, you should begin by directing them up toward the ceiling and aiming them at each of the two corners on their side of the room. By using the two mikes in this way, you will be able to create an excellent stereo reverb effect.

For optimum results, the reverb chamber should be treated as if it were an outboard reverb device. For example, instead of having the guitar come directly out of the amp in the bathroom, you'll have more control over the reverb if you record the guitar through an amp in a different room and bring that clean signal into the console. You can then use the console's effect sends output to feed the amp in the reverb chamber. By then bringing the bathroom mikes into the console on a second and third channel, you have complete control over the blend of instrument and effect that is sent to tape.

This effect can be used for other purposes as well. For instance, you can set the chamber up as described and use the cue send circuits to add the reverb to the headphone mix. Or you can use it as you would any other outboard reverb during mixdown, which would mean patching the effect sends from the tape returns into the amp.

Of course, you can also place the guitar amp in the reverb chamber and add a close mike to the mike configuration. However, this makes it quite difficult to control the amount of reverb, as you probably won't be able to keep the close mike isolated from the effect.

(*Hello* . . . hello . . . hello . . . hello), and each is a single, discrete entity (thus the name "slap" echo).

I'm particularly fond of using slap echoes on vocals because I like the way they sound. They allow the vocal to retain its presence, while at the same time they surround it in an ambience. Plus, slap echoes with multiple repeats tend to give the vocal a sense of warmth and mystery.

I used slap echoes on the Men At Work vocals, and you can hear them on all the Led Zeppelin albums. In both cases, the slap echo was used to create multiple repeats, meaning that after the initial return of the sound, it continues to return again and again until it eventually dies out. However, you can also create a single-repeat slap echo, which is an effect more commonly found in rockabilly music.

Slap echoes can be generated with an outboard tape echo such as a Roland Space Echo. Essentially, the effect is created by recording a signal while simultaneously monitoring it off the playback head. The delay time created by the distance between the record and playback heads becomes, in effect, the echo's delay time. The delay time is then altered by speeding up or slowing down the tape.

Again, as was the case with the spring reverb units, when you are using an echo machine that gives you the ability to internally blend the source and the effect, you're generally better off setting the unit so that the output of the device includes only the echo (or as little of the source signal as possible). This way, you can bring the affected signal back into the console and create the blend using the console circuits. This allows you to treat the echo and the source signal as individual elements and it enables you to EQ each separately.

Another method of creating slap echoes is through the use of a digital delay line ("DDL"). Basically, these units offer the same capabilities as tape echoes, except that instead of using tape, they re-create the sound digitally. They're also a bit more flexible, because the delay times can be set much more precisely.

I happen to prefer tape, because it sounds warmer to me. However, it's strictly a matter of personal taste, as either one will do the job.

Multing/Doubling

Another function of the DDL is what used to be called "electronic doubling" (more commonly called "multing"). This is a process by which the repeat time of the DDL is so short that it almost seems as if, for instance, someone has

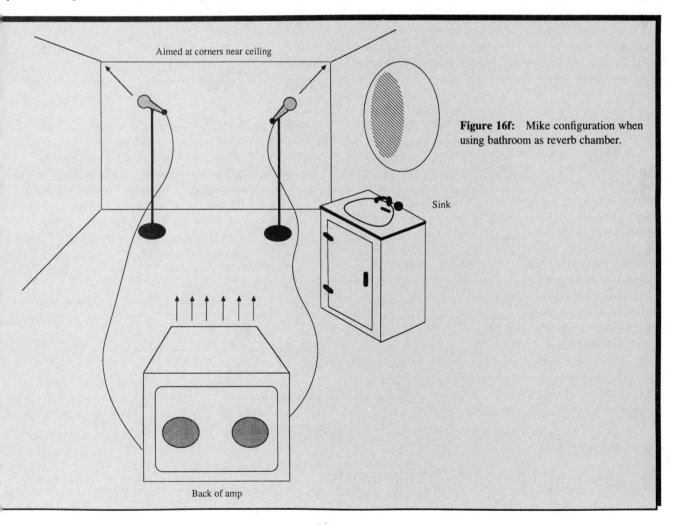

Aimed at corners near ceiling

Figure 16f: Mike configuration when using bathroom as reverb chamber.

Sink

Back of amp

TAPE TIP #35
Creating Echo with Your Tape Machine

If you don't have the money to spend on a tape echo or a digital delay line, but your tape deck has separate record and playback heads, you can create an acceptable slap echo with your tape recorder. This technique is occasionally used in professional studios, although it was much more popular before the introduction of sophisticated outboard effects gear.

The basic concept is quite simple. If you record a signal while monitoring the track off the playback head, there will be a delay between the time the signal is placed on tape at the record head and the time the recorded signal reaches the playback head (see chapter 6, "Track Synchronization"). So if you monitor both the signal that is being recorded and the signal coming from the playback head, you will hear a single repeat.

The best way to generate a tape echo is to send the recorded signal to a second tape machine. For example, if you're recording overdubs, and you want the guitar to be treated with echo in the headphone mix, you bring the guitar track into the console (as you would normally during overdubs) and from there send it to a second tape recorder. You then set that second deck in repro rather than sync (so that you'll be monitoring off the playback heads) and begin recording on it. Then you bring the delayed signal from this second deck back into the console, blend it in with the original guitar track, and send both signals off to the headphone amp.

There are a number of variations on this theme. For example, you can create multiple delays by sending the delayed signal back through the "echo" machine and delaying it a second time. Or if you have open tracks on the source machine, you can create an echo using the same procedure but bouncing internally.

When you create tape delays, you can alter the delay time by altering the tape speed of the "echo" machine. The length of the delay is dependent upon the time it takes for the signal to go from the record head to the playback head, where it is heard as a repeat of the original. So if you speed up the tape, it will take less time for the recorded signal to travel that distance, and the delay time will be shorter.

Yet since most tape decks only have two tape speeds, which means you only have one of two delay times to choose from, their applications are limited. For example, they can't be used for such special effects as phased or delayed reverb, which require extremely short, precise delay times. And since you want to time the delays to fit in with the tempo of the song, you wouldn't want to use one on something as important as a lead vocal unless the delay time conformed exactly to the beat (although if your "echo" machine has pitch control, so that you can vary the tape speed in degrees, this may be possible).

---

sung with himself and doubled a vocal track, or as if there are two guitar players playing exactly the same part together.

This effect is frequently used to fatten up a sound, although to a trained ear the artificiality of the effect is obvious. This is because the DDL creates an identical copy of the part as you go, and this is actually quite unnatural. If you were to have the musician double the track during overdubs, there would be some human error involved, and the part would be played or sung just a little bit differently each time. Still, it's a very useful effect, and I use it quite often.

Another, slightly different form of multing can be produced with a harmonizer. These units actually generate harmonies with the source signal, and you can create a mult by setting the harmonizer's pitch bend so that the return signal does not come back at exactly the same pitch as the source.

Of course, doubling can also be accomplished simply by having the performer record his part twice and panning the two tracks so that they sit either at the same point on the stereo plane or at opposite ends of the spectrum.

Gated Reverb

Another form of echo I use quite often is called a gated reverb. This is a special delay effect, which until the advent of sophisticated digital reverb devices like Yamaha's Rev-7 depended upon the use of a *professional*-grade noise gate and a highly sensitive reverb chamber. However, on these digital units it's simply another one of their programs.

A gated reverb is a reverb that is not allowed to fully decay, as it would naturally. Instead, the gate effect allows the unit to reverberate for a specific amount of time (based on volume), after which the gate closes down abruptly and cuts off the decay. This produces an arresting effect, which I've used with great results on rhythm instruments like the snare drum on Men At Work's "Who Can It Be Now?" (See also Tape Tip #23, chapter 9.)

When setting the decay time on a gated reverb, you should do so in relation to the tempo of the song. Ideally, you want the gate to close before the next beat, because you don't want the reverb from one beat overlapping into the next.

Unfortunately, almost all of today's nonprofessional noise gates lack the sensitivity necessary to create this effect properly, so chances are you'll have little success generating it with pedal effects and spring reverbs.

SPECIAL AMBIENT EFFECTS

All of the previous reverb and echo effects do basically the same thing, which is to create psychological space and re-

Figure 16g: Delayed reverb.

AUX SEND ——— DIGITAL DELAY ——— REVERB ——— RETURN
(145 millisecond
echo desired)
(via
effect return
or input channel)

move the instrument from the plane of the speakers. However, there may be occasions when you'll want to use reverb but won't want to lose the presence of the instrument (in other words, you still want it to be in the foreground). In such cases, there are some special effects you can use to accomplish that purpose.

Delayed Reverb

One such effect is the delayed reverb. This is created by delaying the signal with a DDL and then sending the *delay* to the reverb chamber (Figure 16g). To do this right, you want to set the delay time of the DDL to between 80 and 135 milliseconds, depending upon the tempo of the song and the feel it creates. And you want the output of the reverb chamber to include only reverb (make sure that it does not include any of the unaffected source signal). Then you use the console circuits to control the amount of effect you want to apply to the signal.

By using delayed reverb, you allow your ear to hear the instrument for a split second without any reverb, as if it were quite close, and then the reverb kicks in and produces the artificial ambience you're looking for.

Phased Reverb

Another useful effect is phased reverb, which is created by sending the source through a flanger or a phase shifter before

sending it on to the reverb unit. Thus, the source signal remains unaffected, but the reverb decay becomes phased.

You can also accomplish the same thing by sending the signal through the reverb chamber first and then on to the phase shifter. However, this method offers less flexibility, because it means that everything you send to the chamber will be phased. So if you're treating two instruments with reverb, both will have phased reverb.

Of course, if you want both of those instruments to have phased reverb, then you're not losing anything with this method. But if you only want one of the instruments to be phased, then you'll need to place the phase shifter in line *before* the reverb chamber and send that instrument through the phaser before sending it on to the chamber.

APPLYING REVERB AND ECHO EFFECTS

At this point, we're going to put some of these reverbs and echoes to work and show you how they can be used to add degrees of depth to the individual instruments in our imaginary mix.

As Figure 16h illustrates, we've added normal "room" reverb to the drums and cymbals and to the keyboards. However, since we want the guitar to have sort of a rockabilly sound, we've used a DDL to generate a single-repeat slap echo. Then, in order to make the snare sound nice and big, we've given it some gated reverb, *plus* some regular reverb,

Figure 16h: This is the stereo image we've created in our example mix.

LEFT	CENTER	RIGHT
DRUMS AND CYMBALS reverb		*DRUMS AND CYMBALS* reverb
	GUITAR digital delay phase shifter	*KEYBOARDS* reverb
	BASS GUITAR dry	
	KICK DRUM dry	
	SNARE DRUM reverb and gated reverb	
	VOCAL reverb and slap echo	

and we've kept the kick drum and the bass guitar dry, which is usually the case.

The vocal deserves special consideration, so we've treated it with both reverb and slap echo. However, we've only applied a small amount of reverb—just enough to warm up the vocal a little bit—because we don't want the vocal to lose its presence. Yet the vocal does need to be given additional ambience, so we've also added the slap echo. The advantage of the slap echo is that before the first repeat, you'll hear the vocal by itself. Therefore, the signal won't lose as much presence as it would if you had just added more reverb, which acts on the vocal immediately.

USING OUTBOARD EFFECTS FOR COLOR

Now that we've panned and EQed the instruments, and added depth to the mix, we're going to use outboard effects to add coloration to the recording in order to give it a more pleasant and interesting texture.

Creating a False Stereo Image

One of the most effective coloration techniques I know of is to take a single track and use an outboard device to give it a false stereo image.

A harmonizer is an excellent device to use for this (Figure 16i). What you do is send the track you want imaged in stereo to the harmonizer and set the harmonizer to a very quick delay (five or six milliseconds). If you don't have a readout on your unit, then you'll have to adjust it by ear, but you don't want pitch bend, and you don't want to create an obvious delay, because you want it to sound fairly natural, as if it's in stereo.

The stereo effect itself is actually created by panning the source signal all the way over to one side and panning the harmonizer output all the way over to the opposite side. Then you just keep the harmonizer level equal in volume with the source signal. What you end up with, then, because of the slight delay is a stereo image. And the important thing here is that without that delay, this technique wouldn't work. As we mentioned in chapter 1, you can't record one signal on two tracks and expect it to be in stereo, because in fact it will play back mono.

You can also use a stereo chorus pedal to create a stereo image. In this case, all you need to do is send the instruments you want to be "stereo" through the chorus, then return the two output channels of the device into two separate input channels on the console.

The only difference between this and the way you set up the harmonizer is that in this instance, you don't want the original source signal to be a part of the mix (Figure 16j). Thus, when you set this up, make sure that the console channel carrying the source signal is either turned off or left unassigned, so that the only signal being added to the mix is that coming through the chorus. Then pan the two channels you're using as returns to opposite sides.

As with the harmonizer, I frequently use stereo chorus on instruments that play a support role, such as rhythm guitars.

Flangers and Phase Shifters

Other coloration devices, such as flangers and phase shifters, can be used to enhance the sound of most any instrument. However, because they have a tendency to alter the frequency configuration of the track, they can also be quite useful when you're having trouble making an instrument fit into the mix.

For example, if the guitar is fighting with the vocal, you might want to flange the guitar. This will give it a distinctly different sound, and psychoacoustically it manages to spread the frequency range of the guitar enough so that there's room in the midrange for the vocals.

The same would be true of phasing, which tends to enhance the upper registers of the guitar. In fact, if you're going to be using a phase shifter, it's not a bad idea to accentuate those upper frequencies with EQ, as that's where you hear the swishing of the phaser.

ROUTING THE EFFECTS

Since you've gotten this far through the book, you should already be familiar with routing procedures. In mixdown, however, there are special considerations.

As a general rule, if you want to use an outboard effect on a large number of instruments, you're best off using one of the auxiliary busses (effect sends) on the console, because

Figure 16i: Using harmonizer for stereo imaging.

BUSS 1————————HARMONIZER————————INPUT CHANNEL
(can also use
aux send)

SOURCE CHANNEL   RETURN CHANNEL
assigned to Buss 1   for harmonizer

ON   *ON*

PAN   PAN
(left)   (right)

Figure 16j: Using stereo chorus for stereo imaging.

BUSS 1——————— STEREO CHORUS——————— INPUT CHANNEL A
(can also use   ——————— INPUT CHANNEL B
aux send)

SOURCE CHANNEL   CHANNEL A   CHANNEL B
assigned to Buss 1
OFF!!   *ON*   *ON*
                                                    ↙   ↘
                                                  PAN   PAN
                                                (left)   (right)

they provide a quick, efficient means of sending many sig-nals through one device (Figure 16k).

If you're going to use an effect on two or three instru-ments, but you want to reserve the aux busses for something like reverb, then you might want to send the signals to the device via one of the buss channels that you've used for recording (Busses 1–4, Busses 1–8, and so on). Then you simply return the signal to an open input channel.

On the other hand, if you're only using an effect on one specific instrument, but you don't want to use the aux sends, then you have three different alternatives. The first is to put the device in the line *before* the console, which is a tech-nique I've used at home with compressors. The reason I like this technique is that it allows me to EQ the combination of the effect and the source, which gives me more control over the affected signal.

The second method is to place the effect in the line *after* the signal has left the console channel but *before* it reaches the stereo buss. However, this can only be accomplished if each channel offers direct-outs, because under normal con-ditions the signal would be routed to the stereo buss inter-nally, and there would be no way to break into the line.

Although this technique does not allow you as much EQ control as the previous method, it can be advantageous if the outboard device needs more level than the tape deck is capa-ble of supplying, as the console can provide the needed boost.

The third alternative you have is one that combines the two previous methods and offers the advantages of each. It entails taking the feed from the tape deck and sending it into the console, where it can be EQed. From there, the signal is sent to the effect device (via a direct-out from the channel) and returned to a second input channel, where the *affected* signal can be EQed. Then both input channels are assigned to the stereo buss, and the signals are blended and added to the mix.

Figure 16k: Ways to send effects using console.

1. MANY INSTRUMENTS:

AUX SEND ——————————— REVERB——————————— RETURN
(effect send)   (outboard effect)   (effect return)

2. TWO OR THREE INSTRUMENTS:

BUSS CHANNEL————————— OUTBOARD ——————————— RETURN
                                              EFFECT   (on input channel)

3. ONE INSTRUMENT:

     A.   If the output of the effect is to be EQed

TAPE——————— OUTBOARD——————— INPUT——————— STEREO BUSS
                           EFFECT   CHANNEL

     B.   If input of device needs level control or EQ

TAPE ——————— INPUT——————————— OUTBOARD ————————— STEREO BUSS
                         CHANNEL   EFFECT

     C.   For capabilities of both A and B

TAPE——————— INPUT——————— OUTBOARD ————— INPUT————— STEREO
                         CHANNEL   EFFECT   CHANNEL   BUSS

HOW TO FIX THE MIX

Now that you have the mix basically set up, you want to try a few run-throughs to see how it sounds. If you've recorded everything relatively well, the mix should only need a bit of fine-tuning. For example, you'll probably need to adjust some of the effect levels and re-EQ, which is something you need to do after every step anyway. You will probably need to adjust some of the volume levels as well. However, as we mentioned earlier, you should not have to be riding the faders at this point in order to make something fit properly. You may need to adjust the levels here and there for aesthetic reasons, such as to boost the guitar during a solo or to help out the vocal if a word or two is getting lost, but you want to avoid having to constantly work the levels when you lay down the mix.

Adding Compression

One alternative to riding the levels is to use a compressor, although this is not something you want to do all the time.

Most musicians play with feeling, and sometimes the dynamics this creates can make the instrument appear to drop in and out of the mix. However, if you send the offending track through a compressor, the device will help even out the peaks and valleys of the performance, so that it remains at a more even level throughout the song.

If I'm using a compressor in this way, I'll generally compress the signal before bringing it into the console, as that gives me optimum control over EQ. And since I'll want to use as little compression as possible, I'll set the compression ratio at 4:1, and make sure that the signal never receives more than a 1 dB or 2 dB reduction in gain.

Even at that, you have to be careful. If you overcompress something, it's going to sound very small and quite distant, because a lot of the harmonic frequencies will lose their impact, and the signal's presence will be reduced.

Riding the Levels

No matter how carefully you've set up the mix, you will undoubtedly run across instances where you *will* need to ride the levels. For example, you may want to increase the impact of some explosive sound by boosting the level just before it hits. Or you may need to bring up the backing vocals during the outchorus. In fact, there are probably as many aesthetic reasons for riding faders as there are mixdowns!

This is actually the performance part of the mix, where you're playing the faders almost the way you would an instrument. So the secret is to find that mental state where you're able to listen to the mix almost without regard to what your hands are doing as they move the faders.

Another reason you might want to ride the levels is to avoid using compression on the vocal. However, you may need to do more than just ride the faders if you want the track to sound right. For example, while you may think that words appear to be dropping out of the vocal because it gets too soft in parts, the problem may actually be due to poor EQ levels. So you might want to help out the enunciation of the singer by rolling off some EQ at 250 Hz. Then, if the track still seems to disappear, you can ride the levels.

Above all, you have to remember that at this point in the mix, virtually everything is interrelated: EQ, effects, levels, and so on. So you can't just look to one solution when you try to fix the mix, because there's just too much going on.

ASSESSING THE FINAL PRODUCT

Once you're done with the mix, you should again sit back and have a noncritical listen. Here, you're looking for any elements that sound unnatural to you or that leap out and grab your attention when they shouldn't.

There should be a natural flow to the mix, and as you listen to it, you should have the feeling, from beginning to end, that the song takes you right along with it. There should never be anything in the mix to jar you out of that groove or alter your concentration.

For me, this is the key to what makes a good mix. The blending of elements is really the critical factor—that and the idea that you want to create an ambience that reinforces the mood the music is trying to create.

This doesn't mean you can't do things for effect. If you want the mix to have kinetic movement, you can have sounds leaping out at you left, right, and center, if that's the mood you're trying to create. You may want to use a lot of effects. You may want to *overuse* effects. It's exactly the same concept as splashing a lot of bright colors on a canvas.

On the other hand, if you're mixing a ballad and want a softer mood, then you want to use a musical equivalent of pastels, and you want the music to flow from beginning to end.

Splicing It In to Fix It Up

If you have a mix that works 88 percent of the time, but there's one section that's not happening for you, instead of redoing the entire mix, what you might want to do is remix the section you don't like and drop the new version into the old mix by using the tape editing (splicing) techniques we cover in Tape Tip #36.

With some producers, this is common studio practice, and a final mix may have ten or fifteen cuts in it. However, in general I figure that if I have more than two or three cuts in a mix, then unless it's an incredibly complicated mix that I don't want to do over again, I'm better off taking it again from the beginning. And in the home, I would suggest that one or two cuts be the maximum.

Re-EQing the Master Copy

If you listen to the mix and feel there's an across-the-board problem with frequency response, that there's just too much woof to the bottom end, for example, or that the top end seems to have lost its luster, you'll need to re-EQ your master copy.

One way to take care of this is to alter the EQ on each and every cassette copy you make. However, a second alterna-tive is to copy the 2-track mix onto a second open-reel ma-chine (such as the 8-track or 4-track you used for the initial tracks) and alter the EQ in the process.

In either case, you simply bring the left channel of the mix into one console input module and the right channel into another. Then you pan them hard left and hard right respec-tively and set the fader levels so that both channels register at equal volumes on the meters. Then you adjust the EQ levels as desired and record a second master copy.

TAPE TIP #36
Tape Splicing Techniques
By recording engineer Paul Ray

Every so often it will happen that, during mixdown, you'll suddenly realize that the timing of the song just isn't right. Maybe it needs a longer instrumental bridge or a quicker exit out of the passage. Perhaps you discover that the song sounds better if the chorus repeats twice or that the verses are too long. Well, instead of starting from scratch and rere-cording the whole song, it's possible to edit the material by physically splicing in or cutting out sections of tape.

This editing technique is often used in professional stu-dios, and if you have the proper equipment and a certain degree of patience, it can also be done at home. However, this is not the sort of thing you can just decide to do one day on a master copy of a song. It requires a lot of practice on *throwaway* tapes and a very steady hand.

WHY EDIT?

There are three basic reasons you might want to splice a tape. The first of these is, as we mentioned, to rearrange a song. This might include simply removing or adding a sec-tion of tape, or it might mean moving one section of the song to a different location. In either case, there are two ways to do this: by editing the premix master tape or by editing a version of the final mix.

In general, it's best to edit the premix master, because it will include fewer effects. This is particularly important if you're adding echo during mixdown, because then if you were to splice something out of the final mix, you'd risk cutting out some of the repeats. On the other hand, if you're not exactly sure which way the song sounds best, you may want to have two versions to choose between. And in that case, you'd be better off making two copies of the final mix and performing your edits on one of them.

The second reason for splicing tape would be to generate a special effect. For example, you may want to run a tape loop of an effect or of a rhythm track on one tape deck and record it as an instrumental track on a second deck. Or you may want to record an instrumental track backward onto your master, another procedure that requires editing.

You'll also want to be able to splice tape in order to com-pile a number of songs on one reel and place them in the proper order. This involves separating the songs with lengths of leader tape. You'll need to place leader tape at the begin-ning and end of every reel as well, and, if possible, between each version of the final mix you make during mixdown.

EDITING TOOLS

In order to perform an edit, you will need an editing block, edit tape, razor blades, and a grease pencil (china marker). In some situations, you will also need leader tape.

Editing Blocks:

Editing without a block is possible but difficult. Editing blocks (Figure 16l) are used to secure the tape and to dupli-cate the angle of the cut. All blocks come with at least one angle, while some offer as many as two or three.

You can buy editing blocks at just about any electronics store. However, make sure you select the correct block for the tape width you'll be using (¼ inch, ½ inch, 1 inch, and so on). And never buy a block that has only the "0-degree" angle, as a flat cut makes matching the edits very difficult.

Edit Tape:

Edit tape (or splicing tape) is specifically designed for splic-ing together magnetic recording tape. It's sticky on only one

Figure 16l: Editing block. Select the correct block for the tape width you'll be using (¼-inch, ½-inch, 1-inch, or 2-inch tape).

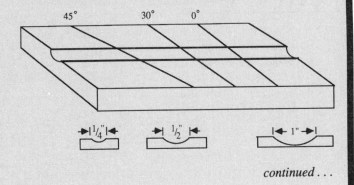

continued . . .

...continued

side and does not stretch easily. Other types of tape, such as Scotch tape or masking tape, should never be used for editing, as they will be too thick and in all likelihood won't adhere properly. Plus, they may leave residue that will clog or otherwise damage the tape heads.

Edit tape comes in various widths and colors, and you should pick whichever is appropriate for your needs.

Razor Blades and Grease Pencils:

Needless to say, the only type of razor blade you should use is a single-sided *safety* razor blade. Generally, these can be found in hardware stores and in shops that carry art supplies.

Grease pencils are used to mark the points on the tape at which you'll want to make the edit. They are used because they are relatively soft, so they won't score the heads, and because they are easily cleaned off the heads when you're through. Use a light-colored pencil, as they leave the most visible marks on the tape.

Leader Tape:

Leader tape comes in a variety of widths, so make sure that the leader width matches the width of the tape you're splicing it to. However, one of the most important things to look for when you're buying leader tape is whether or not the tape includes timing marks. These are black lines that run across the width of the tape at intervals of 7½ inches. Since tape speeds are calibrated in multiples of 7½ (15 ips, 30 ips, and so on), this allows you to cut the leader length according to the interval of time you wish it to represent. For example, if you want to leave a five-second interval between songs, you would cut the length accordingly.

You can use the following chart as a reference:

—At 7½ ips, **1** mark represents **1** second
—At 15 ips, **2** marks represent **1** second
—At 30 ips, **4** marks represent **1** second

HOW TO PERFORM AN EDIT

1. Select the edit points. Where the edit starts (the start of the section to be removed or added to) is normally called the "out." The point where the edited section picks up (the end of the section removed or the start of the section to be added) is normally called the "in" (Figure 16m).
2. Play the tape. As the beat of the section to be edited passes over the tape head, press the "stop" button. This will place the first edit point close to the head you are

monitoring off of. (Note: You can mark the edit on either the playback head or the record head, but be sure that the head you are marking on is the head you are monitoring off of.)

3. You are now ready to zero in on the edit point. If the machine has a lifter-defeat switch, which is normally marked "Cue," this should be engaged so that the lifters do not pull the tape away from the heads. If you have a motor-defeat switch, this should be engaged so that the wheel hubs don't lock.
4. After engaging these switches, rock the tape back and forth across the heads and listen for the particular beat that you want to cut out. During your first few edits, you may have some trouble identifying this beat, so when possible, edit on the beat of a kick drum or snare drum.
5. When you've located the beat, mark the edit point with a grease pencil by drawing a thin line across the tape at the spot where the tape head comes to a point (Figure 16n).
6. Locate the other end of the edit by repeating Steps 2 through 5.
7. Begin editing on either the IN or the OUT. In either case, leave the reels on the machine and pull the tape gently away from the head. Then place it shiny side down into a well-secured editing block.
8. Make sure there are no ridges or bumps in the tape and that the tape is properly secured at both ends of the block.
9. Line up the edit mark with either the thirty-degree or forty-five-degree angle, making sure that the edit mark sits to the left of the cut (Figure 16o). (Note: Which angle you use is just a matter of preference. The forty-five-degree angle makes for a smoother but longer cut, but the thirty-degree angle will be better if you have a lot of material at or around the edit spot.)
10. Hold the tape down with your fingers and make a smooth slice through the tape by inserting a clean, sharp razor blade into the angle guide and dragging it through once. Make sure the razor is sharp, as a dull razor may rip the tape, and most times you only get one chance at the cut.
11. Release the tape from the block and gently pull the two ends apart. Then spool the tape to the next edit point and repeat the procedure.

Figure 16m: The edit.

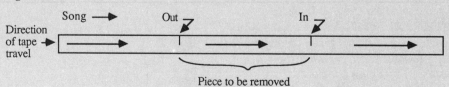

continued...

. . . continued

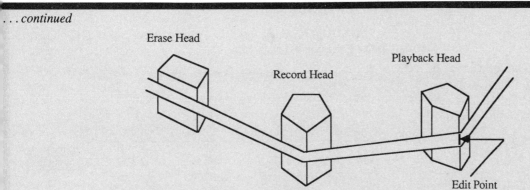

Figure 16n: Marking the edit point.

12. Save the section of tape you've removed from the reel by marking it and hanging it (with tape) on a wall or on a table edge. If it's a long section, you may want to spool it onto an empty reel. In any case, it's a good idea to save these pieces, at least until you see whether or not you like the edit.

13. To resplice the master tape, place the two free ends into the block (shiny side down) and gently slide them together until both ends meet but are not overlapping. Make sure that the OUT is on the left and the IN is on the right (Figure 16p).

14. Cut a small piece of editing tape (about 1/2 inch long) from a roll and press it over the cut. Smooth out any air bubbles with your fingernail. (Note: Editing tape should *not* be applied to the side of the tape that comes in contact with the tape heads.)

15. Rethread the tape onto the machine and play through the edit.

16. If the edit works, you may want to discard any unwanted sections. However, if the edit *does not* work,

you can always separate the splice by removing the edit tape and putting the removed section back in.

17. If you have multiple edits to perform, you should always label the pieces of tape you have removed (remember, all tape looks alike). You can do this either by marking the reel that it's on or by marking the piece of tape you're using to secure it to the wall.

How to Perform an Insertion

If you are inserting a section of tape, locate the point of insertion as you did the edit points (Steps 2 through 5) and splice the tape sections together using the methods described in Steps 13 through 15.

However, if you are inserting a blank section of tape that will be used to create a deliberate pause in the music, or is being used as a leader but is not leader tape, make sure you encode it with bias beforehand. If you don't, there will be an unflattering increase, or gust, of bias as soon as the music resumes.

To add bias to a blank piece of tape, run it through a tape machine that has been placed in record with the input volume all the way down.

Figure 16o: Lining up the edit and making the cut. Edit mark should be to the left of the cut.

Figure 16p: Rejoining the tape.

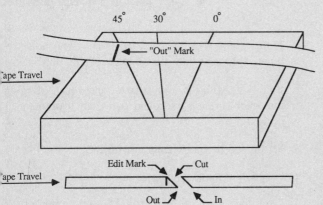

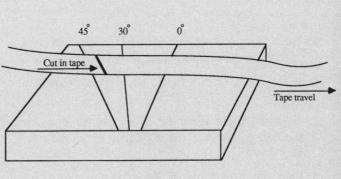

MIXDOWN DIAGRAMS

MIXDOWN
Setting Up the Example 8-Track Mix

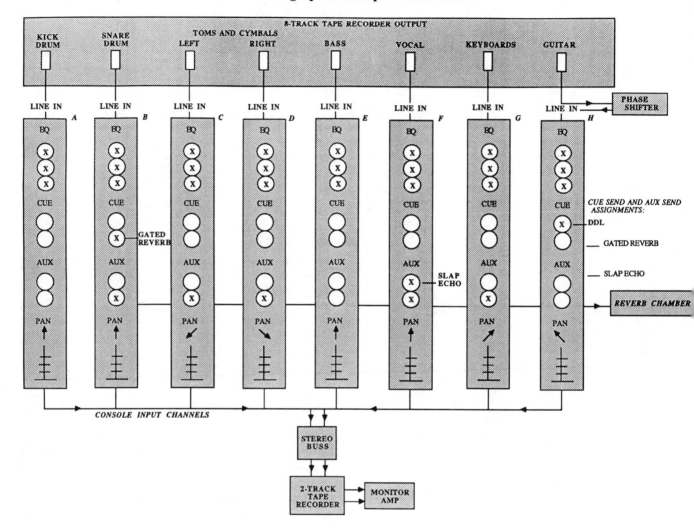

Note: Since a headphone mix is unnecessary during mixdown, the cue sends can be used as aux sends, as indicated.

Procedure:

1. Patch the output of each track into a separate input channel on the console (using line-level inputs).

2. Assign each channel to the stereo buss (frequently labeled "Mix").

3. Patch the output of the stereo buss into the inputs on the 2-track tape deck you're using to record the master copy.

4. Patch the outputs from the 2-track into the line inputs of your monitor amp.

5. Place the source tape recorder in "repro" (take all tracks out of the "sync" mode if your tape deck uses Sel-Sync).

6. If the tracks were encoded (recorded) with noise reduction, be sure they are set to decode on playback.

7. Beginning with the drums, bass, and vocal, bring up the level on each track and pan each instrument as desired.

8. Set the EQ levels for each instrument.

9. Listen to mix and plan application of effects.

10. Patch the output of Aux Send 2 into the input of the outboard reverb chamber.

11. Patch the output of the reverb chamber into the Aux 2 return.(Note: When using a +4 dB console, each effect should be sent to a direct box before being returned to console.)

12. Patch the output of Aux Send 1 into the input of the tape echo unit.

13. Patch the output of the tape echo into the Aux 1 return.

14. Patch the output of Cue Send 2 into the input of the digital reverb device (used for gated reverb).

15. Patch the output of the digital reverb into the Cue 2 return.

16. Patch the output of Cue Send 1 into the input of the DDL (Digital Delay Line).

17. Patch the output of the DDL into the Cue 1 return.

18. Beginning with the drums and vocal, add the desired ambient effects to each instrument.

19. To add digital delay to an instrument, bring up the level of Cue Send 1.

20. To add gated reverb to an instrument, bring up the level of Cue Send 2.

21. To add slap echo to an instrument, bring up the level of Aux Send 1.

22. To add reverb to an instrument, bring up the level of Aux Send 2.

23. Adjust volume levels of instruments as necessary.

24. Adjust EQ levels for instruments as necessary.

25. Patch the direct-out from Channel H (guitar) into the input of an outboard phase shifter.

26. Patch the output from the phase shifter into the line input of Channel H.

27. Adjust the amount of phasing you want applied to the signal.

28. Adjust volume levels and EQ levels of instruments as necessary.

29. Place the 2-track tape deck in record and run through the mix.

30. Listen to the playback of the mix.

31. Make any necessary adjustments and take the mix again.

32. Continue this procedure until you achieve the desired blend of instruments.

33. If, when you're finished with the mix, one section still bothers you, either redo the entire mix or splice in a new version of the offending section.

MIXDOWN TECHNIQUE FOR ELECTRONIC DRUMS
Using All Direct-Outs and Recording Off Sync Code

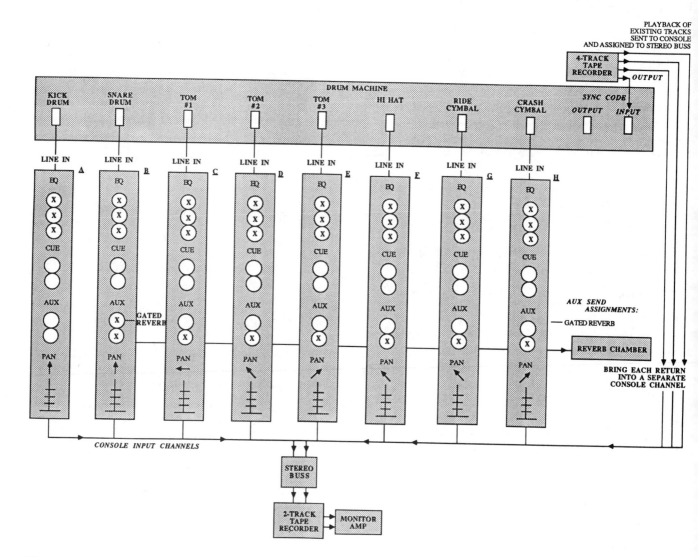

Note: 1. If this configuration were being used for overdubs, the cue sends would be needed to generate a stereo headphone mix for the musicians.

2. Unlike the previous diagram, for this example we've used a 4-track tape format instead of an 8-track format.

Procedure:

1. Patch the output of the code track (Track 4) on the source tape recorder into the "sync code" input on the drum machine.

2. Patch each of the direct-out channels on the drum machine into individual input channels on the console.

3. Patch each of the existing instrumental tracks on the tape recorder into individual input channels on the console (an example of which is shown in the previous mixdown diagram).

4. Assign all of these input channels to the stereo buss.

5. Patch the output of the stereo buss into the inputs on the 2-track tape deck you're using to record the master copy.

6. Patch the outputs from the 2-track deck directly into the monitor amp inputs.

7. Place the source tape recorder in "repro" (take all tracks out of the "sync" mode if your tape deck uses Sel-Sync).

8. If the instrumental tracks were encoded (recorded) with noise reduction, be sure they are set to decode on playback.

9. Place the tape recorder in playback and let the code track trigger the drum machine.

10. Bring up the level on the channels used for the drum machine, set the pan and set EQ levels for each, and create a tentative mix.

11. Beginning with the bass and vocal, add each of the instrument tracks to the mix and pan each instrument as desired.

12. Set the EQ levels for each instrument.

13. Listen to mix and plan application of effects.

14. Follow Steps 10–33 from previous mixdown diagram, but in Steps 14 and 15, use Aux Send 1 for the gated reverb.

Chapter 17

Studio Acoustics

The science of acoustics is extremely complex. In fact, it's almost more of an art than a science. Commercial studios spend enormous sums of money on design, yet it still takes months of postconstruction work by a professional acoustician to get all the bugs out. In fact, Chicago's Auditorium Theatre, which is known for its superb acoustics, was constructed long before anyone ever even thought to make a study of the subject!

Even modern-day acoustic wizards have vastly different opinions about how certain acoustic problems, like low-end room resonance, are best resolved. So instead of trying to achieve a level of acoustic perfection in your studio, you'll have much better success if you concentrate instead on simply improving the overall sound.

Thus, the purpose of this chapter is to provide you with a variety of acoustic treatments that can easily be applied in the home. Most of the techniques offer simple solutions to relatively minor problems, although some *can* be used to make adjustments in the acoustics of garage and basement studios. Still, this material is not meant to be the last word on acoustics, and if you're building a studio, and the room requires extensive work, you should purchase a book devoted solely to the subject.

A SIMPLE, PRACTICAL APPROACH

In most home situations, it won't even be necessary to make major changes in the acoustics. As long as you're recording and monitoring in carpeted, well-isolated rooms, and as long as the wall surfaces and corners in those rooms are broken up by bookshelves, furniture, and the like, the acoustics should be suitable for many different applications. You may occasionally need to enclose the sound source within a tent or surround it with baffles or pillows, but you certainly won't need to overhaul the decor.

And if you have enough such rooms available, instead of changing the acoustics, you can just change rooms. So, for instance, if you find that the ambience in one room is wrong for the track, or for the instrument, all you'll need to do is move to a room that *is* suitable.

In order to find a suitable environment, you'll need to test the acoustics of each room (Tape Tip #37), which often entails moving your gear from one room to another in a process of trial and error. For example, when I first set up a bass amp in my house, I initially tried miking it in a relatively small upstairs room. As it turned out, this room had a hollow wooden floor, and the mike kept picking up a deep, booming rumble. So I moved the amp into my bedroom and tried again. Here the sound was acceptable, but it still wasn't quite right. So I aimed the amp directly into an open clothes closet (Figure 17a), lined the back inside wall with a large piece of carpeting, and close miked the speakers—which meant that the mike was actually inside the closet. And this gave me the sound that I wanted.

I went through exactly the same process when looking for a spot to record guitars. I tried miking them in a stairwell, in a hallway, in the den, and in each of the bathrooms. Ultimately, I found two suitable locations: when I want to get an ambient sound, I record in one of the bathrooms; when I want a dead sound, I record in a small study. And in the latter case, in order to eliminate ambience, I close mike the amp and aim it directly into a pile of pillows in the corner (Figure 17b).

Figure 17a: To eliminate room echoes, you may want to close mike your amp and aim it directly into an open clothes closet.

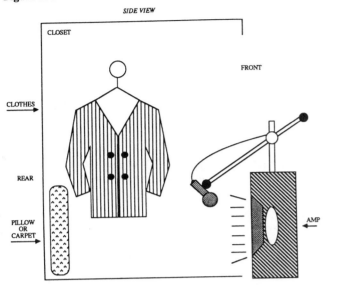

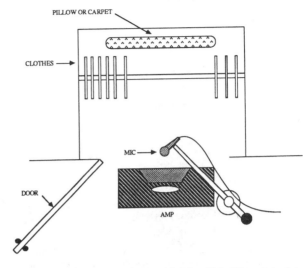

There are many simple, practical solutions like these that you can use at home. Some, like building "tent baffles," are included in this chapter; others are discussed in the chapters on instrumental recording techniques. Of course, they don't work if you're trying to record a stack of Marshalls or a live drummer, but they do provide a viable alternative to some of the more radical methods we cover.

ACOUSTIC BAFFLES

Baffles can be used quite effectively to alter the acoustics of a room without altering the room itself. For example, you can surround a sound source with "dead" baffles to isolate it from room ambience or from the sound of other instruments. Or you can use "live" baffles to increase the reflective properties of a room and create ambience where none previously existed.

One of the advantages of using baffles is that they're movable. So if your living arrangements make it difficult for you to maintain a space that is devoted exclusively to recording, you can always store the baffles until they're needed, and when you're through, you can pack them away and turn your "studio" back into a bedroom. By the same token, if your landlord doesn't even want you putting thumbtacks, much

Figure 17b: Aiming the amp directly into a pile of pillows can also reduce ambient reflections. (*Courtesy of Larry Wichman*)

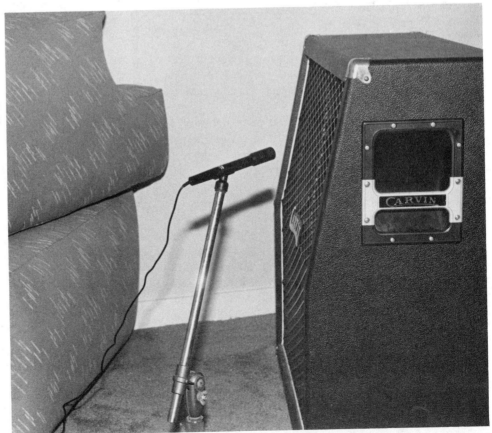

less nails, in the wall, baffles may provide a better solution than looking for another apartment.

In other words, baffles are pretty handy devices to have around.

TAPE TIP #37
Testing the Room Acoustics

It's important that you know how to evaluate a room's acoustical characteristics, because you'll need to test the acoustics to determine how, or even *if,* they need to be altered. And if you plan to make use of the natural acoustics in areas throughout the house, you'll need to determine how live or dead each environment is and which instruments, if any, each might accommodate.

When you test the environment, the idea is to check for the quality and quantity of room reflections. In chapter 1, we talked about the effect these echoes can have on a track and how, by listening, you can determine which are desirable and which are not. However, ambient reflections can be very difficult to judge when you're standing in the room, so it's often easier to record the tests and evaluate the acoustics on playback. The reflections are more clearly defined on tape, and as a result they're more easily judged.

One way to do this is to record each instrument in each available location and see which rooms are suitable for which instruments. This can be very useful, because you will immediately be able to tell whether or not you like the sound you're getting. And if you want to find out if there are any frequency buildups occurring in the room, all you need to do is experiment with EQ during playback and see if there is one particular band of frequencies that consistently needs to be raised or lowered.

The major drawback to this method is that it means dragging your gear from one end of the house to the other, which is nobody's idea of a good time. However, there's an alternative test that can be used to narrow down your choices so that you'll only have to drag *half* your gear through the house. And all it entails is miking each room and testing the echoes with your normal speaking voice.

For example, to check the general room ambience, you position a mike in the center of the room, aim it toward one wall, and *without adding any EQ to the signal,* begin recording your voice. For the first part of the test, stand a few feet in front of the mike and speak directly into it. This will give you an idea of how loud the reflections will appear under close-miking conditions. Then, for the second part of the test, stand against the wall the mike is facing and speak back toward the middle of the room. This will give you a sense of what the distant mikes will hear. Finally, in the third stage of the test, you move to the opposite wall, and without altering the position of the mike, you again speak back toward it. This will make the echoes appear much louder than normal, and as a result you'll be able to judge how warm or how brittle they sound.

"Dead" Baffles

You can make your baffles any size you want, although small baffles will be relatively ineffective in damping low frequencies, since these high-energy waves will pass right around them. Professional studios use baffles that stand anywhere from four feet to eight feet high and are about four feet wide. You may not want your baffles to be this large, but that will depend upon the size of your studio and what you'll be using them for.

To construct the baffle, you simply build a frame out of two-by-fours, fill it with insulation, and cover both sides with one-inch corkboard, carpeting, or fabric (Figure 17c).

Figure 17c: Constructing a "dead" baffle.

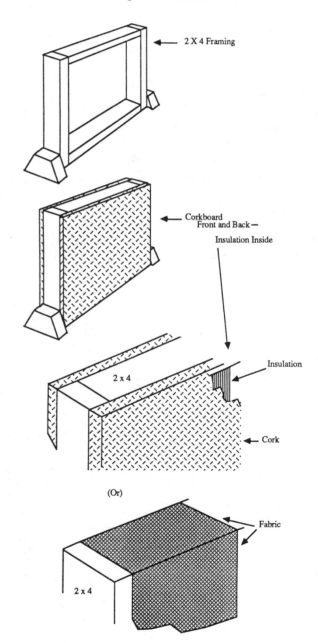

If you're good at upholstery, fabric might look nicer, and it's cheaper, but you'll find that corkboard is more absorptive.

Yet insulation is the real key to a baffle, and if you just stuff it with rags, it won't be very effective. On the other hand, Styrofoam pebbles, which are about twice the size of BBs, form a very dense sound trap. Fiberglass wall or ceiling insulation can also be quite effective, as can thick foam padding.

"Live" Baffles

Live baffles, which are used to *create* reflections, are also rather easy to make. Again, you begin by building a frame out of two-by-fours, but instead of filling in the center of the frame with foam, you cover it with an acoustically reflective material. In our example (Figure 17d), we use bathroom tiles, which can generally be purchased for as little as fifteen cents each, but you can also use mirror tiles or anything else that will give you a nice, bright reflection.

If you do wish to use bathroom tiles, you should first cover the frame with a sheet of plywood at least half an inch thick. And make sure you use screws to fasten it down, because if it doesn't remain tight to the frame, it will rattle. Then you simple glue the tiles onto the plywood and fill in the cracks with grout.

Ceiling Baffles

Ceiling reflections can often cause excessive high-end response in the control room. One way to eliminate this is to suspend a baffle from the ceiling so that it's directly overhead when you're sitting at the console (Figure 17e). In its finished form, the baffle should be about 4 feet square and should hang 1½ feet down from the ceiling in back and about 1 foot down from the ceiling in front. To construct it, you build a frame out of two-by-fours or two-by-twos, fill the frame with insulation or foam, and cover it with padding or carpeting.

And when you hang it, *make sure* it's *secure!*

Tent Baffles

If you record by night in the same rooms you live in by day, you may not want to keep a bunch of baffles lined up along the wall. However, you will undoubtedly need to make some acoustical adjustments from time to time, and when you do, one of the least disruptive methods you can use is to build an acoustical tent like those we've described in the chapters on instruments.

There are many ways to build these tents and many materials that can be used. But the most important thing to remember is that in order for a tent to be effective, it must block reflections from the ceiling and the floor, as well as from *at least* three sides.

Figure 17f illustrates two types of acoustic tents. In the single-tent example, we've used wool blankets for the sides and ceiling, but you can also use thick draperies or even carpeting. The key here is that thicker material will absorb more sound. However, it will also require stronger support. And if you use carpeting, just make sure that the nap, or shaggy side of the carpet, is facing the interior of the tent.

In the case of the double-layered tent, you construct a tent-within-a-tent, and in doing so, you create an air space that serves as an acoustic trap. This greatly increases the effectiveness of the enclosure and thus offers an alternative to using just one layer of thick material, such as carpeting. However, you will need to provide at least six inches of air space between the two layers in order for the sound trap to be effective.

Figure 17d: Constructing a "live" baffle.

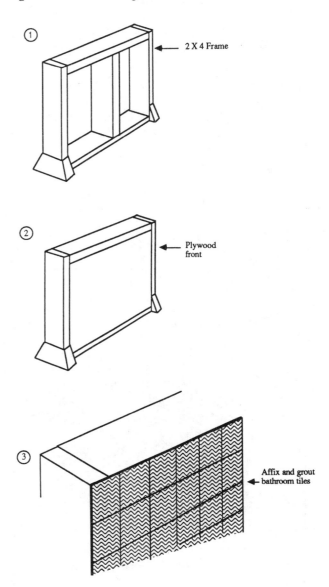

① ← 2 X 4 Frame

② ← Plywood front

③ ← Affix and grout bathroom tiles

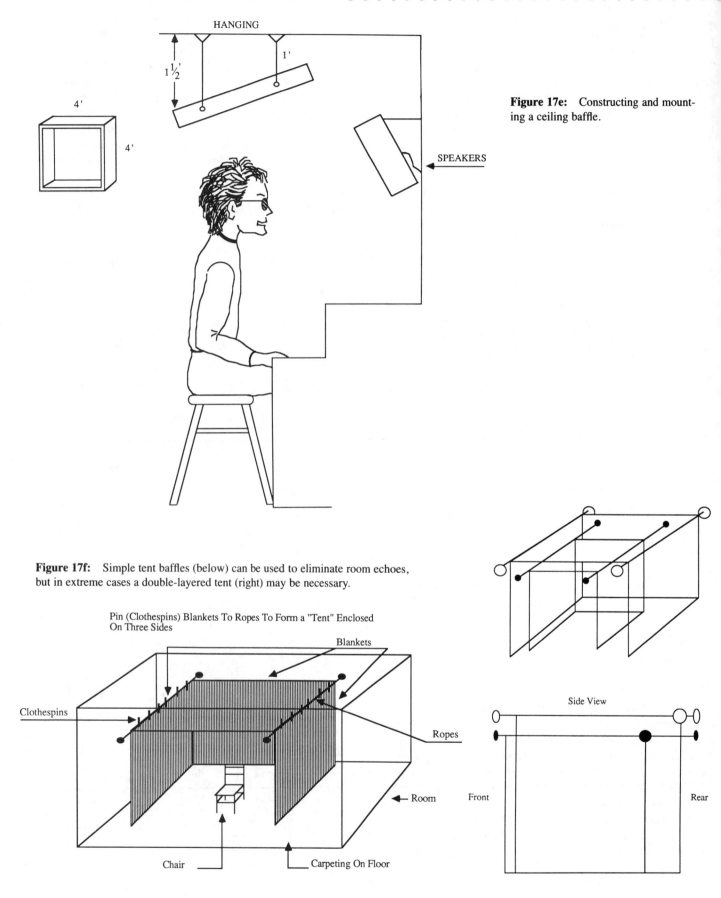

HANGING

4'

4'

1½'

1'

SPEAKERS

Figure 17e: Constructing and mounting a ceiling baffle.

Figure 17f: Simple tent baffles (below) can be used to eliminate room echoes, but in extreme cases a double-layered tent (right) may be necessary.

Pin (Clothespins) Blankets To Ropes To Form a "Tent" Enclosed On Three Sides

Blankets

Clothespins

Ropes

Room

Chair

Carpeting On Floor

Side View

Front

Rear

THE IMPORTANCE OF THE LISTENING ENVIRONMENT

The ideal acoustical environment for recording is one in which there is a mixture of reflections and damping, so that the room is far from being acoustically dead, but neither are the room reflections allowed to interfere with the sound. Uncontrolled reflections can be very harmful. If there are too many reflections, it will sound as if all the instruments have been treated with reverb, and if the reflections are allowed to bounce back and forth between a set of parallel walls, you'll get either a buildup or a cancelation of bass and/or top-end frequencies.

The same is true for the listening environment; if you monitor your work in a room that is acoustically flawed, the tapes won't sound right. For example, if the room generates low-frequency phase cancelation, when you record you'll probably try to compensate for the lack of bass response by boosting the bottom-end EQ. But as a result, when the material is played back in a room with normal acoustics, the bass will overpower the rest of the recording.

Thus, the simplest way to determine how the acoustics in your room stack up is to play your tapes back in a number of different rooms and then at a friend's house. If they consistently sound weird (for example, if the low end is always too loud or too soft), then you've got a problem in your studio that requires immediate attention.

Assuming that you're not setting EQ levels while monitoring through headphones (a definite no-no), and that your tape heads and bias circuits are properly aligned (chapter 4),

the first thing you need to determine is whether the speaker system you are using as a monitor is producing an overabundance of high or low frequencies. This, as we mentioned in chapter 5, is something that should be checked at the time of purchase by hooking up the speakers to the amp you'll be using and listening to an album you're familiar with. However, if you didn't perform this test, the easiest alternative is to play an album through your system at low volume (by keeping the volume down, you remove any influence the room acoustics might be having on the sound). If the record sounds fine, meaning that the relative levels of high and low frequencies are normal, then the problem is not in the speakers but in the room acoustics.

If the problem is one of speaker response, you simply need to get speakers that better match your system (or vice versa). However, if the problem is of an acoustical nature, you can either try to adjust the room acoustics, which we'll discuss in a moment, or you can take the acoustics into account as you record and monitor your work at low volumes.

For example, the acoustics in my home studio are a bit bottom-end heavy. Yet since I'm aware of this, I compensate for it by *reducing* low-end EQ any time I record an instrument like a bass in the room. And during mixdowns, I'll usually set up the mix at a louder volume, which I'm more comfortable with, and then, after making a run, I'll replay it at low volume to make sure it has the proper bass response. In fact, it's a good idea to monitor at low volumes even when tracks are being laid down, because then you won't need to guess at the effect the control room acoustics are having.

SOLVING YOUR ACOUSTIC PROBLEMS

The following checklist is designed to help you find an adequate solution to acoustic problems that exist in either the listening environment or the recording environment. Some alternatives can be used to make minor adjustments in ambience, while others can provide a means to totally alter the acoustics. However, even in extreme cases you should always try using the simple approach first.

SOUNDPROOFING

When we use the word "soundproofing" in the context of a home environment, all we're really talking about is lowering

the level of sound leakage into and out of the studio. Commercial studios spend fortunes constructing truly soundproof rooms, but to be successful they often have to create floating floors that are made of layers of eight-inch concrete slabs, and they have to build uniquely insulated walls that are a foot thick. Obviously this isn't practical for home studios, yet unless you're the exception, you *will* need to find ways to at least limit the leakage.

And remember, while you may be concerned primarily with keeping sound *out* of the recording environment, you also need to be concerned with keeping sound *in*. After all, you're not going to get a whole lot of recording done if the police are knocking on the door and the neighbors are pounding on the ceiling!

PROBLEM
Street Noise Is Leaking into the Studio, or You're Disturbing the Neighbors

CHECK

1. If sound is leaking into or out of the recording area, find a more isolated part of the house to record in. If there are no such areas,

then

2. Close mike the sound source and either aim it directly into an open clothes closet (Figure 17a) or surround it with pillows, a tent baffle, or "dead" baffles. However, if these minor measures don't solve the problem,

then

3. Carpet the floor with thick carpeting and lay padding down underneath. Then cover the
continued . . .

... *continued*

windows with heavy drapes and fill the room with as much absorptive material (pillows, cushioned furniture, and the like) as possible. If that doesn't help,

then

4. Check all doors leading to the outside and make sure that they are made of solid wood (not hollow) and that they fit snugly into the frame.

If not:

5. Seal off any cracks between the door and the frame with weather stripping or rags, and if the door is not made of solid wood, cover the interior surface with acoustic tiles, foam, or corkboard (Figure 17g). If there are any windows in the door, cover them with foam padding (for sliding glass doors, see Step 8).

then

6. If there is a storm door, keep it closed, as the air space between the doors provides an additional sound trap. But if leakage persists,

then

7. If you have storm windows, put them up. And, if possible, sandwich a thick sheet of foam between the outer and inner windows. But if that doesn't solve the problem,

then

8. Board the windows up from the inside with plywood or fiberboard (Figure 17h). And for additional soundproofing, place a two-inch sheet of foam between the glass and the fiberboard (this technique can also be used on sliding glass doors). If you still get leakage,

then

9. Follow Steps 4–6 in "Deadening the Acoustics," page 266.

Sound Is Leaking to, or from, Other Areas in the Building:

10. Follow Steps 1–3, above and seal off any doors leading to the rest of the house in the manner described in Step 5. If you still get leakage,

continued ...

Figure 17g: When you cover the inside of a door with cork, make sure you cover the entire surface.

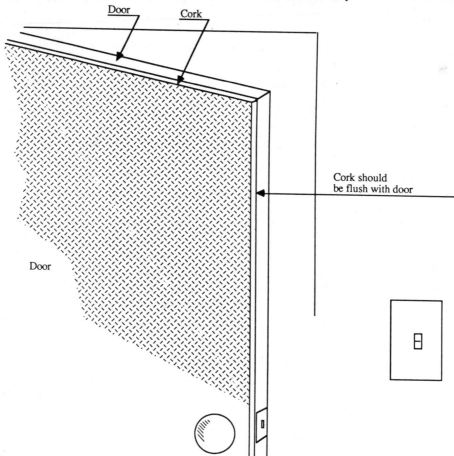

Door   Cork

Cork should be flush with door

Door

Figure 17h: Boarding up a window using foam padding and fiberboard.

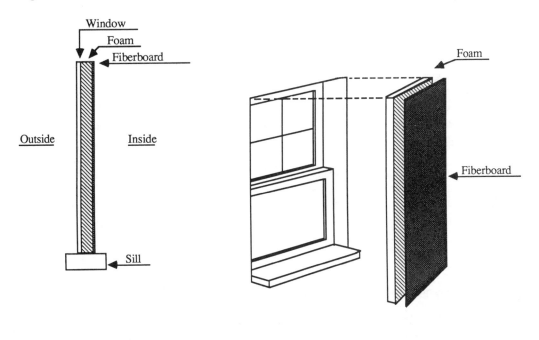

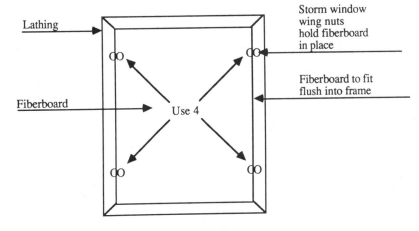

. . . continued

then

11. Check cooling/heating vents for leakage and, if necessary, close them. If the problem persists,

then

12. Follow Steps 4–6 in "Deadening the Acoustics."

Sound Is Leaking to, or from, an Upstairs Area:

13. Follow Steps 1–3 above. If you still get leakage,

then

14. Check cooling/heating vents for leakage and, if necessary close them. If the problem persists,

then

15. Lay carpet and carpet padding down on the floor of the room above you. If this doesn't work,

then

16. Cover the walls, doors, and ceiling with such absorptive materials as acoustic tiles, corkboard, or carpeting.

But

17. If money is a problem, staple egg cartons to the ceiling and cover them with fabric (Figure 17i). Or, if you need more damping, you can create a sound trap by suspending a blanket or a carpet at least six inches below the egg crates.

continued . . .

... *continued*

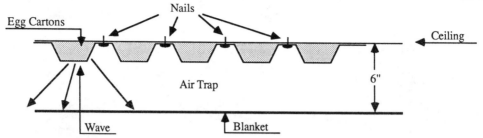

Figure 17i: Tacking egg cartons to the ceiling helps reduce leakage of noise from or to an upstairs apartment or room.

Or

18. If money *isn't* a problem, you can create an excellent sound trap by building a drop ceiling. This should hang at least one foot below the existing ceiling, and it should be heavily insulated.

Sound Is Leaking to, or from, a Downstairs Area:

19. Follow Steps 1–3, above. If the problem persists,

then

20. Check cooling/heating vents for leakage and, if necessary, close them. But if that's not the problem,

then

21. Cover the walls, doors, and ceiling with such absorptive materials as acoustic tiles, corkboard, or carpeting.

DEADENING THE ACOUSTICS

When we talk of deadening the acoustics, we are speaking only of *reducing* the number of ambient reflections, not of eliminating them entirely. In fact, in many cases you'll find that in order to keep room ambience out of a microphone, you'll only need to deaden the area around the sound source, not the entire room.

There are many reasons to deaden the acoustics. For instance, it improves soundproofing, because when you deaden the acoustics, you create an environment in which sound is absorbed. And the more sound that is absorbed, the less sound there is to leak out of (or into) the room. It also provides an equally important means of eliminating ambience from the recording.

Thus, this section includes one set of techniques for deadening the acoustics of the listening environment and another for eliminating unwanted ambience from the recording.

PROBLEM

The Control Room Echoes Are Too Strong:

CHECK

1. Move to a room that is more suitable. But if that's not possible,

then

2. Carpet the floor with thick carpeting and lay padding down underneath. Then cover the windows with heavy drapes and fill the room with as much absorptive material (pillows, cushioned furniture, and the like) as possible. If the room is already carpeted,

then

3. Turn down the volume of the monitor speakers. If that doesn't help,

then

4. Cover the walls, doors, and ceiling with such absorptive materials as acoustic tiles, corkboard, or carpeting. And if the problem persists,

then

5. In extreme cases, instead of nailing the carpet flat against the wall, bunch it up so that it forms ripples, or pleats, that protrude six to eight inches out from the wall (Figure 17j).

Or

6. Nail the carpet to a frame of two-by-fours that is the same size as the wall. Then, tack egg cartons to the surface of the wall and lift the two-by-four framing into position (Figure 17k). Note that the top of the frame should sit farther out from the wall than the bottom of the frame.

The Mikes Are Picking Up Too Much Ambience:

7. Move to a room that has fewer ambient reflections. But if that's not possible,

then

8. Turn down the volume of the amp.

Then

9. Close mike the sound source and aim it directly into a big pile of pillows. If that doesn't work,

continued...

266

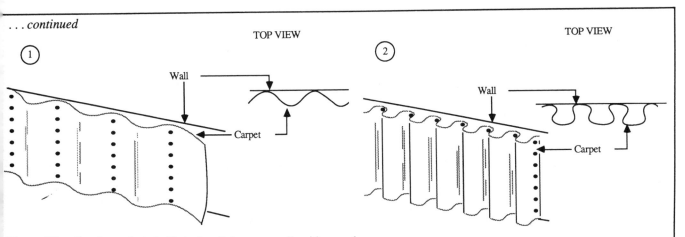

Figure 17j: Creating a pleated effect when lining your walls with carpeting.

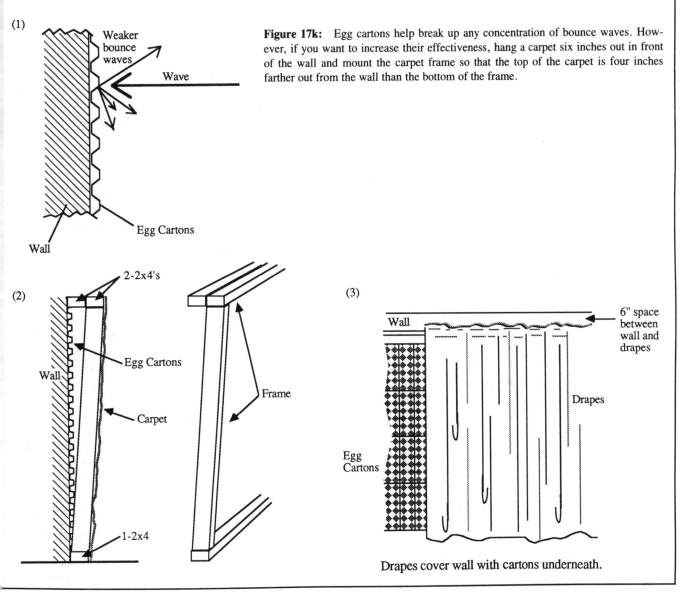

Figure 17k: Egg cartons help break up any concentration of bounce waves. However, if you want to increase their effectiveness, hang a carpet six inches out in front of the wall and mount the carpet frame so that the top of the carpet is four inches farther out from the wall than the bottom of the frame.

Drapes cover wall with cartons underneath.

then

10. Place the amplifier directly in front of an open clothes closet and aim it inside (Figure 17a). Be sure to cover the back wall of the closet with pillows or with a piece of carpeting. And if that doesn't work,

then

11. Carpet the floors, hang thick drapes across the windows, and fill the room with as much

absorptive material (pillows, cushioned furniture, and the like) as possible. If the room is already carpeted,

then

12. Enclose the sound source within a tent baffle or completely surround it with "dead" baffles. And if the problem persists,

then

13. Follow Steps 4–6 in this section (above).

REDUCING FREQUENCY BUILDUPS

In some rooms, the ambient reflections will cause a buildup of individual bands of frequencies, and as a result the room will produce anything from low-end resonance or phase cancelation to high-end brittleness. These frequency "humps," as they're called, may affect the ambience of the entire room (such as when a bass guitar booms every time the guitarist hits a certain note). Or their effects may just be limited to a

particular corner or cubbyhole, or to the area immediately in front of a wall.

In severe cases, there really is no solution short of rebuilding the room. So, for instance, if you're hearing enormous amounts of low-end resonance, the best thing you can do is record in a different room. However, if the problem is relatively minor, you simply need to break up, or deaden, the reflections coming out of corners or bouncing off the ceiling and walls (Figure 17l).

PROBLEM
Disruptive, Low-Frequency Reflections (the Bass Sounds Boomy, or It Disappears Sporadically):

CHECK

1. Move to a room where the ambience produces a pleasant set of reflections (preferably one with a high ceiling). But if that's not possible,

then

2. Turn the volume down on the amp.

Figure 17l: Wave reflections off corners and walls.

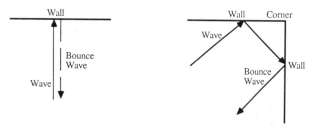

Eliminating right-angle corner reflections.

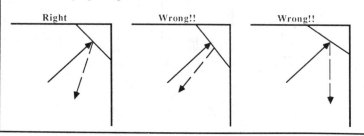

Then

3. If the effect is only noticeable in the room mikes, place blankets and pillows on the area of the floor immediately surrounding the mike, then lay a strip of carpeting down between the sound source and the mike.

Or

4. Try to locate, and eliminate, the frequency hump with EQ. If that doesn't help,

then

5. Place the amplifier directly in front of an open clothes closet and aim it inside (Figure 17a). Be sure to cover the back wall of the closet with pillows or with a piece of carpeting. And if that doesn't work,

then

6. Carpet the entire floor and cover the windows with heavy drapes. Also, fill the room with absorptive materials and position them in such a way as to block off corners and interrupt any long, reflective wall surfaces (for example, pile pillows in the corners, place furniture against the wall). If that doesn't help,

then

7. Build a "house" out of "dead" baffles and fully enclose the sound source. If that doesn't work,

then

8. Line the walls on either side of each corner with corkboard or acoustic tiles. But if this doesn't sufficiently absorb the corner reflections,

continued . . .

... *continued*

then

9. Close off the corners with plywood and cover the surface either with acoustic tiles or with corkboard. Angle the plywood so that the reflected wave neither bounces back toward the opposite corner nor bounces parallel to either of the walls (Figure 17m).

Or

10. Use fiberboard to similarly block off the corners, and fill the space behind the fiberboard with old pillows or pieces of foam. However, if you're still getting low-end buildup,

then

11. Cover all parallel wall surfaces with carpeting that has been bunched up to form ripples, or pleats, that sit six to eight inches out from the wall (Figure 17j).

Or

12. In extreme cases, nail the carpet to a frame of two-by-fours that is the same size as the wall. Then, tack egg cartons to the surface of the wall and lift the two-by-four framing into position (Figure 17k). Note that the top of the frame should sit farther out from the wall than the bottom of the frame. If this doesn't help,

then

13. Cover the ceiling with acoustic tiles or carpeting.

Or

14. If money is a problem, staple egg cartons to the ceiling and cover them with fabric (Figure 17i). Or, if you need more damping, you can create a sound trap by suspending a blanket or a carpet at least six inches below the egg crates.

However

15. If the buildup is being caused by reflections off the control room ceiling, install a ceiling baffle, as described earlier in the chapter (Figure 17e).

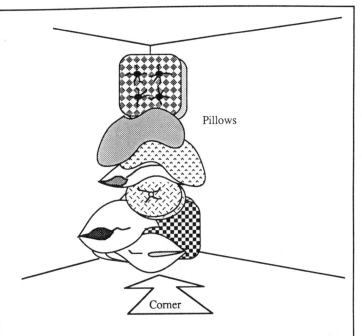

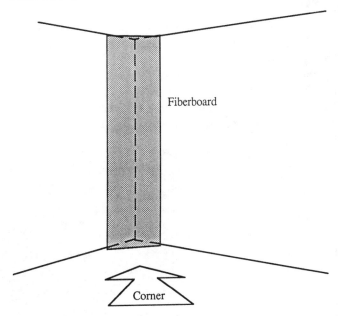

Figure 17m: Blocking off corners with pillows (above) or fiberboard (below).

Disruptive, High-Frequency Reflections (Room Echoes Sound Brittle):

16. Move to a room where the ambience produces a more pleasing set of ambient reflections. For example, if you're using a bathroom, try a hallway or stairway. But if that's not possible,

then

17. Turn down the amp. If it still sounds bad,

then

18. Remove any room mikes you might be using to pick up the room ambience. And if that doesn't work,

then

19. Modify the environment by placing a few cushions or pillows around the room in order to soften some of the reflections.

Or

20. Close mike the amp and aim it into a pile of pillows placed a few feet away.

SUGGESTED RECORDING AREAS FOR EACH INSTRUMENT

There are many locations in the home that have acoustic properties suitable for recording. The following is a list of areas that will often complement the sound of each particular instrument. Yet each location will need to be tested, and in some instances you still may need to modify the ambience slightly.

Ambient Guitar (Loud Echoes):

1. Tiled bathrooms
2. Hallways and stairways (possible, but test first).
3. Large kitchens with tiled floors.

Semiambient Guitar (Soft Echoes):

1. Living rooms with high ceilings.
2. Some sparsely furnished dens or bedrooms.

Nonambient Guitar (No Echoes):

1. Very dead bedrooms, dens, or living rooms.
2. Clothes closets (any room).

Bass Guitar:

1. Clothes closets (any room).
2. Very dead bedrooms or dens.

Vocals:

1. A bedroom or den that has *some* "live" ambience.
2. Clothes closets (any room).
3. Any large, carpeted room (using a tent baffle as a "vocal booth").

Drums:

1. Large, open, carpeted room with a high ceiling.
2. A "live" area with a hard floor and a high ceiling (such as a garage or a basement).

THE REEL WORLD
Shure Brothers' Anechoic Chamber

So, you say you want to deaden the acoustics of your studio? Well, we certainly don't advise attempting anything like what you see here, but if you wanted to *totally* eliminate ambience, this is what it would take.

This photograph (Figure 17n) was taken in the interior of Shure Brothers' anechoic chamber, which is where the company tests the response patterns of its microphones. The strange shapes you see on the walls and ceiling are foam spikes that serve to absorb and/or scatter the sound waves, while the floor (which is not pictured) is a grid that is suspended on springs.

You can't truly know what dead acoustics are until you've been in a room such as this. In fact, it's downright eerie. The acoustics are so dead that when you talk, your voice sounds as though it projects to about the tip of your nose and then stops!

Figure 17n: Shure Brothers' anechoic chamber. (*Courtesy of Shure Brothers Inc.*)

Chapter 18

Buyer's Guide to Studio Gear

Assembling a studio, even a small studio, is a very expensive proposition, and it's often difficult to know what gear to spend your money on in order to get the biggest return in terms of recording flexibility and quality. To some extent, this will depend upon the equipment you already own or have access to, but of greater importance is the amount of money you have to spend and the level of recording quality you want to be able to achieve.

For example, if you only intend to use your gear for writing songs or working out arrangements for a band, the quality of the equipment you'll need, and the amount of money you'll need to spend, will be considerably less than if you want to have the ability to generate demos for recording artists or record companies. By the same token, if you don't have much money to spend, you may not be able to buy all the gear necessary to give you the recording quality you desire.

There are, of course, ways to get around the problem of money. As you'll see later in the chapter, you can often buy used gear that, for certain applications, will perform just as well as a new unit—and at about one-third the cost. Or you can outfit your studio a piece at a time, starting off with the basic gear and adding to or upgrading the system as your bank balance allows. And then there's the chance that you may be able to rent certain pieces of gear that you can't immediately afford.

However, these are all decisions you must make for yourself. All we can hope to do is provide you with an outline of your options and give you an idea of what each means to the quality of your tapes.

WHAT TO BUY... WHAT TO BUY...

The following "shopping lists" are designed to help you determine your purchasing needs. Each is categorized according to the type of recording you want to be doing (songwriting, generating song or record company demos,

and so forth), and each contains a list of the gear you'll need in order to do the job properly.

These lists are meant to provide *general* purchasing "guidelines," so some slight adjustments may be called for, depending upon your specific needs. However, it is important to keep in mind that the audio chain is only as strong as its weakest link, so while your studio should include each item on the appropriate list, you don't want to buy a bunch of cheap outboard gear in order to fill in the gaps. As we've said many times, you need quality gear if you want to produce a quality recording.

It should also be noted that the prices we've included are based on the list prices for new equipment (namely, that gear we've listed as an example), and you should be able to get at least a 15–25 percent break in almost every case. If you buy the gear used, which is covered later in the chapter, you may pay as little as one-third.

On the other hand, these are the base prices, and in the case of tape decks, they reflect the cost of the gear alone—no auto locators, no special setups, or the like. So by the time you add in the cost of all the "extras," you could end up paying half again as much. For example, the Fostex B-16, which is the cheapest version of their ½-inch 16-track, presently lists for $5,900. Yet by the time you add in the cost of optional modifications, you can end up paying as much as $8,900 for the unit. And that doesn't even include an auto locator!

By the same token, many manufacturers offer gear at various levels of quality, and you should check with your dealer to see what else a particular company might have available. For example, TASCAM offers five 4-buss mixers, the cheapest being a $700 unit that's about the size of a Porta-studio, the most expensive being a $3,800, full-on console that features twenty input channels. The same sort of thing is true for Yamaha, which offers an array of consoles. So while you can use these lists as a guide, when you go shopping for gear, make sure you shop around.

And remember that we've listed specific pieces of gear so that you have an idea of the quality you should look for. There are many excellent tape recorders and consoles that we didn't have room to include but would serve you just as well. Thus, these are not the only brands, or the only models, that we could recommend.

NOTE—*No list prices have been given for outboard gear, as the quality and "sale" prices of such gear can change dramatically.*

PERSONAL HOME USE

Applications:

Songwriting
Working out arrangements
Recording live gigs (multitrack cassette format)
Creating song demos for artists and publishers (open-reel format only)
Recording songs for personal enjoyment

Figure 18a: TASCAM Portastudio 246 (*Courtesy of TEAC Corporation of America*)

OPTION #1   **TOTAL COST: $2,150–$2,750**
4-Track Studio—Cassette

4-Track Cassette Deck and Mixer—$1,000–$1,400*

YAMAHA MT44D
TASCAM 246 PORTASTUDIO
FOSTEX 250

2-Track Open-Reel Tape Deck for mixing and masters—$900–$1,100

TASCAM 22-2
FOSTEX A-2

2-Track Cassette Deck for copies—$250+

Microphones—a minimum of two, plus mike stands
Monitor amp and speakers (can use your stereo system)
Headphones—two pairs
Outboard equalizer—parametric or sweepable-band
Reverb—digital or spring
Compressor/limiter

Advantages	*Disadvantages*
Easy to use	Sound quality
Portable	Only four initial tracks**
Inexpensive	
Versatile	

*Some older models can be purchased *new* for as little as $700.
**Although 8-track cassette decks have recently become available at a list price of $2,300.

Figure 18b: Fostex Model-20 (*Courtesy of Fostex Corporation*)

Figure 18c: TASCAM 22–4 (*Courtesy of TEAC Corporation of America*)

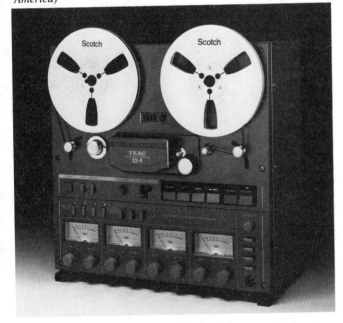

Figure 18d: Yamaha RM804 (*Courtesy of Yamaha International Corporation*)

OPTION #2   **TOTAL COST: $3,850–$6,150**
4-Track Studio—Open Reel (¼-inch format)

4-Track Open-Reel Tape Deck—$1,500–$3,000

> TASCAM 34B or 22-4
> FOSTEX A-4
> OTARI BQII

4-Buss Recording Console—$1,100–$1,800*

> YAMAHA RM804
> TASCAM M208/M308
> FOSTEX 450-8

2-Track Open-Reel Tape Deck for mixing and masters—$900–$1,100

> TASCAM 22-2
> FOSTEX A-2

2-Track Cassette Deck for copies—$250+

> Microphones—a minimum of three, plus mike stands
> Monitor amp and speakers (can use your stereo system)
> Headphone amp (can use headphone jack on console)
> Headphones—two or three pairs
> Reverb—digital or spring
> Compressor/limiter
> Direct box (if using +4 dB console)

Advantages	*Disadvantages*
Standard-gauge heads on 4-track improve signal quality	Only four initial tracks More expensive, as more equipment is required

*See "Recording Console" section in this chapter.

SEMIPRO HOME USE

Applications

Songwriting
Creating song demos for artists and publishers
Creating artist demos for record companies (½-inch
8-tracks and 1-inch 16-tracks only)

OPTION #3   **TOTAL COST: $4,500–$10,750**
8-Track Studio

8-Track Open-Reel Tape Deck—$2,000–$5,300*

FOSTEX 80 (¼-inch format)**
TASCAM 38 or 48 (½-inch format)
OTARI MARK III/8 (½-inch format)

4-Buss Recording Console—$1,250–$2,800†

YAMAHA RM804
TASCAM M312
SOUNDCRAFT SERIES 200

2-Track Open-Reel Tape Deck for mixing and masters—
$900–$2,300

TASCAM 32 or 22-2
OTARI BII

2-Track Cassette Deck for copies—$350+

Microphones—a minimum of three
Monitor amp and speakers (can use your stereo system)
Headphone amp
Headphones—two or three pairs
Reverb—digital or spring
Compressor/limiter
Echo/delay machine
Direct box (if using +4 dB console)
Auto locator (for the 8-track)

*TASCAM's "Studio 8," which combines ¼-inch tape deck *and* console,
lists for $3,995. See Tape Tip #39.

**The ¼-inch formats are less expensive than the ½-inch models, but
the narrow-gauge, ¼-inch heads produce poorer response.

†8-buss console can also be used—see "Recording Console" section.

Figure 18e: TASCAM 48 (*Courtesy of TEAC Corporation of America*)

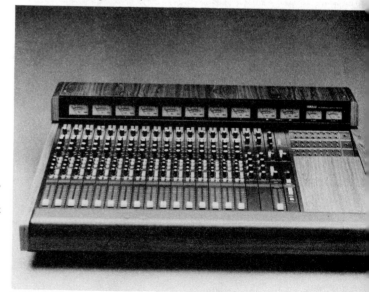

Figure 18f: Yamaha RM1608 (*Courtesy of Yamaha International Corporation*)

Figure 18g: TASCAM MS-16 (*Courtesy of TEAC Corporation of America*)

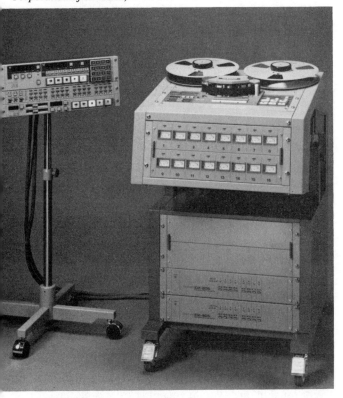

OPTION #4   **TOTAL COST: $13,250–$20,600**
16-Track Studio

16-Track Open-Reel Tape Deck—$5,900–$10,000

> FOSTEX B-16 (½-inch format)*
> TASCAM MS-16 (1-inch format)

8-Buss Recording Console—$5,500–$7,950**

> TASCAM M520
> YAMAHA RM1608
> SOUNDCRAFT SERIES 600

2-Track Open-Reel Tape Deck for mixing and masters—$1,500–$2,300

> TASCAM 32 or 42
> OTARI BII

2-Track Cassette Deck for copies—$350+

> Microphones—a minimum of three
> Monitor amp and speakers (can use your stereo system)
> Headphone amp
> Headphones—two or three pairs
> Reverb—digital or spring
> Compressor/limiter
> Echo/delay machine
> Direct box (if using +4 dB console)
> Auto locator (for the 16-track)

*The ½-inch formats are less expensive than the 1-inch models, but the narrow-gauge, ½-inch heads produce poorer response.
**16-buss console can also be used—see "Recording Console" section.

TAPE RECORDERS

It goes without saying that the tape recorder is the single most important component of your system. A good tape recorder is capable of producing an excellent recording, with or without a mixing console. But if you have a lousy tape deck, you can have the world's greatest console and your tracks are going to sound terrible no matter what.

When most musicians think about setting up a home studio, the first thing that comes to mind is getting the biggest and best *single* tape recorder money can buy. (What musician hasn't dreamed of owning a 16-track!) But to produce a finished recording, you need more than one machine. You need a system that gives you the capability to (1) record initial tracks, (2) record final, 2-track mixes and perform bounces, and (3) record cassette copies. And that means having *three* quality tape decks.

Multitrack "Tracking" Deck

When you're shopping for the tape deck that will serve as your primary, multitrack machine, your decision will probably come down to the number of tracks you can afford, given the quality you hope to achieve.

Take, for example, the situation where you're trying to choose between buying either an 8-track or a 4-track. In this instance, you actually have three choices: a ½-inch 8-track, a ¼-inch 8-track, or a ¼-inch 4-track. The advantage of having an 8-track is, of course, that it has eight tracks instead of four, and the advantage of buying a ¼-*inch* 8-track is that they are less expensive than those using the ½-inch-tape format. However, the *disadvantage* of buying the ¼-inch 8-track is that it uses narrow-gauge heads, so the signal quality isn't as good as what you'd get from either of the other two units.

Ultimately, this means that if you have enough money to buy the ½-inch 8-track, you'll get the convenience of having eight initial tracks, *plus* you'll have good signal quality. However, if you can only afford a ¼-inch 8-track, then you'll need to decide whether you want more tracks or better fidelity, the latter of which you'd get from the 4-track.

In general, I would suggest that you choose quality over convenience, although that may depend upon the specific units you have to choose from. For example, if you're a songwriter, and you want to be able to throw eight tracks down quickly, you would be better off buying the ¼-inch 8-track, as you'd be forced to bounce and combine tracks if you were to use a 4-track, and that might disturb your creative flow.

It should be noted that the same considerations apply to 16-track purchases, since they, too, are available in standard-gauge and narrow-gauge formats.

2-Track "Mastering" Deck

No matter how many initial tracks you have, and no matter how good the primary tape machine is, you will also need a 2-track (or "half-track") deck of *comparable quality* so that you can perform external bounces and generate a 2-track master.

Unfortunately, you can't use a cassette deck for your master copies—unless, that is, you want to set up the mix and record a new master every time you send a tape to someone. A cassette deck just doesn't have the reproduction quality of a good open-reel machine. So if you keep a cassette copy as a master, and you bounce the material to a second cassette deck (for mailing out), you'll lose the recording quality you worked so hard to achieve.

It's also important that your 2-track bounce deck is relatively equal in quality to the multitrack deck, because if you bounce to a tape machine of lesser quality, you'll lose the fidelity you achieved on the initial tracks. This may mean spending more than you had anticipated, but if you don't have the money at the moment, you might check around to see if you can occasionally borrow a friend's machine for your bounces. Or you might look into buying a *used* 2-track, as we discuss later in "Buying Used Gear."

2-Track Cassette Deck

Whether you want to send personal tapes to friends or demo tapes to record companies, you'll need to copy your master onto a 2-track cassette deck. Again, the quality of this machine should closely match the quality of your other decks, although this is somewhat less critical. As we've often mentioned, most record company execs listen to demos on regular home stereo gear, so as long as you're not losing a significant amount of quality in the transfer, your normal home unit should be quite suitable. However, you should check the results on some of your friends' stereos just to be sure.

Digital Tape Decks

As we go to press, digital recording technology has already begun to make its way into the home in the form of 2-track audio cassette recorders that list for about $2,000. Although designed for the average consumer, once they become established in the market, plans are under way to produce 4-track and 8-track versions for the home studio.

As 2-tracks these units may make excellent mastering or duplicating decks for demos, since the DAT (digital audiotape) format effectively eliminates tape hiss and generation loss. However, there are some potential drawbacks to DAT. First, since the machines will only handle cassettes, you won't be able to perform any tape edits on the master. Early decks may not have punch-in capabilities, either. Plus, it's still unclear whether the tape itself will hold up to extensive play. The recording process is the same as that used for video cassettes, which wear out fairly quickly (about 100 plays). Thus, some experts theorize that the sound will begin to degenerate after as few as 50 or 75 passes (others feel that they'll last for up to 200 plays).

Of course, considering the advantages digital reproduction affords, such limitations would be pretty easy to live with. But before you jump on the digital bandwagon and blow two grand, we suggest you check out the performance of DAT recorders and consider whether or not they suit your needs.

Tape Recorder Features and Options

When you're looking for that one basic unit to buy, you should be concerned primarily with the reproduction quality it offers. However, the following features can also be useful and should be taken into consideration.

If you intend to perform any edits that require tape splicing, you'll want to buy a deck that offers a *"lifter defeat"* function. This function disengages the tape lifters, which are the two small metal rods that move the tape away from the heads when the machine is not in playback or record. By retracting the lifters, you can rock the tape across the heads (as described in Tape Tip #36, chapter 16) and locate the exact point at which you want to make the edit.

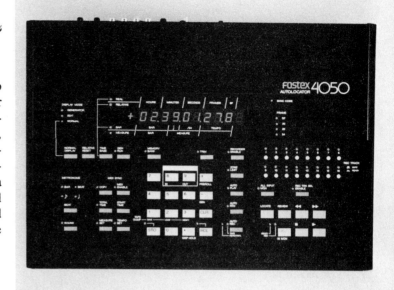

Figure 18h: Fostex 4050 Autolocator (*Courtesy of Fostex Corporation*)

If you buy a machine that offers a tape speed of 15 ips, make sure the deck can accommodate *10½-inch tape reels*. At these high speeds, a 7-inch reel will only hold enough tape for about two songs—if you're lucky!

If you want to be able to lock your machine up to a video recorder, you will want to buy a tape deck that is *"SMPTE compatible."* SMPTE is the time code system used for video-audio linkups, and like MIDI, which provides audio-audio synchronization, it must be recorded on tape. SMPTE code can be recorded on any machine, but if you use it often, the "compatible" machines are far more convenient. To begin with, in order to accept the signal from a SMPTE code reader/generator, these tape recorders have a special input/output jack. Then, in order to make proper use of the time code, the machine has onboard circuits that allow the SMPTE reader/generator to actually take control of the unit's operations. And in order to keep the SMPTE code track from leaking onto an adjacent track, the machine has to be capable of producing very little crosstalk.

Most of the new tape decks, particularly those designed by TASCAM, which is a leader in the field, are SMPTE compatible. However, in some cases, these features are offered as options that are not included in the list price. So if you plan to use SMPTE, when you're checking prices on units that claim to be SMPTE compatible, make sure you're not going to have to pay extra to have the unit set up for SMPTE use.

Remote control is another feature you might want your tape deck to have. Most manufacturers offer them as options on their units, and, depending on your needs, they can come in handy. But if your deck comes with an optional *auto locator,* that's even better. Auto locators are remote devices that enable you to start and stop your machine at specific points along the tape, so that if, for example, you need to keep repeating one particular punch-in, you can return to the same location on the tape each time. Plus, the latest, most sophisticated auto locators, such as the unit designed for Fostex's 8-track and 16-track systems, can actually generate SMPTE time code.

Another feature that is sometimes helpful to have on a tape deck is built-in *noise reduction*. Generally, this is not an essential feature to have on tape decks that use standard-gauge heads (¼-inch 4-tracks, ½-inch 8-tracks, and 1-inch 16-tracks). However, if you're buying a ¼-inch 8-track or a ½-inch 16-track, noise reduction is advisable, because these units have smaller tape heads and thus tend to produce noisier recordings.

RECORDING CONSOLES

Consoles are expensive, and many people try to squeak by with cheap models that offer very few features and little flexibility. However, the console provides a major link in the audio chain, and it is the one piece of gear that can be used to compensate for other pieces of lesser quality. So when you buy a mixer, spend the money and get the best one you can afford.

No two mixing consoles are alike, so before you start shopping around, you should familiarize yourself with the console operations outlined in chapter 5. This will help you determine what size console you need (how many input channels and busses), and which features it should have. Then, instead of comparing the frills, you can concentrate on comparing the *quality* of the units.

In fact, quality should be your main concern. So if, for instance, you have a 4-track tape deck, and you need to choose between an average 4-buss console and an above-average 2-buss unit, unless you need to record on all four tracks at once (such as when you're recording a band), you should go with the latter. Higher-caliber gear will give you better signal quality. And even though it may have fewer features, you can use the information in this book to find ways around the limitations.

Yet realistically, money can be *the* determining factor, and if you have limited funds, you may either want to opt for a used desk (which can be a *very* smart move), or, if you can't find any secondhand gear, you may want to try one of the smaller desks made by companies such as Yamaha or TASCAM (both companies make excellent professional consoles as well).

Input Channels and Busses

Many musicians have the misconception that they need a console with the same number of buss channels (outputs) as their tape recorder has tracks. So they figure that if they have an 8-track tape deck, they need an 8-buss console. While this configuration does, in fact, allow you to record

on all of the tracks at the same time, if you overdub most of your material, and you only record two or three tracks at a time, then no matter how many tracks your tape deck has, you'll only need a desk that has at most four busses.

On the other hand, the console does need to have at least as many *input channels* as there are tracks, because when you perform a mixdown, you want to be able to send the playback from each recorded track into a separate input channel. So if, for instance, you have an 8-track tape deck, you need a console that has at least eight input channels and, preferably, *ten* (two of which would be used as effect returns).

Plus, you have to remember that a channel is only capable of processing one signal. So the larger your productions are, the more input channels you'll need. For example, if you like to record three or four instruments at once, you'll need to use more input channels than if you were overdubbing each of the instruments separately.

Effect Sends

As a general rule, the more auxiliary send circuits you have, the better, because these sends are used to generate headphone mixes (cue sends) and to route signals to and from outboard effects gear. However, many desks come with direct-out circuits and "patch insert points" (see "Additional Features") that can be used to perform many of the same functions as effect sends. Therefore, while you would ordinarily want a desk to have two sets of aux sends (one pair for the cue mix and one pair for outboard effects), many alternatives are available.

EQ Formats

Another important feature to consider is the EQ format. As we discussed in chapter 5, there are basically four types of

---

OVERALL CAPABILITIES

BASICALLY, THEN, IF YOU HAVE A **4-TRACK** TAPE RECORDER, YOU WANT A CONSOLE WITH:

Input Channels: a minimum of *six*
Aux Sends: *Four** (two cues, two effects)
            (*If necessary, you can get away with only two.*)
Buss Channels: a minimum of *two*, a maximum of *four*
EQ Format: *PARAMETRIC* or *SWEEPABLE-BAND*

AND IF YOU'RE USING AN **8-TRACK** TAPE RECORDER:

Input Channels: a minimum of *ten*
Aux Sends: *Four* (two cues, two effects)
Buss Channels: a minimum of *four*, a maximum of *eight*
EQ Format: *PARAMETRIC* or *SWEEPABLE-BAND*

EQ used on consoles, and each offers a different level of control.

Most new consoles come equipped with either parametric or sweepable-band EQ systems. Parametric EQ offers the greatest amount of control, since it allows you to vary the location, the strength, *and* the bandwidth of the EQ you apply. Sweepable-band EQ also provides excellent control, although it doesn't allow you to alter the bandwidth. Plus, many of these sweepable systems only provide *shelving* control (fixed, broad-band EQ) over the very high and very low frequencies, which is something you need to be aware of if you're comparison shopping. So if you notice that the unit has two sweepable controls, *and* a dial that is labeled with a single frequency (for example, 100 Hz), be sure to ask the salesman about it.

Many older desks are only equipped with tone controls, which provide fixed, broad-band EQ. While this system is unusable for our purposes, some consoles, such as PA desks, offer additional, graphic EQ control over the output, and as long as it's an 8-band or a 10-band system, such desks will provide adequate EQ control over initial tracks. They may, however, prove inadequate for complex mixes.

Additional Features

There are a number of additional features you might look for on a console. For example, many of the high-price units provide control circuits that let you monitor playbacks through the buss channels (see chapter 5). This means that you don't need to bring the playback signal in on an input channel during overdubs, and as a result there are more input channels available for, among other things, processing the signal that is going to tape.

It's also helpful to look for a unit that has low-impedance capabilities and offers XLR input jacks. As we've mentioned, you'll get better signal quality from your mikes (even those that operate at up to 600 ohms) if you send them into the console on low-impedance inputs. And if you're using condenser mikes, you should look for a desk that has phantom power circuitry.

Some other useful features to look for include channel solo switches and attenuated (rotary dial) input gain reduction. The latter feature enables you to be very precise with the amount of gain reduction you apply to a signal, and thus it gives you more control than, for instance, a three-stage pad system that only offers three fixed levels of reduction.

You'll also find that some consoles provide direct-out circuits from the input channels. This enables you to bring a signal into a channel, process it, and send it directly out of the channel module. Thus, it effectively gives you an additional send for each channel.

Some of the smaller home mixers provide "insert patch points" rather than direct-outs. Depending upon the manufacturer, these inserts enable you to add effects either to the stereo buss mix (which can be very useful during mixdown) or to the input channel itself, in which case they function as an additional effect send.

MICROPHONES

The number of microphones you'll need to buy for your studio will depend upon how many instruments you record at a time. If you are recording an entire band, then you'll need a whole slew of mikes. However, if you tend to record only one instrument at a time, you'll be able to get away with far fewer.

In general, we would suggest that you set yourself up with a minimum of three mikes: one very good mike for vocals ($300–$800) and two multipurpose mikes ($150–$200 each). This way, you have enough mikes to use triangular miking on the drums, and you have the capability of, for example, miking a piano and a vocal, should you like to write on the piano.

The vocal mike is the most important one to have, as the vocal is the feature attraction, if you will, of the song. Therefore, you'll want to shop carefully for just the right mike, and you should choose the one you personally prefer.

The more expensive the microphone, the greater the difference there will be between it and other microphones in the same price bracket. However, some specific models we can suggest you try out include the Neumann U-89 and U-87, the Telefunken 251, the AKG C-12A and 414, and the Shure SM-7.* However, even though some of these mikes can only be purchased used through specialty outlets (some are no longer in production), they can run you up to $1,000, and unless you're working on artist demos for a record company, and you have pro gear in your studio, you'll be wasting your money on a level of quality you don't need.

Instead, you may want to try some of the higher-priced mikes manufactured by companies like Shure, Beyer, AKG, and Electro-Voice, all of which are highly regarded around the industry. And remember that you don't use this mike just for vocals. It can also serve as the principal microphone when you're using two mikes on an instrument or amplifier.

At the same time, you don't want to spend *all* of your money on one mike, because you'll also want to have a mike to use as an ambient, or distant, mike. In fact, you'll probably want to have two of them available for miking pianos or for background vocals or whatever. These mikes do not need to be as expensive as the vocal mike, but they do need to be high quality. And if you're going to be pairing them together as overheads for the drums or for piano tracks, it helps if they match up well with each other.

Again, Shure, Beyer, AKG, and Electro-Voice are some of the best-known manufacturers of microphones, and you can feel fairly certain of purchasing a quality device from any of them. However, one specific microphone I have a very high regard for, and would strongly recommend you

---

*For most of these mikes, 48-volt phantom power is required.

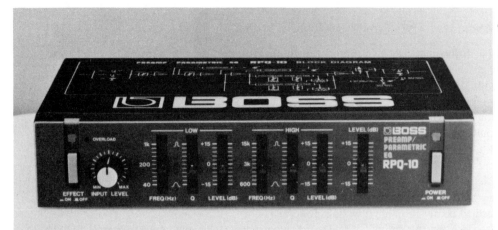

Figure 18i: Boss RPQ-10 Parametric EQ (*Courtesy of Roland Corporation*)

Figure 18j: Yamaha GC2020 Compressor/Limiter (*Courtesy of Yamaha International Corporation*)

Figure 18k: Roland SRE-555 Chorus Echo (*Courtesy of Roland Corporation*)

Figure 18l: Roland SDE 2500 Digital Delay (*Courtesy of Roland Corporation*)

look at, is the Shure SM-57, which is an excellent multipurpose mike. Both TEAC and Fostex also have a line of microphones available in this price range, and you might like to look into those as well.

When you do go out shopping for microphones, make sure you test the sound quality of any mike you want to buy. Just because a mike is expensive, you can't assume it's going to give you the sound you want. For example, you might find an expensive mike that is very bright, which would be fine if it's being used on a snare drum. Yet if it lacks warmth, it won't sound very good on vocals.

You should also ask about the store's policy on returns. Quite often an establishment will let you exchange one mike for another if, after you get it home, you're not satisfied with the quality. This is particularly important with mikes, because it's often difficult to judge the subtleties of a microphone's performance when you're testing it in the middle of a busy music store.

Finally, you'll find that some of the more expensive microphones have variable response patterns. Thus, if you need to use the mike for isolation, you can switch to a cardioid pattern, and if you need a wider field, such as for recording "group" backing vocals, you can switch over to a unidirectional pattern. This is a very convenient feature to have on your mike, and you should look for it if you have need of more than one response pattern.

OUTBOARD EFFECTS

There is such a wide variety of outboard effects gear available, it's often difficult to determine which piece of equipment to buy next. We can offer some general guidelines, which, for what they're worth, may help with your choice, but ultimately the decision will hinge upon which one or two effects are going to do you the most good.

Since the quality of the recorded signal is of utmost importance, your first priority should be to make sure that you have enough EQ. So although it's not exactly an effect, if your shopping list contains an *outboard EQ* device, it should be at the top of the list. Then, to insure the quality of your vocal, lead guitar, and bass tracks, you'll want to buy a 2-channel *compressor/limiter* (Yamaha and DBX make excellent, reasonably priced units). Then you'll want to get a *reverb device,* as it will help you create the "imaginary room" ambience so important to the overall mix.

Next on the list should be either a *harmonizer* or a *stereo chorus,* as these devices will give you the capability of generating a false stereo image. Then, once you have those capabilities, you can turn your attention to such coloration devices as *digital delays* (or *tape echoes)* and *flangers* or *phase shifters*.

You may think we're way off base suggesting that you choose a compressor over some fancy delay device or over a reverb unit, but in many cases reverb is not as important as compression. For example, if you listen to any of the Eagles' albums, you'll see that they used very little reverb on their vocals, and when I recorded the song demo we talked about in chapter 7, I had no reverb at all. Yet it's nearly impossible to record a *good* vocal without compression. Plus, you may be able to use your bathroom as a reverb chamber until you can afford a good reverb device.

On the other hand, once you do reach the point where you're ready to buy ambient effects, you may want to opt for one large, expensive piece of gear rather than a bunch of small ones. For example, a digital reverb device like Yamaha's Rev-7, which presently lists for $1,325, is capable of generating stereo reverb, stereo echo, stereo chorus, and phasing. Plus, it can create special effects like gated echoes, as we discussed in the mixdown chapter.

If you're a guitarist, you may want to opt for a Rockman, which offers stereo echo, stereo chorus, and distortion, rather than buying a delay line, a stereo chorus, and a heavy metal pedal.

However, effect technology is advancing so rapidly that a year or two after a company develops a new, innovative piece of gear, its competitors inevitably introduce a version with more features and a much smaller price tag. So before you take some big plunge and invest a year's worth of paychecks in an outboard device, make sure that it does everything you want it to do and *more!* And do your best to find out what the competition is coming out with the following year—which means going to any electronics shows in your area, talking to people who are up on the field, and reading magazines like *R-e/p* and *Mix* (see appendix A for their addresses).

BUYING USED GEAR

Used recording equipment can be a great buy. It's less expensive than new gear, and even though it's used, as long as it hasn't been *mis*used, it should still be capable of meeting the quality standards it was designed for. So whether you're putting a home studio together from scratch or just looking to buy a few additional pieces of outboard equipment, the bargains you can get buying used gear often make it possible for you to outfit your studio with additional pieces of equipment you could not otherwise have afforded.

Some used gear can, in fact, be just as reliable as new gear. If an electronic component is going to fail, it will generally fail early on in the life of the machine, and the circuits themselves rarely "wear out" from normal, continual use. So if you buy a unit that's one or two years old, and the owner's never had a problem with it, unless you overload the circuits or damage the equipment in some other way, it should perform equally well for you.

HOW TO BUY "USED"

You have to be very careful when you buy used gear, which is why we've included the following list of consumer tips.

After all, it may be said that "you only get what you pay for," but if you're not careful, you can end up with a whole lot less!

1. **If possible, buy from a reputable dealer.**

 Many music stores sell used gear on consignment, and although their prices may be somewhat higher than those quoted by individuals in the paper, you'll at least be able to return the gear if there's something wrong with it. Plus, you shouldn't need to have the unit checked out by a technician (Tip #6).

2. **Buy from a friend.**

 Friends are also excellent sources. For one thing, they won't try to rip you off, and for another, you'll know how well or how poorly the equipment has been treated. *But,* if you don't want to *lose* a friend, be certain to follow Tip #6, and remember that if the unit doesn't function once you get it home, it's *your problem!*

3. **Know what you're buying.**

 Before you go looking at gear that is advertised in the paper, make sure you research the particular unit you're after. And if you're totally unfamiliar with that type of equipment, ask friends and/or go to a music store and learn as much as you can about similar units that are on the market.

4. **Check the list price.**

 First, find out what the list price of the unit was at the time of purchase. And while you're at it, check the list price of any similar gear that is presently on the market. This will give you an idea of the sort of "deal" you're getting, and at the same time you may well discover that a different manufacturer is offering a comparable piece of *new* gear at a lower price.

5. **Test the equipment.**

 Used gear doesn't come with a warrantee, so test the equipment and make sure it works. Also, make sure it performs all the functions that you require (that it's stereo instead of mono, that the attack time is fast enough, and so on).

6. **Have the equipment thoroughly checked by an authorized technician.**

 This is particularly important if you're spending more than $200 or $300 on the unit. You will probably have to pay the fee yourself (so take it to *your* serviceman), but it may keep you from buying a piece of gear that is not worth the asking price. And if the owner balks and says the gear has just come back from the shop, be sure to check the serial number on the unit against the serial number marked on the repair order. (Then have it checked out anyway.)

7. **Try to work out a fair price.**

 Unfortunately, there is no "blue book" value on used gear, but you can get an idea of what the going price is by checking classified ads and by looking in music stores that carry used equipment. Then, if something on the unit *does* need to be repaired, you can try to work something out. For instance, if the heads on a tape deck are badly worn, it isn't likely that the owner will take the full cost of replacing them off the price. However, you *may* be able to get him to split the cost of the new heads.

BEST BUYS IN USED GEAR

There is plenty of used recording equipment around, but not all of it is worth buying. So to help you decide which pieces of studio gear to purchase new and which, if any, to pick up secondhand, we've included the following list of what we consider to be some of the best values in used equipment.

Open-Reel Tape Recorders

Used tape recorders can be a real bargain. A well-manufactured deck that was designed to generate high-quality recordings five or ten years ago is quite capable of producing the same quality today. And depending upon your needs (and the condition of the gear), these units may do the job as well as, or even better than, a new one!

For example, a used open-reel 4-track can cost less than a brand-new 4-track cassette deck, but because the heads on the open-reel machine are larger, they'll give you better reproduction (chapter 3). In fact, this is one reason some musicians who feel they can only afford a Portastudio-type cassette/mixer eventually choose to buy a used open-reel 4-track and a used console. Both systems cost about the same amount of money, but by taking the time to shop around for the appropriate pieces of used gear, they're able to generate cleaner recordings of a higher grade.

Of course, some used tape decks are better buys than others, so if you don't want to end up on the short end of the deal, you should heed the previous list of consumer tips *and* make sure:

1. the unit was originally designed for high-quality recording;

2. it was made by one of the top manufacturers in the industry (firms like TASCAM, Revox, Studer, AKAI, Ampex, and, more recently, Otari and Fostex);

3. it's capable of performing all of the functions that are required.

 This last consideration is an important one, because over the years advances in technology have produced significant improvements in certain recording functions. For instance, you may find that an older deck generates noise when you punch a part in during overdubs, or that the punch-in function isn't even available. Or you may find that the machine doesn't operate at 15 ips, or that it's not designed for high-bias tape. And this means that when you're shopping for a used deck, you need to consider how it's going to be used, because that will determine which features are important and which are not.

In other words, if all you need is a 2-track tape recorder to use for external bounces and master copies, you can forget about Sel-Sync, punch-ins, and the rest, because all you need is a machine that has the ability to produce top-quality stereo recordings at tape speeds of 15 ips.

And if you have any doubts about all this, it should be noted that Larry uses a fourteen-year-old TEAC 3340 4-track in his studio, while I've done some of my song demos on a ten-year-old TEAC 40-4 4-track.

Mixing Consoles

A used recording console can be a great buy—*if* you can find one. Unfortunately, most of the "consoles" that are advertised in the papers are powered PA mixers that are designed to be used with sound systems. So although they can be used in a home studio, they often provide less control over the signal. Plus, you end up paying extra for the amplifier circuits that power the PA speakers.

If you *do* locate a used console, you should remember that it's not a bargain if it doesn't meet your needs, so read through "Recording Consoles" in this chapter before you plunk your money down.

Microphones

Used microphones are another excellent bargain. There are always plenty of ads for mikes in the papers, and even though they may be offered as part of a "sound system" package, many owners *will* sell them separately. And if you live in a big city, check with any audio production companies that rent out PA equipment for live stage performances, as they periodically sell off their inventories at very low prices.

However, the best advice we can give you, no matter whom you're buying the mike from, is that you should *never* buy a microphone you're not familiar with. After all, if you don't know what it's supposed to sound like, you won't know if there's anything wrong when you test it.

And when you *do* plug it in, make sure you wiggle the cable and listen for any buzzes or hums.

Outboard Effects

There are some very good deals to be made in outboard effects, but there are also some bad ones. The prices and the quality of outboard effect units change so rapidly that to get a good deal on the most technologically advanced pieces of gear, you literally have to stay right on top of the industry. So we recommend that, for the most part, if you're shopping for used effects, you stick to relatively standard pieces of gear. And if you want to get a break on some newfangled gadget, just wait a year or two for the competition to flood the market!

The fact is that in most home situations, state-of-the-art technology is overkill. Sure, it would be nice to have a Dolby-A noise reduction system like the ones they use in commercial studios, but you're not going to be cutting a record out of your home, and professional-grade gear just isn't necessary. So what you want to look for is an outboard effect unit that is functional yet effective.

FREQUENTLY ASKED QUESTIONS

QUESTION: What can I do if I buy a piece of gear, but once I get it home and try it out, I don't like it?

That all depends upon where you bought the equipment. Most stores have a "return policy," whereby if you return the unit within a certain period of time, they'll give you credit toward another purchase. This is one reason to buy from a merchant who has a large selection, because if you do need to return something, chances are he'll have some other unit in stock that will do the job. However, it's always best to find out what this return policy is *before* you buy. And while it's rare that a store will have a *refund* policy, some specialty outlets that deal in professional recording gear will, in fact, simply return your money if you don't like the unit.

QUESTION: Is it possible to rent equipment that I can't afford to buy?

Yes. In fact, I often rent a good vocal mike when I'm doing song demos. Quite often, when you're doing a lot of work with one studio, you can establish a relationship with the people, and they'll let you rent some of their gear for a day or two. Or you can call around to the sound-system rental companies in your area, as you may be able to work something out with them.

QUESTION: How important are name brands?

If you're unfamiliar with the type of equipment you're buying, it's always best to go with name-brand gear. However, there are many "brand-name" manufacturers, and not all of them produce high-quality equipment, so it doesn't do much good to go with name-brand gear unless you know the kind of quality that is associated with the name. Plus, you don't want to make the mistake of assuming that just because you're *not* familiar with the company name, the gear isn't any good. For example, Lexicon is a leading manufacturer of professional recording equipment, but they don't advertise in *Rolling Stone*. So unless you're familiar with professional studio equipment, you wouldn't know what kind of quality they offered.

QUESTION: Should I buy an outboard noise reduction device?

Outboard noise reduction is not the first piece of gear I'd buy, but it is worth investigating if you're having trouble with tape noise. Still, you should only need to apply it during external stereo bounces, so at most you would need two channels of noise reduction (if you're getting a lot of noise on your initial tracks, you're probably doing something wrong). To see how this would be done, you should refer to "Example A" in chapter 7, page 115.

QUESTION: How important is it to have a patch bay?

That depends on how complex your studio is. If you have a lot of different effects, and if you're always swapping tape machines around and using different routing configurations, then a patch bay can prove to be quite a timesaver. But if you only have a few outboard effect units, and your setup is relatively simple, you don't really need one.

QUESTION: What should I look for when I'm buying headphones?

Basically, you want a pair of headphones that sound good, but you also want them to be light, comfortable, and durable. If there's generally a lot of noise in the studio, such as when two or three instruments are being recorded simultaneously, then you might want to opt for a pair of "closed" phones that fully enclose the ear. However, "open" phones, which rest against the ear but do not completely cover it, are much more comfortable to wear over any length of time. Thus, as long as you're not having any problems with leakage, they would be the best. And in terms of brands, I would recommend AKG (strongly), Sennheiser, and Yamaha, in that order.

QUESTION: Is it better to buy a digital delay device or a tape echo?

Actually, I wouldn't recommend one over the other, because it all depends on the situation. A digital delay is more flexible, but it doesn't sound as warm or as pleasant as a tape echo. On the other hand, tape echoes are monaural, and unlike the more sophisticated digital delay units, all they can do is create an echo. So if you only want to create a slap echo, then a tape echo unit would be great. But for the cost of a Roland Space Echo, you can buy a digital delay that can be used to create all sorts of different effects.

QUESTION: Can I use "guitar" effect pedals to add effects during mixdowns? Or do I need to buy special gear?

As we've mentioned many times, you *can* use effect pedals on your recordings. However, the cheaper the device, the more noise it's going to make—even if you *are* using a direct box. Therefore, the answer to this question will really depend upon how well or how poorly the particular piece of gear sounds in the given situation. And as we've said all along, you get what you pay for. So if the effect is a high-

---

TAPE TIP #39
An Open-Reel "Portastudio"!

When TASCAM began designing the original Portastudio, one of the earliest prototypes utilized an open-reel format ("The Reel World," chapter 8). Although the company eventually opted to use the cassette format in their Portastudio 144, in 1986 they revived the open-reel concept and incorporated it in the TASCAM 388 "Studio 8" (Figure 18m).

The Studio 8 is an 8-track system that uses a ¼-inch tape format. The reproduction quality of the recorder section is quite good—in fact, it's much better than I expected it would be, given that it only uses a tape speed of 7½ ips.

Plus, it offers full SMPTE compatibility and built-in DBX noise reduction.

The Studio 8 is an extremely versatile recording tool. It can be used for demos as well as for work on videos and films. And although it's not exactly light (it weighs eighty-three pounds), it is compact, so it can be easily stored away.

And if you think this is just a plug for TASCAM, you're wrong. The fact is that at press time, the Studio 8 remains the only unit of its kind. And it's a good piece of gear. Yet if, at the time you're reading this, other manufacturers have introduced their own versions of the Studio 8, we can only suggest that you compare each unit and pick the one most suited to your needs.

Figure 18m: TASCAM 388 "Studio 8" (*Courtesy of TEAC Corporation of America*)

price, top-quality unit, it will likely prove to be quite satisfactory.

QUESTION: If I buy a used tape recorder, are there any particularly dependable decks I should keep an eye out for?

Yes. There are a number of manufacturers who are known for the quality, dependability, and *durability* of their tape machines. Among them are TEAC/TASCAM, Techniques, Sony, Otari, Fostex, and Studer/Revox. However, the following is a sampling of specific models that have proven themselves over the years:

TASCAM 3440-S *(¼-inch 4-track)*
TEAC/TASCAM 40-4 *(¼-inch 4-track)*
TEAC/TASCAM 80-8 *(½-inch 8-track)*
OTARI 5050 *(¼-inch 2-track)*
SONY 750 *(¼-inch 2-track)*
TECHNIQUES 1500 *(¼-inch 2-track)*

QUESTION: Am I better off fixing up my old tape deck or buying a new one?

If your machine is among those listed above, you're probably better off fixing it up, although that will depend upon the amount of work that needs to be done on it. If it's not listed as a classic, and it's *very* old, you'll need to ask your serviceman about the signal quality the unit would be capable of after the repairs. However, as a general rule, be wary of any machine that was manufactured much earlier than 1970.

QUESTION: Is there any difference in operating costs between, say, a 4-track and an 8-track tape recorder?

Yes, and the differences fall into two categories: the cost of magnetic recording tape and the cost of repairs. For example, while a 10½-inch reel of ¼-inch tape costs about $20, a reel of ½-inch tape costs $50, so if you have an 8-track that uses ½-inch tape, your tape cost will more than double. You will also find that repairs on an 8-track or a 16-track unit are more expensive than 4-track repairs, for the simple reason that there are more circuits involved (plus, professional gear will require professional attention). And should you need to replace the heads, they'll be more expensive as well.

QUESTION: Should I buy a +4 dB console or a −10 dB console?

As we discussed in chapter 5, consoles function at one of two different operating levels: +4 dB or −10 dB. However, when choosing a console, this should *not* be a major concern, because both formats are capable of producing a signal of equally high quality. It's just that professional gear operates at a +4 dB level, while semipro gear operates at −10 dB. So if your studio is full of professional gear, a +4 dB desk will be more compatible with the other units, and it will make your life easier. But if your studio is filled with outboard effects that you could use on a guitar, you might do better with a −10 dB console.

QUESTION: What's the difference between a direct box and an input transformer/adapter?

Conceptually, these two devices are the same. They're both transformers that convert signals from low impedance to high impedance or vice versa (see Tape Tip #15, chapter 5). However, the cheap input transformers offered as XLR adapters by electronics outlets are poor substitutes for a professional direct box. The electronic components in these devices are less sophisticated, and as a result they reduce the strength of the signal. And since you have to make up for this loss by giving the signal a bigger boost, you end up with a signal that's noisier than what you would have gotten using a direct box. So while a $10 input transformer may appear to be quite a bargain when compared with a $60 direct box, it's not.

QUESTION: How can I determine the relative quality of a piece of gear by reading the spec sheet?

You should be able to, but in actual fact, any two pieces of gear that are priced about the same will have nearly identical numbers on the spec sheets. However, there will undoubtedly be a difference in the way each sounds, so instead of going by numbers on a spec sheet, try the gear out before buying it.

QUESTION: Aren't all cables the same quality?

No. There is a big difference in the quality of connectors and cables. A great deal of research has been done in an attempt to reduce the signal loss caused by cables, and many cables have been designed specifically for studio work. For example, TASCAM offers cable (TC-410/8) that has been specifically designed to reduce signal loss, and you'll find many different brands at electronic stores and music stores that would also be good buys. One *very* general rule of thumb in such matters is, the more expensive the cable, the longer it will last and the better it will perform.

Glossary

Glossary ∿∿∿∿∿∿∿∿∿∿∿∿∿∿∿∿∿∿∿∿∿∿∿∿∿∿∿∿∿∿

The following is a list of words and phrases that appear in music industry ads, spec sheets, and publications. Each is accompanied by a short explanation that is designed to aid in your understanding of how the term is used. While several of the more technical items are not actually discussed in the text of this book, we felt it would be helpful to include them so that you can also use this glossary as a reference source when reading outside material.

In certain instances, we may not be technically exact in our definition, and in other instances there may be additional applications of the particular word or phrase. However, it is our feeling that it is more important for you to understand the concept than to subject you to what might easily become a confusing, equation-filled explanation. If you want to get the pure scientific lowdown, there are, of course, plenty of highly technical books available.

And if you don't find the word here, you can always try a dictionary.

Acoustics—The sound characteristics (or ambience) of a particular environment. For example, the term "live acoustics" would be used to describe a room in which the sound waves reverberate off the walls and ceiling, while "dead acoustics" would describe a room in which the sound waves are absorbed by the surroundings.

A/D—An abbreviation of "analog to digital," which refers to the process of converting a signal from an analog to a digital medium.

Analog—An "analog" is a close but not perfectly accurate copy of (in this case) a signal or sound. For instance, a signal recorded on tape is an analog of the original sound, and although it may be a nearly perfect duplicate, it will not have exactly the same characteristics as the original.

Attack—This is the initial, sharply delineated portion of a signal. For example, the attack of a drum would be the portion of the signal that is generated by the drumstick at the point of impact.

Attack Time—The amount of time it takes an effect, such as compression, to begin affecting the signal.

Attenuation—This refers to the weakening of a signal or sound wave. It can be used either in the context of a sound wave's natural loss of strength over distance, or it can be used to describe the electronic process of reducing signal strength.

Audio Spectrum—The range of frequencies that can be heard by the human ear.

Balanced Inputs—Low-impedance inputs that are wired with two lines plus a ground and are specifically designed to accept a signal from a balanced source.

Bias—An electrical current that is sent through the tape heads during recording in order to insure that a minimum level of magnetization is going on at all times. This increases the frequency response of the recording by making it easier for high-frequency portions of a signal to reach tape. Yet it also increases tape hiss, because it produces a chaotic "nonpattern" on the surface of the tape, which reproduces as noise.

Block Diagram—A schematic representation of the optional paths a signal can take through a piece of electronic gear.

Bounce—The process of moving a recorded signal from one track to another. An "internal bounce" is one that moves the signal to a different track, or tracks, on the same tape machine. An "external bounce" is one that transfers the signal to a new track, or tracks, on a second machine.

Buss—A console output channel. It can best be described as a means of outbound transport for the signal.

Cans—Headphones.

Channel—A channel is an electronic circuit (or set of circuits) used to process a signal. For instance, on a tape recorder you have record channels (one for each track) and playback channels, and on a console you have input channels and buss channels. On your home stereo, you have speaker channels, and so forth.

Clear Signal—The clean, nonnoise portion of a signal. It represents the "pure sound" you would hear if you could eliminate all electronic hiss.

Clipping Level—The point at which a signal begins to distort. (See Figure G1.)

Compression Ratio—This is a *representation* of the amount of compression that is applied to a signal that has passed the unit's threshold and triggered the compression

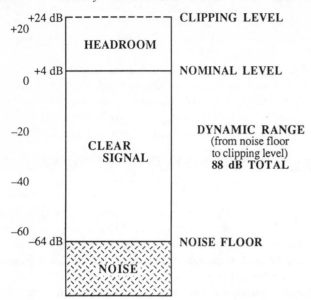

+24 dB ·········· CLIPPING LEVEL
+20
HEADROOM

+4 dB —————— NOMINAL LEVEL
0

−20   CLEAR   DYNAMIC RANGE
      SIGNAL   (from noise floor
                   to clipping level)
                   88 dB TOTAL

−40

−60
−64 dB   NOISE FLOOR

NOISE

Figure G1:   Diagrammatic representation of an electronic signal.

circuits. For example, a compression ratio of two to one (2:1) would mean that once the signal has passed the threshold, enough compression would be applied so that a signal surge of two decibels at input would only result in a one-decibel increase at output.

Crosstalk—Crosstalk occurs when the signal being recorded onto one tape track bleeds over onto the next. This can sometimes occur when you are using tape saturation to compress the signal.

Cue System—A monitor system used to generate the musicians' headphone mix. Basically, the cue send on the console feeds an amplifier, which in turn provides a signal source for the headphones.

Cycles (per second)—The frequency rate of a sound wave. It is interchangeable with the term "Hertz."

Damping—The process of deadening the sound of an instrument by limiting its ability to resonate. For example, you damp a drumhead in order to limit the amount of ringing you hear in the drum.

dB—The abbreviation for "decibels," which is the recognized standard for determining volume level of sound.

Decay—The decay of a note, or instrument, is the process whereby the note, having been struck, fades out. This can be a slow, gradual process, which would mean there would be a long decay time involved, or it can be very brief.

De-esser—A special limiter, or limiter circuit, that is used to cut high-end frequencies. It is called a "de-*esser*" because it is often used to eliminate the vocal distortion created when pronouncing words that include the letter "s."

Defeat Switch—A control that can be used to mute a signal.

Digital—An electronic format that is designed to duplicate sound, while affording extremely accurate control over

any changes you might wish to make in the copy. In simple terms, the digital circuitry analyzes (samples) the signal and then reproduces what it has seen (the quality of the copy being dependent upon the sampling rate of the device). And it does so without adding the tape hiss present in analog copies.

Direct Box (DI)—A transformer that is used to alter a signal's impedance level (from high impedance to low impedance or vice versa). It can also be used to split a signal if it has two outputs.

Discrete Output—A direct output from a channel, which services only that one channel.

Doubling—The process of recording an instrumental part twice and blending the two takes together in order to achieve a fuller sound.

Drop-Out—The sudden loss of signal in the middle of a track. You would say the signal "drops out" of the track.

Dynamic Range (*Acoustic*)—The difference in decibel level between the loudest and the quietest sound produced by an instrument or sound source.

Dynamic Range (*Electronic*)—The difference in decibel level between the noise floor of a signal and the clipping level. When applied to a piece of gear, it refers to the amount of clear signal the unit is capable of processing. (See Figure G1.)

Dynamics—The decibel level produced by any given instrument or sound source.

Effects-Loop Circuitry—A mixing console circuit that is used to add an effect to a signal or a group of signals. When the effect unit is plugged into the circuit (via effects send and effects return jacks), it literally functions as a loop, splitting the signal off from the mixer and sending it to the effect, then returning it to the mixer, where it is blended with the original signal.

EFX—A popular abbreviation for "effects." It is used when referring to an outboard effects unit or a console's effects send circuitry.

Envelope—A representation, over time, of the volume of the signal generated by an instrument. In a sense, this represents the "life" of the signal, from the point of attack to the point of decay.

Fidelity—In music electronics, this term indicates how faithful a reproduced signal is to the original. For example, a "high-fidelity" signal would be a very true representation of the original sound.

Filter—A device that is capable of removing or reducing a select band of frequencies within a signal.

Flamming—An undesirable audio occurrence in which one of the instruments used on a rhythm track strikes slightly behind the others. It is caused primarily by the improper application of delay.

Flat Response (Curve)—This term refers to frequency response and is normally associated with optimum performance levels. For instance, a flat response curve on a graphic EQ unit would be one in which all faders were set in a straight line at "0." In turn, a speaker cabinet that exhibits a flat response will give equal treatment to all frequencies (it won't emphasize a particular band of high or low frequencies), and this produces the best-possible fidelity.

Flutter—A rapid fluctuation in the flow of tape across the heads of a tape recorder. It literally gives the recording a jerky, flutterlike sound and is caused by irregularities in the tape transport system.

Foldback System—"Foldback" is a term used in England to describe the mix that is being sent to the monitor speakers in the control room. However, it can also apply to the headphone mix that is being generated for the musicians.

Frequency—In general terms, "frequency" is the rate (how often) at which something repeats. In acoustic terms, it is the rate at which sound waves repeat over time. The greater the number of repeats, the higher the frequency. And the higher the frequency, the higher the pitch of the tone that is produced. Consequently, high-frequency waves are very short, and low-frequency waves are very long (up to fifteen feet).

Frequency Response—When used on spec sheets, this phrase refers to the range of frequencies a unit is capable of reproducing. However, when used in terms of an instrument or a signal, it refers to the range of frequencies *being* produced.

Fundamental Tone—The band of frequencies (usually between 300 Hz and 800 Hz) that makes up the basic tone (or "body") of the instrument.

Gain—This refers to the strength (or volume level) of a signal.

Generation Loss—The loss of signal quality that can occur with each succeeding generation, or transfer copy, of a recording. This does not mean that a master tape will lose more and more quality every time you copy it, but that the copy itself may be of poorer quality than the master.

Harmonics—Acoustic overtones that represent the upper and lower octaves of a note. When a note is played, the harmonics ring out along with it, and this, combined with other overtones, gives an acoustic instrument its particular sound. (See **Overtones**.)

Headphone Mix—The monitor mix that is sent to the musician's headphones during initial tracking and overdubs. Often, this mix will contain effects not given to the recorded signal (or to the existing tracks), in order to make the music sound more exciting in its premixdown state.

Headroom—The distance (in decibels) between the nominal level of a piece of audio equipment ("0" on the meter) and the clipping level, at which point it distorts. (See Figure G1.)

Hertz—A unit of frequency that is used to measure the frequency rate of a sound wave. In terms of application, it is a universal standard for frequency levels.

High-Bias Tape—A grade of recording tape that has been designed to reduce the amount of bias a recording deck needs to apply in order to achieve high-frequency reproduction. Since less bias is required, you get less noise in the recording.

High Impedance—This is one of two impedance loads. Most tape recorders, amplifiers, and electronic instruments operate at high impedance. However, a high-impedance signal does not "travel well" and loses quality over long distances. (See also **Impedance** and **Low Impedance**.)

Hz—An abbreviation for hertz.

Impedance—The technical definition of impedance is "an opposition to AC current flow, measured in ohms." However, the subject of impedance is quite complex, and there are entire books devoted to it; so for more information see one of the books listed in appendix A.

ips—The abbreviation for "inches per second." It refers to the speed of tape across the tape head.

K—The abbreviation for "kilohertz" (1,000 hertz).

Line Level—The voltage level at which a signal is processed by electronic circuitry. The line level for most tape decks, for example, is −10 dB, which means that the device needs to see a minimum of −10 dB of signal strength in order to process the signal properly.

Low Impedance—This is one of two impedance loads. Professional studio gear and most microphones (600 ohms or less) operate at low impedance, and since a low-impedance signal will not deteriorate over long distances, it is useful for running signal through lengthy cables.

Masking—Masking occurs when the sound of one instrument gets blocked out by the sound of another, because both exhibit the same basic frequency response patterns. This is something that must be carefully watched for in any mix situation.

Modulation Effects—Sound effect devices that use the principles of signal modulation to create an effect. Such effects would include phase, chorus, and flange.

Monophonic—This term is used to describe an instrument, such as a synth, that is capable of playing only one note at a time (thus, no chords).

Mult—The process of electronically multiplying or doubling a signal through the use of a digital delay or a harmonizer.

Noise Floor—The level (in decibels) where the "noise" portion of a signal ends and clear signal begins. (See Figure G1.)

Noise Reduction—This term is commonly used to describe circuits, or pieces of electronic gear, that are specifically designed to enhance the signal-to-noise ratio of a signal. Two of the most popular noise reduction systems are manufactured by Dolby and DBX.

Nominal Level—The optimum level at which a signal is processed in a particular piece of gear. For instance, if the piece of gear has a VU meter, this level would be represented by the "0" mark, past which the meter goes into the red. (See Figure G1.)

Outboard Device—An external signal processing device (EQ, compressor, reverb, and so on) that is used in conjunction with a console. For example, if a console doesn't have enough onboard EQ, you may want to use an outboard EQ device as well.

Overdub—The process of adding additional tracks to a song. It is accomplished by monitoring the already existing tracks, along with the track that is being laid down.

Overtones—These are sympathetic frequencies above the fundamental tone of a note, which give the instrument its particular sound characteristics. For most instruments, these overtones can be found in the frequencies above 800 Hz (the fundamental tone of most instruments is found in the 300 Hz–800 Hz range).

Pan—A mixing control that gives you the ability to send a signal anywhere from the far left to the far right of the stereo spectrum.

Phase Cancelation—The loss of signal quality, usually in the low frequencies, that occurs when two signals (or microphones) are out of phase. As a result, when each signal is played separately, the high ends and low ends may sound perfectly balanced, but when combined, either the bass, treble, or midrange tones of the signals seem to disappear.

Phase Shift—The relative movement of a pair of signals that are sweeping in and out of phase. The effect that is created sounds like waves.

Polyphonic—This term is used to describe an instrument, such as a synth or a piano, that is capable of playing more than one note at a time. Thus, it is capable of playing chords.

Pop Filter—A device that is used to reduce the "pop" made by a microphone when the singer pronounces words that begin with letters like "p" or "b."

Ports—Another term for the inputs or outputs of a unit.

Print a Track—The operation of recording (printing) a signal onto tape.

Proximity Effect—This term is used to describe the increase in bass response exhibited by a microphone as it moves closer to the sound source. However, it can also be used to describe the decrease in signal definition that results. For instance, a singer may hold a microphone right up to his mouth in order to give his vocals low-end strength, but in so doing, he loses much of the crisp, high-end definition of his voice.

Punch In/Punch Out—The process of inserting new material into a previously recorded track and recording over part of the track in the process (AKA "drop in" or "dub in"). This is often used to fix a weak portion of a track that would otherwise be quite acceptable.

Quantize—A drum machine function that enables you to subdivide each measure into specific increments (quarter notes, eighth notes, and so on). When you create a drum pattern in real time, this allows the machine to correct for any slight mishits.

Release Time—This refers to the amount of time an effect, such as compression, acts on a signal before "releasing" it.

Resonant Frequency—Any particular frequency that will cause an instrument or string to resonate even though it has not been struck. For example, when a tuning fork is struck and then pressed against the body of an acoustic guitar, it will cause any strings that are tuned to its pitch to begin vibrating. The tuning fork, then, is said to produce the resonant frequency of that string.

Roll Off—The process of reducing the level of a particular band of frequencies. For instance, when applying EQ, you can be said to "roll off" the level of certain frequencies.

Sampling Rate—The rate at which a particular digital circuit samples, or analyzes, a signal.

Sel-Sync—This term is short for *Sel*ective *Sync*hronization, a tape recorder function originally introduced by Ampex that allows you to monitor an existing track off the record heads, so that any new track you add will be in sync with any existing tracks. This is generally known as the "sync" mode.

Servo Control—A particular type of tape transport system that provides an extremely steady, accurate flow of tape across the heads. It also makes variable pitch control (variable tape speed) possible.

Shelving—An EQ treatment that affects every frequency above (high-frequency shelving) or below (low-frequency shelving) a designated band of frequencies. For example, if you use shelving to boost EQ in the high end of the spectrum, the boost will affect all the frequencies from, for instance, 10K up—although the point at which shelving begins (in this case 10K) varies from one piece of gear to the next.

Sibilants—Sounds produced in the high-frequency ranges. This can include everything from whistles to cymbals to the upper harmonics of a string instrument, as well as to the sound of the letter "s."

Signal Pulse—The duration of a sound, from attack to decay, as it exists as an electronic signal.

Signal-to-Noise Ratio—This describes the quality of a signal by comparing the total amount of signal (in decibels) with the amount of noise (in decibels) it contains. It is generally used to determine the processing efficiency of electronic equipment, as the higher the ratio, the more efficient the unit.

Slap Echo—An echo that, unlike "reverb" echoes, has sufficient delay time to allow the repeat to be heard as a duplicate of the original signal. In this sense, all long-delay tape echoes and digital echoes are slap echoes.

Slew Rate—Basically, this is the amount of time it takes an amplifier to fully amplify a signal, relative to the amount of amplification it is capable of generating. In automotive terms, it's sort of how quick it gets from zero to sixty. . . .

SMPTE—The electronic code system used to synchronize

audio to video, video to audio, and audio to audio. Basically, the SMPTE code is one continuous electronic "word" that is twenty-four hours long but changes "characters" every 1/3,000 of a second. When this code is printed on tape, it enables you to lock up the machine with a second deck that also reads SMPTE.

Solo a Track—The process of isolating a channel on the console and sending it through the monitors totally by itself. It is used to check the quality of the signal in question and/or to set EQ levels.

Splitter—Any device that splits the output of a signal so that it can be sent to more than one location.

Spooling—The process of preparing a tape for tails-out storage. It is performed by threading the tape directly from one reel to the other (although on some decks you need to thread it around the tape heads) and running it forward at a normal "play" tape speed. By doing so, you get a tight, flat layering of tape on the take-up reel, which will help maintain the integrity of the recording.

Standing Wave—An undesirable acoustical phenomenon that occurs in low frequencies when a sound wave bounces back and forth between two parallel walls. As a result, the waves keep bouncing back on themselves, and they never have a chance to die out. This can create a buildup in specific frequencies or phase cancelation.

Stereo Spectrum—The three-dimensional audio field created by a stereophonic signal. Basically, it consists of a surface plane that stretches from speaker to speaker and a field of depth beyond this plane that stretches as far as you can be made to imagine.

Sustain—The process of electronically holding a note by extending the normal decay time of the instrument—sometimes indefinitely.

Tails Out—This refers to a reel of tape that has been stored without being rewound, so that the beginning of the song is actually at the other end of the tape. This is a normal practice in professional studios. In turn, a tape that is stored "heads out" is one that has already been rewound and can be put directly onto the machine and played.

Talkback—A console circuit that allows the engineer to speak to the musicians, either via their headphones or through monitors set up in the studio.

Tape Loop—A continuously running loop of tape that can be used either in a record or a playback context. For in-

stance, tape loops are used on analog echo units in order to provide a continuously running source of echo. However, a loop can also be used as a playback vehicle in instances when an instrument simply repeats the same part over and over.

Threshold—The point at which an effect unit "kicks in" and begins affecting the signal.

Track—The linear portion of tape (running the length of the reel) that is used to record the signal from one channel of the tape recorder. If the tape deck has four record channels, the tape will be electronically divided into four strips, each of which will represent one recorded track.

Tracking—A common term for the process of recording tracks and overdubs prior to the mixdown stage of recording. For example, someone might say he is doing "some initial tracking" on his material.

Transient—A sharp sound of extremely short duration, which results from the striking of an object or the hammering (picking) of a string. It is the attack of a sound that is produced percussively.

Transient Response—The ability of a circuit to respond to the transient. Poor transient response means that the equipment does not react quickly enough to capture the entire peak of the transient.

Transport System—These tape recorder components control the flow of tape across the tape heads.

Trim—Console controls that allow you to alter the strength of a signal that, depending upon the control, is either entering or leaving the unit.

Waveform—The physical shape or structure that a frequency has when in the form of a sound wave.

White Noise—A signal that contains all audible frequencies, just as the color white contains all visual colors.

Wow—A gradual speeding up and slowing down of the flow of tape across the heads of a tape recorder. Unlike "flutter," which is a rapid fluctuation in speed, wow creates a slow, rolling inconsistency of motion and pitch.

Y-Cord—A patch cord used to split an output signal so that it can be sent to two different inputs. It is called a Y-cord because it is literally shaped like a "Y."

Zero Locate/Auto Locate—These terms refer to a feature of most tape recorders that allows you to automatically rewind or fast forward to a specific location on the tape.

Appendixes ∿∿∿∿∿∿∿∿∿∿∿∿∿∿∿∿∿

Appendix **A**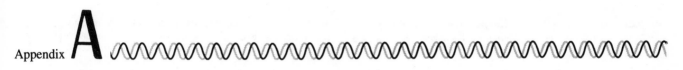

Bibliography
Reference Books and Magazines

TEXTBOOKS
The following textbooks provide material that can be useful should you require additional technical information.

Alton, Everest F.
ACOUSTIC TECHNIQUES FOR HOME AND STUDIO
Tab Books
Blue Ridge Summit, PA
1978
—An excellent, easy-to-read textbook that covers specific acoustical problems in the home studio environment.

Clifford, Martin
MICROPHONES: HOW THEY WORK AND HOW TO USE THEM
Tab Books
Blue Ridge Summit, PA
1977
—A good book for beginners; includes simple, complete explanations for each type of microphone

Davis, Don and Caroline
SOUND SYSTEM ENGINEERING
Howard W. Sams & Co.
Indianapolis, IN
1978
—Offers detailed information concerning the techniques of setting up sound systems both at home and in concert halls.

Eargle, John
SOUND RECORDING (2nd Edition)
Van Nostrand Reinhold Company, Inc.
New York, NY
1980
—Covers the technical aspects of recording and is relatively easy to understand. However, it lacks detailed information on electronic effects and mixing consoles.

Keene, Sherman
SHERMAN KEENE'S PRACTICAL TECHNIQUES
FOR THE RECORDING ENGINEER
Sherman Keene Publications
Hollywood, CA
1981
—Provides excellent reference material for advanced studio work and explains most technical material in a way that can be easily understood if you already have some background in the subject. Designed to serve as a studio engineering course book, the bulk of the text is devoted to working with professional-grade gear.

Olsen, Harry F.
MUSICAL ENGINEERING
Van Nostrand Reinhold Company, Inc.
New York, NY
1959
—Though extremely dated, this is a fine book for theory, as the author has attempted to make the technical aspects of recording understandable in nontechnical terms.

Runstein, Robert E.
MODERN RECORDING TECHNIQUES
Howard W. Sams & Co.
Indianapolis, IN
1974
—Though a relatively old book, it presents a fine account of studio theory. In fact, it is often one of the texts used for studio engineering courses.

Tremaine, Howard M.
THE AUDIO CYCLOPEDIA
Howard W. Sams & Co.
Indianapolis, IN
1976
—A very complete reference book of some 1,700 pages. However, it's expensive, and it contains little, if any, how-to information. It will answer most any technical question, but only in technical terms.

Turner, Rufus P.
IMPEDANCE
Tab Books
Blue Ridge Summit, PA
1976
—An extremely technical book, but one that does an excellent job of covering the subject.

BOOKLETS

The following booklets (twenty-five pages or less) are recommended sources for background material. Generally, they cover a limited amount of subject matter in a brief, concise manner.

TASCAM
ARE YOU READY FOR MULTITRACK?
TEAC Corporation of America
7733 Telegraph Road
Montebello, CA 90640
1986
—An excellent booklet for beginners that presents an overview of the multitrack recording process. However, the bulk of material has already been covered in this book.

TASCAM
REFERENCE DATA
TEAC Corporation of America
7733 Telegraph Road
Montebello, CA 90640
1985
—Provides a relatively easy approach to such complicated technical subjects as impedance and signal strength (dB's).

HOME HANDBOOKS

The following publications offer alternative views on home recording techniques. However, having bought this book, you really don't need them.

Anderton, Dave
HOME RECORDING FOR MUSICIANS
Amsco Publications (Music Sales Corp.)
New York, NY
1978
—A fine book for its time, it provides a mix of information on home recording techniques. However, much of the gear available today was not available in 1978 and is not discussed. Still, the theory portions of the book are good, and it includes instructions for building electronics gear at home.

Rosmini, Dick
THE MULTITRACK PRIMER (Revised Edition)
TEAC Corporation of America
7733 Telegraph Road
Montebello, CA 90640
1982
—A fine book for beginners, as it covers a great many aspects of recording. However, some of the technical information included can be difficult for a novice to understand.

PERIODICALS

The following trade magazines provide a considerable amount of useful consumer information. Though oriented toward commercial studio operations, much of their editorial space is devoted to keeping up with current trends in recording.

R-e/p (RECORDING ENGINEER/PRODUCER)
1850 Whitley Avenue
Hollywood, CA 90028
—Interviews with professional engineers and producers. Coverage of audio, video, and concert-hall production. Reviews new products and provides in-depth articles on specific types of equipment (such as digital delays, computer software, and so on).

MIX MAGAZINE
2608 9th Street
Berkeley, CA 94710
—Regional listings of recording studios across the nation. Interviews with celebrities. Coverage of both audio and video production. Reviews of specific types of gear (such as cassette recorders for the professional studio, equalizers, and the like).

db—THE SOUND ENGINEERING MAGAZINE
1120 Old Country Road
Plainview, NY 11803
—Coverage of audio production and reviews on new gear. Also, a section on small pro studios that includes general tips on techniques and how to run the business.

Appendix B

Corporate Index

The following manufacturers, wholesalers, and retailers contributed, in a professional manner, to the content of this book. Should you wish to receive further information about their products or services, they can be contacted at the address indicated.

AKG
77 Seleck Street
Stamford, CT 06902

AUDIO-TECHNICA US, INC.
1221 Commerce Dr.
Stow, Ohio 44224

CARVIN CORPORATION
Dept. 85B
1155 Industrial Avenue
Escondido, CA 92025

CROWN INTERNATIONAL
1718 W. Mishawaka Road
Elkhart, IN 46517

E-MU SYSTEMS, INC.
1600 Green Hills Road
Scotts Valley, CA 95066-4542

FENDER MUSICAL INSTRUMENTS CORPORATION
1300 E. Valentine Drive
Fullerton, CA 92631

FOSTEX CORPORATION
15431 Blackburn Avenue
Norwalk, CA 90650

THE GUITAR CENTER
14760 Ventura Boulevard
Sherman Oaks, CA 91403

HARRISON SYSTEMS, INC.
Box 22964
Nashville, TN 37202

JBL
P. O. Box 2200
8500 Balboa Boulevard
Northridge, CA 91329

MARSHALL AMPLIFIERS (UNICORD DISTRIBUTORS)
89 Frost Street
Westbury, NY 11590

NEUMANN MICROPHONES (GOTHAM AUDIO CORP.)
741 Washington Street
New York, NY 10014

OBERHEIM SYSTEMS CORPORATION
2250 S. Barrington Avenue
Los Angeles, CA 90064

OTARI CORPORATION
2 Davis Drive
Belmont, CA 94002

PEARL INTERNATIONAL
P.O. Box 111240
Nashville, TN 37222-1240

REMO, INC.
12804 Raymer Street
North Hollywood, CA 91605

R-e/p MAGAZINE
P.O. Box 2449
Hollywood, CA 90078

ROLAND CORPORATION
(also Boss Products)
7200 Dominion Circle
Los Angeles, CA 90040

SCHECTER GUITARS
2605 Andjon Street
Dallas, TX 75220

SCHOLZ RESEARCH & DEVELOPMENT
P.O. Box 191
Lincoln, MA 01733

SHURE BROTHERS
222 Hartray Avenue
Evanston, IL 60204

SIMMONS GROUP CENTRE, INC.
23917 Craftsman Road
Calibasis, CA 91302

SOUNDCRAFT ELECTRONICS
1517 20th Street
Santa Monica, CA 90404

TEAC/TASCAM CORPORATION
7733 Telegraph Road
Montebello, CA 90640

TOA ELECTRONICS, INC.
480 Carlton Court
South San Francisco, CA 94080

VALLEY ARTS GUITAR
12162 Ventura Boulevard
Studio City, CA 91604

WESTLAKE AUDIO
7265 Santa Monica Boulevard
Los Angeles, CA 90046

YAMAHA INTERNATIONAL
P.O. Box 6600
Buena Park, CA 90622

And a Special Thanks To:

Derrick Pilkington and Jean MacMaster
AKG

Bonnie Lawrence
AUDIO-TECHNICA US, INC.

Jackie Reeves
CARVIN CORPORATION

Margie Scudder
E-MU SYSTEMS, INC.

Dan Smith
FENDER MUSICAL INSTRUMENTS CORPORATION

Mark Cohen
FOSTEX CORPORATION

Rita Vikes
JBL

Bettina Feiner
UNICORD DISTRIBUTORS

Jerry Graham
GOTHAM AUDIO CORPORATION

Beth Menze
OBERHEIM SYSTEMS CORPORATION

Jeff Philips
OTARI CORPORATION

Todd Mauer
PEARL INTERNATIONAL

Lloyd McCausland
REMO, INC.

Mel Lambert
R-e/p MAGAZINE

Barbie Clark
ROLAND CORPORATION

Dee Hoyt
SCHECTER GUITARS

Max Ann Buchanan
SHURE BROTHERS

Bill Threlkeld
SIMMONS GROUP CENTRE, INC.

Erika Lopez
SOUNDCRAFT ELECTRONICS

David Oren
Bill Mohrhoff
Anders Madsen
John Bliese
TEAC/TASCAM CORPORATION

Christina Foran
TOA ELECTRONICS, INC.

Al Carness
VALLEY ARTS GUITAR

Glen Phoenix and Deborah Jenkins
WESTLAKE AUDIO

Phil Moon
YAMAHA INTERNATIONAL

Appendix **C** 〰〰〰〰〰〰〰〰〰〰〰〰〰〰〰〰〰〰〰〰〰〰〰〰〰〰

Sample Tracking Sheet

Tracking sheets provide an easy means of keeping a running account of the instruments each track contains, the effects that may have been added, and the EQ treatment applied to the instruments. Feel free to Xerox this sample tracking sheet (over) for your home use.

ARTIST_____

TITLE_____

CLIENT_____

1	2	3	4	5	6	7	8
9	10	11	12	13	14	15	16

Index

INDEX ~~~~~~~~~~~~~~~~~~~~~~~~~~~~

About the Authors 〜〜〜〜〜〜〜〜〜〜〜〜〜〜〜〜

Peter McIan is a highly respected record producer/recording engineer who's worked with such top recording acts as Men At Work and Mr. Mister. His critically acclaimed production and engineering efforts on Men At Work's record-shattering *Business As Usual* and *Cargo* albums earned him numerous awards, among them being named one of the top five Producers of the Year by *Billboard* magazine. McIan is also a songwriter and recording artist. He's written songs for Pat Benatar and Barbra Streisand among others, and his solo album, *Playing Near the Edge*, was rated one of the year's ten best by *Cashbox* magazine.

Larry Wichman is a free-lance writer/musician whose articles and short stories have appeared in such national publications as *Men's Look, Oui* magazine, and *Hustler*. His library of home recordings dates back to 1964 when, as a drummer, he began taping his band's live gigs and basement practice sessions. Over the years he's maintained a small home demo studio which he uses for songwriting.